Germaine Greer was born in Melbourne, Australia, and educated at the universities of Melbourne, Sydney and Cambridge. Her doctoral thesis was on Shakespeare's early comedies. From 1967 to 1972 she lectured at Warwick University, while working in the Underground press and co-presenting a television series. The publication of *The Female Eunuch*, in 1969, and the notoriety that followed, eventually led to her resigning from the University to write and make lecture tours. From 1979 to 1982 she was director of the Tulsa Centre for the Study of Women's Literature. Her books *The Obstacle Race* and *Sex and Destiny* are both available in Picador. She has lived in the United Kingdom since 1964.

Germaine Greer

THE MADWOMAN'S UNDERCLOTHES

Essays and Occasional Writings 1968–85

PICADOR

published by **Pan Books**

While every effort has been made to acknowledge first publication, we have been unable to establish this in every case. In the event of any inadvertent omission or inaccuracy, please write to Pan Books, Cavaye Place, London SW10 9PG. We will be pleased to rectify any errors in future printings.

'The São Francisco' reprinted from *River Journeys* with the permission of BBC Publications, a division of BBC Enterprises Ltd.

The publishers acknowledge that certain articles in this collection were originally published under different titles.

This collection first published 1986 in
Picador hardback by Pan Books Ltd. This
edition published 1987 in Picador paperback
by Pan Books Ltd, Cavaye Place, SW10 9PG

9 8 7 6 5 4 3 2 1

ISBN 0 330 30149 7

Printed in Great Britain by
Richard Clay Ltd, Bungay, Suffolk

For Sonny and Gita,
who put up with it all.

Contents

Introduction

I can't remember why Emilio and I decided to go south in the summer of '67. Emilio was studying at the Faculty of Architecture in Venice, where we had both learnt to detest tourists; maybe we hatched the project in the hope of experiencing a tourist-free summer. When I got to Venice, I discovered that while I'd been completing the residence requirement for a Ph.D. in Cambridge, Emilio had been falling out of love with me. He was very kind about it, but I was so stunned by the inconstancy of a man who could fall out of love with me when I wasn't even around to bore or annoy him, that I had to refuse his hospitality. My still-unpacked bags were loaded on to the back of a *facchino* and I marched blindly off to take the next train down the Adriatic coast on my own.

Everything had been arranged, with a cold-blooded thoughtfulness that hurt much more than neglect would have done. At Rossano Scalo I was to meet the father of one of Emilio's friends, who had found me somewhere to stay, a 'very nice' room in a poky modern flat above a scrapyard, between the coast highway and the railway. Nobody understood why I wouldn't take it; the flat had a flush toilet and hot and cold running water. It was modern, it was clean, it was close to the cinema, the bars and the 'dancing'. It was hideous.

Jammed against me in the Fiat *cinquecento*, as we hunted for a suitable dwelling up and down the simmering plain of Sybaris, was the nearest Emilio's friend's father had come to a young woman in twenty years. From time to time he would utter a kind of muffled groan and thrust his hand between my legs. For three days we searched, tears dripping off my face as I sat there, helpless, with the fat old man's hand between my thighs, unable to repulse him with sufficient violence because in my estimation the offence did not warrant real ferocity, although it compounded my desolation dreadfully. Besides, the old man was my only hope of finding anywhere to live, for I had neither licence nor sufficient money to hire a car of my own, supposing such a thing was to be had.

After three days we came upon an isolated clump of stone buildings in sight of the sea.

Along the west side of the dirt road ran a long two-storey building with windows only on the upper floor. The windows were shuttered against the blaze of late morning in the *mezzogiorno*. We went around to the other side and found a series of crumbling stone staircases leading up to small balustraded balconies, called, in Italian, *ballatoi*, dance floors. The old man panted up the middle one and felt among the stones of the balustrade for a key. He kept clicking his tongue and shaking his head. 'It won't do,' he said as he pushed open the door. I squeezed past him and went in. The door gave on to an almost empty room. On one side was a cavernous stone fireplace. Under the window at the far end stood a gas bottle and on the grease-spattered table was a three-burner gas stove. There were two blue-painted chairs. I opened the shutters and looked out over the cornfield flaring golden in the heat.

There was only one other room, much larger, with two windows in each exterior wall. I opened them all. On one side the cornfield blazed; on the other the windows were shaded by a grapevine growing on a pergola, framing the view of a vast *uliveto* planted with the oldest olive trees I have ever seen, each with a girth of eight or nine feet. I closed the shutters on the cornfield side so the room filled with the refracted glow of the sunlight on the olive trees filtered through the green gloom of the leaves. A soft draught moved through the slats. The house was perfectly oriented from north to south. In the morning the west windows could stand open, and in the afternoon, the east. At midday the sun stood directly over the narrow eaves so that I could open all the windows and still keep cool. The peasants thought I was mad. They never opened their windows at all, especially at night.

This, then, was my bedroom and workroom. There were five beds in it, each with its own shapeless mattress made of coarse homespun and filled with corn shucks. The shucks were astonishingly noisy and the homespun was very hard on skin, especially sunburnt skin, but the mattresses were always beautifully cool. The floors were made of ancient terracotta tiles, crazed into a million fissures. I knew that if I sluiced them with well-water each morning the transpiration would keep the rooms fresh. The walls were coated with velvety whitewash. There was no running water, no electricity.

Outside, the inhabitants had begun to appear. Most went about their own business, with nothing but the usual time of day to indicate that they were not so much going to the well as checking out the newcomer. Only one woman, with the red-gold hair left behind by the Normans in southern Italy, stood and frankly stared. A troop of ragged, filthy children stood with her and she held a baby face down on her hip. A small girl detached herself from her mother's skirts and came up to take my hand. Her breathing was loud and the dirty little hand in mine was too hot.

'This is just what I'm looking for,' I said.

My guide was aghast; what would I do there, miles from town, with no car, among these uncivilized people? I didn't know myself, but anything was better than his hand between my legs, so I unloaded my bags and waved him out of my life.

I was sure that the peasants would have been impressed and excited to see so tall and elegant a young woman, with a bright red typewriter and many books, coming to adorn life in the *frabb'ca* with her presence. In the event, my arrival was rather overshadowed by that of the water truck. The roadway was suddenly full of people. The young wife from the house opposite and her three children all appeared with demijohns and stood waiting to have them filled. The shepherd's wife, who lived on my side, lined up behind her with her two daughters-in-law and her unmarried daughter. Her last-born, a bright-eyed boy called Mario, always known by the affectionate diminutive, Mariuzz', came to tell me, in proper Italian, to make sure I got clean water from the council truck, for the well was polluted. The elegant foreigner was thus obliged to make her first public appearance struggling with two thirty-five-litre demijohns across the roadway and up the stairs. So she learnt her first lesson; for people living at subsistence level, she travels slowest who travels alone.

It was not possible to be friends with everyone in the *frabb'ca*. I soon discovered that nobody talked to the family in the house opposite. The wife was considered stuck up; she was much younger than her hard-working husband who had taken her without a dowry. The implication was plain. Besides, the first person to take an interest in my welfare was the shepherd's wife and so before I knew how matters stood I was commandeered for her faction. I had not been there many hours before Mariuzz' and the unmarried daughter were standing on the *ballatoio* peering in through the open door. 'What do you want?' I said, rather crossly, for they had interrupted my first working session.

'*La mamma* sent us to keep you company,' they said.

'I don't need company. I don't get lonely.'

I tried to explain that I needed peace and quiet to work but they looked both hurt and puzzled, so I gave up. Although they heard it every day, they never associated my typewriter with work. Their notion of what a Ph.D. thesis might be, remained as insubstantial as their concept of England, which they could identify only with *l'alt'Italia* which was as far away as their minds would reach.

The shepherd and his family lived at the north end of the long building, on two floors. The ground floor, which should have been used only as a shed or storeroom, was their kitchen, that is, the room in which they spent all their waking hours. The floor was earth and the only ventilation came from the door. They were better off than the red-haired woman, who lived with her children in two such *fondi*, because they had a room upstairs which was crammed with beds spread with the women's snowy dowry linen, homespun sheets and crocheted bedspreads. How they washed off the toil and squalor of each day so that they were clean enough to enter such beds I shall never know. Nine people slept in that room: the shepherd and his wife slept in one bed, the daughters-in-law and their babies in two, Mario and his elder brother in another; only Rosetta, the unmarried daughter, had a bed to herself. The room was so small that the only way to get around it was to climb across the beds. I, who had always had a whole room to myself, could not imagine how they could endure such crowding. I felt guilty in my larger room with five beds to choose from and wondered if I shouldn't offer to share it. It was some time before I realized that they couldn't imagine how I could sleep in such echoing loneliness and with my windows open too, so that the bats and the foul night vapours could enter freely. The noise of the smugglers' trucks coming and going to the beach was bound to wake me. Seeing the windows open they would know I was watching them, a sure way to get myself into serious trouble. Nevertheless my windows stayed open. I learned from the peasant women to wake in the cool gloaming at four o'clock, and attend to bodily necessities before the men awoke. Lunchtime was the end of the working day; in the afternoon, while the peasants slept behind their shutters, I took the children to the beach and washed them under the guise of teaching them to swim.

We had nowhere but the sea to bathe in – and none of the peasants had ever entered it – and no way of disposing hygienically of human waste. Yet I never found excrement underfoot except once, in the house of the red-haired woman. I have seen more people relieving themselves in the streets of London in a single day than I saw in three months in Calabria. Every day the peasant women waged war against dirt, except for the red-haired woman who had long ago given in. She and her husband used to copulate on the filthy floor in full view of their children and anyone else who might be passing the open door of the *fondo*. The little girl with the cough, who became my special responsibility, had inherited her mother's regular features and a paler version of her red-gold hair; I didn't know enough to tell whether she had inherited her mental retardation as well. Her father was addicted to the filthy adulterated wine they sold in the *bottega*; when the fit was upon him he would spend hours trying to devise ways of killing himself, stringing up nooses made of rotten twine, trying to make knives out of old tin cans. Occasionally he would prostrate himself in front of me or try to carry burdens for me, under some hallucinated impression that I was a courtesan, for somewhere in the Calabrian scheme of things the notion of the *hetaera* was still alive. We were, after all, living among the invisible ruins of Sybaris.

Cleanliness was so high a value in our dusty community, that the dialect word for 'beautiful' when applied to objects was the Italian word for 'clean'. When Rosetta was given a crocheted dress to wear to the Assumption Day celebrations, she hardly dared to touch it. '*Quant'e p'lit*,' she kept saying.

The first time I went to eat with the shepherd's family in their windowless kitchen, I was appalled. A column of flies danced above the battered table, a thousand more crawled across it and over most other surfaces in the room. The women could barely squeeze past each other in the confined space, especially as two of them had to carry babies who couldn't be put down on the dirt floor. The meal consisted of a *piatto unico* of pasta flavoured with marrow flowers and plenty of olive oil and garlic. The home-made pasta tasted of dust and sweat. I had been invited to share this humble repast because it was considered a slap-up dinner. Another treat could be had if one of their hens laid an egg, a rare event in the summer heat; they would fry baby marrows and break the single egg into them, unless they sold the egg to me to get a little cash for some other necessity. The staple of their diet was bread, solid, grey bread which was all the men took to work with them, with an onion or a tomato to be sliced on top, a millimetre of tomato or onion on three centimetres of bread. And a thin, harsh wine that tasted of rusty nails.

It did not at first occur to me to doubt that these people must envy me, with money (however little I had, it was still more than they) and freedom and education. When Mariuzz', who became my official escort, would perch on the low wall of the *ballatoio* and ask with concern, 'Where is your husband?' I would answer patiently, 'I don't have one.' Then his voice would drop to a whisper, as if he was asking something deeply shameful, 'Why did your mother send you away?' I tried a hundred ways of answering that one, but to Mariuzz', not loving your mother above all earthly things was unimaginable. If I tried to explain that I left home at eighteen and neither my mother nor I ever tried to make contact, his face became haggard with trying to understand such a nightmare. 'What can you have done?' he would wail, hoping, I dare say, by finding out, to avoid such an unspeakable fate himself. Every few days the questions would arise again, and every time I made a hash of answering them.

I went on feeling superior to people who wore sweat-sodden woollen vests in the blazing heat and never ate green vegetables. I ran to the sea each day to amaze the dolphins with my Australian crawl and sprinted back in my bikini, displaying the *corpore sano* to go with my *mens sana*. Emilio's friend brought his middle-class cronies to meet the *straniera* and they took me spear-fishing for the huge octopuses that were almost the only things of any size left in the chilly Ionian sea. I got hold of a bicycle and pedalled furiously up and down the roads, while old ladies cursed me and spat at my flying legs.

The first inkling I got that I might have been more insular and unsophisticated than the people I had inflicted myself upon, came when I was sitting on the beach one day with Rosetta. We were talking about love and marriage. Rosetta told me that, when the time came, a young man would come to her father's house to *chiedere amore* and her father would ask her if she wanted the boy who came. And she would answer no until one day she answered yes. Perhaps she would answer yes the first time, if they had seen each other, *guardato amore*, she said. It is *guardare amore* if a woman looks a man full in the eyes. (I was having a lot of difficulty in learning to behave like a *persona seria* and not to *guardare amore* with the butcher, the baker and the candlestick maker.) I started to remonstrate that this was no way to choose a husband, and that they should date, get to know each other, that she should get to know other boys, and on and on. Rosetta heard me out, and then she said simply, '*Da noi si fa cosi.*' She never tried to preach her lifestyle to me, and she was never tempted to judge her life by my criteria. She had no preconceived notion of backward or primitive, no prejudice equal to my blind assumption of superiority. I stopped trying to teach her and began to learn from her instead.

Those three months destroyed all my certainties and taught me the reality of the pluralism I had always argued for intellectually and never really understood. If I had thought that literacy equalled intelligence or that education equalled wisdom I should have been incapable of learning the lessons of that summer. My experience as a teacher in an inner-city high school had shown me the folly of trusting to our systems of classifying human beings according to social status and intelligence quotient, but I still shared the common assumption that the products of good nutrition, housing and education represent some kind of progress from inferior to better. Three months living with some of the poorest peasants in Europe turned that certainty upside-down and it has never righted itself.

As far as the *marchese* who employed the shepherd and his son was concerned, as far as the fat white parish priest was concerned, my neighbours were *incivili*. The *marchese* housed the oxen that drew his plough, because they were pure-bred animals like himself, better than the shepherd and his family. The priest badgered the people with his notions of virtue. I sat in the rose-pink chapel of the *marchese*'s Venetian red palace and listened, incredulous, as the priest explained the action of grace as being like that of a refrigerator where we put the meat to stop it going bad, to people who had no electricity supply, no refrigerator and no meat. His plump cheeks shone as he urged the people to acts of self-denial, these people whose lives were founded on the most rigid self-discipline, poverty, chastity and obedience, more binding than any the priest had vowed to observe.

The poverty was bottomless; each year the peasants had a little less. They had no land to grow their own vegetables and no money to buy them with in the town market. All around us were the market gardens, but in the market there was only fermented fruit, the tattered outside leaves of salad, and diseased tomatoes, all inedible and ruinously expensive. The good stuff was picked and packed at dawn each day by the peasants and sent to the North, as they went home to meals of pasta and bread. One evening I decided to go under the wire and through the *uliveto* to the *marchese*'s kitchen garden. There wasn't much they could do to a foreign national if they caught her stealing food, I reasoned. In the garden there were lettuces of all shapes and colours, peppers, carrots, cucumbers, celery and parsley; I filled my apron and ran back through the olive trees. The shepherd's family knew where my gifts had come from, but nobody made any reference to my thieving. I found out that the people did know how to use fresh vegetables, which are more important in the Italian diet than meat, and I also began to realize how irrelevant to the poor are the laws made by the rich. Once I had defied them, I became trustworthy. I had complained to the *finanza* about the smugglers; two officers had come to see me, with the sole result that everyone, except my friends the shepherd and his family, knew without doubt that I was a prostitute.

The peasants were not only oppressed by the laws of the rich, they were also victimized by the criminality of the rich. Corpulent gentlemen, who were making their millions distributing the fruit and vegetables of Calabria to the citizens of Turin and Milan, along with contraband cigarettes and heroin, liked to visit our part of the world for a little sportive fishing. This consisted of hurling home-made bombs into the sea. The detonation would send every fish, from the largest to the smallest, floating belly up on the surface. The corpulent gentlemen would wade into the sea and pick them up. The fishermen had protested when this genteel amusement had first been practised in their waters, knowing that not only their present livelihood was being threatened, the fish population of the sea was being completely eradicated. That night, the hulls of the fishing boats drawn up on the sand had been smashed in. Now the fishermen could only watch helplessly as their livelihood was destroyed. The children and I would walk along the shingle when the men in their white Mercedes had gone and collect handfuls of dead small-fry to make fish soup. The peasants didn't dare physically to defy the men from the North, or their servants, who were desperadoes covered with home-made tattoos, most of them disfigured by premature explosion of the bombs they made by stuffing tin cans with dynamite. Any appeal to the authorities would have been worse than useless for the police were in hock to the Mafia, known in our parts as *'ndrangheta*; besides, if ever the peasants found themselves in real trouble, they had more to hope for from the assistance of the Mafia than from any legal entity.

To be on the wrong side of the law was inevitable. To invoke the law was to bring upon us the whirlwind. Our only hope was to defy the *bombardieri* collectively. It began when I refused one day to come out of the water when the bombers arrived. The children went fleeing back home to wake their sleeping parents and tell them of the drama on the beach. I stood in the water. The bomber lit his fuse. As he had already lost an eye when such a bomb had exploded above the level of the water, it seemed likely to me, not that he would throw the bomb while I was still in the water, but that he would injure himself, so I gave in. But I did not hold my tongue. On and on

I nagged, following the white Mercedes up the dirt road crisscrossed with viper tracks.

The showdown came within a few days. When I had gone into the bamboo hut the children had built for me on the shingle, so that we could rest after our swim and listen to the story of the most beautiful frog in the world, a zoological and entomological fable of deep philosophical import, I had sat upon a strangely crackling something which turned out to be a polythene bag full of dynamite sticks. Which of course I decided to confiscate, with a view to forcing a parley. I had no sooner balanced the bag on my bosom and tied my bathrobe tightly over it, than the bombers appeared through the heat haze, marching along the waterline. I turned to run, and screamed to the children to run home as fast as they could, for the men were armed and I didn't know how the struggle might end, but they stood stock-still watching the men gain on me. They watched goggle-eyed as the men pulled off my bathrobe and snatched at the plastic bag I was hugging to my almost naked bosom. Then at last they turned and fled.

'This dynamite is ours. You're a thief!' said one of the corpulent men. 'Go tell it to the police!' I sneered just as the bag shot out of my arms and I fell hard on the shingle. The *mafiosi* got back into their white Mercedes and moved off up the dirt road that led through the *frabb'ca*.

I gathered up my own and the children's things and limped back home, more shamed by my defeat than hurt by my fall. I felt that the men had knocked me aside as casually as one might swat a fly. But when I came in sight of the *frabb'ca* I saw something truly wonderful. All my neighbours, even the landowner's steward and his ritzy wife who were staying with us in *villeggiatura*, were crowded in the roadway. Through them ran a narrow passage where the big cars had to run the gauntlet. Everyone was carrying some implement: a hoe, a scythe, a *forcone*. They didn't brandish them, just gripped them and held them very close to the paintwork, watching silent as the drivers inched along. When the big cars had passed the well and the hedge of prickly pear that marked the boundary of our territory they speeded up and disappeared in a cloud of dust. They never came back.

What happened was never discussed. In fact it was the culmination of a long period of building up trust. When the children had first followed me to the sea their parents had worried about my sense of responsibility for them, as well as my ability to save them if something went wrong. They interpreted my fury with the *bombardieri* as protectiveness of the children, when it was at least as much concerned with the fishermen and the fish. A child could have been hurt if a bomb had exploded above the surface of the water, but the fishermen were being hurt and the fish were being exterminated.

At the feast of the Assumption, called in Rossano by its Greek name, *achieropite*, I got my middle-class *cavalieri serventi* to drive the children to the celebrations in Rossano. We were sitting drinking almond milk in the town square when I realized that we had been surrounded by familiar-looking men, the sea bombers. The children hushed and watched nervously to see what would happen. One of the corpulent gentlemen came up and offered me the money to pay for the drinks. 'They're paid for,' I said, but he thrust the money at me anyway. It was an awkward moment, but we were saved by Mariuzz', who took the 10,000 lire bill thrust under my nose and hared across the piazza and into the cathedral. 'Thank you,' I said and bowed, trying ineffectually to be dignified in a yellow minidress of see-through crochet. Mariuzz' came back grinning. He had put the money in the poor box.

Mariuzz' was eight years old and my regular escort. He was one of the most sensitive, wise and light-hearted individuals I have ever met. I was never bored in his company, not even during the long walk to the market (for I eventually decided to stop making an exhibition of myself and be as other women). He knew how to listen and he knew how to discuss, and yet he was a child, not a small grown-up. He was always busy, never bored or fractious. He never asked for anything, but was delighted with every small thing he got: a pen, a notepad, and finally, as a going-away present, a goat. It was typical of him to want something that would be of benefit to his whole family. The bane of his life was his sheep, which was anyway soon to be slaughtered. At all hours I would hear Mariuzz' attempting to reason with his sheep, 'Look, you stupid creature, you have all this to eat, why did you eat mother's flowers? They don't even taste good, I bet . . . How did you get your rope all tangled round your neck? . . . Please, please, you foolish beast, keep out of trouble. Look at that olive tree! You know you're not supposed to even like olive leaves. I can't take my eye off you for ten minutes.' And in his nagging I would hear the exact words his mother and sister-in-law used to scold him, repeated in unconscious parody.

As I observed Mariuzz' I observed too the upbringing that made him the person he was. His baby niece was never 'put down' while she was awake but lived her entire waking life in someone's arms. She was not shy or possessive of her mother because there were so many arms all anxious to hold her. It was assumed that any visitor to the house would be hungry for the touch of baby skin, and so on my first visit she was plumped in my arms and promptly let out a loud fart which delighted everyone hugely. She had no dummy; when she was insecure or fractious she was given the breast. I began to watch out for peasant children who sucked their thumbs or dragged around stuffed animals or security blankets and I found none. Mariuzz's little niece had no toys but she had a dozen people to play with; watching her, I realized that toys are hideous things, decoys we use to deflect children from their natural love-objects, and I felt ashamed.

Mariuzz's little nephew, her cousin, was toddling and being toilet trained by the simple expedient of dressing him in shorts with a split between the legs; to avoid soiling all he had to do was squat. He was learning at his own pace to squat in appropriate places. If he blundered, a broom whisked the results off the dirt floor and there was no fuss. One evening as we all sat around the table talking politics I watched as the children listened, actually listened. As their bright eyes followed the conversation around the table, they seemed awed and interested rather than annoyed by a discourse they couldn't understand. Even Mariuzz', as he felt sleepiness overtaking him, turned into my body and curled up inside my arm as unselfconsciously as a cat. It was an hour before his old mother picked up her beloved youngest son, her *beniamino*, and carried him up to bed still fast asleep.

Ever since I met those children, I have been conscious of children as members (or otherwise) of a community, and have formed an unconscious habit of judging lifestyles by their integration of children. I have seen peasant families at work and at play and in the grip of the most terrible suffering, surrounded by their children, children who were more like Mariuzz' than like the children of my friends. I have seen children closing the eyes of their dead parents in Ethiopia, children supporting their families by fishing or begging or wheeling and dealing in Brazil and India, children fighting a war in South-east Asia, children embedded in a collectivity, children with old people who always have time for them, with young uncles and aunts to induct them into their own youth culture, children who have laughed when I have asked them if they would give up life on the streets of Calcutta and come home with me to live in comparative luxury and change work for school.

And I have watched those same children being shipped out of their communities, rescued from hunger, disease, illiteracy and the threat of early death. I have seen children who had no clothes to speak of, who slept all night at the breast, whose only riches were skin contact and security in the enfolding arms of the family, stuffed into padded ski-suits, encumbered with vast bags of disposable nappies and bottles of formula, and several changes of clothes, propped in the laps of women who had no recourse when they writhed and wept than to poke the teat of the feeding bottle into their mouths, laying the groundwork for our psychoses, turning a small human being into a self-absorbed consumer. If I were to rescue such a child and strip it of its synthetic cocoon and hold it against my skin, I would be guilty of our newest stereotypical sociopathy, child abuse. When I wrote in *The Female Eunuch* that I would want any child I bore to be brought up in Calabria, all kinds of people who should have known what I meant, scoffed at my elitist snobbery. What I meant was that if I brought up any child of mine as most of the people I knew brought up theirs, I should end up liking it as little as they liked theirs, which would be, for me, the worst catastrophe, for the more I see of human beings the more I believe that for most human females, their greatest love affair is with their children. In our society this is not so, and in our monstrous arrogance we believe that it ought not to be so in other societies. Reforming institutions take it upon themselves to teach the subject we know least about, family life, to people who have no intellectual defence except their own poise and dignity. My months in Calabria were the beginning of an apostasy; in the twenty years that followed I have become a heretic, preaching as angrily against masturbation as the paradigm of human happiness as ever Savonarola fulminated against the pleasures of the flesh. All because, long ago on the banks of that ancient sea, an illiterate sixteen-year-old defended herself and her people against my jejune criticism.

Rosetta, as an unmarried daughter, was responsible for the laundry. She was a moss rose, with fair skin and flushed cheeks, freckles scattered across the bridge of her nose and a dark down on her upper lip. Her life was hard, for every week the heavy homespun sheets were washed in cold water by bashing and thrashing them against flat stones around the well. The men's overalls were clean on every day. She had never eaten a meal in a restaurant, she had never gone to a dance, she had never seen a movie, she had never owned a pair of sheer stockings, she had never been to a hairdresser or tried out make-up. But there was always a spring in her step and I would hear her singing fit to bust as she pounded the wet clothes.

I wondered about the source of her apparent happiness. It wasn't that she didn't know about the lives of teenagers in consumer society. Her parents had a television set which was turned on every evening after dinner especially for the programme of commercials called *Carosello*. She had seen young women, gorgeously dressed and lusciously made-up, being wooed by pop stars by candlelight or in moonlit gardens or in fast cars, and had kept her head. She did not see herself as prevented from having such a life by poverty and ignorance; she was untouched by envy or discontent.

At first I refused the invitations to join the crowd sitting outside in the cool, watching the television set through the kitchen doorway. Then I joined in but refused the seat they offered me in the front, because I wanted to watch them watching. They regarded the posturings of the actors and presenters in much the same way as we might watch endless couplings of spiders or sticklebacks; the rich were some kind of exotic species, sometimes barbaric or ridiculous, never to be identified with. Mostly they watched silent, for they are a taciturn people, but every now and then a laconic comment would bring hoots of laughter.

The more I thought about it, the more this level-headedness seemed to me to derive from the very severity of the Calabrian moral code. As long as they adhered to this discipline, and their group cohered, they were able to resist the cultural onslaught of the North. They knew that the cult of honour was despised by Northerners, and that the law of Italy did not distinguish between crimes of honour and common criminality, but then they did not recognize the civil authority. The institutions by which the state hoped to tame these people, the courtrooms and the schools, were instruments of foreign domination. My neighbours didn't try to impose their morality on the whores and gigolos of the North, so why did the North try to meddle with them? Honour was their only psychological defence against the squalor and humiliation that, in their powerlessness, constantly threatened them. It was not a real defence, in material terms, but it was a spiritual defence. If they had abandoned their costly code they would have been stripped of their last possession, their self-esteem. I decided that Rosetta danced when she walked because she had a dazzling self-image; she knew she was a pearl of great price.

This is not to say that Rosetta saw herself as some sort of sexless untouchable. She was intensely aware of sex all around her, but her awareness was not muddled with sentimentality the way that mine was. I have told elsewhere how one day, as we sat on the beach shingle, an almost naked boy riding bareback came clattering past us in a shower of spray. I was winded by the astonishing beauty of the sight, but Rosetta was excited by a particular detail that had escaped my eyes completely, the boy's erection. He was, like all the boys at Mirto, one of Rosetta's cousins; I often wonder if he was the one who came to *chiedere amore* for she is married now and lives in town.

Listening to Rosetta describe it, explaining how, if any of her cousins was to commit an act of moral turpitude, generally but not solely understood as a sexual transgression, she too would have *la condotta macchiata*, a stain upon her reputation, I felt both appalled and impressed by the rigour of such a code. I began to understand a little of the character structure which develops inside this kind of collectivity and of the effect on behaviour of the consciousness of the continuity of the individual. It took a catastrophe to show me how far this went.

One morning, when I came with my bucket for water to douse my floors, I found the steward's wife and the dairyman's wife standing one each side of the well. Their buckets were filled but still they stood, rigid, trembling slightly. I walked between them and lowered my bucket. My heart was pounding. Walking past their eyes was like walking through a wall. When I was safe upstairs I came to the window. The women were still standing, staring at each other. Then one spoke with measured theatrical violence; what she uttered was the most preposterous insult. Minutes passed and the women stood silent. Then the other spoke, and again, projecting her voice as if she spoke from behind a tragic mask, she said the unsayable. Behind half-closed shutters the inhabitants of the *frabb'ca* watched in total silence.

Mariuzz' came quietly up and stood holding my hand, watching for an hour until the flyting match was over, and the women left the stage. Then he explained. 'The dairyman has been caught stealing milk. He's been doing it for more than a year, fifteen litres off the top, every day. He's to be turned away today. He's gone for a cart to take away their things.' That morning the dairyman's eldest child, a twelve-year-old girl, had crept out at first light and found the steward's wife's only laying hen, strangled it and thrown it on the stairs where she would find it when she came down to the well. 'Why?' I cried, mystified. 'Why should anyone do such a thing? How does that help the situation?' '*Per dispetto*,' said Mariuzz' reasonably, as if it explained everything.

I watched as the little girl carried out the first of her family's poor possessions. Her face was as set and blank as her mother's had been. I wondered if anyone had told her to enact ritual defiance of the steward who had destroyed her father, and I decided not. The house was soon emptied into four small boxes. The dairyman's wife, his big daughter, his son and his baby daughter, whom I had never known to be either silent or still, seated themselves on the boxes. All day we went about our business in silence as the tragic family sat there, unspeaking, staring sightlessly across the roadway, unflinching when the hot wind stirred up the dust. No one made any sign of compassion. I wanted to take them water to drink, but I couldn't repeat my mistake of the morning. The pageant had to be acted out in all its stony grandeur. It was as if the family's moral survival depended upon this unbroken defiance and if I had offered them my noncommittal compassion they might have broken down. The cart came for them at dusk and heads high, without a tear, the children left the only home they had ever known.

The events of that terrible day left me with a kind of vertigo, which came back whenever I got a glimpse across the spiritual landscape in which my neighbours dwelt. One day the shepherd's daughters sat down with me to write to their husbands, away working in Germany. I imagined myself prompting them into little playful turns of phrase, hoped for some insight into Calabrian eroticism. The women leaned over the children sleeping in their laps to gaze at the marks I was making on the page, and dictated: '*Caro sposo, La mamma sta bene . . . i figlioli stanno bene . . .*' I thought of the culture the men were being exposed to, the facile intimacies and expensive amusements that would milk the money they had gone to earn to give their families the basic necessities of life and health, and suddenly felt breathless with rage. The stilted letters I was penning could hardly compete with the constant seductiveness of life among the rich foreigners. Here amongst the ruins of Magna Grecia the women would be keeping alive a culture and a system of values that nobody wanted, unless their men were as staunch as they, which I rather doubted. How would the men be when they came back, if they came back? Would they demand that their wives bleached their hair and painted their lips, and wore sheer stockings and used contraception, so that their calm beauty was destroyed. I didn't want these overwhelmingly female beings to become merely feminine and learn to flirt and cajole where once they were stern and silent.

I had thought that life in the *frabb'ca* would be dreadfully dull. I had wondered how I would fill my days. That was before I found myself rising in the grey-violet pre-dawn with the shepherd's wife, washing myself at the well, watching the sun come out of the steel-grey sea as I sipped my thick black coffee, hurrying to finish the day's ration of rewriting (for I was finishing my Ph.D. thesis) before the day's dramas and disasters overtook me. The excitement was intensified when I succumbed to a quartan fever akin to typhoid, so that every fourth day I had to abandon my work and toss about on the homespun mattresses until the hallucinations wore themselves out. Then I was glad I had five beds, so that as one became saturated with sweat I could roll on to the next one. While young fools of my generation produced terrifying symptoms by ingesting poisons of various synthetic kinds, I was taken to extraordinary realms by a bacillus carried from human excrement on a fly's foot. I swelled to the size of a mountain and shrank to the size of a pin, flew and sang and fell through exotic configurations, in the intervals between agonizing convulsions on the heavy earthenware *vaso*, whose lethal contents I had to dispose of in the fields when the fever subsided. When the burning and shivering stopped and I could see again only what was there, I stayed enthralled by clarity. There was nothing to me in biochemical mindbending and bullshit psychedelia that did not have the slimy scent of death about it. I hated being out of touch, isolated by the solipsism of delirium, unable to communicate or comprehend. The first time I was offered a joint I had to crawl to the lavatory and barely managed to lock myself in before voiding completely upwards and downwards. The years of social smoking were an unending ordeal, the combination of marijuana and sex an obscenity.

I went back to Mirto Foresta last year. Rossano Calabro has changed. The fields where I watched the harvest and the stubble-burning have been turned into truck farms where lettuces and table grapes are grown under acres of polythene sheeting so that Scandinavians may eat them all the year round. The citizens of Naples like to come here in *villeggiatura* and have built a thousand blocks of gimcrack little flats all along the stony beach. When I came by, the sea was wild and raised itself to show like palest jade against the mackerel sky before pitching itself upon the rolling cobbles. I stood in the sandy roadway where the shepherd's wife blessed me before watching me walk off to the train station. Where we used to watch television, and where the shepherd's wife had once thrown a knife through the neck of a viper that had crawled out of the prickly pear towards her grandson, someone had made a small flower garden, marked out by bricks laid on edge.

The steward from the farm recognized me. The shepherd's family had gone to live in town, he said. Only Mariuzz' lived in the old house now, and he had made the flower garden. He would have been twenty-six. I felt a cold fear that the coming of the fair stranger that summer had deflected the course of his life; it seemed all wrong that he should be keeping an English flower garden around the old house where nine of them had lived together. I didn't dare wait to see what my little *cavaliere servente* had become but climbed into my old Ford and went on my way. I should be glad that this part of the *meridione* has developed and Mariuzz' has a car when once he could hope for no better than a goat. I am certainly glad that the *latifonderia* has collapsed and the shepherd got to own the two rooms he lived in and can one day sell it to a Neapolitan holiday-maker.

Most of all I am glad that the summer eighteen years ago, when my heart was bruised enough to be sensitive to such subtle impressions and there was no love egotism to block out the view, I was delivered up to those people as they were then. I could have gone on with my academic career, convinced that nothing else was so worthy or so distinguished, applying the values of the hothouse to the vast anguish of humanity, but that they saved me from such a fate. They made sure that I always heard a different drummer. They made no attempt to impress me, nor were they likely to be impressed by me or my Ph.D. I had to test my cleverness against their reality, so much more like the reality that most of the world's inhabitants know than my own; seen from their perspective my lucubrations appeared no more germane than polo playing or stamp collecting. Given their deeply serious view of sexuality, I must have seemed like a child using sex as a toy, a distraction, a pastime. While I had no more intention of abandoning my view of sex as harmless recreation than of failing my Ph. D. (it being far too late for either course of action) I was never tempted to call my way 'normal'.

The experience of those three months underlies all my thinking, to an extent that can surprise even me, even now. I realize that my dissatisfaction with the theory of the feminine mystique stemmed partly from the view of another kind of womanliness, of women as adults, women as workers, women as female rather than feminine, that I absorbed that summer. My critique of the nuclear family is based upon my experience of the multi-woman family as a better place for child-rearing and for the avoiding of much female neurosis and psychosis. The track of the Calabrian experience can be found in my critique of sexual morality in our time, in essays like 'A needle for your pornograph' and 'The expense of spirit' and 'Seduction is a four-letter word'. I might not have found our sexual morality so crazily confused, if I had not had the opportunity to live with people who have simplified and streamlined sexuality in order to knit this wild strand into their social fabric. This process, by the way, is not primarily religious; my Calabrian neighbours were all anticlerical. Delinquency in sexual matters was possible, but only on condition that its perpetrators dropped out of the social structure generations of peasants had created for themselves. There was an alternative society of casual, commercial sexual encounters which resembled the permissive society in all particulars. The so-called sexual liberation of our time seemed to me then, and seems to me still, to be the intensification of the focus on self-pleasuring, and is fundamentally masturbatory, hence its reliance upon external stimuli which work on sexual fantasy. The appeal of self-gratification as the key to self-realization was and is its adaptability to marketing.

When that summer ended I went back to England, took my job as an English lecturer at Warwick University, and huddled in an expensive furnished bedsit, waiting in vain for one of my colleagues to invite me to meet his family or eat a meal with them, finding them immeasurably more parochial, squalid and *incivili* than my peasant neighbours, learning to despise their costly but graceless and dreary way of life. As an over-qualified, overworked and above all unmarried female I was as much of an outsider at our white-tile university as I had ever been in Calabria, but the consequences were quite different. I had no choice but to identify with the students and involve myself in the explosion of co-operative anarchism that all too briefly convulsed our institutions of higher learning. I got a part I didn't want in a television series, got some extra income, rented a studio in London, and wrote a book that drew more heavily than immediately appears upon the Calabrian experience, *The Female Eunuch*.

I meant to stay at the university, but when teaching began to bore me, I decided to quit before I had begun to bore my students. Besides, I wanted to escape from the stereotypes imposed by our society, and look for new possibilities in different human contexts, above all, for a different notion of woman, for it seemed to me that consumer society could never regard human qualities as anything but commodities. It is curious now to find myself considered an architect of the permissive society, when at the time I was one of its bitterest opponents – not that I was in favour of institu-tionalized repression, rather I longed for a less banal and commercial approach to sexuality.

'Flip-top legal pot' is one of a group of articles that I wrote for the underground magazine *Oz*, run by Richard Neville and friends. I had first met Richard when he was editing *Oz* in Sydney; my career as a journalist had begun as a reporter and drama critic on *Farrago*, the Melbourne University magazine, continued in *Honi Soit* at Sydney University and *Varsity* at Cambridge. It was but a small step to contributing (unpaid as ever) to the underground press, which was run not only by the same types of people, but by the same people. In my experience free copy is always worse treated than copy that has been paid for, and cheap copy is always treated worse than expensive copy; the underground press was no excep-tion to the iron law of capitalism that decrees 'If you fuck for a dime, you can't complain if someone else is getting a fur coat.' In the years that followed, *Oz* was to print my stuff in everything but black and white, culminating in their treatment of the essay on the death of Jimi Hendrix, which was printed in Day-glo pink and Day-glo green over a photograph. This is, in effect, its first publication. I had my first experience of spiking with *Oz*; the obscene letter to John Gorton was never run, for obvious reasons. The joke was, and is, that the issue was seized for obscenity notwithstanding. *Oz* missed out on the opportunity to run Britain's first-ever piece of loony feminist nonsense.

One of the hallmarks of the underground press was that it always printed far too many words in such a format that nobody could, or would, read them. Seldom has journalistic talent been so squandered. Nevertheless, my Cassandra pieces got up everybody's nose; while Richard, who was not so much a revolutionary as the ad-man for the revolution, faithfully followed every new gimmick – flower power, marijuana mysticism, LSD lore, the little red book, Maoism, TCP, black power, gay power, yoga, feminism, macrobiotics, alternative medicine, paedophiles' rights – he had to deal with a Cassandra in the basement, whose pieces always added up to the same message: 'You're full of shit.' He ran them, amid the millions of minute words that lay on the pages of *Oz* like sand on a beach.

When *The Female Eunuch* began to take off, which was not until a year after its first publication, I too became flavour of the month, and I got my own number of *Oz* to edit, hence my editorial, 'The politics of female sexuality'. The days of unpaid journalism were almost over for me, for soon after I began writing a fortnightly column for the *Sunday Times*, alternating with Jilly Cooper. In order to keep tinkering with my pieces by the *Sunday Times* subeditors to a minimum, I adopted a strategy of filing at the last moment, beetling down to the Reuters office in Saigon or Delhi or Bangkok on the Friday before my publication day. This ruse did not work too badly and our relationship continued fairly uneventfully until I submitted three pieces adding up to a sustained argument for abortion on demand, here printed for the first time in sequence. The paper took the view that it was just too much harping on the same string; in fact I was very well aware that my future as a columnist depended principally on my ability to entertain the couple under the Habitat duvet on a Sunday morning, and so I had interspersed my more bitter animadversions with frivolous columns about moped riding and going knickerless. These, of course, were the only ones anyone ever remembered. 'Does Miss Greer's mind ever rise above her navel?' they used to ask. Such flightiness produced the now fixed idea that I was an architect of the permissive society.

'My Mailer problem' (so named in ironic tribute to Norman Podhoretz's 'My negro problem') is my own account of the New York Town Hall debate of 1972, in which I attempted to define the problem of women and creativity in terms of the sexist concept of the artist as supermale, here impersonated by Norman Mailer.

'Seduction is a four-letter word' was my first attempt, and rather a prosy one, to improve thinking on rape. For it, by way of purchasing golden opinions, *Playboy* awarded me the title of 'Journalist of the Year' and a lucite plinth with a medal embedded in it. The effect on the rape debate was absolutely nil; neither thinking nor legislation improved. As long as women are isolated, and emotionally dependent upon men's interest, petty rape continues to be a fundamental characteristic of sexual relations. I broached the subject again in a review of Susan Brownmiller's book (1976) and yet again in the *Spectator* in 1982. Changes are beginning to be made in rape law, notably in Australia.

The essay on 'body art' was to have been put at the front of a book of photographs by my dear friend, Barry Kay; the publishers were unable to find a co-production deal to their liking and abandoned the project. The disappointment was one of many crushing reversals in Barry's professional career which hurried his decline and untimely death. It represents another stage in my thinking about peoples, in this case, an argument about body decoration as more beautiful when serving a collective purpose, than when reflecting self-preoccupation. In groups like the Nuer, whose body art is unsurpassed, the decoration is applied to the whole body by comrades and expresses not only the creativity of the owner of the body, but its interpretation by his friends and kin. Body art in consumer society is either narcissistic or commercial, and often undertaken in a spirit of body-hatred rather than celebration.

The essays on Brazil, Cuba and Ethiopia represent my coming of age. Something like a coherent system of values is beginning to emerge after my years of wandering, although I have certainly not arrived at a set of articles of faith, and never will I hope. In visiting all three places I encountered three important absolutes, which established outer limits to my intellectual system, uncertain though I still am about what lies between.

The question is often asked of me now, 'Are you still a feminist?' as if it were possible for me to be anything else. Everything I learn reinforces my conviction that the only corrective to social inequality, cruelty and callousness, is to be found in values which, if we cannot call them female, can be called sororal. They are the opposite of competitiveness, acquisitiveness and domination, and may be summed up by the word 'co-operation'. In the world of sisterhood, all deserve care and attention, including the very old, the very young, the imbecile and the outsider. The quality of daily life is what matters, the taste of the food on the table, the light in the room, the peace and wholeness of the moment. Perfect love casteth out fear. The only perfect love to be found on earth is not sexual love, which is riddled with hostility and insecurity, but the wordless commitment of families, which takes as its model mother-love. This is not to say that fathers have no place, for father-love, with its driving for self-improvement and discipline, is also essential to survival, but that uncorrected father-love, father-love as it were practised by both parents, is a way to annihilation.

When I went upon my travels around the world, I was seeking the firm ground under the dizzy dance of technological genius, the matrix that is the ultimate source of all our human brilliance. Wherever I went I found it in the commonalty of women, who often failed to recognize me as of their group, and left me with the men as an honorary male, unsexed by privilege. It never occurred to me to assume that woman in technological society was happier or worthier than women in other worlds, nor would I ever have supposed that women's liberation involved the jettisoning of their history, their traditional occupations or their forms of creative expression. I travelled, not to bring the gospel of liberation to the heathen, but to learn from other women what women are and can be. With a couple of magnificent exceptions, anthropologists in the past have been either actually male, or unsexed as I was by their isolation from women and women's concerns. As an amateur I was unbound by the discipline of anthropology and open to the glimpses of a female world through the mask of masculine social organization. Women spoke only the local patois, seldom the official language, let alone English. Women talked in concrete terms of day-to-day experiences, because they knew nothing of ideology or the use of words for mystification. In everything I was their pupil; in everything I have written I hope can be found the imprint of my love and respect, admiration indeed, of poor women, women's women.

1968 – 1969

Flip-top legal pot

Oz, October 1968

The Legalize Pot Rallies, organized by SOMA, of whose advisory board Jonathan Aitken, now a junior minister in Mrs Thatcher's Government, was a member, took place in Hyde Park in July 1967 and 1968. The campaign was abandoned in February 1970.

Legalize Pot rallies are so beautiful; hundreds of doe-eyed painted people stirring slowly under the soft sky, bound together by their sense of gently daring in a common cause, holding smoking incense sticks like they were precious aphrodisiacs or opium pipes at least. Not less beautiful, but probably more so, because their beauty is not compromised by utility. If pot is legalized it won't be capitulation to this kind of demand: when our masters decide to have pot on their side it is dubious whether it will be to our ultimate advantage.

It is clear that nobody wants to be penalized for doing something harmless and pleasant, but do we really want our pot legal?

Champions of legality do, because the law against marijuana is too clear an example of the arbitrary nature of the law, but to many of us, the notion of law itself is antipathetic. The law exists, we are told, to protect life and property. It protects life by outlawing abortion, euthanasia and suicide, i.e. it insists on life even when it is unbearable to the liver. It cannot be proved ever to have prevented a murder or an assault, and can be proved to have legally killed and to have penalized those who refused to fight and kill. Police brutality is legal massacre.

In the interest of life, the law proscribes marijuana as a dangerous drug, less habit forming than tobacco and coffee and considerably less harmful to the organism than alcohol and aspirin. If the law did protect life or could protect life against war, madness or disaster perhaps there would be some point in wooing legality, but there seems to be no point at all in respecting what is merely the safeguard of property. Many of us do not believe in the inalienable right of property, to the extent that we possess little or nothing, and do not complain when it is used or carried off by others, and tend ourselves to use and carry off the goods' of others, especially department stores and bookstalls, and yet I do not find posters saying 'Legalize Theft'.

Everything that I do can be guaranteed to annoy a guardian of the law in a certain frame of mind, and yet I cannot join any movement to 'Legalize Offensive Behaviour'.

It would be less soft-headed, and consequently more beautiful, if equally futile, to rally in Hyde Park under the banner 'Fuck the Law'.

The signers of petitions to legalize cannabis go to some lengths to distinguish themselves from the criminal classes. Of the thousands who would sign, and maybe did, the publicized names were priests, members of parliament, pop intellectuals, jurists and doctors, stooges of the establishment, some of whom were so rosily innocent of the irrational nature of arbitrary opposition that they cried out in amazement when they were passed over in the race for more eminent positions within the Establishment. Others were so firmly entrenched that they didn't have to worry. You can't revoke MBEs.

The rest of you, stop and consider before you rally again, what legalization would mean. Our masters will not legalize marijuana until they have worked out how to control it, which means how to exploit it. When the cigarette companies have finally lost their battle to conceal the relationship between smoking and lung cancer, they will begin pressurizing for legalized marijuana (and ought to be designing the scene right now). Their economic pressure is more powerful and more subtle than the unintelligible ravings of a few unamplified hysterics among the doe-eyed crowds of Hyde Park. Governments get a useful slice of revenue from cigarettes, otherwise tobacco would already have been outlawed. The potential rake-off from pot is enormous – it's even more than what goes to the pushers.

Then the advertising campaign will begin: all the young executive prestige shit will gather round the kind of joint one smokes. They'll come in flip-top boxes and be lit with Dunhills, photographed on malachite bedside tables, with automatic pistols and platinum cufflinks. All the slow ritual of rolling a joint, the gentle rhythm of passing it from lip to lip . . . all the communion of the shared conspiracy gone. The smoke won't be as good either, adulterated with commercial products, dry and stale from being too long in the packet or the shop or the machine.

Maybe it won't happen that way; only one thing is certain: if pot is legalized, it won't be for our benefit but for the authorities'. To have it legalized will also be to lose control of it.

The alternative is to join the criminal classes and be done with it. Regard the law as your enemy (it is actually impartial to all but itself) and take steps to lick it. The negro, prevented from joining the whites on his own terms, closes the ghetto to the white man. The pot smoker may reject legality and work instead to promote law breaking in that form, as far as possible with impunity. To begin with, Stop Getting Caught.

Any London con can tell you that you're more likely to get caught when you aren't doing anything wrong than when you are, so it's nonsense to think that you need not develop any routines to protect yourself because you're not doing anything wrong. The law is not concerned with right and wrong. Any criminal knows that the police will manufacture any evidence that they cannot find, and better it should be pot than detonators and gelignite, or heroin. He also knows that in all but the rarest cases (like if you're a bishop in mufti) it is worse than useless to claim having been framed. Learn how to deal with the police. The great evidence-manufacturing industry is part of that legality pot smokers are so anxious to get on the right side of. Fuck it. (One way you could fuck it, if you are caught, is to insist on the exact amount you were carrying being declared in court, so the cops don't keep half of it to plant on somebody else.)

Most criminals know the law very well: pot smokers don't bother to find out. You should know exactly how little you have to tell the fuzz. If the cops stop you on the street asking what's in your paper bag, especially if it's obviously records, pause, before letting them search the rest of you, long enough to hurl your gear into the nearest front garden or down the grating or into a crowd, or somewhere. Even if they find it, it's a different matter to prove that it's what you threw. Even if you're not carrying anything you could throw something else just to confuse things. Another way is to carry some harmless substance like basil leaves or sugar cubes or sugar pills, so that they think that they've found the gear and don't bother to fit you up, and only after tests discover their error. The tests are too documented and too public to be rigged (I think). Learn the criminal's rule: to protect your own, especially your connection, and don't, as one idiot did, toss your gear to someone else when you're getting busted. Remember, ignorance of the contents of a parcel is no defence. If you're in a public place which is getting busted, drop the gear on the floor because it can't be traced to you and the management is for it anyway, that's if you can't drop it in the can in time. Awful to think of the stuff the fuzz gets hold of for free. Don't leave gear at home: if you must have it around it's safer on you, especially if you're staying with a friend. Don't stockpile it: let the pushers do that, for them it's a calculated risk.

There are more ways out and we must develop them. If, like Mafia and Prohibition, we succeed well enough in breaking the law and not getting caught, it will paradoxically have more effect in getting pot legalized, than all the pious ejaculations and gormless pleas for gentler sentences, because people cannot be allowed to get away with things. We have certain advantages over criminals of a less self-conscious type, so let's use them.

If, after all, you really must have your pot legal, you can always get a prescription for tincture of cannabis, an innocent corn cure, and have your own bottle of filthy green liquid and your own little spoon.

A groupie's vision

Oz, February 1969

Musicians, like other men, have always had women, but something in their way of having them was different by virtue of their being musicians, like it would differ again for airline pilots and lighthouse keepers. In the years BB (before Beatlemania) there were two kinds of musicians' birds – the musos' old ladies and the scrubbers. The rock-and-rollers picked up and put down the local goers like meals, perhaps storing a little woman at home, protected from the knowledge of her husband's promiscuity and the lunatic fringes of his sexuality. The scrubbers suffered all his aggression, all his loneliness and self-doubt. The jazz musicians had a different scene. They toured less often and less spectacularly and played to a discriminating clientèle that came to listen. They were deep into their music, and so perforce were their women. Marriage was not common, but monogamy was the rule. It was a hard life for the birds, because they never went out at night except to listen to the old man's sets. There wasn't much money so they worked in the daytime, and fought fatigue and loneliness sitting in a dark corner where the club owner would not find their presence intolerable. They came to listen instead of waiting at home in bed because musicians were not often verbal in those days of separated media, and the only way they could hear the message of love was through the music. But cool jazz was cool. The message was often cold, inner-directed, and musos often lost their birds, not often to each other. Some of them took up a pose of embitterment, and took it out on the scrubbers. Lots of them drank or pilled up. One or two kept a wife in the suburbs. And took that out on the scrubbers too.

'The first boyfriend I ever had,' said Dr G, the Daytripper, 'was a jazz drummer, the best. I was with him for a year, and I never danced with him, that was one of the things it meant. I couldn't even dance to his music in front of him. Seems like I sat that whole year. In the end I became the hat-check girl in the club. Then he took a long gig in another state. On his last night in the club he sang a blues song just for me, about having a girl ten foot tall, and I cried myself blind in the hat-check room. The rag merchants talked all through it and then they all clapped their hands.' She knitted her brows. 'Then somebody told him I had been with somebody else, 2,000 miles away, and he just dropped me cold without another word. Can you imagine that?'

But the post-Beatle era was dawning and the media were drawing closer to each other for the fusion which is now. Music became commercial and creative, not only notes but words, not only sound but physical onslaught, sight, movement, total environment. The jazz musician's love affair with his instrument moved out of his hand and met the rocker's violent cruel sensuality at tenderness junction, and the girls sitting wiped out against cold nightclub walls in quiet clothes arose with their listening eyes and danced alone, opened out their beauty in the various light and sex flowed back into the scene and lapped all around them. Where all the currents intersected and flowed forward and back, there he was, the musical revolutionary-poet calling all to witness the new order and achieve the group grope, astride his thousands of volts, winding his horn while the mode of the music changed and the walls of the city fell and everybody burst out laughing. The women kept on dancing while their long skirts crept up, and their girdles dissolved, and their nipples burst through like hyacinth tips and their clothes withered away to the mere wisps and ghosts of draperies to adorn and glorify, and at last the cunt lay open like a shining seapath to the sun.

So who did it happen for? Not for everybody. For the musicians it happened, and for those same girls who dragged out their lives flattened against a leaf of sound, for their sisters and their daughters. The women who really understand what the bass guitar is saying when it thumps against their skin, a velvet-hard glans of soundwaves, nuzzling. To understand and face the possibilities of annihilation OM without flinching. To be limitless. Infinite. Bounty as boundless as the sea, and love as deep. Here's how it happened for one: 'I was very slow to turn on to pop. I turned down an invitation to a party for the Beatles. I moved from jazz through blues, skirted folk music, and ended up with Bach and Buxtehude, Monteverdi and the great madmen. Hobnobbed with guys who were called *composers* and wrote operas and ballets and stuff. Started to go to concerts of contemporary music and talk about it. Sang Carl Orff. The song that made the difference was 'I Can't Get No Satisfaction' and the original resensifiers were the Stones. I pay attention. The walls of the city begin to shake.

'It was evident that there was a pop conspiracy to blow the minds of my generation. I was interested but not involved. I only began to understand the group symbol when I met Simon Dupree and the Big Sound in a TV studio. The place was full of smoothies and groovers using cool and calculating every move. The sounds of sucking filled the air, when these little guys blasted off, singing what was really an old number, "Reservations", I remember, and his underpants showed. And he sweated a lot. And his sound blew out all the crap and BBC gumshoes, and I knew I was on his side. You know what it's like; all the technicians regard rock stars as freaks, the management regards them as charming, grubby, mental defectives. They do their thing and don't give a fuck. The message is sent. When

I was being dressed for some change or other in some tight little thing that squeezed all my boobs up, I looked up and they were all looking at me with a kind of hot innocence, and I suddenly realized that groupiedom was possible. But the stitches were still in. Just say, it occurred to me. They all went off and took a train to Aberdeen or somewhere, some gruelling bloody awful tour.

'The first pop star I actually pulled was an entire accident. I was at this ball in the country (the best scene for a calculated "hit" now I come to consider it) and I was having a dreary time because my bloke was utterly spaced out, so I made myself mildly conspicuous [we should point out that Dr G's six feet and other freakish attributes make inconspicuousness a more significant achievement] and sure enough, in the first break the lead singer of the group turned up next to me and stayed there, which was all right except it was a nowhere group who were not getting it together and I didn't dig him. I started to kind of edge away and I walked into the lead singer of the star group and we went into this crazy improvised routine, as if we'd known each other for years. When it's right that's how it is. You recognize each other and you play in tune. Because you start that way there are no hang-ups, no ploys, well, no ways of exploiting each other. If you fuck, you do it with the carnal innocence of children or cats or something. When you've watched a man calling his call and you've heard it and know what it means, there are no limits; the night you spend together is limitless too . . . you might go off for a few days to a few places, but it's immaterial if you're still together . . . Sounds like a poor line in cheap mysticism, but that's how it can be. Usually you separate quite soon, because there are things to do, more things to have and do, and maybe it happens again a few times, maybe months apart. It's a bit like a jam session I suppose. Or a supergroup. Maybe he's married or got an old lady: that's like his regular scene. He knows he can blow good things when he's with you, sometimes, things he can only blow with you, so you get together. That's how I like it. Monogamy is death for me.'

She's laughing but she means it. She explains that she's very promiscuous but out of the hundreds of guys she's made, relatively few are pop stars, but most of the pop stars are names to conjure with.

'I guess I'm a star-fucker really. You know it's a name I dig, because all the men who get inside me are stars. Even if they're plumbers, they're star plumbers. Another thing I dig is balling the greats before the rest of the world knows about them, before they get the big hype. Because I have to follow my judgement, not the charts, you dig? Now take Magic Terry, he's a star which your telescope hasn't picked up yet. We met at a party in New York and he said he wanted to come and read poetry at my apartment. I believed him, although it seemed unlikely, and he came and he did this amazing thing, this ENORMOUS poetry, which he's going to do soon (if he doesn't die or something) with the best hard-rock backing money and his judgement can get, and that is the best. When it happens it will all happen to me too, whether I'm there or not. The great thing about star-fucking is that every time you play a record, or just dig his thing again, it's all there, like he was there.'

I spy on her by looking through the records scattered round the turntable: they are the names I expect, with a few notable exceptions. I had seen her sharing Jim Morrison's spotlight at the Doors concert so I asked why there were none of their records there.

'I suppose I went there to get some Jim Morrison. I never know until I experience the thing properly whether it's a good thing or not. Jim Morrison was a terrible bring-down, I mean, he was there coming on like a fucking sex kitten, pouting and wiggling and slipping out of his clothes. He thought he was singing to teeny-boppers and kept throwing them the drumsticks and stuff and everyone froze with embarrassment. The vibes were so bad that he started to have trouble getting it together. He went upstage and tried to bring himself on jigging the maracas up and down with his elbow down here so he'd have a stand to show the customers, and then he goes leaping down to show it to everyone and it's gone.

'Most commercial groups are a terrible bring-down: it must be like fucking a whore, you know. You watch them standing there slapping their instruments with these terrible fixed expressions. Can you imagine sex with Andy Fairweather-Low or that podgy guy from the Amen Corner, or is it the other one? Jesus, I never know which is which. That night, the Doors communicated their impotence to all of us, and we sneaked home furtively, separately, ashamed of liking that LP so long ago. What a disgusting hype they are.

'Most groups are hypes, sure. That ought to be irrelevant. Like you and I both publish to earn a bottle of wine, you write *The Wanker's Manual* and I write *Reality Sandwiches*. But when a group is nothing but a hype, as I believe the Doors are, when they make love and revolution *commodities*, assassination is called for. Mind you, there are other kinds of motives for star-fucking. Maybe if someone turned Jim Morrison on properly the Doors would open. But I'm really not a groupie reformer, for God's sake.

'But do you know I find Engelbert very horny-making. He's so evil you know, getting all those lonely housewives to cream their jeans, with his tight high-fronted shiny mohair trousers with just a touch of rubber hose. So fucking evil.'

She's still laughing, and I start her off on a different tack and she stops.

'I don't know, I mean everybody uses the sacrament acid, most people some of the time. I only ever once went with anyone on horse, and I remember it was as absolutely magical, I nearly turned on myself. He was as strong as a hawk, as light as a feather. His breath was as sweet as a child and his skin was hot and smelled like sunlight. He slept and woke and made love and slept as easily as if it was happening every day instead of every hour. He was amazingly high energy, and unutterably tender. I thought it would be all monkey-on-my-back stuff, but it was unbelievably potent and delicate. I still feel very involved with him although I never see him. I heard he fell off a bandstand the other day and cut his head. He gets sick a lot and he's unhappy I think. That's a drag, not being able to help. I guess it's unemancipated or something but I won't call him. I only hope if it gets really bad he'll think of me ... I love him you know, him and a thousand others as they say.'

She is laughing again, but I am glad when the phone rings, and I put on a record while she talks.

What a bring-down ... when she comes back, I ask my last question. I phrase it awkwardly and the Doctor squeezes her fleecy hair up in her hands and laughs again.

'It's not a matter of *minding* balling the whole group. They're not like the ton-up boys who'd hold a girl down while they all fucked her: that's the fascist sort of homosexual kick, like where the leader fucks the girl in the glare of their headlights and they all jack off and stuff. I'd never be likely to wind up in that situation. But I'd love to be one of a group in a loving sexual situation. I just don't know very many groups who can get it together. The Airplane seem in love and listen to each other a lot, but *Rolling Stone* tells me they get uptight about sharing birds. Now *RS* is not always right, any more than a penis is always called a Hampton Wick, but I haven't often come across a group that were so together that they could make that scene. Probably the MC5 are near it. I had to go to sleep in their hotel after Elektra had had to ring me up to get Rob Tyner to a conference, and they slept two to a room with the doors open and everyone walked through. I found out I really *really* liked being able to hear other people balling close to me while I was, and I was very pleased; you see, the group fuck is the highest ritual expression of our faith, but it must happen as a sort of special grace. Contrived it could be really terrible, like a dirty weekend with the Monkees!

'When you asked me that question, you made like you thought that it was a kinky sort of thing, well it isn't you see, because kinkiness ... it's the great British disease. Kinkiness comes from low energy. It's the substitution of lechery for lust. You don't really feel desirous so you turn yourself on with cute variants like rubber mackintoshes and nuns' habits ... Lots of pop stars run a sort of playboy scene where they lie about, being the rich tycoons, having skilled whores go to work on them, sort of refining sensations like learning about caviare. Look at the image Tom Jones puts out on his TV show, a sort of fat, noseless Hugh Hefner, real consumer sex in self-seal plastic wrap. But the groups I dig, and who are likely to dig me, are high energy, high voltage tenderness! There are no taboos, you can do anything anywhere, from excess to excess. Rolling Stone speak true when he say The Happy Nation sucks. Frank Zappa's an odd case though. I fancy him like mad. Have you seen the photo on the American sleeve of Ruben and the Jets? Here they made it too little, but the big photo reveals that Frank Zappa is a Grade-A-High-School-Prom-Heart-Throb!

'I dig everything he does, except when he goes into his paranoid why-am-I-explaining-you-don't-care-or-understand routine, but I'd think twice about balling him, because Ed Sanders told me that he has the same perversion as Tyrone Power on *Hollywood Babylon* and somebody else told me that that means he's a shit fancier! How can you get that together for God's sake? I don't really believe it. It's probably meant to frighten off all but the brave and resourceful. Still, maybe I'm not that brave and resourceful. Nevertheless, because I really respond to his vibes, I want him, shit or no shit, because that's how it is if your body and soul and mind are hooked up. I'd fuck Shakespeare, except that he specially asked that his bones not be disturbed.'

She jumps up to get ready to go eat at the Macrobiotic (because she likes it!) and rattles on while she fluffs out her hair, about the *café-au-lait* groupies of New York, brittle and loveless, but beautiful and entertaining, or the softer girls who still hunt among the minstrels the familiar lineaments of a husband and cry by silent telephones in lofts along the Bowery of the necessity of being into your own thing; of getting back into your body so if you understand or admire an artist, your nipples erect when you read a line of him or hear a bar of his music (like berries under the brown gauze of her long dress whipped with old lace) so Norman Mailer's penis blossoms in her head, stopping suddenly to swoop and kiss me on the mouth, with her hand cupping my breast as naturally as a nest a bird, a kiss full of promise of a 'day when we shall come to life among the flowers of Beulah, sprung in unity in the Four Senses, in the outline, the circumference and Form, forever in the Forgiveness of sins which is Self-Annihilation', and notice that she has changed her record

'I'm so glad
I'm so glad
I'm glad
I'm glad
I'm glad'.

Dear John

Unpublished

In 1969, John Gorton, Prime Minister of Australia, became involved in a series of scandals, one engineered by journalist Geraldine Willesee who claimed that he was feeling her up when he should have been at a conference with his American allies, at whose behest he was sending Australian troops to Vietnam. The others involved his ambitious and influential secretary, Ainslie Gotto. This, the first ever cunt-power piece, was considered too hot even for the Underground press which was already subject to police harassment (see 'The million-dollar Underground.')

Dear John,

How proud and pleased we renegade Australians were to learn that you're really one of us! That you, dear crumple-faced John, have the rich temerity to be a fucker! Spear-fisherman, yes, that has the electorate's sanction; glutton-drunkard-execrable poet enjoyed your eminence for years, but a *fucker*! Why, this means that, in your underpants at least, you support the sexual revolution! Hooray! Or do I cheer prematurely O distinguished cocksman? I am not of course referring to your charming lady-wife, for the matrimonial fuck has not the same subversive significance, but to your glorious affrays, attested with customary indirectness by such unimpeachable sources as *The Times* (London) with Ainslie! Your amazing gropings and grabbings with Liza! Your hot knee-tremblers with Geraldine! To think that, there on the Kokoda trail between the little legs of your boxer shorts, insurrection pounds unseen! Do your colleagues guess that your fingers smell sweety-sharp from your last pre-penetral generosities? Can they imagine the sweet alchemies now working in the moistest crannies of your anarchic tool? Where will it lead you next, O glorious goatman? (Will you console Zara? Perhaps you have, probing her secret wound with your honey wand, your big, spotted groper lying between her swaying weed-clad walls. Did you give her head-of-state ha-ha? Not that she wouldn't have been used to it, before something got her old man – an eel? a shark? NKVD? CIA? You, you old horn-swinger you?) The surge of seed in your corridor of power, spent between the thick lips and kinky hair of the cunts of all the world. You know, of course, that all cunts are *coloured*, don't you? Don't you? Think of them, the velvet lips hidden in a black, nappy old beard, there, baby, between her tanned and golden-downy legs, for cunt power is black, baby, black, and it's my cunt is telling me to write this letter, white man.

I'm not going to go on now about what you've done to my woman-people, boss-man, because the nicest thing you do to us is fuck us and I'm afraid you might stop! But in exchange for the tongue-baths, for your one strength which to your press secretary it is death to reveal, I'm going to give you a warning. So far my poor sisters are unradicalized: a wife is an Uncle Tom, that's clear, but the others who gave you cunt-room are just silly. They felt like some cock-of-state to tell their sisters about (how they *laugh* at you big-fella white man) but if you don't stop playing your double game (which only you and us cunts and *The Times* know about) you better get clever, my battered satyr, and your chances are slim.

A cunt won't *black*mail, whitemale, that's *your* style; we have our own ways.

As long as you send our young brothers, our young lovers, to strangle their souls, petrify their hearts, twist their heads out of shape killing and torturing women and babies in Vietnam, knot up their manhood and dry out their sperm in showers of napalm, to forget the blind and gentle cock and learn the supersonic rifle and the flame-thrower, for that long you're not safe, and probably for longer. That old black anarchist between our legs doesn't think your way, massa, doesn't prevaricate with reason, sahib, she just feels, and one day she's going to recognize your calloused old dick, and her toothless mouth will turn to steel and close and close and close in a new orgasm, pulp up your foolish tassel, pulverize, homogenize, vitamize you, gulp you up and shit you out for ever. Give it up, you with the scars on your thighs, give up the war game. We know it's nice playing tin soldiers with real men, talking strategy and joking in parliament about the torture of Vietnamese women (what would you like to do when they death-rattle and their cunts are tight with terror and hate, eh? Jiggle jiggle?), but your pleasures are incompatible. The day is coming when they'll tear you apart, I promise you. One day the women of the world will fill their cunts with razor blades for the likes of you: the strong, golden thighs of some Sheelagh or Valmae will crack your ribs and crush your much-thumped chest. You'll bleat around the world then, Merino bell-wether, but the cunts will be locked, and you won't have the key –

watch it Johnno,

Germaine

The million-dollar Underground

Oz, July 1969

'*Rolling Stone* is not,' cried Jane Nicholson, 'repeat *not* an Underground paper,' as *Oz* and *It* were busted. 'Well,' the friendly policeman might have replied, 'you use four-letter words like rock and fuck and dope, don't you?' Poor baby. It's awful to be misunderstood. Of course, you only want to talk about music and fucking and dope. We know you have no intention of overthrowing this Vichy government; nothing is clearer than that English *Rolling Stone* presents no threat to any political institution of any kind. Well, sister, events of the past weeks should prove even to you that *Rolling Stone* had better develop some political principle and some subversive know-how, because when the Man decides he wants you for saying fuck and all that, he isn't going to check with the Underground whether they claim you, let alone whether you think you belong.

Recent publicity in *Melodymaker* (yet) for the Lyceum filled the Mecca magnates with terror and disgust. When Mick Farren fronted down there with a chick shortly after Tony Wilson's mild rave (which was mainly about how much more comfortable it was than the Roundhouse) he was barred from entering because they didn't want any 'superfreaks', were not Underground, didn't want to know. After some aggro they were let in free, just as arbitrarily as they had been excluded.

The real reason why Miss Nicholson and Mecca Ballrooms want to dissociate themselves from the Underground is that they have to make money. Both want to be allowed to keep on making it, and that means keeping in with the cops and with the users of dope, rock and sex. Society will permit a brothel but not a houseful of happy fuckers: the kids will be allowed to have their fun at the Lyceum within limits and at a price. Lyceum means high school, I believe, and this one is a four-and-a-half-million pound shit-heap, with flesh-coloured tights and writhing stucco ornaments more obscene than anything the Underground has ever spontaneously emitted. To see hippikins and hippettes milling miserably around among the Mecca gorillas who hate them almost blurs the memory of police collaboration at the Roundhouse, and UFO seems another part of summer '67. The Midnight Court (once associated with John Peel's name without his consent – a trick more Underground than above board) at the Lyceum is doomed because the Underground that they milk for a pound a head will keep using it as a rendezvous to pick up dope, or sleep in or freak out in, despite the fevered protestations of the square management. The management will co-operate with the police to show their good faith, and the police, to show theirs, will close it down. Who the hell cares?

Despite the two English issues which were contemptible it would be sad if *Rolling Stone* goofed, as they are sure to do if they try to serve the cause of rock and the Establishment simultaneously. In America it is clear that this divided loyalty is a no-no, as Janis Joplin pointed out with her comment on the meaning of long hair there and here, because persecution is less subtle and resourceful than in England. In England Miss Nicholson is tempted to please everybody all the time if she can get away with it, but she's playing poker in the dark. Once a paper admits any principle of censorship for survival, the we-don't-want-to-do-it-but-we-don't-want-to-lose-the-printer kind of censorship, it jeopardizes the integrity of its editorial principle. It's better to print and be damned, because you'll be damned anyway. It is actually impossible for any paper worth reading to satisfy all the Man's requirements for trouble-free journalism, so it's strategically better to give him as much trouble as possible. The bitterness of the situation may be gauged from an example. Some issues ago *Oz* deleted an article which gave them, in a deliberately disgusting form, a scoop, a possible libel (unlikely) and a more possible reaction from the printer. While still bleeding from this self-imposed wound, *Oz* was busted for something no one expected and lost the printer and 6,000 copies after all. If *Rolling Stone* continues to print only what is acceptable to Woodrow Wyatt's North Riding Publishers, you'd be better off giving your two-and-six to the old guy failing to play the recorder in Sloane Square.

The Underground is not simply some sort of scruffy club that Jane Nicholson and Mecca Ballrooms have refused to join. It's where the life is, before the Establishment forms as the crust on the top, and changes vitality for money. It's humus, the matrix that the city fathers pin down with foundations, spread asphalt over and crush under piles of glass and steel and concrete. Where it reappears in the overground it is known as dirt. It is used as a repository for waste, shit, offal, dead bodies. From circumference to circumference through this old terrestrial ball whereon we all in darkness crawl it extends, the wormy, undermined, inter-mind Underground. Most things that live in it communicate by smell and feel. Some are so primitive that their systems of sexual distinction and forms of copulation are utterly confused. They crawl and grope in the humming darkness, their unmapped, unremembered paths intersecting occasionally and tunnelling on. No signposts because there are no strangers and nothing to point at. You may take refuge there from the catastrophes of the overground. No fallout in the alleys where the moles root their lives away.

Analogy between subversion and the behaviour of badgers led to the coining of the term to describe groups formed in secret to undermine tyranny, particularly groups with a large organizational network, which, like a mole's system of tunnels, is impossible to trace, even if intersected. The term was used for the non-Establishment newspapers, for UFO and Middle Earth, because they were set up by consumers to satisfy their own requirements, which were not the acceptable ones of profit by exploitation. The political content of these manifestations was at first negligible, and in some cases still is, but confrontation is political awareness, and by trying to do their own thing, the phenomena now described as Underground pretty soon discovered the machinery of repression. The political character of the Underground is still amorphous, because it is principally a clamour for freedom to move, to test alternative forms of existence to find if they are practical, and if they are more gratifying, more creative, more positive than mere endurance under the system. This partly explains the lack of ideology which combines so oddly with the growing peevishness of the Underground, peevishness now developing into belligerence, with the threat of violence.

It is commonplace to remark that a politically decided elite may use the force of this generalized discontent to establish a more repressive system still, but so far the difference between Bolshevik revolution, Maoist revolution, Trotskyist revolution and revolution for the hell of it, has only resulted in grotesquely confused skirmishing within the Underground. The Establishment, however, will hope in vain that the Underground will destroy itself: the signs of internal dissension are the signs of continuing life; complacency and inertia are qualities prized only by the Establishment.

It is in our interests to let the police and their employers go on believing that the Underground is a conspiracy, because it increases their paranoia and their inability to deal with what is really happening. As long as they look for ringleaders and documents they will miss their mark, which is that proportion of every personality which belongs in the Underground. That is what responds to the peculiar poetry of rock, and feeds on the insecurity of the unlimited possibility. To silence that, it would be necessary not just to kill all the prophets of the new king, but to utterly eradicate the memory. The people who belong to the Underground all the time are very few, but almost everybody has spent a season there. The Establishment has to draw nourishment from it, and so plunders and is plundered by the Underground. Despite the venal patronage of Elektra, Transatlantic, Polydor, EMI, Track, Apple, the Inland Revenue and Radio 1, the Underground remains uncharted, unreliable, unrewarding and irresponsible. If every head who clamours to be of it today were to deny it tomorrow it would exist still. Miss Nicholson may tell the fuzz anything she pleases – her cunt knows better.

Mozic and the revolution

Oz, October 1969

When Joshua fit the battle of Jericho the walls came tumbling down. That's revelation. The Holy Ghost talking. So it can be done. The way to crack a mirror or shiver a wine glass is to find the right frequency and pound it. Like those strobe lights that picked up the B-rhythms of some kids dancing around in Ealing or somewhere, and threw them into epileptic fits. TC knows a cat in Australia who used to make strange music, sitting between two huge columns and singing into them and feeding and feeding it back and back. Finally, he burst a blood vessel in his head and now he's crazy. If you sit a man with a bucket on his head and let a water tap drip on to it, he'll be crazy within hours. The Japanese taught some Australians that. Music has charms to soothe a savage breast, as Congreve noticed. Music hath alarums to wild the civil breast as well, as Tuli Kupferberg pointed out. It is partly a matter of the mode of music, but then as well, something to do with the ears the music exists in. He that has ears to hear, let him hear. The bell tolling in the desert makes no sound.

What then, is the mode of revolutionary music in October 1969 and who's it for? Mick Farren is right to agonize over the superficiality of the rock revolution. The Underground is falsely complacent, living on an exaggerated notion of its own importance and effectiveness, which Mick Farren tirelessly deflates and derides. He looks back with furious nostalgia at the time when ugly, desperate, grinding songs were million sellers. When shopgirls, mechanics, storemen, packers, gas fitters, wharf labourers and their girls, found dignity, lust and anger in the music of rock. It is painful to hear the skinheads saying, as they look over the crowds, past the enclosure where the beautiful people bask in a cloud of Mick Jagger's spittle, 'Well, the Stones are one of us, arnay?' Expensive drugs, more expensive butterflies, dead mates, Baby Jane Holzer's dildo, no, baby, the Stones are not one of you. By Marianne Faithfull's sacred Mars Bar they are not one of you. They are being protected from you by the Underground's favourite scapegoats, the poor old phoney Hell's Angels. In the official souvenir of that concert, there is a photograph of the groupies' enclosures backstage, which features, in filthy yellow plush trousers, Ibiza vest, chain and dilly-bag, the Underground impresario himself. The expression on his face sums up the whole blind alley of revolutionary music. 'Why isn't it working?' those hot eyes are saying. 'What the fuck happened?'

Why did Mick Jagger not tell those quarter of a million people to take over the city? Why did they behave so well and pick up all their garbage? They were celebrating their togetherness, boasted the Underground. They showed the parent generation how they were gentle and loving and co-operative. Mick Farren knew that that was not how it was. The phenomenon had been contained. No one need be afraid of the Rolling Stones any more. They couldn't change a thing. They didn't want to change a thing. They arrived at the head of the pop wave, expressing the vague discontent of their generation. They were rewarded with money and initiated into the fancy vices of the upper class: drugs, buggery, cruelty and vicarious violence. Home videos of the Aberfan disaster with 'Yes sir, that's my baby' for a backing. Loving, gentle, co-operative, my arse. Still, it was genuine. The greasers, the rockers, the mods, the skinheads, the hippies, the yippies, all of your genuine working-class youth would have been corrupted in the same way. Only the bourgeois revolutionary can spurn the insidious rewards this society offers to successful subversion. Only the middle-class rebel yearns for the proletariat.

> Someone told me times are changing
> But looking all around it seems the same
> Buying selling running hiding
> Wondering if the world has any shame
> Looking from my window
> Blank faces queue for something new to come
> But nothing ever changes
> And their dreams all wither in the sun

(The Deviants. Transatlantic)

The rock revolution failed because it was corrupted. It was incorporated in the capitalist system which has power to absorb and exploit all tendencies, including the tendencies towards its own overthrow. The Rolling Stones have been absorbed and their music has been corrupted too. 'Honky-tonk Woman', like 'The Salt of the Earth', is merely a new perversion, a kind of self-conscious slumming. It stinks. And yet, even if Frank Zappa has had to throw Mick and Marianne out of his house in Laurel Canyon, Mick Jagger is still a better man than he, because the deficiencies in his revolutionary theory do not matter, because the corruption and faggotization of his own character are irrelevant. What is only important, is that the Rolling Stones found the frequency, they sounded the chime, they dripped the tap on to the bucket, they cracked the mirror and busted the glass. 'Satisfaction' can never be unwritten. It has been heard, for there were ears to hear.

Frank Zappa is more intelligent and a better musician than any of the Stones, and that is probably why he would never risk immolation as a pop hero. For Mick Jagger is a victim, after all, and it makes little difference whether he is aware of the fact. Though, when he chooses to dance in a studded dog collar and his white clown suit, perhaps we may assume that he has an inkling. Zappa may enjoy his artistic and other sorts of integrity, but he will never make a contribution to the revolution of sensibility which is the prerequisite of political revolution. The converted seek out Zappa and learn more about their attitudes from him, but the Stones helped thousands of kids to bust out. What pains Mick Farren, and it pains him terribly all of the time, is that the bust-out was so trivial in its immediate effects. So his music dashes itself against the horns of a polylemma – every proposition has its *but*. Music must reach a mass audience, *but* it will then become commercial. Music must please those who hear it, *but* it must not make the unbearable bearable. Music must be violent and exciting, *but* it must not provide harmless expression for violence and frustration. In such a conflict, Mick Farren's Deviants could only use music as a weapon. Time, harmony, rhythm were a bunch of Uncle Tomisms. The Deviants were offensive. Mick screamed, Russ battered. When the equipment collapsed, or silence ensued for any reason, Mick bawled at his audience, pleading with them to tear the hall down, to fuck or shit, telling them the home truths about the management, libelling, protesting, complaining, cursing. But the audience remained an audience. They listened. They stood still, patient under barrages of feedback and Mick's incomprehensible yelling. They wanted to have a good time and there was this wheezing Jeremiah begging them to hate something. They were too good mannered, even to hate him. Mick ended up hating nearly all his audiences. He meant to yell at their parents, but he ended up yelling at them.

> We are the people who pervert your children,
> Who lead them astray from the lessons you taught them,
> We are endangering civilization,
> We are beyond rehabilitation.

(*The Deviants. Transatlantic*)

But they aren't endangering civilization. It's all a fantasy. The Stones could claim this, they still could, but they never would. Mick Farren is convinced, passionate, sincere and unsparing of himself in his service of the revolution, and that's just what's wrong with him. Electronic music was a glimpse into the possibility of liberation, not expounded, but demonstrated on the nerves; kids began to dance, to leap and their want was born. Mick Farren understood the phenomenon politically, intelligently. He is still the best critic the English Underground has, and like Jeremiah he ought to be heeded. But he cannot sing. He cannot sing because, although he has a freaky throat, he cannot *hear*. And he never did hear what rock music really was, in terms of guts and glory. He is an impresario, but he does not understand exactly what it is that he's peddling, any more than any other Denmark Street wheeler dealer. The most significant part of the rock revolution, because it did happen, was that kids got into their bodies. Music is a curious medium. Utterly abstract in its construction, but completely sensuous in its apperception. Tunes, rhythms can only be conveyed by exact mimicry. They are not ideas. Mick Farren writes lovely prose, he has good, tough, sharp ideas, but he is not and never will be into his body. He is a victim of one of the meanest tricks that our sick civilization plays upon the body-soul hookup, chronic asthma. As a result of it, he is addicted to a particularly brutal form of stimulant. This tyrannical dance with death has too much to do with the kind of music he makes, and with the deadly, if microscopic, efficiency of the Pink Fairies' operations in fucking up other people's music. King Crimson are still apologizing for the gig they did at the Speakeasy, which is the only regime which the Pink Fairies will ever upheave, because they were put off and harassed by a more-than-usually drunken and drugged Twink, Steve, Tooke and Mick Farren.

But something has happened. The Deviants are no longer Mick Farren's Deviants. Under all the bullshit flummery of the Pink Fairies, something was really happening. A leather giant with a deformed arm and a natural Charles II mane, leans into the mike and says with a maniacal smile, 'Let's have some fun', before he drives off on deranged lead guitar. That's it. That's the pulse. He has it. The bass player can find it from him and Russ boxes out the frenzy on drums. The words are inaudible. The band practises these days. They dig it. They are into it. Soon their audiences will fuck without being told. The Deviants have discovered music. They used to be frail and pious. Mick's yelling was still preaching after all. Now Paul Rudolf's 'Let's have some fun' could set up a sympathetic vibration in the foundations of the Home Office. Mick has responded to the pressure, which looks these days like bouncing him clean off the stage, with a change in the group's public image. He is no longer *il Duce*. Russ and Sandy and Paul talk to the papers too. Mick has swapped 'The-Pink-Fairies-are-organizing-a-musical-attack-on-authority, like-the-MC5-in-Chicago- (sic) a-strategic,-organized-and-effective-attack-on-the-straights'-type bullshit for the 'If-Nat-Joseph-thinks-you're-sincere-he-just-lets-you-get-on-with-it-your-way'-type bullshit.

Factory has yet to publish its deal on the Pink Fairies, with its special record and all that. If it does, it really ought to change its name to Fantasy. The basic weapon of the Pink Fairy conspiracy is conservative. The machine-gun that will rip open a policeman's chest and furnish Mick Farren with a satisfactory orgasm at last, is the weapon of the straights: to kill a man is simply murder; it is revolution to turn him on.

It is not the groups who call themselves Underground who will provide the music that will shake the walls of the city. It is not the polemicists who choose a microphone and electronic backing to continue an argument, who will enlighten the straights who continue to be born. It is not the best musicians and it is not the worst. But it will be done with music.

> Beware a man who is not moved by sound.
> He'll drag you to the ground
> Come dance with me, come dance with me in [Wilson's] land
> Come dance with me, we'll beat that hoary band.

(Tuli Kupferberg)

1970 – 1979

The slag-heap erupts

Oz, February 1970

The 1969 second wave of women's liberation movements were very much a manifestation of those sinister forces in our society which we call the media. While pulling in millions of pounds, dollars, lire and what-have-you by brainwashing women into demanding the emulsified fats, perfumed deodorants and disinfectants, liver-corroding analgesics and other consumer products which are as necessary to keep our economies on an even keel as the threat of war or anarchist insurrection, the newspapers kept up their circulation, and thus their sale of advertising, by inventing a new sensation – women's liberation.

Valerie Solanas got them at it first by shooting Andy Warhol, although they could not get as much out of that as they might have liked because the matter was *sub judice* for quite a while. Still, that tactic meant that Girodias got round to publishing *The Scum Manifesto*, which is still most of what most people know about women's liberation. It did not take long for other women to grasp the principle of Solanas's shock tactics, especially when they saw young blacks exciting WASP paranoia by similar means on every campus and in every subway.

When the House Commission for Un-American Activities was officially called a witch-hunt, one group of radical women suddenly realized that that was what they wanted to be, so WITCH, Women's International Terrorist Conspiracy from Hell, was formed. Ballyhoo was their business and from the beginning they were good at it. Dressed in black and riding broomsticks they hexed the Chase Manhattan Bank, distorting the familiar slogan (You Have a Friend in the Chase Manhattan) in a fashion fatuous enough for J. Walter Thompson himself (You Have a Fiend in the Chase Manhattan). When they bewitched Wall Street the market obligingly suffered a frisson of five points and then pulled itself together again. Bra burning and invading the annual Bride Fair in Madison Square Garden were good fun and good copy too. Nowadays WITCH is a little leery of the Tactical Police Force and has gone underground and anonymous, a heavy fate for ballyhoo.

Betty Friedan's National Organization for Women takes itself much more seriously than WITCH, although after Valerie Solanas showed them how, they ran around with slogans like 'A Chicken in Every Pot and a Whore in Every Home', until they managed to weed such vulgarity out of their ranks and into extremist movements like the Radical Feminists and the October 17th group where it belongs. Mrs Friedan did not want to endanger her beautiful relationship with Congress; after all, a bird in a congressional committee is worth a thousand in the bush. Nevertheless she capitulated to the media by 'forcing' (you recognize the journalese cf. 'frost hits railways') the *New York Times* to demonstrate its freedom from male chauvinism by desegregating the want ads. Of course, she could not 'force' anyone to desegregate jobs. The immediate result was that more women wasted more time reading about, applying for and getting rejected for jobs that they had had no chance of getting in the first place.

The problem is at least partly one of image and self-image. Men don't really like women and that is really why they don't employ them. Women don't really like women either, and they too can usually be relied on to employ men in preference to women. Playing weird pranks in Wall Street was at least an attempt to multiply the probabilities and break down the stereotype of the female image. However, such a strategy relies upon a superhuman freedom from paranoia. Valerie Solanas had to shoot her man to get him to take more than patronizing notice of her. So Abbey Rockefeller and Roxanne Dunbar teach karate to the Boston Women's Liberation Movement. When nobody likes you, and you really don't much like yourself, the most predictable reaction is to turn nasty and attack before you are attacked. Unfortunately, as any skinhead could tell Miss Rockefeller, cowardice and steel-tipped boots, broken bottles and safety in numbers are more effective than the karate you can learn in debutantes' finishing schools. Alas, women don't like each other enough even to want to travel in packs like the Chelsea supporters.

The real reason why female liberation is a hot number in the Sunday mags and the glossies is because it smacks of lesbianism, female depravity, freakishness and solemn absurdity. The tone of the reportage is most commonly derisive. The karate experts want to censor their meetings, regarding all the female journalists, who imply that they are ugly, frustrated, poor things (as Irma Kurtz did for London and Julie Baumgold for New York) as Aunt Tomasinas who capitulate to the enemy. The only perceptible result of the non-tactic of excluding the press is that the journalists need not observe even the minimal restraints of courtesy and the accounts of the meetings read more like descriptions of witches' covens than ever.

And yet, militant women owe a great deal to the media that guy them. The average housewife is dulled and confused by her day-to-day diet of pulp journalism and crap television. She does not catch the nuances of contempt that swill around the images of Abbey Rockefeller splitting a board with her head. Threading her way through clouds of clever-clever verbiage she retains the overwhelming impression that 'something is happening here' even if 'what it is ain't exactly clear'. Most of her life she has served fashion without demur, and now the media have created the fashion of female liberation. At last the fucking media look as if they are hoist with their own petard.

The trend is based on a tiny reality. Betty Friedan started NOW in 1966 and its membership even now (1970) is not more than 3,000 odd. The nucleus of the Boston Women's Liberation Movement is twelve and the national convention called out 500. The average local group counts twenty-five as a bumper turnout. The groups divide and subdivide every few months. Names proliferate: New York Radical Women, the Feminists, the Redstockings, the October 17th Movement, New Women, Cell 55 and so on. As far as the newspapers are concerned, new names mean new stories and so the phenomenon grows. Most of the groups are more or less academic, workshops with reading lists, research projects, discussion groups. The prescribed texts are confused and repetitive. The membership is mostly educated middle-class women who have rebelled against male chauvinism in the new left, with especially complex problems of priorities and strategies. It is argued on the one hand that oppression of women is the prime example of class oppression, and that women cannot be emancipated until private property has been abolished and the state has withered away and on the other, as many learned while fighting for the rights and opportunities of blacks, that you cannot be liberated fighting other people's battles. Russia, China and Cuba all used women's bodies to fight their anti-colonial battles and once the new regime was established, put women right back in their place again. Of course, most women are not radical leftists or unmarried university students; the luxury of such theorizing is not accessible to them at all. Mrs Smith, who tends a bottling machine by day and husband and kids morning and night, has no use for a reading list, however fascinating.

In England the situation is a paler and more confused reflection of the American scene. Middle-class suburbs boast their Women's Liberation Workshops, but finding out about them for the uninitiated is virtually impossible. Agitprop import the publications of the New England Free Press, but when I rang up it took two hours before anyone could tell me that most of the advertised titles hadn't arrived yet, and nobody knew how I could get back-copies of *Shrew*. Calling the Tufnell Park Women's Liberation Workshop proved no more fruitful. When an energetic bunch of women from Warwick University joined the Miss World demo, chanting and dancing rings around the police, the Tufnell Park ladies clung quietly to their banners (saying 'We are not sexual objects' – a statement no one appeared inclined to dispute) and begged them to desist. *Shrew* officially deplored the demeanour of the interlopers, but reminded itself, noblesse obliging, that the Warwick women may have been working-class house-wives who knew no better, the people they meant to help, in fact. The Coventry group is almost unique among gatherings of privileged young women in that it is actually attended by working-class women who tell the organizers how it is.

Many militant women show too plainly by their inefficiency, their obesity and their belligerence, that they have not succeeded in finding any measure of liberation in their own company. They are still beset with middle-class sexual scruples and cannot find any alternative to the phoney concept of female sexuality as monogamy and child-bearing, except, as some extremists have advocated, masturbation, lesbianism or celibacy. These alternatives are more compulsive and repressive than the despised heterosexual confrontation; the consequence must be that the movement is debilitated, because repression consumes energy which might be used creatively. Masters' and Johnson's vindication of the clitoris is assumed to be the elimination of the vagina, and the sexual response of the middle-class American of the 1960s, hung about with electronic monitors and watched by strangers is assumed to be a physiological absolute. Rather than multiplying possibilities in a liberating way, militant feminism too often reduces them, imprisoning the new women in a wilderness of theory that itself grew out of a hopelessly distorted situation in which clear sight was an impossibility. Rebellious women have always been able to find liberty, independence and culture in nunneries, but that never changed reality for the mass of women. Confrontation is political awareness. A woman who cannot organize her sex life in her own best interest is hardly likely to reorganize society upon more rational lines.

Men are the enemy. They know it – at least, they all know that there is a sex war on, an unusually cold one. They have no perverse desire to remain enemies. If women liberate themselves they will free men of their neurotic dependence and the fearful inauthenticity of sexual relationships. A hidden factor in the situation is the desirability of the tearaway girl, the unpredictable virgin, the proud bitch. Many men hate brassières and vaginal douches and the other impedimenta of women's humiliation as much as women do, and more. They are as tired of guilt as we are of shame. The bourgeois perversion of motherhood has been attacked by male psychologists and obstetricians; ought we not to heed them? SDS and IS men may be chauvinistic, and may reap female adulation and their reward for conspicuousness in the movement – we have all seen Tariq Ali marching with his blonde harem. If radical women had the guts and imagination to look beyond their epicene middle-class environment and start to fuck for sex instead of ego and prestige, they might discover a different ethic among the working class. Working-class women are often more literate than their husbands. Working-class men don't regard educated women as ball-breaking competitors; they have no respect for most of their learning, which is irrelevant. Women automatically take on the class of their husbands; it's good Marxist strategy to mate 'down' instead of 'upward'. Some of radical women's academic skills could actually be used in the service of the class they say they want to enfranchise. It must be a more attractive prospect than typing, distributing leaflets, making tea for and falling into bed with, some arrogant IS male.

So far, the self-appointed leaders of female revolution have remained the dupes of their middle-class education, and their demands are circum-scribed by cautious notions of equality with middle-class men. Their organizations are built on political structures derived from the patterns of male grouping. At the very worst, they fall for the colossal male perversion, which is where it all began, the perversion of violence. The only genetic superiority that men have is their capacity for violence, which in this age of preparation for total war has taken on an institutionalized form. We all need to be rescued from the computer-aimed nuclear phallus that kills without passion. What women must do is invent a genuine alternative.

The cunt must take the steel out of the cock and make it flesh again. Female masochism must be eradicated if male sadism is to become ineffec-tual. The masochism is not essential to the female psyche nor the sadism to the male, but the existence of either entails the existence of the other.

There are signs that it is happening, but slowly, and so far without prophetesses and not in the workshops and chapters of the spasm called the Movement.

Strenuous February

International Times, 13–26 March 1970

On 11 February 1970, radical students occupied the registry of the University of Warwick, where I had been teaching English since 1967, and discovered that the Vice-Chancellor had been keeping political dossiers on staff and students and sharing information with the security officers of Coventry-based industrial plants. In the ensuing uproar, individual departments held general meetings of staff and students. A meeting of the English school attempted to reorganize its constitution on the principle of one person, one vote, whether staff or student, even to the extent of setting curricula on the anarchist principle of unanimous acceptance. At an extraordinary general meeting of the whole staff and student body on 17 February the four resolutions of the English department were proposed and passed by a huge majority. Senior academics called an emergency meeting of the Assembly, the rubber-stamp organization of all the teaching staff, which characteristically failed even to censure the Vice-Chancellor and barely passed the motion agreeing not to discipline the students involved in the invasion of the registry. The Association of University Teachers sent down the national secretary to pour bureaucratic oil on the troubled waters and no action was ever taken on the matter of political surveillance of teachers, which is doubtless still going on. By Easter, as the article gloomily predicts, the students' brief burst of political energy was spent. In 1972, although knowing that, as retrenchment became actual cuts in an already inadequate programme of tertiary education, I would never get another university job in England, I resigned.

The universities have at last recovered from the retrenchments of the summer and the annual influx of innocence; student action has once more reared its shaggy, unwashed head. This year the dragon's teeth have been sown at Warwick; new-grown warriors are travelling up and down the country explaining to student unions the scandal of the confidential files and its likely implications. In happening upon such an issue the radical students found themselves a formidable weapon in the *realpolitik* of a permanent struggle.

The left conservatives solidified with a form of political action which they had long ignored or reviled, and the liberals, woolly and not so woolly, voted staunchly for motions which in other circumstances would have made their hair stand on end. The militant minority won majority support.

Even Jack Straw took up the cudgels. The issue of academic freedom excites high moral fervour, especially if it is not very clearly understood that it has never existed. The thought that big business interests in the Midlands might be exercising covert influence on academic appointment and selection at Warwick University, as well as providing facilities only for the kinds of research that benefit it directly, can be relied upon to excite a majority, even the famous silent majority which never attends any kind of political meeting, or expresses any political view.

Nevertheless, the files are not the issue, and the direct and indirect influence of fairly shady magnates is not the issue. It would be nearer the mark to say that the Union building was the issue at Warwick University, but only a part of the truth to say that Toryism in the academic establishment, mixed with a little jiggery-pokery over dinner in the Vice-Chancellor's house, is the reason why the Union building never eventuated. The facts of the case are more dismal, if less shocking.

If Warwick University were the only business university in the country there could be no explaining the action taken by students in Oxford, Sheffield, York, Lancaster, Manchester, Sussex, Southampton, and God knows where else by now. Even if the administration of Warwick manages to stonewall long enough to escape any kind of significant exposure, which might well ensue if Lord Radcliffe does his job properly, the problem will still remain. It is easy to protest against the universities acting as induction centres for the executive ranks of the motor industry: it takes more insight to see that they are fast becoming induction centres for the biggest business of all, the nation that must show a profit. It might be argued that they have never really been anything else, and certainly it is true that he who pays the piper expects to call the tune. But the piper was not always paid by the government, and when he was paid, he often managed to play his own tune nevertheless. Those people who care for the principle of education realize that it can never be adequately safeguarded, but is the centre of a continuing conflict with interests irrelevant to it; notwithstanding, the pressure of contouring of the universities, so that the right kinds of graduates are produced at the right speed, becomes more perceptible every year.

One of the ways in which academics sought to identify the pressure upon them to turn out better and cheaper products is in the placing of academic salaries within the purview of the Prices and Incomes Board, which promptly set about identifying the academic *product*, challenging the universities to justify their existence in those terms. The immediate result was a series of questionnaire forms of all the colours in the rainbow, forms which claimed either randomness or protection of anonymity, nonsensically enough, while setting out within their own terms of reference the classes of work done by academics, research, undergraduate teaching, graduate teaching, administrative work and so on. Academics were asked to identify the kind of work they were doing, first of all within a nine-to-five spectrum, then, more realistically, within a wider spectrum over seven days a week, and that is too much like an inquisition into private affairs. None of these interrogatories ought to be filled in: the presuppositions are false, and the information sought is misleading, and therefore cannot be used to good effect, even if it were to be apparently justified by a rise in academic salaries. But many academics did not feel the insidious threat of such scrutiny; some sabotaged it by swapping their questionnaires around, or by filling them out in ways calculated to show impossible statistics; more just didn't manage to do them. The joke was in circulation that there ought to be a category in the questionnaires called 'Time spent answering questionnaires'. If the point of time-and-motion study on academics could have been overlooked, it is not possible to overlook the meaning of the suggestion that the academics should absorb the shock of the impact of public demand on an inadequate system, with their own bodies – one survey included an unanswerable question about whether students would suffer if academics were asked to take a fifty per cent increase in their staff–student ratio! There is no shortage of trained teachers to cope with greater student influx, especially at the points where it is heaviest. Historians and literature teachers are severely limited in their bargaining power and freedom to move by the widespread unemployment among qualified graduate teachers. A reader or senior lecturer is virtually immobilized, because as a higher paid worker, he is the last to be required by penny-pinching departments. Inexorably, the pressure of demand to study first degree courses in arts, is reflected in the demand from good graduates to continue their education.

If we consider how the market principle would operate if applied consistently, we would have a clearer idea of the direness of the peril threatening the education principle. The supply of students far exceeds the demand, especially in the arts and humanities, where they are also most radical: academics are similarly replaceable: only typists and cleaning staff are virtually irreplaceable, and the administrative staff, who are represented in the academic assemblies, know that very well. The letter from the staff of the registry which appeared in the *Coventry Evening Telegraph*, denouncing the vandalism of the 'future brains of Britain', reflected all the traditional animus against self-styled intellectuals, privileged youth, and long-haired lefties, as well as the extraordinary isolation which prevails at Warwick between those whom the students call the 'fools on the hill' and the humanity swarming in the hollow a mile away where stand the halls of residence and the social building called 'Rootes Hall'. Prestige used to be the compensation for the poverty of academics; in an economy of market values, prestige, wealth and bargaining power are inseparable.

Consider then, in this wider context, the University of Warwick. It was designed to be a battery of 25,000 students, before cuts in the programme stalled it at 1,800. The pressure of demand for university places is stronger than was anticipated, and it is applied to the wrong places. Education is a luxury: the arts and humanities are the points at which the pressure was strongest. Unfortunately these are the areas which yield the least return for the investment; they do not produce a marketable commodity like expertise or vocational training. Statistics rarely show the whole picture, which must include the numbers of applicants for degree courses in arts and humanities, the proportion which may be accepted and the quality of their qualification for admission, as well as the number and quality of the degrees awarded. In 1969, Warwick produced twice as many degrees in arts and humanities as in science, and yet capital expenditure on the sciences amounted to seven times as much as was spent on the main resource for the arts and humanities, the library. The disproportion was not simply the result of the injection of private monies. In endowing the Barclays Bank Chair of Management Information Systems, the Clarkson Chair of Marketing, the Esmee Fairbairn Chair of the Economics of Finance and Investment, the second Clarkson Chair (Economics) and the Volkswagen Chair of German, the Institute of Directors Chair of Business Studies and the Pressed Steel Fisher Chair of Industrial Relations, private grants were only following the patterns of government policy.

The most insidious effect of the autonomy of the academic body may prove to derive from the financing of almost all undergraduates by their Local Education Authority. Obviously, it is a good thing that indigent students can be financed through university so that they do not have to divide their attention between study and some menial employment: however, the ultimate effect of receiving a grant is that students are under considerable pressure to consider themselves mini public servants, with unspecified duties towards their employer, the taxpayer. It is a rare situation when a vice-chancellor is reminded that he has an obligation to the taxpayer, even though it clearly outweighs that of the whole of the rest of the academic body. It is already possible for a LEA to withdraw a grant on the grounds that a student has been in trouble, and soon it will be avowed policy. A student who feels that he must withdraw from the university, or change his course, is instantly bedevilled by the problem of the reaction of his local authority. If he fails to make the best of his time at university, and by this is universally meant taking a good degree, he has the moral guilt of having squandered an opportunity which some other deserving person would have turned to full advantage, that is, profit. Too many drop-outs means that the university must examine its selection procedures. It is easy to see the productivity principle operating here: it is even easier to feel it when you sit in a room in the Warwick battery, a room which is just, but only just, big enough, with enough light, a healthy bed, and a uniform temperature, a room which opens on a blind passage just wide enough for one to pass, and a window that looks across to an identical window, or out upon the blank, dispossessed fields of the Coventry perimeter, stretching behind the posh commuter houses on the Kenilworth Road, where the Vice-Chancellor lives.

Just as there is a limit to the efficiency of the administrative gestapo, there is a limit to the application of the profit principle at Warwick. The feed system is run in the name of efficiency, and it would be nice to think that its policy of controlled scarcity and utter monopoly was enriching someone, but the fact is that it is not. The food is not bought cheap: it is expensive food ruined and sold for high prices. Most of it is filler, starch and fat, so that the students do not grow thin, but flaccid and apathetic. The buildings are so heated and dried out that students struggle to stay awake; in the library the man-made fibre in the carpet packs so much static in the dry air that putting your hands on the steel book shelves can fling you clear across the gangway. The students like to pretend that all this is deliberate: more depressingly, it is simple incompetence and false econ-omy. The end boards of the books in the library are curled and cracked from the bad heating, but no one knows how to change it. Subscribers to the conspiracy theory like to think that the dirty white loo tiles which have been used as universal cladding were the result of a shady deal between the architect and the V-C, and rejoice grimly whenever a fifty-pound lump of masonry crashes to the ground. The real explanation of those crashing tiles is stupidity. The windy fields of Warwick just aren't New Street Station. If anybody has been rapped for these expensive mistakes, the academic body knows nothing about it. The mistakes of the academic body on the other hand are discussed all the time.

A battery is not a community: when the students began to claim some-thing like a campus, a building designed for them, to be administered by them, they already knew that in the list of productive priorities it ranked pretty low. Some academics argued the case for them in interminable and powerless meetings, pleading that a sense of self-determination, responsi-bility and coherence as a group was a necessary condition of education, but they too must have known that the cause was a lost one, however long they were allowed to divert themselves by entertaining it. What employer finan-ces his own workers' direct action committee? The students were supposed to absorb knowledge, rambling head down over the academic pasture, intellectually fattened as quickly and cheaply as possible: why should they demand a free range? No one really believed the parboiled herd had the energy to press their demands so far as to invade the registry, bust open locked doors and files, write dirty words in the Chancellor's loo, nick his booze, and eat the biscuits they found in the typing pool. When they did, the authorities had to use the stun-gun of an injunction on the stampeding creatures, while waving the red rag of student violence before the sleepy mother herd of academics and readers of the *Coventry Evening Telegraph*. It was a minority of militants who sacked the registry at Warwick, and it was just as well for them that they found the scandalous files, because otherwise their brothers and sisters would cheerfully have watched them railroaded out of the university. As it is, confrontation is proving to be political awareness, and academic liberals are finding themselves on the left of safety, protected only by solidarity; from there it is only a step to radicalism. Students who thought that it was almost the best of all possible worlds, have learned about the press, about university government, about the law. This battle could still be lost: the students may not have the energy or the money or the endurance to stay in their pokey rooms right through the vacation so that Council cannot discipline the 'ring-leaders' in secret; the academics may lose themselves in their own poor syntax and procedural wrangles about standing orders – even when they have legislative power, which is seldom – the Vice-Chancellor may prove to be on the right side of the law, if on the wrong side of morality and public opinion. But the battle has begun: each day that passes solidifies the academic left, and outlines the essential issues more clearly. Nevertheless, it is as well to remember that, regardless of who wins the next election, the academic employers will soon have their big gun; law and order are emotive terms, like violence. Those who support the words must find that they have espoused the realities of ignorance and impotence, so that education is further away than ever.

The last three weeks at Warwick have accomplished more education than the last three years, especially about the nature and function of laws and orders. The slight advantage that the academic body has gained by discrediting the administration must be pressed hard, so that the inevitable retrenchment will not succeed in depriving the students of all room to manoeuvre. The students have abandoned ignoble ease for strenuous liberty: the experience may prove to be their only reward.

The politics of female sexuality

Oz, May 1970

From Female Energy Oz, for which I was guest editor.

One of the chief mechanisms in the suppression of female humanity is the obliteration of female sexuality. Historically the process can be traced in the change in the iconography of women. In the Middle Ages women were characterized as lustful, allies of the devil weaning men from God and noble intellectual pursuits; woman-hatred had a virtue which is lacking from more recent forms of stereotyping in that it allowed the women energy, diabolical energy, but energy nevertheless. The rise of the Protestant commercial classes brought with it a change in the characterization of women: they became chaste guardians of their husbands' honour, emblems of prestige and possession. The historical process can be observed in microcosm in the growing up of every female child. From an unknown quantity as an infant human being, she passes through a sexual phase, which the Freudians describe as masculine; her pre-adolescent sexuality is explained as an infantile stage of penis envy, which ought, if due process is observed, to dwindle into the passivity of the mature woman. From subject, she declines into object, and her status as toy for man's delectation is indefatigably illustrated in the popular imagery of sexual intercourse, the missionary position, big boobs, suspender belts and all the paraphernalia of pornography.

In order that women might become sex objects rather than sexual people, sex itself was devalued. Instead of extending through all forms of communication into the 'highest pinnacle of the human spirit' (Nietzsche) it became 'a momentary itch' (Amis). Women lost spirit and were made flesh. Desire was localized in the male genital, the visible doodle, the tag of flesh that could become as hard as a fist. The interpretation of souls and bodies became the pummelling of one lump of meat by a harder lump of meat. Sexuality became as masculine a virtue as packing a good left. No one thought to object that in the sexual battle the bigger and stronger picked upon the smaller and weaker. Women like asses were made to bear. If the softer flesh was further tenderized by pummelling, the tremulous dangling thing in which the male located his sex was safe from any threat, except the anxiety which was the unavoidable result of having invested male sexuality in a lump of meat in the first place. In his efforts to allay his anxiety that his tassel might not turn into a fist when required, that it might be smaller than the man-next-door's, the male forbade comparison to his woman. From her he extracted fidelity. Fast vehicles, bombs, male bonding were called into service to allay his persistent phallic anxiety. Women lost interest in all of it, the competitive sports, the war game, the games of darts with the boys.

The female genital organ, in keeping with the desexualization of her whole energy and the obliteration of her desire, became a mere hole, troops for the use of. Receptivity, which is no more passive an act than eating, became synonymous with passivity. In their anxiety to suppress suspect receptivity in themselves, men developed aberrations in the regulation of their eating habits, became unable to regulate their digestion, compulsive about food; their bellies and bowels ulcerated. If gentleness was like feminine passivity, activity had to distinguish itself by becoming aggression. The world was conquered, knowledge was raped, virgin countries were exploited. The only becoming attitude for the masculine hand was a fist, and the only position in love or war was on top.

In order that the pork sword might be seen to rule the world unchallenged, women obligingly hid their sex, at first with a hand and a glance of simulated alarm as the goddess of love rose glistening from the waves. The devices for minimizing the organs of femaleness became more sophisticated; women began to wear knickers, then to deodorize their genitals, douche them, shave them, pluck them. Modesty rotted their innocence. They learned to prize smallness, inaccessibility. Their rich juices were discouraged from flowing. The clitoris, which no stretch of the imagination could make part of any mere hole, was ignored and forgotten. Women were to have no more understanding of sex than a Bechstein has of Beethoven. They wished no more than to be played upon by a master, to be his favourite instrument upon which he might father masterpieces.

Girls of a more 'primitive' age have sung the praises of their 'deep fringed purse' and mocked the man who tried to plumb them. They could boast of the fury of their venery and the comfort of their lust but the permissive women of our pill-safe age can only allow the Hell's Angels to prove their valour by not vomiting when they suck menstrual blood from them, or wank the boys who walk them to the bus stop, or let them have a fuck without too much palaver. The relaxation of sexual taboos has not even been a reform, let alone a revolution. Revolutionary woman may join Women's Liberation Groups and curse and scream and fight the cops, but did you ever hear of one of them marching the public street with her skirt high crying 'Can you dig it? Cunt is beautiful!' The walled garden of Eden was CUNT. The mandorla of the beautiful saints was CUNT. The mystical rose is CUNT. The Ark of Gold, the Gate of Heaven. Cunt is a channel drawing all towards it. Cunt is knowledge. Knowledge is receptivity, which is activity. Cunt is the symbol of erotic science, the necessary corrective of the maniacal conquest of technology. Skirts must be lifted, knickers (which women have only worn for a century) must come off for ever. It is time to dig CUNT and women must dig it first.

To dig it is to know it. To know it is to feel it, the clitoris so complicated and so clever, as thrilly as a high-tension wire. In its nest within a nest like the word within a word. The bud in its calyx in the vales where the big lips cleave away from the slopes of the Mount of Venus. This is carnal knowledge.

It is absurd that women can only name their sex by the terms of phoney objectivity, the scientific terms which seek to push away the reality of the thing by talking about it in foreign tongues, clitoris, labia majora and minora, the glands of Bartholin for God's sake! The only other terms they may employ have been deformed by centuries of sadistic male use. You cunt, gash, slit, crack, slot . . . Women have no names of their own for what is most surely their own. It ought to be possible to establish a woman's vocabulary of cunt, prideful, affectionate, accurate and bold.

But it is not enough to know what it is called. Women must know above all other people what it is. Feeling it with the fingers serves to accomplish much, but more must be known, of its prettiness, its varying expressions, of how it smells and how it tastes, so that women's magazines cannot frighten us into believing that what lies between our legs is rotting meat. There is no substitute for confrontation: women must become expert in their own complexities and, because there is no knowledge without standards of comparison, the cunts of others. It is no more true that all cunts are the same when you get down on them than it is that all cats are grey in or out of the dark.

Of course it is not true either that cunt is honey-pot, jelly roll, sugar pie, or a wooded garden or any of the other euphemisms which seek to extol it in terms of something else. It is more wonderful than candy or baby food, more extraordinary than caviare; we will have to learn to describe it, not in terms of what it is not like, but in genuine comparisons. One eighteenth-century anatomist, seeking a way of describing the elegance of the cervix, said simply that it was like the mouth of a tench fish, or the head of a new-born puppy.

To know cunt, it is also necessary to know how it works, and what it can do. While Masters and Johnson have done much to dispel absurd presumptions about cunt, they could not be better than their subjects and there is no reason why we should believe that what American middle-class women taped to electrodes could do, is all that could have been done. Tahitian girls can draw the penis irresistibly and keep it firm and eager for a whole night. Ladies doing exercises to correct urethral incontinence found that their new muscle power increased their enjoyment of sex. Some heroines of folklore have caught pennies with their cunts and picked up bottle tops from a table. Vaginal insensitivity may be the status quo of the sexual research labs; that too is not absolute. Women can devise simple exercises which will help them to isolate the musculature of the vagina, the clitoris and the labia, by masturbating with no hands.

When little girls are eventually told about their organs, they are told only about reproduction, with grim, shiny diagrams which leave out the clitoris, present the vagina as a slack tube, and make no mention of lubrication, female erection, and above all, none of pleasure, of how to give it or how to get it. It is not surprising that such a great number of women never find out what is in it. The tremblings which greeted the showing of sex films in school would become an earthquake if schools began to teach the arts and reflexes of pleasure. Since they cannot transmit pleasure in any of their academic fields, in poetry or music, we may safely assume that sex will be less fun when it is taught in school than it was before. It is up to mothers to introduce their little ones to something which they themselves might have come to know too late. Knowledge of carnality must be visceral, not academic.

To know cunt is to love it and to love it is to care for it. To care for it is not only to avoid the maltreatment of it by such gross practices as inserting needles or bottles into its tenderness, but to keep it free of the germicides and deodorants which upset its balance and obliterate its essential character. Unfortunately, doctors, male or female alike, seeing as the science of medicine is still male-controlled, are at best not interested, and at worst positively loth to attend to the inconveniences which cunt occasionally suffers. Whereas the penis is taken seriously, especially when it is clear that the origin of a patient's complaint is essentially inorganic, cunt is treated as a crude mechanism, apt to function badly for long periods without any significant consequence. Any woman can recount her own horror story of a doctor's failure to examine her properly, of his brutal use of the crude and cold speculum, screwing the tender membranes of the perineum, shocking her cervix with the smear swab.

Not fifty years ago, it was accepted medical practice to perform neurectomy or clitoridectomy on women who were habitual masturbators, and to hurt women sharply who became erotic during examination. It is still on to cut cunt to ribbons and treat the formation of scar tissue as a slight inconvenience. If women are to reconquer their sexual pride they must find a way to make cunt as important in medicine as cock is. There are doctors who are gynaecologists because they are into cunt, although most of them sooner or later are therefore struck off. These are the ones who should be the health officers of the women's movement. As things stand, they are more likely to be avoided by the militants who confuse sex roles with sexuality.

So much for taking care of cunt, and setting it in contexts of dignity and joy. There is then the question of communicating with others through it.

It is difficult to say lovely things when you are being belted in the mouth. For many women it has become a question of struggling for an expression of their own sexuality in a situation which is basically sadistic. Any fuck in which the heavier and stronger party makes the smaller and lighter take his weight is sadistic. If Henry Clay could be squashed by his white women of uncommon size into a bedside mat, so enacting yet another fantasy of male terror, most women are half-squashed most of the time. The missionary position is the one adopted by all Mailer's, Miller's, Spillane's, Bond's, Jackie Collins's heroes and the one which is always filmed, even if Ingrid Thulin moans her head off in simulated ecstasy.

From any point of view the missionary position is a bummer. The degree of variation possible, even when the gentlemanly male takes the weight on his elbows, is much smaller than in any other position. Suppose the man does prop his darling's arse up with cushions and fires into her cunt from a kneeling position, or indeed into her arsehole; he is still grinding her in a lonely fashion, whether panting into her ear or into the nape of her neck. The rhythm is established by him and everything depends on the degree of his control. Madame gasps and murmurs in polite appraisal of his virility.

So why shouldn't he lose control once in a while? Twice? Often? Why should not cunt descend on cock, especially seeing that women can take the cock from above without needing to take the weight anywhere but on their feet or thighs? Once a woman throws her leg over her lover she has accepted responsibility for her own sexuality and recognized it as an integral part of her personality and her intelligence, and not merely a function of meat. Once she is poised over her lover, male or female, she is able not merely to claim the right of orgasm but espouse the sweet responsibility of giving pleasure. She can see her lover's whole body from an angle, and touch it anywhere, embrace it and kiss, or lean over it or away from it . . . The variations are infinite.

While it is true that male–female relationships in our society are perverted, it is not a revolutionary solution to eschew all such contact. Although it may be argued that the reproduction of female sexuality coincides historically with the development of capitalism, it does not therefore follow that female sexuality can only be reconstructed when capitalism is defeated and the proletariat dictates. What is certain, however, is that the patriarchal state could never survive the re-conquest by women of their own sexuality. The patriarchal family structure, the outward expression of the conjugal missionary position, would not survive the advent of self-regulating pleasure-seeking femaleness. It is only by reinstating genuine potency in themselves, that women can avoid falling into the sterile perversion of male sexuality which is violence. Violence confuses aggression with power. Cunt-power is the only form of power yet devised which can avoid this arid syndrome.

Hey, Jimi, where you gonna run to now?

Oz, October 1970

On 22 September 1970, three weeks after the Isle of Wight concert described in this piece, Jimi Hendrix died of inhaling his own vomit while in a nembutal sleep. He was twenty-five years old.

It was no surprise that Jimi split. He was a long time dying and he gave us adequate warning. He cut his wrists when he was a poor boy eating shit to make out, and when he was making out, he was eating more shit than ever. The first time I ever saw him was, after all, like the last. He was trapped by a huge dooby crowd on a high stage in the corner of a cattle shed in Spalding. The air was hot and rank because all the sliding cattle-doors were shut but one and there were no windows. As usual, an unlimited number of tickets had been sold and the promoters had split, leaving the kids to struggle in the heat and the dirt while the police snooped round them with dogs trained to sniff out the drugs that none of them had the money to buy.

We got in, in the chaos, for nothing, and there was Jimi caught like a bright bird underneath a corrugated-iron roof in the stink of cattle shit and sweating English youth. The crowd was so dense that those who fainted couldn't even fall down. Jimi was wrestling to get his guitar in tune and cursing the Orange gear that they had to use, as crappy then as now. The kids were festive and abusive. Jimi began to play and the sound was terrible so he stopped. They jeered so he stepped downstage and yelled, 'Fuck you. I'm gonna get this guitar in tune if it takes me all night.' Then, as now, they didn't care whether 'Hey Joe' was in tune or not. They just wanted to hear noise and adulate. They wanted him to give head to the guitar and rub it over his cock. They didn't want to hear him play, but Jimi wanted, as he always wanted, to play it sweet and high. So he did it, and he fucked with his guitar, and they moaned and swayed about, and he looked at them heavily and knew that they couldn't hear what he was trying to do and they never would.

He dropped down into the Isle of Wight like the sick man lowered through the roof of the house to be cured, hopping from his helicopter minutes before he was due on stage, slipping into his psychedelic minstrel-clown's gear, freshing up his gum and walking out on stage into nowhere.

Nothing was changed, except that the promoters had discovered that they didn't even have to supply a roof any more. The police were still there. The crude drugs were still there and, as always, the brutish adulation. In front of the stage all he could see were the film cameras, the press, the bedraggled groupies with their blank, hungry faces, and the politicos as ruthless in jockeying for position as the cameramen. Where was it to come from, the feedback that would turn him on in reciprocity for all the turn-ons he gave us? His guitar pleaded for resonance from the people, but in the vast stormy darkness there was not so much as an echo. He kept glancing over his shoulder to Mitch who was as lost as he was, to Billy Cox for some power, but he had to look back into the blank darkness again. 'Hell, I just ain't came,' he kept saying. What was there for him to come on to?

> I know what I want
> But I just don't know
> How to go 'bout gittin' it

It had always been like that even when the psychedelic rock millennium had seemed closest at hand. The groupies had always been further into prestige-fucking than honest sensuality. The freak-dancers had always danced most extravagantly when the cameras were on them, and the cameras had always been there. The musicians had always felt the pressure of the hype at their backs. But somehow we were deluded that the phenomenon of the Woodstock nation was bigger than all of that. We thought we had enough real energy to come through. We thought we had soul. We thought Clapton had soul too. By the time the Rolling Stones drew a quarter of a million in Hyde Park we began to realize that we were mostly tourists, kibitzing on someone else's happening. The Stones invited people 'to bring tambourines, bells, clappers, anything and join in'. But in the end nobody got their yayas out, though they all watched hopefully to see if anyone else did. The Stones released their butterflies and read the poem on the death of Keats that David Litvinoff found for them, because, as Bill Graham said (and who knows better), Mick Jagger is one hell of a showman, but the smell of death was stronger than the smell of pot or spunk or incense, as Altamont was to prove. Like lots of other people, Jimi tried to keep the good idea of love and peace and mixing alive. In the last interview with 'Seen and Heard' he chanted all the familiar slogans and put down the people who said that the Isle of Wight festival of music was bummer, but he was using his panhandling voice.

> Is this love, baby? or is it just confusion?

Jimi probably would have dug Kathy Etchingham's promptitude in getting on his funeral bandwagon ('Jimi Hendrix – the truth', *People*, September 20, 1970). After all she was only into him for money and maybe revenge for the bad times. She had always said that a mama must keep an eye on the main chance, and Jimi knew the sense there was in that. He might find it harder to forgive Mike Jeffries for releasing stuff that he would rather have suppressed, so that people will say that he was overrated and he couldn't really have been the best rock guitarist in the world. Even then he would have dug that the Electric Lady's bills have got to be paid. We might piously cry that the gross commercialism of the op-pop-rock industry ground him to death, but really it wasn't that. It was the power of death in us, the people.

Let me stand next to your fire.

Our fire was never alight. Jimi burnt himself up and kept himself going with artificial energy waiting for it to come, but he saw it turning to paranoia and servility. He heard love and peace abused, the new cop-out words, and felt the loathing of the hypocrisy getting stronger in him than the hope. He provoked his own Altamont time and time again and the people grovelled and adulated as blindly as ever. At Monterey and Woodstock the spontaneity held a moment and flowered and he and his guitar rode on the wave mightily. He was no leader; he could not make it for us, and that is what we all mistook. 'Move us! Move us!' we bawled, and lapsed back into our torpor and wrote clever-clever and down-down. We missed our moment and the spontaneity died.

How many times was it like that? How many times did Jimi try it on with friends and find he had nothing but fans? How many times did he start to rap charming with his bush-baby eyes and his ready smile and that fast sharp patter only to find no comeback but fawning? How often did the rapping change to panhandling and then to sneering because his friends were nothing but an audience and they didn't know the difference between the panhandling and the straight rap? How often did the caress and the compliment change to insult and assault? His foxy ladies turned to slags and pigs in a second. He tried testing to see how much shit people would take before they would give him a flash but they went on and on tolerating him. Everyone still maintains that Jimi was charming, gentle, disciplined even, always punctual. Even his reported last message (actually from Herbert Dannemann in Düsseldorf) was a glib lie. 'Let there be peace. Love each other and do not be hard and cruel.' *Nil nisi bonum.*

Within hours of his death the hard bright line of Hendrix is being blurred by the mediocrity of the medium that must transmit it. Being blurred by us. Our love is so feeble that it can only grovel and submit. Our peace is black inertia, the dull ass's hoof.

Is it tomorrow or the end of time?

Jimi had often talked about his death, but he can hardly have foreseen how crummy it would be when it happened, choking on his vomit in a chick's rented apartment. He may not have wanted us to grieve for him but we had better grieve for ourselves. We have lost the best rock guitarist we ever had because we did not know how to keep him. The awful fright and the dead sense of ageing that the newspaper dodgers gave us on Friday afternoon had better be a shock current to galvanize us to save our nation. If Jimi is going to live tomorrow we have to make up our minds to live today. 'There ain't no life nowhere', unless we make some. People are going to tell us that Jimi's death is the end of an era. Others are going to tell us that, like Bird, Jimi lives. There's no point in cheap kitsch metaphysics. Hendrix is dead, a heap of offal in a morgue, a heap of electronic paraphernalia for future marketing, and a bunch of slick hip biographies.

No doubt there are those who will maintain that Hendrix was finished, burnt out. That there was no more great music to come. On the evidence of the Band of Gypsies and the Isle of Wight they might seem to be right. Even if they were right about the music, a lot of people would still hurt, because Hendrix was a great man. Some other people are going to regret his dropping out because they had a lot of money on his back. In fact the best music of Hendrix was still to come. The last but one time he was in London, he was working on an album with Steve Stills and one night he jammed with him at the Speakeasy in the early hours of the morning when all the ravers had gone home, all the clowns were gone to bed . . . There was no freaking, just the three of them, Jimi, Steve and Billy Cox (as well as Twink who was so far out he finally vanished altogether). Jimi played like a musician, utterly absorbed in the sound, his whole body still except for his big hands on the guitar, feet together, head on one side, with huge, listening eyes black in his pale face, and the sounds were amazing. It was not a matter of discipline. He was at peace and potent. We sat there in the gloom, feeling strong and lucky, knowing that under the hype and the bullshit there had been a genius all along. I don't think anybody clapped even. There was no need. Jimi knew why we sat so still. Not even the cloacal fug of a groovy nightspot could blot out what was going down. He played as long as he wanted to. Nobody shouted, nobody paid. He was playing real good for free and he was happy.

> Music, sweet music
> Wish I could caress
> The rest

We let him slip down the energy drain. Can we build fast enough to close it before we disappear ourselves? Can we sweep up the pieces of yesterday's life?

> I think I'll go turn myself off and go on down;
> Rilly ain't no use me hangin' aroun'
> Music, sweet music . . .
> Wish I could caress . . .
> And kiss kiss . . .

Welcome the shit-storm

Oz, January 1971

While awaiting trial for obscenity and corrupting minors for publishing Schoolkids'
Oz (No. 28) which was actually edited by the minors themselves, the three editors
suffered a police raid on the Oz office, and confiscation of papers and files; Richard
Neville's home was also raided. He was done for a tiny quantity of cannabis and
spent Christmas (1970) in gaol. The virgin leader of the Tory government was, of
course, Edward Heath.

We've always known that the shit would eventually hit the fan. The
permissive society was a journalists' catch phrase that confused parents had
begun to believe in. One of the reasons why the Tories and their virgin
leader won by a landslide at the last election was that the rednecks of
England thought that the long-hairs were getting away with murder.
Wilson gave the vote to the eighteen-year-olds in a last-ditch attempt to
stem the tide of reaction. What he did not bargain for was the degree of
reactionism among the eighteen-year-olds themselves.

The Underground was beginning to feel (until recently) as if it was
operating in a vacuum. Its gestures had become louder and more rhetorical, more deadly serious than before, so that more than one power-player
paused now and then to wonder whether he hadn't overshot somewhere
and ended up nowhere. Our energy was all draining out into the void,
meeting no obstruction, never bouncing back. Repressive tolerance was
killing us. The Underground press cast about for new sources of energy,
decided to grow despite all Alan Macusson's dire predictions.

But what was needed to foster new growth was a little judicious pruning.
That need coincided with the decision of the Tories to score two new
public-relations victories, by 'smashing the unions' and 'eradicating the
Underground'. Government without the trade unions is impossible, as the
Tories well know, so the whole rigmarole is meant to display an intransigent, authoritarian attitude which the mass of the British population will
welcome as the proper face of government. To win the allegiance of the
readers of the *News of the World* this government will flirt with real
economic danger and find it worthwhile. The public-relations value of
appearing to send all the pot-smoking, cunt-lapping, ad-men for the
revolution to Brixton, or even Parkhurst, is enormous. All those bitter

45

people who envy those who never fought a war or even did national service will feel vindicated.

However, the enforcers of this policy are not as sophisticated as their masters. Driven on by the same kind of burning moral indignation that the governors are trying to appease, Inspector Luff and his familiars decided that as a really crushing punishment, Richard Neville was to go without his presents and his Christmas dinner, even if the slippery bastard was impossible to gaol by legitimate means. So they had him busted for the second time, while he was still on remand for charges relating to their first bust. But in appearing to persecute the Underground so ruthlessly, they did in fact no more than is routine for people from the Underground who do not edit papers. Inarticulate grubby kids who look as if they might not have any fixed abode are refused bail as a matter of course. The Underground media freaks might have been feeling isolated from their readership because of their increasing absorption into the Establishment. Hooray hooray. 'At a stroke' Inspector Luff reintegrated the Underground, by treating hitherto unconvicted and always very well-defended Richard Neville like an old lag.

By crushing *Oz* the ground is made more fertile for *Ink*. By encroaching upon what more naïve moderate folk have always thought of as their civil liberties, the police and their masters are forcing a polarization on the general public. The backlash against permissiveness is about to provoke its own backlash. Even the prostitute press will be sympathetic to a cause of crude censorship, which has involved confiscation of material prepared for the defence of the Schoolkids' *Oz* charges. Christmas Day in the gaol-house is a great line for the 'human interest' purveyors.

The really exciting thing about all this unlooked-for manuring is that shit is an Underground medium. It is doubtful whether the virgin Prime Minister and his ten thousand sainted followers can handle it as well as we can, arse-fuckers that we are. At least they've stopped laughing at us, which means that we can go back to laughing at them. We don't have to thrash ourselves into a frenzy of revolutionary fervour any more: we can evacuate the pockets of the Establishment where we have been allowed to play and bring it all back home to the Underground. We can be illegal. We can conspire. We can come closer together again as the space around us closes. There are more of us now but that's nothing compared to how many of us there'll be tomorrow. Eradication means plucking up by the roots – but our roots are what they'll never get at, they're sunk down somewhere inside of every family in the British Isles. Whenever the virgin Prime Minister takes his solitary pleasure he pours out a libation to the underground.

Women and medicine

General Practitioner, 8 January 1971

As a result of gradual raising of consciousness, it is now illegal to advertise proprietary medicines in the manner described here.

It is assumed as a kind of rule of thumb among doctors and others, that women are particularly prone to psychosomatic disorders. Few doctors are liable to perpetuate the old nonsenses about greensickness and hysteria, yet a doctor faced with implacably psychosomatic symptoms in a female patient is still quite likely to suggest that she get married, live a normal life, have a baby, have another baby and so on. Really, the GP is not to blame for the limitations of his approach. He has no option but to attempt to reconcile his female patients to the limitations of their existence. He cannot even spare the time to follow up with an examination of the whole family situation, or even to examine the aetiology of his patient's symptoms over an extended period.

The root of the problem is that female patients use their doctors in a special way, as father-surrogates or simply as confidants. Bred to a filial role from their earliest childhood, they are encouraged to carry it over into the passivity of the mature female. Besides, in the modern nuclear family there is really nobody else to talk to. In order to avail themselves of the doctor's consulting room they must be able to show themselves as physically ill. Being ill deserves sympathy and attention outside the doctor's surgery and it is the condition of entry into the doctor's surgery. Being ill is without moral stigma – being unhappy is an admission of failure.

Obvious and superficial as such an account must seem to any trained man who has day-to-day dealings with such cases, it is a more hopeful and profitable line to take than the one that supposes that the malingering of women is something to do with their endocrine system and its fluctuations. An altered bias in the consideration of female ills could affect the commonest assumptions about the menstrual cycle, so that symptomatic treatment of menstrual ailments could be superseded by a more radical therapy of adjustment. What did come first, after all, the menstruation or the tension?

There are no official figures on the subject, so that it is impossible to establish that women seek medication from their GPs more frequently than men. Apart from the evidence of haphazard observation, we can establish on *a priori* grounds that women are more likely to seek medical aid than men, and to visit more frequently. They are persuaded that they are delicate, despite their greater resistance to the ills that wreak most havoc on their male companions. They have no objection to appearing weak or silly and relying heavily upon the doctor's authority. They tend to rely upon medication: if it works, they take more of it. Out of the two hundred and forty-six million prescriptions dispensed every year, nearly seventy million are for preparations acting on the nervous system, painkillers, tranquillizers and antidepressants, the largest single group in the total figure.

There have been several outcries in the recent past about growing addiction among housewives: the All-Saints Hospital unit in Birmingham claims that the numbers are on the increase and that they have had no success in weaning housewives off barbiturate addiction. A GP in Croydon confessed that he was supplying more and more of his female patients with more and more of what the general public calls 'drugs' and that he could not see any feasible alternative. When the Department of Health published its pilot survey of patients attending the euphemistically named day hospitals the figures showed that women outnumbered men by two to one, and there were more housewives than the total male attendance. The largest group of women were suffering from depressive pyschoses or involutional melancholia, and the improvement rate was disappointing. For nearly all of them the day hospital was the latest stage in a history of disorder; we can only speculate as to the form in which their distress was first observed by a GP. The largest group in the day hospitals is the smallest group in psychiatric hospitals, the married women between twenty-five and forty-four. The disparity might mean that depressional and melancholic states and 'nervous breakdown' are most typical of female distress and most ineptly dealt with by the existing systems of detention. Women are not maniacs or idiots, either by nature or by chance, but they do need help. That help cannot come out of a bottle, nor can it be supplied by the most patient and gentle doctor. It will have to come from the women themselves and a radical change in their situation and prospects.

The known extent of female hypochondria and drug reliance is nothing compared to the unknown extent of compulsive behaviour in housewives. Recent experiments on caffeine addiction showed unmistakably that women who drank coffee as part of their morning routine were distressed physically if it was omitted. (Women who did not normally take coffee were distressed if they did take it.) Such reliance may seem trivial, but it is part of a pattern of reliance which is openly exploited by the manufacturers of proprietary medicines. The consumer of such medicines is almost invariably characterized as female. Reading marketing research reports on successful selling campaigns, I was appalled to notice that in cases of new analgesic preparations the impersonal consumer was characterized as *she* quite unselfconsciously. Morris J. Gottleib, psychologist, describing the successful marketing of one proprietary line and analysing it as a paradigm, announced without a qualm that 'What one should do is to address himself to the compulsive in all of us'. The aim is not only to persuade the customer to buy a product once, but to induce a need which ensures that the market, responding to the iron law of capitalism, goes on expanding. Users must be created and *kept*. In 1969, Beechams spent £5,342,201 on inducing such needs in the general public. Among the most heavily promoted items were Beechams Pills, Beechams Powders, Fynnon Salts, Iron Jelloids, and Phensic. A glance at any newspaper, especially at the women's press, will show how painkillers are presented to women over and over again as relievers of tension, freeing them from headaches and releasing them to new participation in the joys of life. Anadin spent more than £565,000 in 1969, Aspro £278,000 and so on. The advertising centres on the image of the distressed woman surrounded by crying children, and the miraculous calm which ensues from the instant relief provided by the drug.

It may seem hysterical exaggeration to point to the dangers inherent in unlimited consumption of phenacetin and acetylsalicylic acid, but in as much as the vendors aim at constant use for their products over a period of fifty years (for the basic A.P.C. recipe has not been bettered, and the newer analgesic preparations have failed to oust it from the mass market) it seems that some caveat ought to appear on the packaging of such preparations. Ten years ago in Australia, I remember the scare when cases of liver deterioration were traced to the effects of huge consumption of the Australian version of Beechams Powders, known as Bex, which some women were taking at the rate of three or four powders four or five times a day. As children we used to laugh at the way our parents prescribed 'a cup of tea and an aspirin' as the panacea for all ills, but the Aspro millions ought to have taught us something more about drug-peddling to the defenceless.

The headache is the favourite lever for selling analgesics, but other products address themselves to ills arising from abdominal tension and inculcate the daily use of laxatives and still more market 'zest' in the form of iron, or yeast, or simply alcohol. The target is always dependence and the daily use, 'the compulsive in all of us'. What the advertisers exploit is the female 'self-image' (in their own jargon) and the cause of their success is the cause of the doctor's too frequent failure when dealing with women. In this country the National Health Service is a natural curb on the degree of medication which can be doled out to individuals. The half-joking prejudice about the private practitioners' malingering female clientèle has some basis in reality. In the USA, where doctoring is big business, female abdominal operations outnumber all other forms of surgery.

When a woman arrives in the surgery she comes from a world in which her insecurity and low self-image are ruthlessly exploited. The barrage of propaganda telling her that she is too fat is now equalled by the costliness of the plugs telling her that she is too smelly. Until mid-1966 the problem of vaginal odour did not exist. In 1969, £126,000 was spent in creating awareness of it, and in 1970 the figure has been doubled. Doctors inherit the problems in the surgery: the feminine dependency which makes them such a valuable market makes them his problem. Like the vendor of proprietary medicines the private practitioner can make great capital out of it. The GP working on capitation fees cannot afford to capitulate to the feminine demand for help and support. He cannot even discover what compulsive patterns have already been set up or how much the symptoms of distress which he now sees have been aggravated by acquired dependency.

The GP is not necessarily a moralist or a social reformer, and in any case the limitations on his position as a healer of physical ills do not allow him to give radical advice to his patients. He cannot be blamed for supplying the only remedies for female malaise which lie within his power, but perhaps if he were free of the prejudice that women are mystically prone as a sex to psychosomatic disturbance, and if he were less likely to take a conventional moralist line with women who are plainly 'maladjusted', he would at least not be contributing to the situation as it exists. A rebellious woman has all too often to count her doctor among her opponents: obviously rebellion in an unfree society is not necessarily better for health than unwilling conformism, and doctors ought not to be obliged to cast their lot with one side or another. Perhaps they could try by other means to break down women's dependency on them, hoping thereby to lessen dependency in other fields. It might go some of the way if they could discuss problems frankly with the patients themselves.

Doctors are proud of their authority, and to that extent they perpetuate the situation in which women resort to them in order to share responsibility which they find crippling. How many times have women detailed inconsistent and plainly hysterical symptoms to their doctor and been given tranquillizers or stimulants under the impression that they were getting direct medication for some organic ailment? Doctors are loath to tell patients about the nature of drugs because of the problems of psychological dependency, but the outcome of such practice is very often real dependency, both physical and psychological. In prescribing drugs which are unknown to the patient, the doctor does take full responsibility for what happens, and it is precisely this opportunity to pass the buck for their own circumstances which women cannot afford. It may seem like the deepest contempt to prescribe placebos for what cannot be cured and must be endured, and doctors are understandably unwilling to do it, but they should be no less unwilling to prescribe potent drugs which can only act upon the sufferer and not her situation. It is a measure of the disintegration and confusion of our society that such problems so often end up on the doctors' cards: perhaps it is in the interests of doctors themselves to speed the coming of a new world.

The Wet Dream Film Festival

Suck, 1971

In November 1970, an organization called Self, the Sexual Egalitarian and Libertarian Fraternity, mounted the First Wet Dream Film Festival in Amsterdam, and invited me to sit on the jury. The wrangling which broke out after Otto Muehl had been prevented from carrying out the torture of a goose as part of his act at the festival, provided an occasion for me to attempt to define the principles behind my editorship of Suck, *which ought to have been the first non-sado-masochistic sex-paper. As I was the only editor who held those principles, the collaboration – and the paper – were short-lived. The article quoted here, to which my remarks are an answer, appeared in* Friends *22, 19 January 1971.*

Albie Thoms, film co-ordinator for the First Wet Dream, wrote an article defending Otto Muehl for *Friends* newspaper (London).

When Germaine Greer saw it she freaked-out and sent us her reply typed between sections of Albie's piece pasted on notepaper.

Albie's article in *cursive* script.

Germaine's answers in non-cursive script beginning with 'e.g. the following'.

In a cultural climate where everyone prides themselves on their freedom, permissiveness, and unshockability and where sufficient mystification for anything is that it 'freaked the straights', Otto Muehl's work comes as a reminder of just how tame and nice it all really is.

For the last ten years now he has been getting on his acts of extreme sexual violence and filming them; whatever event he takes part in, his actions dominate and provide the main talking point. But although he provokes an amazing amount of bullshit

---

e.g. the following

---

the important thing is the experience – one of his functions is to re-forge links between experience and its representations, links that have almost snapped in this technological media cocoon we have built ourselves.

Friends magazine?

Below, Albie Thoms, the Australian film-maker, makes his own very personal appreciation of Otto Muehl.

Thus ends the anonymous introduction, and thus, in the strain of authentic bullshit, the appreciation begins:

Otto Muehl is an artist so powerful that his work is never presented without creating 'that awe-ful fear that is most stirring'.

The function of the artist being to frighten or art an excuse for anything. Pretentiousness is the keynote.

At the London Underground Film Festival in September, his intention to stage an action was sufficient for authoritarian heavies to muster against him, censoring his art with hints of violence should he persist.

Muehl's art being violence censored by the hint of violence? A well-tried and vindicated guerilla tactic. Albie is no Black or White Panther.

In Amsterdam, people had watched a celluloid orgy

What film was that? If there was any orgy there I wasn't at it, nor was Albie. The point of this remark seems to be that you have to pay for your pleasure by condoning the infliction of pain.

of cocks and cunts for three days under the careful supervision of police

True – the police were the only ones watching the films.

who ensured that all present were members of the élitist Sexual Egalitarian and Libertarian Fraternity.

Elitist is a good word to describe any group which pays to join. Joining was the condition of having a festival at all. If Albie didn't approve he was involved enough in the organization to have protested. But he didn't withdraw his labour and he didn't issue membership cards for free to the élite who came without the bread. Others did.

Muehl once again exposed the sham libertarianism of the self-appointed bourgeois avant-garde.

The bourgeoisie is born, not appointed, even by itself, and as for avant-garde, Albie is the first one to have applied such a term – he'll call us Bohemians next!

Drawing into the open the hidden moralism of underground intellectuals, revealing their confused puritanism and their conditioned authoritarianism.

The people who were present were not all underground or intellectuals, and many of them are more aware of puritanism and authoritarianism than Albie gives them credit for. The perpetrators of the crime against Otto Muehl haven't stopped worrying about it yet.

In Amsterdam I was pushed and jostled by a man who punched and kicked Muehl's female assistants, bodily throwing them out of Kosmos – Amsterdam's subsidized meditation centre. I was unable to prevent this brutality without resorting to violence myself. While begging, pleading, attempting to reason with the man, I was pushed aside as he crazily attacked the bodies of the two girls who minutes before had performed an exhibition of liberated sexuality that disturbed the audience and drove some to irrational activity.

The man who pushed and jostled Albie also belted Heathcote when he leapt at the goose – he was an organizer of Kosmos, not of SELF and it is only fair to point out that the exhibition of liberated sexuality we had just seen was in fact an exhibition of violence, involving the manhandling of two girls and a bloke by Otto, and his pissing all over their bruised, naked bodies – 'art' it may have been – liberated sexuality it never was.

Muehl is driven by some inexplicable urge to rub the faces of the bourgeoisie in their own shit.

The bourgeoisie are driven by a not-so-inexplicable urge to resist, especially as the shit is not theirs but Otto's.

Initially his work engaged genital sexuality, covering fucking couples with eggs, flour and paint in material actions that were logical extensions of action painting. In the repressive atmosphere of Vienna this was branded as pornography and Muehl was gaoled.

The connection between this and the preceding sentence, which can only be inferred, is revealing of some confused puritanism in Albie himself – so who's surprised!

Not deterred by the harsh treatment of his work, Muehl went further in exposing 'the pornography of the businessman' and included anal sexuality, sadism, masochism, and coprophilia.

Art becomes journalism! Muehl exposes by doing – do I expose coprophilia by eating shit? Do I expose someone else's coprophilia by eating shit myself?

Further gaolings, fines and censorship followed, but at the end of the 60s, the bourgeoisie had seen the marketing possibilities of pornography, legalized it in Denmark and tolerated it in Germany, Sweden and Holland.

The commercial value of pornography has collapsed with legalization. The market quickly reached saturation and the high prices which scarcity and proscription had made possible for a tiny outlay, which means huge profits, plummeted.

In Germany, Muehl found his most enthusiastic supporters: intellectuals who related his work to Freud, Reich and Jung;

Ah! so Muehl is a member of the élite and the self-appointed bourgeois avant-garde all the time? Well, any old shit can be related to Freud, Reich and Jung. The problem is to find things that can't be.

art experts who saw him as the most significant practitioner of newly acceptable erotic art.

Crème de la crème – art experts yet! This is bullshit of an old and venerated stamp.

Last Christmas in Braunschweig, a former Nazi centre, Muehl pushed beyond the tolerability for pornography that liberal Germany permitted. He performed a burlesque of religious festivities that included a butcher slaughtering a pig on stage for Muehl to use in his sexual happening. Intellectuals of the city petitioned for his arrest and the burgomaster demanded police action.
Since then he has dispensed with the butcher and performs his own ritual execution of birds on stage. In London he announced his intention to use a chicken in his action Oh Sensibility, *but authorities at the NFT (who had already permitted Peter Kochenrath's film of the Braunschweig action) prevented it from taking place.*

Shame to those who stop Otto doing this thing – although presumably he could have gone and done it at home or elsewhere. What one protests against, you see, is enforced *assistance* as an ignorant and unwitting audience is made accomplice to an act performed before it. I need not feel guilty watching a film of a massacre because I wasn't there, helping by failing to intervene; I may watch the film and retain the right to despise the film-maker. What would you do with the Nazi archives otherwise?

An attempt to stage the action at the Underground ghetto New Arts Lab was similarly banned.
The repressive treatment of Muehl in London instigated minimal self-criticism. But at least one vegetarian moralist saw the naïvety of his position in condemning Muehl while sitting calmly with friends who devoured a chicken dinner.

Poor bullied vegetarian moralist! Food is a better motive for brutality than art and in any case the chicken eaters were not forcing the vegetarian to relish their food; presumably they had not forced him to serve them with chicken either. The parallel is invalid, because spectatorship at an act performed under these special circumstances involves a different kind of participation. Otto Muehl kills birds for our sport. The chicken eaters were not practising upon a live chicken for the sake of shocking or delighting the vegetarian.

But the sexual libertarians of Amsterdam (particularly the visiting super-groupies from London)

i.e. Mike Zwerin, Jay Landesman (who defended Muehl), Heathcote Williams, Anthony Haydn-Guest, Richard Neville, Daniel Topolski, Danny Hughes (who cursed the interruption of the show), oh and me . . . Albie came from London too, didn't he?

couldn't reconcile their supposed belief in freedom with their opposition to violence and so resorted to the very thing they decried in order to save the life of a goose. They supported their physical attack on Muehl by calling him fascist, and threw him off the stage and robbed him of his goose in a calculated act of sexual repression which prevented Muehl's sexual performance.

So the super-groupies turn out to be Heathcote and Anthony. Their act was so far from being calculated that neither of them understands to this day quite why he did it. The act was thus: Heathcote sprang up from his seat, shook off the bigger people who grabbed him and leapt at the goose, held aloft by Muehl who was bigger than he and on a higher level. He succeeded in snatching it, and was brought down by the opposition, so that contrary to every journalist's instinct Anthony reverted to schoolboy morality and ran off with the goose. Yah! Sucks! Boo! to the bully. The underdog is alive and well and living on a barge in Amsterdam. It was bloody good fun, and we cheered like workers at a melodrama. Muehl flapped around the stage brandishing his knife. Come his last truly great performance he will gut himself and fuck his own liver. What is life where art is concerned?

Sexual libertarians congregated at the Amsterdam Wet Dream Film Festival to exhibit their tolerance and generosity. (Gee, I thought they came to watch dirty films.)

Instead they exhibited intolerance, selfishness, greed and frustration.

As well as hunger and thirst and fear and bewilderment and curiosity and kindness and cowardliness and most human passions to be expected in a gathering of that kind. Albie's antipodean moralism is cruder than most.

Summoning up all the strength of their collective unbalanced egos, they vented punishment on Otto Muehl, who has probably suffered more than all of them combined.

Nobody punished Otto Muehl – somebody stole his goose. If you allow that the act was a collective one, then you must allow that if the goose had been killed that would have been a collective act too. But we didn't want to do it. And we didn't want to do it more than Albie did want to do it. Life is a better motive than art any time. Heathcote stole the goose because we wanted him to. How do you avoid censorship of that possibility if not by enacting it?

People born after the demise of fascism called Muehl a Nazi,

Dutch people who lived through the German occupation turned grey when Muehl began barking at them in his Hoch-deutsch accent and pulled a pregnant girl out of the audience and flung her about. If any of us consider fascism to be dead, they don't and they were there.

not realizing that after the Anschluss he was forced into the Hitler Youth and into the German army to witness the massive human conflict undertaken in – the name of freedom. They did not know that after the war anti-German mobs almost killed Muehl because he was in German uniform.

I called him a Nazi, when fighting with Jay Landesman who claimed that Muehl was an energy release (like a smack in the mouth or a police raid). I meant it figuratively; I had to wait for Albie to tell me that it is literally true.

And they probably didn't know the suffering and indignity inflicted on Muehl in gaol and elsewhere because as an artist he defies the taboos of a society that controls the lives of its members in the name of the omnipotent state.

One of the reasons that *SUCK* exists is to deny that there is any moral value in suffering. Albie's adherence to this puritanical notion would appear to sanctify such political prisoners as Adolf Hitler. The bullshit rears its head again. Muehl ought not to be gaoled because he is an artist, it would seem. And Albie called us élitists!

Perhaps these élitist authoritarians will stage another Wet Dream Festival in Amsterdam and look beyond the narrow confines of their own ego trips to the people around them, denied the privileges they have extracted from the state. Perhaps they'll extend their freedom to other people in Amsterdam and stage a festival that will liberate people from the tyranny of commercialization of sex.

Seeing the shit-storm flying after this festival gathering thickest on those who worked hardest for it, one could hardly expect them to try again. The notion that it would take no more than another festival to liberate people from the tyranny of commercialization of sex is outrageous. The planners of the festival are themselves not liberated, any more than Muehl was. Each step is only an experiment and some will be fruitless and others mistakes. We have only instinct to go by, after all.

If they do, I hope they will remember Otto Muehl and his courageous performance this year. I hope they recognize the greatness of this artist and have the courage to invite him to perform another live action.

Muehl comes without asking, and takes his chances – we are not élitists. He can organize his own festival, here, there, anywhere; that's harder than commandeering groups convened for different motives.

Otto Muehl taught people more about sexual freedom than all the films shown at the festival.

The films taught us that we are not very sexy. Muehl would have taught us that we are full of hatred, fear and impotence. We denied it. We may be wrong. He was not the only teacher. We were not his pupils. Albie respected Muehl's art, and sat at his knee. How Muehl must have laughed at him. Pompous, pretentious preacher-man from down under, where the censorship is most brutal and there is no class but the bourgeoisie.

He is a great artist and I feel privileged to have seen his work. I return to my own country inspired by his freedom and by his courage (Albie Thoms).

Friends, organ of the White Panthers and other fist-shaking elements added a pious rider to mitigate the bombast of this ending.

At the Wet Dream Film Festival in Amsterdam in November the censors were a fellow playwright and a journalist, both English, and apparent subscribers to the libertarian ideals of the festival. Their predetermined violence on Muehl took place during his performance, interrupting his work and stealing his props, which failed to deter Muehl from improvising an ending to his action which showed his contempt for his oppressors and his superb ability to create art which shatters the most jaded sensibilities.

(This has got to be a paper tiger – what has the Underground to do with words like 'superb ability to create art'? How did they decide upon predetermination? The treatment for jaded sensibilities is not to shatter them, after all.)

Our cause is sexual liberation. Our tactic the defiance of censorship. Thus expressed our aims are political, for the patterns of sexual interrelationship are created by, and in turn support, the other social structures. The approved sexual relationship in all Western societies is exclusive, possessive, colonizing, exploitatory; sex is recognized as intimately connected with violence, for the power of the one over the other must be enforced and enforceable. Butch rules bitch, pimp rules whore, man rules wife, queer rules queen. Like the most insidious tyrannies it is spoken of as a natural law, nature red in tooth and claw.

This organization, which is as clear and universal as if it were indeed the expression of an irrefragable law, has at its central pole, pain instead of pleasure. The pain of sexual frustration, of repressed tenderness, of denied curiosity, of isolation in the ego, of greed, suppressed rebellion, of hatred poisoning all love and generosity, permeates our sexuality. What we love we destroy. Censorship is the outward and continuing expression of this distortion of the human erotic faculty. It is the one public point at which we can join battle with what enslaves us. Defiance of censorship is an emblem of the removal of the swaddling bands that have deformed our sexual personalities and it is our faith that they must be removed absolutely as a first prerequisite of freedom and new growth. But when leg-irons are first removed the prisoner cannot walk.

SUCK itself is no more than the creation of one tiny area where we may say freely how it is: what flows through *SUCK* is unliberated sexuality, much of it heavy with hatred and cruelty and desire of death. Most of it is fantasy, and hugely derived from the fantasy machines developed by commercial pornography to reinforce the sexual status quo. *SUCK* too must carry its burden of whips and chains and ironhard cocks ploughing the wombs of women in agony, because we have rejected all censorship, even our own. But we do not need to censor our own comments upon the sexual status quo.

The Wet Dream Film Festival was not a festival of liberated sex and could not of itself liberate anyone, for it is axiomatic that one can only liberate oneself. It was the beginning of something which might develop into a collective celebration of sex, but, much as *SUCK* itself, it was originally an experiment. Its problems were the problems of *SUCK* but felt much more keenly because felt simultaneously and together. Firstly, we were committed to showing a great number of commercial porn films, made to exploit the misery of the deprived and the perverted, at minimal cost, badly shot, worse played by the unhappy actors blackmailed by force or lack of money; dingy, murky, spotty, choppy film, sex without dialogue or soul or body. The effect of such films is calculated turn-off, throwing the viewer back into himself, isolating us all from each other. Removal of restraints in Denmark had produced glossier porn, better lit, better shot, but the flesh was still meaty, lit up all pink like a butcher's shop, and the plots were vestigial, the characters depersonalized. But at least the commercial porno films were aimed at a sexual response, however desolate and specific. The Underground films were not even genital: either they celebrated sex in narcissistic and 'artistic' ways or they offered a sort of commentary on decadent social mores. The hypocrisy of getting kicks out of the depiction of depraved sex while retaining the right to disapprove of it or satirize it was the worst turn-off of all.

The process was most stunningly illustrated by the films of Otto Muehl who enacts all kinds of infantile and sadistic routines and then puts the fantasy back into the head of a straw man from the bourgeoisie. As every other judge on the panel knows, I believe that there was only one film which brought heart and mind and sex to swell and strain with yearning, one film only which would have liberated me to drink the sperm of every man and sip the juice of every woman in the room, Genet's *Chant d'Amour*.

So all the members of SELF were poisoned. We sickened and slumped incapable of bridging the gaps between each other. We saw our hideous impotence so clearly that it seemed that the festival had betrayed revolution and had driven it into another world. We were guilty with each other. By the end of the third day we could hardly hear each other's voices. There had been the beginnings of a different blooming, which has since been criticized in the aftermath of bitterness and guilt by other people who never got that far.

Heathcote and I had come late to one of the drearier sessions, so we had to sit on the wrong side of the screen, which was no hardship because half the films were projected backwards anyway. Otto Muehl was showing, and we felt impatient with the cruelty and clod-hopping 'satire' because we had been getting in to each other. We took off our clothes as a protest and began rolling about knotting and unknotting like sea-creatures; people came up quietly, melted their clothes off and joined in. The sea-plant grew and its arms multiplied. Then suddenly our very own commercial porn-film unit arrived, sending ahead their researcher whose clothes we removed so that she became part of our anemone. But we could not digest the arc-light and the projector or the cupidity and voyeurism of their masters, so we wilted and shrank into ourselves. We found ourselves shivering. Only Heathcote remained, dancing like some faun or satyr against the body-loathing of Otto Muehl. We needed magic and only Heathcote had it. As events later proved.

Confrontation is political awareness. What we discovered at the Wet Dream Film Festival is that we will have to generate enough energy in ourselves to create a pornography which will eradicate the traditional porn by sheer erotic power. We know it needs money (for was it not to pay expenses that Jim Haynes sold our innocence to commercial porn-makers?) which can be raised, and now we know that it needs genius and energy too.

We must commission films, make films, write, act, co-operate for life's sake. The battle against sadism and impotence is more desperate than we ever believed. We must begin the struggle within ourselves, carry it into the political sphere. It is mere hypocrisy to suppose that we are more liberated than others, and sheer puritanism to feel guilty that we are not. Just as Heathcote stole the goose, we will have to steal away the victims of capitalist sex, away from death to life. Those who depend upon violence and pain for their orgasms will protest. Let them. Traditional commercial pornography keeps their fantasies well supplied; there is never any lack of torturers and sufferers.

Our task is much harder. All our skills tend to death: we must reverse them and struggle with a new-born baby's strength against the black inertia of the old law.

Look up Heathcote! Bill! Jim! We can only perish in the attempt.

Oz trial post-mortem

Unpublished

The *Oz* trial was political all right, but to say so boldly is to utter no more than the anarchist maxim, 'All prisoners are political prisoners.' The *Oz* trial was political in the same way that Nixon's decision to ignore the conclusions of his own Commission into Pornography was political. By doing so, he persuaded vast numbers of voters that he was an upright man, not to be pushed around by a bunch of depraved highbrows and long-hairs. He was the one to clean up VD and the drug menace and crime on the streets. The tacit appeal to ignorance and bigotry was part of his courtship of the reactionary majority, like his decision to forbid abortions in army hospitals, which he later modified to a demand that army hospitals be bound by the code of the state that they are in. (When he justified this move in terms of his *personal* belief, nobody laughed.) What Nixon knew was that New York, LA and San Francisco are not the country and that the Woodstock nation is a hated minority, for whose persecution he would gain rich rewards in voting power. However, the war and the shameful mode of its waging have provided him with an explosive situation; he cannot be sure how many shot university students the country can bear at any one time. The First Amendment is being thoroughly exploited by the papers ever since Ellsberg, so Nixon must look longingly across the Atlantic, where Edward Heath can play the scourge of God with a free hand.

So the politics were not of the kind that comes of a fear that *Oz* and its readership might overthrow the state, for if there were any such possibility, which is to say if *Oz* had a large minority following, or particularly militant supporters, or powerful friends, it would not have been possible to conduct the persecution the way Luff did, or to put Argyle in charge of the case. Part of the point of the trial was to show that *Oz* was of little consequence. Convictions and gaol terms were absolutely necessary, not that Argyle would be required to do any more than follow the dictates of his conscience in applying the law as he understood it, which given the law of obscenity as it stands, is his prerogative, for the ascription of obscenity does rest quite securely with the judge's and the jurors' aesthetic sensibility. The politics were in the choice of Argyle, father of a raped girl and well able to trust his own conscience in spite of four weeks of evidence. I dare say he would like to have ordered most of the witnesses to take medical and psychiatric tests too, yet if you reminded him that in Russia political dissidents go into mental hospitals he would be suitably horrified.

The *Oz* trial was a public relations exercise for the Tories. The public chastisement of *Oz*, however gratuitous and fanatical to the liberal mind, would persuade those voters who read the *News of the World*, that this is the government to clean up Piccadilly Circus and smash strikes. The swiftness, thoroughness and ruthlessness of the descent, unhampered by any petti-fogging concern for civil liberties, showed that this administration knew how to be tough. Any pious liberal outcry could easily be ignored, for the realities are on the side of the political opportunists; if Felix Dennis puts the readership of *Oz* at 500,000, we could, by using the same ratio of circulation to readership, put that of the *News of the World* at 70,000,000.

Before repressive tolerance became a tactic of the past, *Oz* could fool itself and its readers that, for some people at least, the alternative society already existed. Instead of developing a political analysis of the state we live in, instead of undertaking the patient and unsparing job of education which must precede even a pre-revolutionary situation, *Oz* behaved as though the revolution had already happened. By adroit use of the concomitants of privilege – culture, charm, personableness and expert defence – the tribe of *Oz* got away with what Mick Ryan and Joe Bloggs of Moss Side thought a little worse than murder. *Oz* went into the trial in the same manner, staunchly refusing to succumb to paranoia. Perhaps politics is in large part necessary paranoia; certainly the inspiration to call Marty Feldman as an expert witness on comedy was foolhardy and impolitic in the worst way. The more the trial looked to liberal eyes like crushing a butterfly on a wheel, the more impassive and reliable did retribution seem to those whose convictions had long been outraged, and whose outrage had long been fanned by the gutter press.

But the butterfly shall not be crushed, even by the wheel. *Ink* and *Oz* both continue, and they must take every advantage of the removal of misleading tokenism in developing their critique of oppression. The powers that be must be shown to have done their damnedest and to have lost. If we are revolutionaries at all our first duty is to survive; we may take stock of the smallness and feebleness of our political stature, but as long as we have a growing point this knowledge can only be good for us. If we recoil in dismay that so few people in England gave two hoots for Richard and Felix and Jim, and allow our efforts to be circumscribed by fear and tremulousness in the future, then we really have been whipped by twelve jurors and a senile judge. Perversely, we might even take heart that the country is not solely ruled by the privileged, that power is still with the people if only in so deformed a way. Our task is now to persuade the readers of the *News of the World* to care about us; those who say in their hearts that it is impossible have denied the validity of their own revolt. Those who think it can be accomplished in a single lifetime are fools.

Body odour and the persuaders

Sunday Times, 25 July 1971

Sometimes, in the course of my indefatigable search for truth, I dip into the volumes of research findings in marketing and consumption which are beginning to gorge the shelves of academic libraries afire with the new disciplines of commerce. (That *afire* is a Freudian interpolation which honesty bids me leave unchanged.) Fascinating reading they are too, of the hair-on-end variety. Imagine, your job is to persuade folk to munch more of a particular brand of, say, codeine tablets. Yours not to fuss about whether they need the tablets, or whether the tablets can do them any good. Cheerfully the problem is posited, 'How to sell more of Xanadun?' and pat comes the answer, 'We must stimulate a demand for regular, repeated and if possible escalating dosages.' In this spirit the advertising campaigns are organized; all problems of the organism are mustered under the heading *tension*. A logo is devised - perhaps a line drawing of the human (female usually) head and shoulders gripped in cruel hands of tension. On TV the diagram is fleshed out by children whimpering in the background, while mother grimaces at the camera in what might be an agony of codeine withdrawal.

The most sinister aspect of the chatty amoral style of the professional persuaders, is that when they are forced to refer to the helpless, psycho-analysed, dopey buyer of anything that is sold right by a pronoun, that pronoun is usually *she*.

A habit-forming drug is a perfect commodity, and heroin, of which very few doses are enough to ensure the need for regular, escalating consumption, is the paragon. In the New York subways one may see beautifully designed, five-foot-high posters showing, in four colours, back lit and immaculately photographed, all the beautiful drugs one may buy in any school playground. And above or below, that infallible sales gimmick, 'Don't'. It is hard to believe that the New York anti-drug campaign has been organized by an agency unaware of the persuasive power of their graphics and the perversity of their wording. Even the choice of the subway as the best exposure for the posters speaks volumes for the prejudices of the organizers of the campaign. The machinery of advertising is geared to sell; it cannot be applied to extinguish an existent demand for which the product exists in enormous quantities and the highest quality. It operates automatically in the same old way – 'Buy, buy' say the heroin posters, 'and you too may be the possessor of this larger-than-life brawny arm, and this snazzy tourniquet. You too can be a hero and get your picture in the subway. Dig my gleaming syringe.' Incidentally, if you didn't know before, the picture tells you how to use the tourniquet and the needle, just like the other picture told you how to tell uppers from downers and bush from grass.

Now the buyer of heroin may not necessarily be a *she*, even though prostitution in New York is now largely a matter of earning enough to pay the heroin bill (it's easier on the pimp that way) but it is usually the member of an oppressed group, perhaps poor, perhaps black, perhaps female, perhaps all three. When it comes to the overfed consumer classes, the inert and the susceptible buyer is usually assumed to be a woman. There are good reasons for it; poppa earns and momma spends. Cars, tools, machinery, sports equipment will be sold to *him*, but nearly everything else, especially fashion, cosmetics and luxury goods, will be sold to *her*. There are exceptions, but they prove the rule. You'd be surprised to find an ad for a car or a circular saw in *Woman's Own*, which might be why they'd put it there. Perfume might be advertised in *Playboy* (promise her anything, but give her Arpège) but not Iron Jelloids or washing-up liquid.

One of the most gripping exploits which one may read in the annals of market research is that of the brilliant boffins who hit upon the plan of solving the problem of 'spare capacity' in the toiletries industries by inventing the problem (at one and the same instant as its solution) of vaginal odour. The poor buyer could be relied upon, however many years she had been upon this earth, to identify with the malodorous but pretty women who snuggled belly to belly with young men in the advertisements. The combination of fantasy and self-doubt worked like a charm, a spell. Few women thought to consult their doctors and fewer to follow their advice. Doctors, after all, are against all sorts of femininities – high heels, tight clothing, false eyelashes. The feminine deodorant sold.

But all did not go well. Magazines that once carried fifteen pages of vaginal odour per issue began to run articles that began in a paranoid vein, 'Feminine hygiene did not spring full-blown from the minds of Madison Avenue' – well, nobody thought it did, after all they did not invent the bidet. In the course of such articles curious facts came to light, 'Since the area is generally covered with clothes, panty-stockings, *et al*., the perspiration can't evaporate . . .' The answer would appear to be 'remove clothes' rather than 'squirt with chemicals'.

More unwillingly, perhaps, comes the warning (in brackets). 'Doctors caution not to use (vaginal deodorants) just before intercourse, or undue irritation may occur.' What horrors could be masked under *undue* – due irritation can be bad enough. Suddenly the whole rationale collapses; those ads that said 'You don't sleep with your teddy bear any more . . .', that showed bare-ass couples leering at each other, all imply that copulation was the deodorants' *raison d'être*. After all, it's not as if the streets had been littered with those overcome by vaginal fumes. From the start it had been an *intimate* problem. And what is the point of *mentholating* vaginal douches if one's lover is not an aficionado of the cool-as-a-mountain-stream experience?

Miserably the articles go on to say 'Most doctors concur that douching should not be done more than twice a week.' Easy to say that, since most doctors concur that douching should not be done at all, if the mucous lining of the vagina is to be kept intact and vaginal flora undisturbed.

A representative of a consumer association wrote to me recently asking if I could cite tests and so forth to justify my anti-VD (Vaginal Deodorant) campaign. After there were no tests to establish the existence of the problem, I am asked to cite tests to prove its non-existence, a pretty improper proceeding. Actually it has turned out to be a hilarious party game, 'Design a consumer test for vaginal deodorants'. Will your sample take account of age, race, social and sexual status? How will you arrange your negative control? What means of measuring odoriferousness will you adopt? One imagines a variety of wine-tasters or tea-blenders called in for the job. Is it too much to expect that they be happy in their work?

A needle for your pornograph

Sunday Times, 22 July 1971

Once, in the throes of research and anxious that I should not assume what I had set out to prove, I decided that I needed some porno photographs – not just tits'n'ass but the real sado-masochistic nitty-gritty. Whenever I went into Soho porn shops the attendants pointedly ignored me, and as the stuff I wanted was not on display, I knew I could never get it that way. So I delegated a friend who went off on his errand with zest, after practising in front of the mirror his imitation of an addict of *le vice anglais*.

He slunk into the first likely shop he came across and lurked about until the assistant asked him kindly what he wanted. 'Got any discipline and bondage?' he muttered. 'Just hang on a moment,' said the assistant, 'I'll fetch the guv'nor.' In his innocence my emissary had a sudden fear that he might be taken up by the law, so he began to edge towards the door, but this furtiveness only engaged the assistant further, 'No, no sir, don't rush off. He'll be here directly.' When the guv'nor materialized he was a great fat personage, all nods and becks and wreathing smiles to put my friend at ease.

He asked my friend to follow him as he led the way out of the shop, into a nearby doorway and up three flights of stairs. A much-locked door was opened and the porn merchant displayed his wares, spread thinly upon several tables pushed against the dirty walls. Swallowing his disgust and anger and ever more anxious to escape, my friend snatched up six packets at random. 'Six quid,' smiled the merchant. He paid and fled back to the restaurant where we were waiting.

Each packet held three photographs of women, women bound, women gagged, women lashed to bedsteads, to racks, with whips, scourges, knouts, by other women. Their eyes were always turned to the camera, empty, meek, expressionless, like the eyes of laden donkeys. Even when they were obediently making as if to scream, the blankness of their eyes did not change. Besides manacles, leg irons, spiked belts and gags, they wore immensely complicated and constricting underwear of satin, rubber and lace, high heels and stockings. Their faces were heavily made up in the style of the fifties, when apparently the pictures had originally been taken. More blotched, yellowed, furry images it would be hard to find, poorly printed on the cheapest paper, and for eighteen photographs my friend had paid six pounds.

The exploitation of the customer's shame is only the last stage in a chain of exploitations. The women whose faces were so plainly visible must have been coerced, if only by poverty, but more probably by blackmail. The thousands of copies printed of their images had made fortunes for their owners for fifteen years or so. There was no element of art, of drama, of excitement or participation; they were not beauties, but women one might see any day in the supermarket, their bodies marked by child-bearing, hard work and unsuitable clothing. Somewhere behind the hypnotic camera the *metteur-en-scène* had stood, commanding them to hold their wooden postures in a tableau of cruelty and despair. His only concern was the mechanism of the fetish, the quaint designs of torture, for in his market all other shortcomings would be forgiven as long as the dominant motif was correctly rendered. Illegality itself would justify the high price; the true porn merchant receives his danger money many times over.

When its outer ramifications are so easily uncovered, it ought to be a relatively simple proceeding for the police force to track down the men who have made fortunes in this business (provided of course they are not any of them, directly or indirectly, policemen). Such men are guilty of fraud, coercion and extortion, although what they are most likely to be accused of under the law, is purveying obscene articles. The latter judgement would depend upon the judge's aesthetic sense, but any accusation on the former grounds would have more substance. The real guilt of the fat proprietor of the porn shop is most like that of the men who rob alcoholics when they are helpless and then force them to commit crimes in exchange for a ration of booze or like the straight who turns women on to prostitution by hooking them on heroin. The core of the crime is not the means, the alcohol, the drug or the sex, but the exercise of power over others for gain, the heart and soul of gangsterism.

And yet is not salesmanship an exercise of the same kind? Does not a market researcher study the ways in which a potential buyer can be got to want a product which he did not need before? What more does my merchant of porno pics do than satisfy a need in the population at the highest price he can command? He need not even admit to the greater responsibility of creating a need where one did not exist before. But he does exploit the secrecy and guilt which only illegality could assure.

But justice traditionally addresses itself to the commodity rather than its purveyor, and so it merely increases the market value of drink, drugs and sex. The Mafia remains enthroned in the heart of America because it is primarily a very good family business, which takes very good care of its own. The efforts of the law-enforcers to stamp out heroin and prostitution are a useless expenditure of energy and funds, as long as the rationale of competition and individual gain, regardless of the requirements of the community as a whole, is tacitly accepted.

It is quite certain that the purveyors of pictorial discipline and bondage make money, but it is very much less clear whether they corrupt or deprave anybody. The group who first saw the photographs when my friend threw them down on the restaurant table was of a normally polymorphous and sexually enquiring cast, but we all gazed blankly at what seemed to us to be utterly unerotic. We were looking at a key for which we had no door. Without the already developed need for it, such stuff was merely incomprehensible and dreary. The real agent of corruption in these cases is probably not in the least pornographic, perhaps a repressive upbringing, in which corporal punishment has become associated with pleasure. As Angelo discovered in *Measure for Measure*, nothing corrupts like virtue.

Now, can you explain to me why the three young men who published *Oz* 28 are in prison?

Sentimental education

Sunday Times, 9 September 1971

As a result of persistent criticism, the DHSS eventually abandoned the practice of spying on unsupported mothers with a view to ascertaining whether they were actually unsupported, or de facto *wives defrauding the state. The extent and manner of the surveillance involved not only a gross invasion of privacy, but virtual suspension of all the victims' civil rights. The description of militant action given here is largely based on the American experience.*

Goodness, I despair of women sometimes! Take, for example, their wretched obtuseness in this matter of social security benefit for the unsupported mother. Plainly, all the expenses of support and administration would be spared the state, and ultimately the taxpayer, if the unsupported mother would quietly become supported without clamorous recourse to paternalistic authorities. She and her issue could be most efficiently and discreetly supported by the proceeds of prostitution.

By way of favouring this particular private enterprise even beyond the extent to which this government generally favours private enterprise, it refrains from levying any tax upon whores' earnings and imposes no tiresome controls of quality, no Weights and Measures or Trades Descriptions Acts, to hamper the small businesswoman.

Her work can be carried on in the home while the thus supported children sleep, or, if the habitation is too confined, almost anywhere else. Initially, outlay is minimal, and, provided the entrepreneuse can avoid takeover by a pimp or organized exploitation by the underworld, it remains so.

For years now the servants of the people have laboured to help the unsupported mother grasp these elementary facts. They have set spies outside her house, so that the instant a man sets foot inside it, his movements can be speculated upon. If he remains overnight, as far as the social security men can ascertain (or guess), it is assumed that the little woman has caught on and – bingo! off welfare. But like as not the silly goose has not twigged and even now cannot take the hint.

But the SS are patient. Over and over, they challenge their sluggish pupil. Surely that man who stopped by to play cards or take the children to the football match, while mother drew a breath and washed her hair, could be (should be) contributing to the kiddies' support. A poor woman should never be so improvident as to give away what she could sell. Her tutors in private enterprise chat with the children about their 'uncle' or their 'dad', and the children uttering wishes and fantasies of a 'normal' home, unwittingly betray their mothers.

What the children leave out, the neighbours fill in, parked cars, people coming and going, the length of missis' skirts.

Doggedly the hounds prepare the dossier that proves that the unsupported mother is two-timing the state. (If not, why not?) When the chips are down, every woman must realize that she is sitting on her fortune.

But no, she doesn't realize. She pleads that she doesn't know her male friends intimately, that they are poor and hardworking themselves, that if she expected every man who spoke to her to undertake the support of her children, she would live in silence – except for childish chatter.

Now the SS men are not so thick that they cannot see at a glance that she does not live in luxury provided by a dual income. When her benefit is stopped she is likely to starve, unless the Welfare send someone by with the daily food money. But the Welfare too is committed to the education of the poor. Sorrowfully but sternly they stay away, hoping that hunger will drive the bemused creature to productive labour. She is more apt to sit at home and cry.

In case she should be ashamed to get out and hustle with the children in the house, benevolent powers intervene to remove any older children (who might catch on) to State care and damn the expense.

So far, the surveillance of these improvident patrons is costing many times what it would cost to maintain her children, but so great a value have independence and entrepreneurial skill in a Tory world that Social Security does not begrudge a penny.

Even yet such women cannot understand the point of this prodigious activity at public expense. They pursue their children through the State departments and make awful scenes, weeping and tearing their hair. They trudge to the Welfare, begging for a food allowance, while their children scream in fear and bewilderment, howling for the sequestrated sibling. The Welfare mournfully considers the possibility of dispersing the household once and for all.

At home the object lesson is unsparingly continued. Instead of comprehending the avuncular role of the man lurking under her bedroom windows, and learning from him the pragmatic realities of the role of women under capitalism, the by now demented woman calls the police. Everybody is very nice to her but no policeman comes.

Her days become a dreary round of humiliating scenes with the Social Security and the Welfare. The Housing Department, by way of showing solidarity with their colleagues, produce a timely threat of eviction. Still the crazed woman does not see.

No one takes so crass an attitude to the education process as to say in so many words, 'Woman, all this pain could have been spared if you had simply foregone welfare and supported your issue by the work of your loins. What else was marriage but support in return for sexual service and cohabitation? What is now so repugnant in the notion of being paid piecemeal, on a casual instead of a permanent basis? You could support your children better that way, and raise your standard of living. It's like piecework, it depends how quick you are.'

Why is it that unsupported mothers cannot see the glories and high morality of the private enterprise system? Instead of imbibing the salutary truths demonstrated so tellingly by the clerks who give and take away, they have lately taken to combining in claimants' unions and such, adopting an illegal posture, resisting eviction, harassing the spies, occupying government offices, combining, heaven help us, like the frame-breakers and Chartists of old, to defend their interests as a class. Why, trespassing spies may be beaten, purveyors of hearsay evidence rebuked. Chaos will certainly come again.

Nowadays, women's houses are not lonely, for other women come to lend a hand, co-operating in freeing each other to get about. When men come by, the women are not left in compromising circumstances, speechless before the lewd implications of the public servants. They have a defence against spying and evidence of their own. Their old teachers hang about in the hope that the feckless women might be running a lucrative orgy business, but such has not so far been the case. Vulgar economics has become political economy. Opportunism has been beaten by principle.

History will explain why the women have chosen the method of combination and mass action in preference to individualism and personal profit.

Perhaps, after all, freedom and dignity were motives for becoming unsupported mothers in the first place, but freedom and dignity are words with which the Social Security has little to do.

The expense of spirit

Sunday Times, 10 October 1971

I have just done rather an odd thing. Indeed, I have been casting about in my mind for a mode in which to convey its oddness, and I decided I had better ask you to imagine a civilization in which eating had ceased almost altogether. Moreover, it was officially reprehended, as a sort of bestial regression. That should not be so difficult, for we are no longer astonished by the astronaut's mini-bulk diets and the attempts to circumvent the approaching food crisis. In this imagined society, then, nourishment exists, but not the great pursuit of eating nor the great arts of the kitchen. But human nature is to some degree irrepressible and so clubs spring up in special areas, the Reeperbahns and Sunset Strips of our imaginary towns. There one may, by dint of paying very large sums – entrance fees, cover charges and minimal consumption (an alcohol pill or a saline injection) – actually watch actual people actually eat.

Great pains are taken to depict the building up of appetite; first a glossy sucking pig with an astronomical price tag is shown in various attitudes before the audience, lit with changing tints. Blackout. Then a series of tableaux of gluttonous people leaping towards a roast chicken on a string, slithering up a greasy pole towards a Virginia baked ham, vainly embracing a sumptuous dessert imprisoned in a block of ice. Closer and closer come the actors to the point of really putting food into their mouths and masticating. They drool, and the public address system relays prodigious sounds of slavering and stomach growling. They thrust imitation bananas and pawpaws into their mouths and slobber about them. They pretend to eat.

Everything is leading up to the last stage in the hour-long show, when four people will put food in their mouths, chew and swallow, thus, one assumes, initiating the whole process of digestion and defecation.

The eaters are not prodigious trenchermen; they may even have trouble tolerating the unfamiliar food when it is in their mouths, but they mime huge pleasure. When they are to slaver they fill their mouths with jelly and let it dribble out. Sometimes they are droll, they go to bite a tomato which explodes in their faces or they don huge rubbery false teeth which bend about instead of biting. One might wonder if they really eat or if they go backstage to be sick and collect their pay. Does their union demand colonic lavage? Perhaps the saddest thing is that they must perform this act four times a night.

The audience does not rise from its plush seats clamouring for food. It does not suck its fingers, pick its nose or bite its nails. It simply watches and vaguely recollects a form of pleasure it might have known but need no longer strive for.

Have you guessed what odd thing it was that I did? I went to a club called Salammbô in Hamburg and watched people perform the sex act or make love, as it is sometimes obscurely expressed. The club belongs to a Marseillais whose laurel-girt profile dominates the decor. His great nose is quite the only priapic event in the environment, and his huge, melting eye in shiny paint the only moist or tender thing. Six girls and three boys lackadaisically disport themselves for the amusement or whatever it was of the nearly all-male clientèle. The six girls, as one might expect, are on stage five times as long as the boys and the exaggerated sexual moaning and squealing which comes over the sound system is all female. When the men are on stage they are clustered about by women, like the heroes of a *Playboy* advertisement.

Of course such spectacles are necessarily costly; we were supposed to be let in free, but each paid fifteen DMs to get in, five for a cover charge and fifty for a half-bottle of Scotch. If prices were not normally much higher, the club would attract the wrong kind of clientèle and it would have to be closed, we were told. Only the rich may have their vices with impunity.

The format of the show purported to be a history of the sexual revolution from the New Economic Policy, signified by a naked lady on whose body was projected a hundred-dollar bill and subsequently a marksman's target trained on her pudenda. 'If you would reach the mark,' the commentator quipped, 'you must aim fair and square with a hundred dollars!' The combination of pecuniary with sadistic motivation characterized the tone of the whole establishment. The social history took us through a series of fantasies about the aphrodisiac effects of marihuana (which had us all laughing hugely, although the audience of visiting merchants was silent), via a celebration of Manson and his harem to the Act itself, performed by a masked executioner with a whip. 'Sexual freedom is here!' howled the commentor. Lord! how we laughed.

But we went away chastened. There had been so much of that tiresome manipulation of floppy male flesh which is ninety per cent of blue films, so much dismal female solitariness, that we sat down by the Alstersee in the first frost of the year and reflected sourly upon the nature of the phenomenon. Marcuse would agree with Mrs Whitehouse that pornography leads to fear and dislike of sex (experienced as impotence and boredom); the phenomenon is called repressive desublimation. The trouble is that nobody, not Mrs Whitehouse or her friend the Pope or Lord

Longford or me, knows how to distinguish pornography which turns you off from erotic art which turns you on. But I do know of a bronze tessera in the Bargello which they would lock away for ever from the light of day, a tiny thing full of holy fire. To see that now, is to feel potent, sexy and full of grace.

Lady love your cunt

Suck, 1971

Suck was founded in the summer of 1969. My reason for joining the editorial board was that we needed an antidote to the exploitative pornography of papers like Screw *and* Hustler. *I tried to insist on using male bodies as often as female, invading the privacy of the editors, naming names in sex news, and developing a new kind of erotic art, away from tits'n'ass and the peep-show syndrome. Most of the contributions were the sinister, sadistic ravings that all sex-papers invite. My co-editors were quite happy to let me expound my utopian sexual theories and utterly indifferent to them; the art-work was never better than hippy art-nouveau. After a particularly egregious rip-off, I withdrew my services and the paper folded along with the rest of the alternative press.*

Because nobody else is going to. Primitive man feared the vagina, as well he might, as the most magical of the magical orifices of the body. Primitive man includes all those born before the birth of *SUCK*. Mind you, *SUCK* may appear to carry on the tradition, for it is rumoured that the Exhibitionists' Association (which has its headquarters in Streatham) has taken out a block subscription because the first issue featured forty-eight limp cocks and their smiling owners. Poor old cocks, not even genuine sexual implements, pissing tubes modified to pass seed, like worker bees' egglaying tube modified to form sting. How much more sweat would it take to get forty-eight smiling women to squat over the hapless cameraman? Most of the hassle for fellows trying to do the decent thing arises from the females' intransigent modesty about cunt. It looks bad. Shave it. Pluck it. Cover it with your hand, and pretend you dig touching yourself. It smells bad. Wash it. Scour it. Douche it. DEODORIZE it. It tastes bad. Wash it some more. It's sloppy. Mop it. It's dry. Lubricate it. The language of pornography is full of cunt-hatred. Fuck it. Stick your weapon in it and punch it around, boy. Get into her womb. (Shit, man, the head of the cervix is impenetrable and prettier than the head of your flattered penis.) Drive it up her, until she moans with pleasure.

Maybe it will be bearable if you shoot Coca-Cola up it, or champagne, fill it with milk, orange juice, honey, brandy (Jesus!), melted ice-cream, pitted cherries, oysters, small fish, caviare . . .

If you doubt that the cunt is hated and feared by most of the population, how will you explain the hundreds of thousands of pounds spent in persuading women that they have an intimate deodorant problem?

Up to twelve or thirteen colour pages are spent in every women's magazine in stressing that cunts smell bad, not just when dirty or menstruating, but all the time.

This fiction allows them to persuade women to buy a barrage of moistened pads to wipe the vulvar area, of chemicals to put in their douche water, of aerosol sprays, all of which are potentially harmful. In fact, the vagina is naturally sterile, and is kept that way by a delicate balance of natural flora, which can be seriously affected by bombardment with these commercial products, so that pruritis and leucorrhoea can result. A completely monogamous woman I know used a vaginal deodorant in San Francisco this year and suffered the most agonizing inflammation of the nymphæ as a consequence. The doctor who was called by the management of the Hilton told her that she had venereal disease, so that she spent hours cursing her absent and defenceless husband. Of course the medico did not examine her, but haven't you noticed that doctors will go to enormous lengths to avoid examining cunt? Even a woman who may be suffering from anxiety or trivial pruritis has an inalienable right to pathology, not to mention the woman who has as traumatic a symptom as the faithful wife of my example. The National Health Service is a difficult machine to operate. The doctor's overwork and greed mean that he doesn't want to have to get the gloves on, put you on the couch and push his finger up and tell you impatiently to relax. His cunt-hatred makes his unwillingness immovable. Most doctors are incompetent in this area of diagnosis, and squeeze and push away with no real idea of what the normal anatomy would feel like, let alone any abnormal condition. Shop around until you find a doctor who has good hands and knows how to listen to a pelvis. If you want a swab taken you just have to scream and refuse to get out of the doctor's office until he takes one.

What is so infuriating is the certainty that if a man takes his cock to the doctor with a pimple on it, his phallic anxiety is taken to be as significant as any actual illness he may have, because cock is lovely and important. But cunt is messy, rubbery, insensitive and greedy. Slap it down. Make sure examinations hurt, especially if you have any suspicion that your patient digs what you are doing. Don't heat the speculum and don't worry if the cold aluminium hinges and the screws pinch the tender membranes of the perineum. In America fifty years ago, doctors deduced masturbatory habits from the coloration and confirmation of the vulva, and treated the mania, which was of their own invention, by clitoridectomy on a massive scale. There are modern parallels. Doctors love telling women to refrain from sexual intercourse. The lengths of time prescribed for abstinence after curettage or treatment of infection are ludicrous. Hospitals shave cunts at any opportunity, and usually with cold water, no soap and a blunt razor with an underpaid and vengeful moron at the business end, who is sure that you are only in hospital because you have been having a good time using that same cunt.

There have been doctors who loved cunt, but when they are discovered they are usually disgraced and struck off for some contravention of medical etiquette or morality. If you should hear of such a doctor, go to him. If he's not a nut, keep going to him. You'll never have such a happy and healthy cunt as when your doctor is actually fucking you. He need only be interested in it, really. Your average doctor is interested in cock because he's got one – cunt is a troublesome irrelevance, usually.

I remember once, after some irresponsible butchery in a public hospital when I had to keep coming back for further treatment, I was anaesthetized on the slab with my legs in stirrups, when one doctor said to the other, 'Come here. Look. Isn't that a beautiful cervix?' I got better much quicker, I'm convinced.

Of course, I should have had to go to the doctor less frequently if I had discovered how to get my mojo working in the first place. Cunts have extraordinary powers, but the effect of constant indoctrination, Freudian monosex, is to convince women that their cunts are mere holes. Most women would be surprised to learn that the women of Tahiti can draw the penis into them with irresistible force, and keep it there working until it bleeds. Complaints about fit are further indications of ignorance, for cunts can expand or contract in the most surprising way.

Tightness and looseness are both indications that they are simply not responding. Well, at best, you might argue, cunt can only respond to claims and pressures from cocks. Not so. Discovery that all female orgasm originates in the clitoris has been treated as discovery that the cunt is irrelevant. Not so. If the cunt is behaving effectively it brings direct pressure to bear on the rest of the clitoris. For example, you can masturbate no hands. This ability is not so much skill in controlling as a liberation of muscles repressed since infancy. It is not either the acquisition of a courtesan's skill, like fellatio, for this muscular dance gives pleasure to the owner of the cunt and to any friend who happens to be inside it at the time.

The clitoris is the only purely sexual organ having the function of pleasure only; nevertheless many of the abilities of the vagina are not directly connected with the passage of the neonate, and sperm may reach the womb without even being deposited inside it. All that clipping, sucking, sluicing, slurping, rolling, nipping, fluttering is the merest pleasure.

Daily masturbating no hands is the easiest way to develop the muscles of the pubococcygeal region. Think of something nice and contract the buttocks rhythmically. Keep it up for about half an hour or until you come. Next day vary the movements.

Gradually you will find that you can isolate the various functions more and more, and thereby produce an astonishing variety of feeling. The method has the advantage that fingers, fingernails and other foreign bodies are not brought into contact with delicate membranes. Sensitivity is increased, not diminished. It can be done on the bus, the tube, in the office, schoolroom, or in church. You can even focus your attention on some member of your immediate environment and circumvent the essentail egocentricity of common forms of masturbation.

If you supplement this exercise with the ones recommended by Dr Erna Wright in *Periods Without Pain* you might even succeed in making the whole pelvis awake to love and beauty. Of course, Dr Wright would be upset if girls started to do her exercises for lecherous motives, just as doctors who suspect that their female patients derive erotic stimulus from examination *deliberately hurt them*.

Erotism has become so confused with sadism, that many women masturbate in ways that are positively injurious. Apart from the dozens of cases in which girls have introduced pencils and needles into the urethra, less obvious damage is done by the usual crude methods of digital massage. Men too often imagine that thrusting a fist into the vagina and jerking it around is pleasant, and too often they gouge about with uncut and dirty nails.

Sadism is the necessary outcome of the belief that one sex is passive and suffers sex at the hands of another. If we are to escape any of the hideous effects of this mythology, effects which include war and capital punishment, we must regain the power of the cunt.

CUNT IS BEAUTIFUL

Suck it and see. If you're not so supple that you can suck your own fanny, put your finger gently in, withdraw and smell, and suck.

There. How odd it is that the most expensive gourmet foods taste like cunt. Or is it?

Squat over a mirror or lie on your back with your legs apart and the sun shining in, with a mirror. Learn it. Study its expressions. Keep it soft, warm, clean. Don't rub soap into it. Don't dredge it with talc. If you must douche it, do it with coolish water. Give it your own loving names, not the fictions of anatomy books, or the condescending diminutives that men use, like pussy, twat, box, or the epithets of hate, like gash, slit, crack. What we need is a genuinely descriptive terminology of cunt.

WHY NOT SEND US A PHOTOGRAPH OF YOUR OWN CUNT, WITH YOUR NAME LABELLED ON? If you can't get a photograph printed, send us the film, and your labels marked on a drawing and we'll do the rest. The results will be published.

If all else fails bring it to us and we'll kiss it for you.

Send photos to our new address: POB 2080, Amsterdam, Holland.

My Mailer problem

Esquire, September 1971

It was early on in the career of *The Female Eunuch* as the forever out-of-print English bestseller that I heard that Mailer wanted to debate with Kate Millett and me in a benefit for the Theatre of Ideas in the New York Town Hall. It seemed such an extraordinary recognition for a new writer that it never occurred to me to refuse, although within days I had heard that Kate Millett had done just that. I never did hear her reason, although I privately rejected other people's versions of it, that Kate was afraid of Mailer, that she was gentle and shy, that she was exhausted and disgusted after being long enmeshed in the machinery of publicity. It was not until I acquired a copy of *Harper's* March 1971 that I began to see that there were legitimate and persuasive reasons for having nothing to do with the liberation of Norman Mailer. *The Prisoner of Sex* is itself a counteroffensive in among 'the radiation of advancements and awards in the various salients, wedges and vectors of that aesthetic battlefield known as the literary pie'. For Mailer, Women's Liberation had become simply another battle of the books in a war in which he had been campaigning all his life. I had already discovered the seedy side of Grub Street, in the curious selection by editors of pregnant women to review my book; in the cursory readings which supported the subjective bias of reviewer after reviewer, even those who praised me; and in my own bitter quarrel with publishers who printed only five thousand of my book at the outset and bound only half of them, never set to reprint more than two thousand at a time, and fixed a price for the book too high for most women to afford. This squalid arena was where GI Joe Mailer liked best to fight; unfortunately he persisted in confusing paper pellets and bullets of the brain with real blood and iron, so there was no telling where this armchair militarism might lead him.

It was this failure in perspective which led him to be so easily convinced by no less a guardian of truth than the editor of *Time* magazine, that 'he was, as he knew all too well, perhaps the primary target of their attacks'. The grammar of this idea must have come from Mailer himself. One could hardly imagine anyone actually saying, and on the telephone too, 'You are, as you know all too well, perhaps the primary target of their attacks.' Even editors of *Time* are not so certain of *perhapses*, one would hope. But if we continue with Mailer's narrative we find him tamping down the masochistic rage to occupy the direct line of fire, and replying demurely, 'No, he

had not realized.' How could he, after all, realize? With misery, disappointment, frustration, injustice, poverty, helplessness and despair for the
women to wage war against, how could a man with a chink of discretion in
the massy structures of his ego imagine that *he*, little he, represented a
primary target (with or without a quaver of perhaps)?

But the editor of *Time* exhorts him to face it like a man and so talks
himself plumb out of a cheap story. Mailer instantly twigs that to offer on
the telephone the meat of a possible book to figure as one of a hundred
snappy anecdotes which make pre-masticated mass-circulation news 'is
improvident. He would be giving up substance – which is to say not making
money . . .' But stronger than the need for money to run his complicated
life and support his ambitions to be a great actor and film-maker, he
needed to draw the women's fire. Luxuriating in the presumption that 'a
squadron of enraged Amazons, an honour guard of revolutionary (if we
could only see them) vaginas' had ambushed his ghost phallus and were
chewing it half to death, he unwittingly betrayed his deepest fantasy, that
his talent, alias his phallus, alias 'firm, strong-tongued ego', three sides of
the equilateral triangle which constitute the Mailer godhead, soared above
them all. The last temptation was, as far as the women could be concerned,
the greatest treason.

> Now he was tempted. To be the centre of any situation was, he sometimes
> thought, the real marrow of his bone – better to expire as a devil in the fire than
> an angel in the wings.

The imagery is drawn from the morality play and perhaps it applies even
better than Mailer was aware, for the Devil is a burlesque character,
heralded by squibs and crackers, absurdly pretentious and deluded, forever
denying his gnawing grief and fury at having lost the love and the sight of
God. The battle of the books would also involve a skirmish with the High
Media; the book would require publicity, publicity means film and television. The pseudo-debate in the Town Hall would satisfy all needs. There
would be a book in it, and a film too, with luck and good management.

His genius was to mobilize on the instant.

Long before *The Prisoner of Sex* dealt the final stroke to *Harper's*, Mailer
was setting up his own morality play, in which he could enact his own
sparagmos by being torn apart by a horde of women, for he would not risk
being outfaced by a single woman. When Kate Millett refused to join in, I
assumed that there would be no debate, for quite other reasons, for I still
considered myself too insignificant to provide adequate opposition. Nevertheless I embarked on a needling campaign which committed me to the
eventual confrontation long before I ever saw the egregious confessions in
The Prisoner of Sex. It became a standing joke that I would seduce Norman
Mailer and prove to the breathlessly waiting world that he was as I had
opined to Felix Scorpio, the world's worst. When Piers Burton asked me

on his television show why I had such a high opinion of Valerie Solanas despite her attack on Andy Warhol, I minced out a crack about attempting to kill people not meaning that you're a bad person. 'Norman Mailer stuck a knife in his wife and no one would deny that he's a great writer.' More and more often I was being asked what I thought of Norman Mailer, and my replies became more and more Byzantine. Ultimately, in a rash of alliteration I announced that I wanted to carry him like a wounded child across the wasted world. In an article for the *Listener* I wrote that I half-expected him to blow his own head off 'in one last killer come' like Ernest Hemingway. Like Muhammad Ali I was softening up my opposition in advance with rhetoric.

Imagine, then, my consternation when the New York women asked me to boycott the whole shindig. Kate's refusal had been followed by Ti-Grace Atkinson's, Gloria Steinem's, Robin Morgan's. Robin had said she would come if she could shoot Mailer, citing the particulars of her licence to possess a firearm, which is one way of putting a stop to phoney revolutionary theatricals. I have always felt rather Nero Wolfeish about my word, given now so long before in ignorance. Moreover the affair was going onward, Diana Trilling and Jackie Ceballos were speaking. My withdrawal would have one certain effect of withdrawing support from them, even if the public was ever to understand my motives, which was doubtful. 'But why,' argued the women, 'should we give an account of ourselves to Norman Mailer? Why should he run the show, he adjudicate?' They might also have asked, if any of us had known what was going on, which we didn't, why Mailer should have acquired the book for New American Library instead of McGraw-Hill, the usual publisher for the Theatre of Ideas, and why Mailer had put up most of the on-the-spot expenses of Pennebaker's filming of the night's entertainment. The Mailer–Women's Liberation title fight was being set up for maximum exploitation, yet none of the women knew anything about it.

Meanwhile I was in training, reading and rereading *The Prisoner of Sex* in an attempt to assess my opponent's form. There was no argument there to discredit the women's cause, although plenty to discredit Mailer, as he obviously knew and did not care, in his divine or diabolical desire to go all the way. Every page bespoke the terrors of the dying king, reaching further and further back beyond morality, beyond Christianity towards the long-dead, if not always imaginary, age of heroes to which the prisoner yearned to belong. Mischievously I decided to apply his fine words of compassion for D. H. Lawrence to himself:

> . . . yet he was locked into the body of a middling male physique, not physically strong, of reasonable good looks, a pleasant-to-somewhat-seedy-looking man, no stud . . .

For all I knew he was a silvery maned bull of a man with electric blue eyes, and yet I knew that the words would apply, for the tragedy of machismo is that a man is never quite man enough. (I had every intention of using the words against him in the Town Hall, indeed I have them written on a file-card still, but when I saw how cruelly apt they were, my heart quailed with pity and I thrust the card to the bottom of the pile.)

> For his mind was possessed of that intolerable masculine pressure to command, which develops in sons outrageously beloved of their mothers – to be the equal of women at twelve or six or any early age which reaches equilibrium between the will of the son and the will of the mother is all but to guarantee the making of a future tyrant, for the sense of where to find one's inner health has been generated by the early years of that equilibrium – its substitute will not be easy to create in maturity. What can then be large enough to serve as proper balance for a man who was equal to a strong woman in emotional confidence at the age of eight? Hitlers develop out of such balance derived from imbalance, and great generals and great novelists (for what is a novelist but a general who sends his troops across fields of paper?).

Granting that Mailer himself is a great novelist (for failing to do so merely minimizes the seriousness of the situation and the radicalism of the changes that need to be made) we may safely grant that, on his own admission, the rest of the syndrome described also applies to him. Certainly his aesthetic imagination is still dominated by war and the imagery of war, whether he was wondering whether women are the aggressors in a primal war between the sexes, or stealing concubines from the potentates of *Time* magazine, or thinking of Bella Abzug's bosom as redolent (among other things) 'of the firepower of hard-prowed gunboats'. And yet the wars are not real wars –

> . . . for one senses in his petulance and in the spoiled airs of his impatient disdain at what he could not intellectually dominate that he was a momma's boy, spoiled rotten, and could not have commanded two infantrymen to follow him, yet he was still a great writer.

Unlike Hitler, or the great generals of history, the artist is a fantasy achiever. Moving his troops around on paper, he achieves in fantasy what he could achieve in no other way: honour, power, riches and the love of women. Only as an artist could he manage to steal women from Nabobs of the High Media, from Shago Martin or Miles Davis. The man who boasts of the men he stole his women from is still deeply involved with those men, acutely aware of long-gone juices that he is stirring in the captured cunt. But how to convince Mailer of the element in himself that he exaggerated in his description of Lawrence, his own obliterated and outlawed femininity? How could he bear to hear that his love-letters to great pugilists in the columns of the daily press are the outpourings of a boxers' groupie, who does not even rate ten minutes in the toilet with his idol? All the violent men I have ever known have had a craving for gentleness but every puny drunk in every bar thought it cute to bait them; to appease their foolish masochism (for fighting and fucking are in their sensibilities so confounded), the strong man must knock down the weak and earn his own contempt. If he resists or allows himself to be beaten he must endure the contempt of others. Mailer's truculence is of the weaker sort, like a drunk ordering the other drinkers in the bar to put up their dukes. In challenging the women's movement he put himself in danger, for theirs is a fight for life, no holds barred. He was as likely to face a tyre lever or a broken bottle or Robin Morgan's revolver as the Marquess of Queensberry's rules. He may have no realistic idea of his strength but the women's movement is very aware of its physical weakness. As long as Mailer sees his spirit as a triumvirate of phallus, ego and talent he cannot discern the fantasy nature of his conquests. He can have no mercy on his own defect in physical competitiveness. His old age threatens to disgust him: perhaps, like Hemingway (and Hitler), he will not have the courage to see it through. The women's movement offers Mailer the only escape from his own worries about his thickening waistline and the incipient 'humphreys of his ass', not to mention the growing capriciousness of his fast-rusting barb (another diabolical image, for only the Devil has a penis of barbed steel).

The concept of the worshipped feminine which holds *The Prisoner of Sex* in thrall is the Omnipotent Mother. To this day Mailer's relationship with his mother is important: when he confesses that he cannot live without a woman, it is not just sex and company that he needs, but nurture. The near-equal war,

> a brutal bloody war with wounds growing within and the surgeons collecting the profit from either sex

is still the antagonism between the formidable mother and the questing boy-child. The goat-kicking lust which drove Miller into one cunt after another is 'man's sense of awe before woman',

> his dread of her position one step closer to eternity (for in that step were her powers) which made men detest women, revile them, humiliate them, defecate symbolically on them, do everything to reduce them so one might dare to enter them and take pleasure of them . . . So do men look to destroy every quality in a woman that will give her the powers of a male, for she is in their eyes already armed with the power that she brought them forth, and that is a power beyond measure – the earliest etchings of memory go back to that woman between whose legs they were conceived, nurtured, and near-strangled in the hours of birth.

Memory might more reasonably be expected to go back as far as the giantess who had control of these vengeful satyrs when they were first struggling to discover the world. Mailer's explanation of abuse of the female is only another version of the description of rape as an act of revenge against the oppressive mother. What Mailer will not heed is the cry of the mothering sex that they are depleted by this attritive war of the sexes, by the endless duplication of Oedipal dependencies and hostilities, that they wish no further part in the primal war because, unremarked by their antagonists, they have borne great casualties. To an abused woman it is a bitter blasphemy to explain, as Mailer would, that her humiliation is enacted simply to prove the 'power and the glory and the grandeur of the female in the universe' for she feels only the female in her debased self. What does it mean to the woman raped and bashed to learn that her assailant did it to show that the power of the feminine 'can survive any context or any abuse'? Not that it's even unusual – many a rapist says 'I love you'.

More and more women are refusing to be doting mothers, looming over their children like mountains to be scaled as a first lesson in exploiting the universe. Part of their motivation may be found in Mailer's description of the formative years of the young dictator. The women's defection from the most exaggerated form of motherhood ever to be developed is timely. Next time round Hitler will be a machine, developed by male conquest as the most efficient method of subduing the peoples of the earth. Our only hope is that we have yet time to breed a generation which cannot be ruled in such a way or seek such a way to rule. We have no more need of great generals, for war is no longer fought by men but by machines against men. Machines are not mortal nor do they feel pain, so they must perforce win the war, unless the last of the fantasy heroes can acknowledge his weakness and his terror and beg pardon. Children in a trance frag their commanding officers these days because their war is waged against the war machine, not Nixon's fabled enemy. The fight for life against the machine is women's fight too, and it is from this essential struggle that Mailer's games seek to divert them. Perhaps, after all, it is necessary to knock him down and out of the way.

While women are deciding to withdraw their co-operation in the process of developing fiercely competitive children with swollen egos in the interests of ecology, artistic as well as sexual and political, their children themselves are formulating their own critique of competitiveness and acquisition. But Mailer finds the new personality boring and frightening in so far as its sexuality is inquiring and polymorphous. The rejection of monolithic standards of excellence in university courses has already broken down the tiny sacred society of truly great writers which he lusts to join. Concepts of aristocracy are breaking down all over and Mailer's chagrin swells when he considers that he was maybe just about to make it, with his Great American Novel. It is ironic that student interest in him was one of the ways in which students pushed courses in American literature out of shape. It is sad that he himself does not realize that the immense pressure that the literary machine brings upon genius has already turned him into Superhack, poet laureate without the bays. The young are the only ones who will forgive him for this major prostitution but Mailer retreats from them into the past and the right wing, speaking coldly of a crowd in the jail of New York with blacks and Puerto Ricans overcrowded in their cells, and ghettos simmering on the American stove, a world of junkies, hippies, freaks, and freaks who made open love at love-ins, be-ins, concerts, happenings, and on the stage of tiny theaters with invited guests . . .

and more coldly still of the new revolution,

that ill-mannered, drug-leached, informer-infested, indiscriminate ripping up of all the roots, yes, spoiled young middle-class heroes with fleas in their beard and rashes doubtless in the groin . . .

What are these but the same old hot imaginings of the beleaguered Puritan bourgeois? Merely another version of 'long-haired, dirty and unwashed', a description that the real McCoy thought applied to Mailer until he paid his dues and bitched the left wing on call. Horrible to imagine that these scruffy young folk have no trouble with their erections, that their semen flows like branch-water. But most horrible of all to think that they don't care whether Eldridge Cleaver writes better than Mailer or not, they just want to know what both are into, whether they will serve a purpose. Suddenly, wryly, but foreseeably, Mailer abandons the Jewish troublemakers, Hoffman, Rubin and friends (and me) and takes up with Podhoretz and the Jewish Establishment, passing his groin inspection with colours drooping at the mast.

This defection kindles a flame of anger in me that will stand me in good stead for our bout together. Those same revolutionaries whom he now reviles as fascists provided him with another book and a film, and of both he was the hero. With me, on the other hand, he finds that he can agree because I breathe sweet liberalism, Cambridge (England) and Golden Square. My publishers are delighted and I am disgusted. He quotes the worst parts of my book and embeds them in non sequiturs. More than ever I am desirous of drawing him into range so that I can knock him down.

Yet all the time I wonder whether he ought not to face his own wives and mistresses on the stage of the Town Hall, for Women's Liberation is a personal issue. In supplying spokeswomen we bely the real nature of our activity, for we are not yet another crazy bureaucracy in the making, nor is there ideological orthodoxy among our ranks. We are no pseudo-army issuing dispatches. How shocking and valuable might it be for Mailer to hear the grievances of his women before an impartial observer, without the possibility of overbearing them by the threat of violence or eloquence. What fun it would be to accept all his thrasonical challenges and then unveil to him his own womenfolk, including his dark and velvety daughters, and ask them what they think of him. If only pity, the curse of women, would not tie their tongues. And then, unexpectedly, for it was arranged, but not by me, I met Beverley Mailer. She had driven from Provincetown to New York, with a beautiful brown boy who wanted to hear her brother play guitar. She was gallant, a little wry and regretful, mildly astonished that Mailer had been so careless of her actress's talent when he had had so much opportunity to indulge it. She smiled and shrugged her shoulders and I knew that without help now it was likely to prove harder than ever, but she had preferred the prerogative to try. I trembled, wondering if I had the right to present her cause, but afterwards Dick Fontaine told me that as we left she winked. I took that as my OK and secretly regretted my covetise of her brown musician.

When at last I met the great man he was sitting in a snot-green dressing-room at the New York Hall, lit like a matinée idol, being photographed by a very apologetic (and rather plain) professional. Mailer feigned butch embarrassment, while I wondered if the star treatment was altogether normal, for Mailer does not strike one as a great photogenic. I was asked to pose beside him. 'You're better looking than I thought,' he said. 'I know,' said I, remembering his descriptions of women's liberationists, and his absurd insistence upon my English lectureship. Later he was to tell me that my picture on the book looked like any other uppity Jewish girl, so he was relieved to see that I was a shiksa (except that that was wrong too – I am like God in his last despairing suspicion, half-Jewish). My convent education prevented me from saying how disappointed I was. I expected a hard, sort of nuggety man, and Mailer was positively blowsy. I contented myself with saying that his eyes were less blue than certain retouched colour photos had led me to believe. Ever since, Mailer has fended off any question about me by some appreciation of my looks, especially my wonderful crooked fang. With him being so gallant, it ought to be difficult for me to explain that my old editor's telegram begging for an option on the story of the Mailer bedroom farce for his underground paper had to go unanswered. I was, after all, defective in Oedipal sentiment. I liked Mailer, but not enough. I disliked him too, and that not enough either.

When we were all assembled before the glittering, turbulent crowd of those rich enough to pay twenty-five dollars a head for the stalls and ten dollars a head for the circle, I felt for him right enough, for the devil in the fire is absurd. There was almost no way in which he could appear sympathetic. It was evident at once that he was the carnival barker who had drawn in the crowd of diamond-studded radical-chic New Yorkers, and that the *Village Voice* would approve of anything he did, but it was also evident that he would not be able to do anything right. As moderator he was principally time-keeper of the speeches and controller of the audience. He was bored by Jackie Ceballos's speech and grated his question, after an over-expanded compliment, whether there was anything in her and NOW's programme that would give men the notion that life might not continue to be as profoundly boring as it is today.

Then it was my turn. I was so tense traversing the space between the chair and the lectern that I tripped over the air. My fox fur, which I had worn for fun and satire because it cost a pound, I stuffed somewhere on the floor, thus exposing my ten-shilling dress and the chromium women's liberation symbol that Flo Kennedy had given me. This was the ensemble that was so wildly reported as elegance, furs and jewellery, by the humourless and unsophisticated New York press. My Australian/English/American hybrid accent was also taken for the true accent of Cambridge (England) which, to the best of my knowledge, has not existed since returned soldiers were admitted to the university after the war. Once safe behind the lectern I clung on tight and launched my shot out over the crowd and (I hoped) into Mailer's sagging bosom. 'The creative artist in our society,' I wailed, 'is more a killer than a creator [Remember, Norman, your notion of the artist as a great general?] aiming his ego ahead of lesser talents, drawing the focus of all eyes to his achievements, being read now by millions and paid in millions [How does that grab you, Superhack?] Is it possible that the way of the masculine artist in our society is strewn with the husks of people worn out and dried out by this ego? [Will this serve, Beverley?] The achievement of the male ego is at my expense. I find that the battle is dearer to him than the peace would ever be . . . [in my quoting voice] "The eternal battle with women both sharpens our resistance, develops our strength, enlarges the scope of our cultural achievements".' And so on. In my convent-bred obedience I did not go beyond my time. Was it my imagination or did Mailer turn to me with clenched teeth, when the applause was silent (why did those people applaud, I wonder, for they cannot have accepted what I said) and charge me with diaper Marxism. As an old anarchist I take that as a compliment. The infancy of Marxism is profoundly more relevant than anything since betrayed.

From then on the evening was simply fun, except for the cries of the women who asked what I was doing there, and whether Women's Lib. was only for rich bitches and so forth, as if we were grossing a bent nickel from the whole detestable circus. Jill Johnston's poem was exquisite and outrageous, much the most entertaining thing that had happened, if only the love scene at the end had not been quite such an anti-climax. It served to blow papa Mailer's cool, though, and that's just as well. Jill promptly vanished, and we had to endure some querulous questioning as to what we had done with her. In New York paranoia knows no bounds.

Diana Trilling's attack on *The Prisoner of Sex* was careful and beautiful, if only she had not considered it so necessary to dissociate herself from the rest of the women's movement so clearly. How much one might have wished to have said that Mailer's was a 'free-wheeling solipsistic fancy to ask for the constant apotheosis of sex in parenthood' (yes, yes, like an old Olympian whose loves could lengthen the night and always made children!)

And so the evening wore on in skirmishing and foolishness, with some of the best contributions coming from the floor, from Cynthia Ozick and Betty Friedan. The most publicized incident occurred when a cockerel by the name of Anatole Broyard was allowed to ask the last question and he put it to me: 'I would like to ask Germaine Greer, as having a peculiar aptitude for this question, to describe, perhaps in the form of a one-act play, what it would be like to be a woman and to have the initiation and consummation of a sexual contact so that now we can get down to the particulars of the evening . . .'

Now if it be possible to strut in one place, he was strutting and smirking like a popinjay. Mailer's hackles rose at the same instant as mine (and at that moment I lost my rancour towards him) and when I went for the fool he murmured 'Attagirl!' or 'Sick him!' or something. The dozing columnists were only just aware that something was wrong when I was already furious so they never did find out what produced the kind of feminist fury they had waited all night to see. The *pappagallo* tried to rescue his question: 'I don't know what women are asking for. Now suppose I wanted to give it to them . . .'

For God's sake. After a whole night's wrangling. What does one do with these men?

That night will be chiefly memorable in my life because, when I was escaping from the continued interrogations and clamour at Westbeth afterwards, my cab was being driven by a corrupt child of my own generation, with a white angelic face (marked a little from experiences on the streets and in reform school) who was to become famous on the West Coast as my 'bodyguard'. (The experience was ultimately costly and therefore valuable.) The Town Hall extravaganza sickened me in retrospect: it was not even effective revolutionary theatre. What the kids were to initiate the very next day in Washington was to run round the world like St Anthony's fire. Stories of impromptu prison camps were to cause old wounds to ache as tired Europe watched the hardening of America into the most reactionary power on earth. The holocaust was drawing nearer. I left for the middle West and the crazy questions, 'Are you a communist – answer yes or no'. What was one to do about Mailer's defection? Was it worthwhile to win him back?

I heard that Mailer wanted to continue his debate with me on the Susskind show. I was pleased, for it seemed like the answer to my question. I should have been better pleased to have gone fishing with him and refined our dialogue in an old-fashioned gentlemanly way, but we were both creatures of the media, and our master called. A phone call at midnight in San Francisco changed everything. My dear editor had discovered by diligent enquiry that Mailer had acquired the film rights and the literary rights of our conversation from David Susskind. So much for his respect for his adversary. The money angle was bad enough, but the editorial angle was even worse. Bit by bit the facts about the Town Hall set-up were emerging. Mailer had been the draw-card, according to his agent, (although on the night he generously ascribed that role to me) and consequently had certain claims which Shirley Broughton, representing the chief beneficiary, the Theatre for Ideas, was charmed to recognize. The women would be taken care of – some proportion or other would be made over to them, but no trouble had been taken to secure an agreement. The matter passed into the hands of McGraw-Hill's corporation lawyers, representing my interests. I realized that I had foolishly assumed that Mailer would treat me as an equal, despite my own clear apprehension of his role among the High Media; I remembered the warnings I had been given, by Abbie Hoffman and Gloria Steinem and others. I quarrelled with David (the cab driver – not Susskind) who could not understand why I was so upset. Gall and wormwood.

On the day of the proposed taping, Mailer called me. He kept saying that he had been writing for thirty years and asking me if I thought he could perform a theft so picayune. Moreover, he had given up all the rights to anything and everything. We commiserated over the boredom of editing transcripts and the difficulty of satisfying everyone. He pretended to be mad at me for allowing my big corporation lawyers to intervene, and all I could think of was that if they had not intervened I never would have known what was going on. I kept saying mechanically that when the lawyers were satisfied I would be satisfied too. The lawyers were never satisfied, as ·it happened.

That night we met at Marion Javits' house for dinner. I was hectic and miserable, and Mailer twitted me for being less good-looking than at our former meeting. In truth I felt awful, watching the Filipino houseboy appearing and disappearing to the tune of the bell under the hostess' chair, eating the paella prepared by a lady who had not sat down to table with us. And yet all the time I was struggling like a neglected and ugly daughter for my father's esteem. I was waiting for him to say he was sorry, to confess to a wounding and careless gamble, but he never did. He rallied me with minor unkindnesses until I recklessly spoke loving words to him like I might have to my own indifferent father, who only ever praised me to other people. 'I love you,' I kept saying, with the unsaid corollary, 'so why do you treat me this way?' – the classic question of revolting women! He was bewildered, mistrustful. Going downtown in a cab I announced my intention of visiting a friend, and was left alone at once. Mailer went to drink in a tough black bar on the Hudson, and I to walk a shaggy dog in Union Square, with my brothers, David and Jimmy, the Hell's Angel. They sensed my misery and bore me company, all three, through the short night in my shabby suite before I was to leave for the 'Today Show' and The National Press Club Luncheon in Washington, where I was to be guest of honour. Even there the phantom of Mailer pursued me. 'If you, Norman Mailer and Edward Kennedy were the last three left on earth, whom would you choose?' My answer surprised me by its bitterness. 'It would be better that the human race should perish than that either of these men should be its father.' What visions of Mailer's beloved primitive were set adrift by the speculation! Kennedy and Mailer setting each other tests and initiations, quarrelling over the woman as the spoil, hitting upon the fine idea of clitoridectomy and infibulation as the best safeguard for the breeding female, and forever fighting, fighting each other, their sons and me.

When at last I fled from New York to my fastness in the Tuscan hills, one more attempt was being made to rescue the love affair of the century from total collapse. Mailer had rung the Cavett show and suggested that as a sequel to appearing on adjacent nights, we should appear together. But I was tired of keeping his stage fire alight, tired of contemplating the cruel mysticism which drives him through so many mythical bioscapes, where the sperm battle for the consummate egg like Argonauts in search of the Golden Fleece. And bored, bored with the foolish assumption that the ovum is the subconsciously absorbing artefact of the woman, while the man's four hundred million sperm, already equipped with memory, will and understanding are produced at no psychic cost to himself. What was Mailer, after all, but a typical patriarch, friend of the foetus and oppressor of the child? All that remains of his title fight with the women is a hundred and twenty quarto pages of transcript and a few reels of film which no one has any right to use. And there let it rest. 'When the revolution comes it will not be on television. It will be live.' Mailer won't be there and no one will miss him.

Going without

Sunday Times, 19 and 26 September 1971

Lately I've been thinking that I was getting rather hip where clothes are concerned. I've finally managed to accumulate some that I like, mostly oldies, but most important, they are all comfortable. I don't own a bra or a girdle (or these days a *tight* but that's another story). This complacency was shot from under me by a simple question my brand-new and very respected lady doctor put to me, when preparing to examine me in her 'office' at an elegant address in the East Seventies in New York. 'Why,' she murmured, 'are you wearing pants?'

Now this is no hippy homeopath or herbalist. My doctor wears no charms or beads or sandals, but a good silk dress of Mediterranean length, and greying hair in a simple coil on top of her head. She waited for an answer and I cudgelled my brains for a rational answer, but all that came to mind was a vignette of my mother saying, 'What if you were knocked over by a car?' Obviously, if going without means that one is more cautious in traffic, there's much to be said for it. So I didn't even try saying, 'Well, if I were knocked down by a car . . .' 'It's very hot,' she prompted, 'and your skirt is quite ample.' Now once warmth is rejected, as a reason for wearing knickers, what else is there?

I suppose we can give modesty as a reason, provided we accept modesty as a reason for doing anything. But it still won't stand up, because pants themselves are not meant to be seen. If a hurricane were to develop in Bond Street, so that women's skirts were instantly tweaked over their heads, there would be so much other havoc going on that few people would have the leisure to observe whether what was revealed was lingerie or flesh. By the time pants get to be seen, the hour for modesty has passed, be it in the boudoir or the fitting room. (I'm not so sure about the fitting room, but if going without pants means we buy fewer clothes then that is another argument for.)

In any event, knickers are themselves erotic, which might be an argument for retaining them, but not from a woman's point of view, because it is not women who turn on to them. Undie shops run a staple line in playful pantees with clefts in the crotch and cheering inscriptions upon them, all diaphanous and vivid in black and white or red or leopard-skin for the truly *farouche*. But apart from the sportive aspect of the knicker, there is also the sinister power of the pant glimpsed at an impressionable age in circumstances of great excitement and guilt, or whatever it is that reduces men to knicker lovers amassing huge piles of them clean or worn, in the corners of rented rooms, begging them from beloved women as an essential prerequisite of sexual satisfaction. If there are no knickers there can be no knicker fixations. Some liberals might think this an impoverishment of the sexual environment – I doubt if the underwear fetishists themselves would agree.

The symbolism of clothes is very muddling. Many women's liberationists have eschewed the skirt for the boiler suit, claiming that skirts mean immobility and availability. Now I know boys who are more intrigued by a front zipper than anything else. A woman in a boiler suit is like a hermit crab, you must wonder and fantasize about her shape. Only reality is an antidote for fantasy. In any case, clothes do not actually influence availability. If all that stands between a male chauvinist and the accomplishment of his desires is a knicker, then you've had it. On the other hand, if you know karate, it doesn't much matter whether you're wearing pants or not. Clothes as protection haven't worked since the knights discovered that their armour hampered them so much that they could be hacked down by the meanest foot-soldier. Ideally, women should not be judged by their clothes any more than men. As long as women are judged easy or provocative because of their chosen mode of dress, they are being judged as beings with significance only through their relation with others. The older generation is often puzzled that women who fling off their clothes at rock concerts are not raped; they do not understand that the connection is not with provocation but with freedom.

One reason I did mumble out to the doctor was, cleanliness, you know, subway seats and all that. But a moment's reflection in the light of her smile revealed that pants are not very hygienic in themselves, or much of a protection against infection, if infection were to be so easily got, which it is not. So, with a great sigh, I put my knickers in my bag and marched off down Third Avenue, all unbeknownst to the passers-by breasting a new frontier in a life marked like a tree-trunk by lines of small emancipations.

And yet it was not a new feeling. Long ago in a hotter country, when I was very poor and had few pairs of pants, I was used to going knickerless, but my man would check me up, when he got wise, by running a finger from hip to haunch, feeling for the ridges through my clothes. Then he would march me home, or into a store, so that I could be decently equipped for the day's enterprises. It became a running battle between us, and I guess, if I'd thought it through I'd have realized the significance of the fact that my pants were a good deal more important to him than to me. But we must crawl before we can walk, and later on I accumulated vast stores of pants of all colours, because, unbelievably, I have a tendency to mislay them. I once left twenty-four pairs of pants in a farmhouse in Sicily. I'll never know how the peasants received them.

The troubling thought that remains is that perhaps fewer women wear pantees than I thought. When some friends of mine were working on a construction site underneath a makeshift footbridge in the city, they assured me that one in three women went without. That was in the summer too.

If I had had no pantees I would not have to remember the horrid sight of twelve little stretchy ones all in luminous colours, hanging on the line in a neat row, with all their crotches cut off in a single unbroken line. I was so shaken by the implied threat, that I locked myself in the bedroom until my man came home and we kept the blinds down for ages.

Towards a standard of morality

Sunday Times, 7 November 1971

The archangel Raphael has not been getting much work these days, unlike Michael who has all that judging to do. That is, he didn't until the Kennedys appointed him patron of their Joseph P. Kennedy Jr Foundation, set up by Joseph P. Kennedy Sr in remembrance of his eldest son, who was lost in the Second World War. Now Raphael is in charge of retarded children, the unvalued scraps of humanity who need a powerful advocate. His handsome unisex silhouette presided this weekend over the Kennedy International Awards and International Symposium on Human Rights, Retardation and Research, to which for some reason I was invited. The only other participant I was truly anxious to meet, Ivan Illich, decided against coming at the last minute. Perhaps he too had been disgusted by the flamboyant expenditure which produced, for example, three telegrams of welcome, each of a hundred-and-fifty words. At any rate, Eunice Shriver told me by way of explanation, his wasn't a very good reason. I doubt if she'd have thought much of my reasons either, if I'd slunk off when the desperate wish formed itself. As it was I bore the patronage of the Kennedy dynasty and the archangel Raphael almost as long as I was supposed to.

The first occasion was a working dinner at the Shrivers' at which the academics and scientists found themselves mixing with such unworldly folk as Mother Teresa of Calcutta and Jean Vanier, founder of villages for the handicapped. 'How many children do you have with you now, Mother?' someone asked Mother Teresa reverently. 'Fifty,' she answered simply. Fifty, I thought in despair, and there are 200,000 non-retarded children already sentenced to death in refugee camps in India. Of course, Mother Teresa was entitled to her award, and to Malcolm Muggeridge's eulogy, but how could her great sanctity suffice to save the rest of us from the enormity of our shared guilt? How can we explain the compounded wrong of our continued inability to intervene in this case of human distress? Was our technology necessarily frivolous and inhuman, more considerate of dead stones in the sky than of living men?

When I lamented the luxury of indulging in discussions of fine points of ethics and human rights when millions of fully developed and capable human beings were pleading for help in vain, the bishop at our table murmured, as he speared the soft thigh of his guinea-fowl, 'Pakistan is simply the first of the irreversible disasters. The problem is simply beyond our resources.' Surely, I objected, the problem was a political one, not to be shuffled off as an ecological disaster. 'Do you not think,' the Bishop's bland voice resumed, 'that the first great ecological disasters will appear to arise as a result of political manipulation?' I supposed I did, but – 'You,' said the professor next to me, 'are the sort of person who grieves for the masses on the other side of the world, and is indifferent to the suffering of a single retarded child.' He beamed in full consciousness of virtue. I thought it was not so, but the argument *ad hominem* permitted no reply. The fumes of hypocrisy began to rise, dimming even the outline of Mother Teresa's simplicity.

The next morning we crept like vermin along the blank acres of red carpet between the sheer marble cliffs of the Kennedy centre, to watch one of our ethical conundrums presented to us in a film: a mongol child is born with no opening between stomach and intestine. The hospital consults the parents, pointing out that if they do not operate the baby will die, and offering the parents the chance to refuse permission. The parents reject the child, and for fifteen days he starves to death. The hospital did no more than was legal. Technology could do no more for the tiny boy than starve him to death. An ignorant mother would have given him the breast, not discerning his abnormality. He would have aspirated her merciful milk and died at once. In the modern hospital the guilt was compounded time and again as more and more people came into contact with the child. No one had the courage to kill him outright, and no one had the love to defy the law and his parents and save his life. The panel toyed with the problem, refusing to blame anyone, searching for a formula, in the same way that financial wizards have searched for ways of going off the gold standard and staying on it at the same time. We were after a floating standard of morality. The panellists seemed more anxious to relieve their consciences than anyone had been to relieve the child's pain. One of them mentioned the Vietnam war, by way of pointing out that the right to life is not accepted in Western society. 'Mere demagoguery,' muttered the doctor behind me. 'That has nothing to do with it.' If it had nothing to do with it, why did it have nothing to do with it?

At lunch we were entertained by retarded children, who had been taught various skills. And behold a boy came out, amid the clattering of dishes, and roared pop songs into a microphone, keeping his eyes fixed on the light above him. What, thought I, of the melodies that thronged his brain before they taught him to yell 'Dream the impossible dream'? A troupe of black children tumbled for us on the too-narrow stage, coming down with back-breaking thumps when their rubber mats shifted. An Indian boy, one of the handful that remains of his whole tribe, danced a prairie chicken dance and a war-dance for us. His soft, small feet flew and pattered like leaves on the wrinkled carpet. His porcupine roach with its whirling feather slipped further and further over his face, but he danced on, his black eyes narrowed in pain or disdain. 'What would you reckon their IQ at, Bob?' one medico asked another. 'Could be anything,' he replied. Of course it could; they might have been pigeons playing ping-pong, if it were not for the faculties that were unteachable, their tenderness, their pride, some wild thing still imprisoned there. It is better to fly than to play ping-pong.

Some of the humanists on our panel did not manage to control their sense of outrage well enough to eat their lunch. When the time came, we put our academic hats on, and argued politely with B. F. Skinner, the man who invented the teaching methods that get pigeons to play ping-pong and retardates (as they are called) to control themselves, and with Jose Delgado, the man who can make monkeys yawn by inserting electrodes in the brain and sending stimuli. And in the evening we watched the Kennedy family honouring Skinner and Mother Teresa, in between sonorous readings from David Frost's clipboard. When we got to the point of applauding a sickly song of Donovan's about Je-sus and Ma-ry, immediately after a film of retarded children on an outing to Lourdes, I sneaked out and fled down the barren canyons of the Kennedy centre to the fresh air. A phrase of Camillo Torres' floated unbidden into my mind: 'The Catholic who is not a revolutionary is living in mortal sin.' Could that have been Illich's unsatisfactory reason for staying away?

Saigon

Sunday Times, 5 December 1971

In other times and under other foreign domination, the women of Vietnam were born to be either wives or concubines.

The cult of ancestor worship meant that a woman's function related always to the continuity of the family, and so she had, in the course of her life, three duties: as a daughter she had to live for her father; as a wife she had to live for her husband; and as a widow she had to live for her children.

Confucius said: 'Among the three sins against filial piety, the gravest is to lack male issue.' Any woman who so lacked had to countenance her husband's keeping of a concubine. Any concubine who brought forth sons had to hand them over to the legitimate wife.

The four virtues of the Vietnamese woman were modesty, douceur (sweetness and gentleness of behaviour), neatness in appearance and hard work. In the Chinese characters which were adopted by the colonized Vietnamese, the ideograph for woman also meant broom. The concubine also served as nurse and servant, unable to complain or protest, always silent, subservient and gentle. She had to make the head of the household happy, conciliate his wife and earn the children's trust.

Even the legitimate wife had to describe herself as 'Miss So-and-so, accepted into the household of the Such-and-such family'. Her devotion to her husband had to be absolute, even though the marriage was arranged by the parents of the couple. She was expected to give her life for her husband if need be.

A Vietnamese woman's work extended to all 'domestic' fields – agriculture, marketing and commerce. Her husband busied himself with 'public' affairs – mainly, one supposes, by chatting about them over a pipe with his friends. The women tended the rice paddies in the heat and the rain, sheltering under their conical hats secured under the chin with a broad strip of cotton. The women trotted through the streets balancing laden baskets on their shoulders and cried their wares in the market-place. Their labours were not made easier by the requirements of *Nu Tac*, which states that they must be noiseless, that they must not let the panniers of the *adu dai* fly up as they walked, that they must not show their teeth when they smiled.

Nowadays you will find the women of Vietnam in the fields, in the market-places and hawking all sorts of wares in the streets. You will find them laying roads around the US Army HQ in Long Binh, behind a sign that says 'Men and Equipment at Work'. Long queues of women wait inside and outside the gates of the big bases: they are the hootch-maids who wait upon the GIs. They must check in and out each day so that the authorities can be sure that no female is left inside after dark, being, as authorities are prone to be, subject to a misconception that sexual activity is strictly nocturnal.

Given such constant traffic on and off the bases, it is not surprising that security is bad. The hootch-maids are the principal source of heroin – 'Ever noticed how they arrive with their hair all done up and leave with it down?' asked one soldier I met.

Occasionally a hootch-maid buries a grenade in the doorway of a hut. More often she tends her five GI charges with smiling humility. Supplying sexual services in addition to other menial duties, some of the women come to polish their boots and scrub floors in miniskirts and false eyelashes.

In the dozens of bars in downtown Saigon, in Tu-Do Street and Plantation Road or anywhere else the rich American military come to find a good time, there are the bar-girls. According to the statistics supplied by the Students' Union of Saigon, there are 200,000 bar-girls, prostitutes and irregular wives of Americans. Hanoi claims that there are 400,000.

In the plushier zones they are all well made-up, elaborately coiffed and prettily dressed. The by-laws of Saigon demand that they all wear white and register on the payroll of the bar (or restaurant as it must be called) as waitresses. Their real duty is to persuade the customers to buy them a 'Saigon Tea', a weak mixture of crème de menthe, water and ice. If the client decides that he would like to spend the night with one of the girls he must pay the Mama-San, who runs the bar, 5,000 piastres, about £5, of which the girl of his choice may claim half.

Most of the girls are between sixteen and twenty. They are at pains to disguise the crass commercialism of the operation by their sweet modesty and charming manners. They play games, plying the soldiers with flattery learned from the book of *English for Bar-girls*. The men play along with their archness, and stories abound of the loving hearts and deathless loyalty of the bar-girls of Saigon.

If an American and a Vietnamese girl find that they get along well together, he may take out a cohabitation permit, which will protect her from arrest if she is stopped by the police.

Many already-married soldiers have established Vietnamese women in apartments and had children by them. When the time comes for the men to go home, these women find themselves worse off than the concubines of old. In the post office in Saigon you may see, any day, queues of girls nervously waiting to put in collect calls to the United States.

Those soldiers who decide that they would like to marry their Vietnamese girlfriends are obstructed at every turn.

The Vietnamese soldiers are so poorly paid that they can hardly afford to compete with the Americans for the attentions of their own womenfolk. The bar-girls and their clients turn blind eyes when maimed Vietnamese soldiers come into the bars, begging with the aid of a typewritten official letter, which is their only recompense for a lost limb.

Not all the women in South Vietnam have had to capitulate to the American presence. Women were more than half the 83,899 communists neutralized by the Phoenix Programme.

While some women were having their breasts enlarged with silicone implants to please the troops, others were fighting against the corruption of their country. Many girl students have disappeared into gaol, like Vu Thi Dung and Nguyen Thi Thu Lieu, as a result of demonstrations against President Thieu's electoral tactics. Tiny, ailing Madame Ngo Ba Thanh is condemned to indeterminate detention, although she has never been charged. She is guilty only of attempting to organize the beleaguered women of Saigon.

All of them, the go-go dancers, the prostitutes, the widows whose president misappropriated their meagre funds, the dead, the imprisoned, are casualties of American policy in Vietnam.

If the Americans were to vanish tomorrow, the scars of their presence would not heal for a generation.

The new maharajahs

Sunday Times, 16 January 1972

In 1964, without much deliberation or trepidation, I upped and left the country where I was born, for the first time and for ever. I thought I never missed Australia except when I caught sight of the Blue Mountains in the background of 'Skippy the Bush Kangaroo' or found myself dawdling in a glade of eucalyptus, anywhere from Los Angeles to Agadir. Then, likely as not, I would snivel a bit, but I never formed any firm resolve to go home, mostly because I never had the money for a two-way ticket, for I'd have to be certain of getting away again. Besides, it is one thing to miss the country and quite another to miss its people. Not that I am not fond of Australian people, for nobody is dearer to me than certain expatriate mates. It is something to do with the combination; for example, an Australian journalist can be the best in the world, but not if he writes for an Australian newspaper. So one is left cherishing Australians overseas, missing smells and shapes and skies, and utterly unable to go home, that is to say, to Australia. Ironically, there are Australian families who mean England when they say that, although they may not have been there in three generations.

I went home slowly, lingering in India, Laos and Vietnam, beating down my squeamishness in the face of wall-to-wall humanity, growing accustomed to the face of poverty and the lineaments of life below subsistence level. From the whorehouse in Saigon to the politician's mansion in New Delhi, the intricacies and contradictions of Asian life unfolded themselves slightly, so that I could glimpse an enormous pattern that I could never master or despise. The maharajah waved his ringed hands and was brought the same foods that the servants were eating elsewhere in grosser helpings, by a one-eyed boy in rags. Why, I wondered from the depths of my crass snobbery, did they not employ handsome fellows in smart clothes and teach them to cook fine food? My host would have answered, as he scooped up rice and dal with his right hand, 'Because in India there is forty per cent unemployment and a lad like this is the last to find work. We do not spend money on liveries but on employing more servants so that we support more people.' In a household of three, bedevilled by forty servants, we did not actually need even two of them.

For all his riches, the maharajah of my example, who is a composite figure, lived among the poor, was familiar with them, ate the same food, taught them to read and write, provided them with medical care and treated them with respect. But he is none the less the most hideous example of inequity and oppression that the Anglo-Saxon mind can summon to its view. Although he could not afford to drink Scotch because of the exorbitant taxes put on all foreign imports of anything at all, although he could not find a tailor to make his Western-style clothes to fit him, although he could not own a house worth more than five thousand rupees, he had been paid his own weight in gold and silver for centuries; he was a gilded repository of wealth, even if the wealth could never be converted into useful goods and services. A good democratic Australian would hate his guts.

When our brand-new, spotless jet decanted us at the brand-new, spotless lounges of Kingsford Smith airport, in all our smart travelling ensembles and matched luggage (no mattresses or bursting baskets or wriggling sacks or crying babies) we might have been en route to a jet-set maharajah's private party. We even got disinfected before we were allowed to leave the plane. There was no crowding or jostling as we made our way through glittering corridors to be driven to the city for two dollars and fifteen minutes. As we glided through the new motorways we spied evidence of wealth on every side, the wealth of the ten-and-a-half-million maharajahs of Australia. Almost all the houses were beautifully maintained, painstakingly renovated at greater cost than if they had been demolished and begun again. Two-and-a-quarter-million houses in Australia are occupied by their owners, eighty per cent of the total number of private houses. Two-and-a-half-million dwellings have television. Inside the houses, the inhabitants, with their 2.09 average of nuptial births, keep a cocktail cabinet and a dozen bottles of beer (in the fridge) and eat meat with most meals. Outside the house is a garden, which absorbs a good deal of energy that might otherwise be misdirected into communal activity like expressing curiosity about politics or anger about conspicuous graft and collusion in high places. And a car.

Not far from any house is a pub, where men forgather to smoke and drink while the wife gets the kiddies down. There will probably be a two-up school and a tote office not very far away as well, because Australians are proud of, and loyal to, their working-class culture, even though not one of them would claim to be a worker so defined. Everyone is the proprietor of something – a car, a greyhound, a blockaland, his own home and a TV that feelingly persuades him that he is, and ought to be, affluent. Those who are not have only themselves to blame. You will also hear that an Australian woman can do anything she wants, if she so chooses, even though her basic wage is fixed at three quarters of a man's and her real earnings amount to an even smaller proportion. Less than two per cent of the children of the third of all married women who work, are given any kind of organized day care, and no child-minding expenses can be claimed for tax deduction. Notwithstanding, if you are poor in the you–beaut country, it is your fault.

There are poor in this country: there are the unemployed, the blacks, the unsupported mothers, the dull-witted and the confused, but they do not rub shoulders with you on the uncongested boulevards and plazas of the urban centres. Their run-down habitat is not well enough served by public transport for them to come into town much, and as they have no money to spend anyway, who cares? The mass of the well-to-do live in Shangri-la, mercifully cushioned from reminders of gross inequities in their democracy, which is still called that although the country has been ruled by the same party regardless of drunkenness, crassness, pederasty and incompetence for the last twenty-three years.

Oh, but ease is so easy, when newspapers keep you ignorant of anything transpiring in the real world, when every table groans beneath food and wine, set in the garden under flowering trees. I have become a lotus-eater, sunk in the warm sands of Bondi, gloating over the flaxen hair and elegant bodies of the boys dancing along the waves. Security and well-being do lend a kind of hearty innocence – where else in the world is a generous man defined as one who would give you his arsehole and shit through his ribs?

'Sex and society – whose rules?'

Sunday Times, 27 February 1972

'Sex and society – whose rules?' is the portentous title of a debate in which I am to spar with a well-known churchman on Australian television tomorrow evening. Besides the ominousness of the assumption that present moral conflicts are nothing more than a tussle between would-be rule-makers, there is, I suppose, something engaging in the impression one might derive from this formulation of sex and society as some kind of game. Perhaps it is a choice like the one that various Australian states have made, between Australian Rules, Rugby Union and Rugby League. It might even be supposed that I, as the opponent of the pop preacher on the programme, was about to defend a brand-new set of conventions for the conduct of sex and society; am I expected to outlaw the forward pass by the masculine initiator or to drive the missionary position out of play by heavy penalties?

The fact that I am a law-breaker does not entail the notion that I must be a law-maker. Because I ran away from my own husband and find monogamy the most incomprehensible perversion of all, I am wrongly assumed to order all other women into a life of promiscuity. Because I do not wear a brassière and do not believe that women ought to feel obliged to wear such an unbecoming garment, it is said that I have ordered all women to throw away such underwear, to burn it even. The sorry fact is that I am not so compulsive in my attitudes that I would spurn all forms of breast binding at all times. On horseback, even I wear a tit-bag. Nor do I jeer at my sister who is nursing her infant and must keep her bosom well supported or leak milk all over her clothes.

People like those who devised the title of the debate do not only imagine that I have drawn up the book of rules for sex and society in the future, they are also unfailingly irritated with me, when they find out that I have not. It becomes my responsibility to provide new norms for behaviour in a world where the nuclear family does not exist, where men are not expected to keep families and women to work for nothing, where work and play are no longer distinguished, although no such society exists to be realistically discussed and it is extremely difficult to foresee how it may come into being. It is not enough to argue that hastening the decay of the nuclear family may of itself be a moral activity with a moral aim, and that new values will emerge in response to new conditions that we will encounter as we work towards it. 'That won't do,' I am told. 'What are you going to put in its place?' New straitjackets must be designed to replace the old, otherwise the unfortunate lunatic must remain bound in the current mode. The champions of rules and repressions draw their best hope from the inability of the bound man to adjust to sudden freedom. They see him staggering and flailing his arms, and so he is bound again, possibly more efficiently than before. This is the process that can be seen in all the toing and froing over liberalization of laws against obscenity, marijuana and abortion – even the prohibitions against homosexuality. Now that homosexuals are not afraid to declare themselves and to behave spontaneously in public, we may even find that the reform of the laws against homosexuality between consenting adults is reviewed. Even the most liberal will lament that the extravagant demeanour of extremists has provoked a backlash, and fail to see that we may only have our freedoms in so far as we refrain from exercising them.

It is a common liberal point of view, that most sets of laws and rituals have developed as a response to existing economic and other conditions; what is not so often understood is that as soon as they become codified and cannot bend to accommodate new conditions, the laws become anachronistic, tyrannical and absurd. The Jewish dietary laws made a good deal of sense when they were first distilled from the pooled wisdom of the elders of the chosen people, but when they become mere ritual observance, they also lose their moral function. The process is astonishingly rapid: in order to retain their relevance to contemporary reality, laws must be under constant critical attack.

Morality is essentially connected with choice, with the exercise of will itself responding to information and observation of the consequences and conditions of action. As soon as a rule is invoked in order to short-circuit the process of individual confrontation with reality, morality has been abandoned.

Those people who claim that other people need rules and leaders or else they will behave outrageously and destructively both towards themselves and others, are denying the whole structure of assumption upon which our concepts of democracy are based. They believe that certain sorts of people, priests and pundits, have special moral insight or expertise, which applies perfectly well to circumstances of which they have no direct experience. So doctors, psychiatrists, churchmen, sociologists and law-makers are better able to make the correct decision about the termination of a pregnancy than the pregnant woman herself. They pre-empt her moral responsibility for her own behaviour, even though they may as a result condemn her to a life of guilt, resentment and inadequacy. Although those who took the decision for her are to blame for that, it is she and her kin who must bear the punishment and the compounded guilt. By this spurious assumption of responsibility for an action for which they will never have to pay, such moral arbiters pervert the course of morality, cripple the spiritual life of the whole community.

The imposition of my set of rules would be no less perverting than that of anyone else's. What we need, in order to become morally agile and strong, is to shake off the ruinous carapace of half-believed, ill-remembered and misunderstood religion and its monstrous excrescence of dead and murdering laws, and so free ourselves to grapple with new problems. There is no other way to develop the spiritual muscle which will build a new morality. That morality may very well be neither monistic nor prescriptive.

We will also need to find again the value of doubting, the courage which is required that we may refuse to codify difficult decisions out of their difficulty. How else will we ever know how to act on the issue of one man's kidney machine costing as much to run as wiping out glaucoma in the children of the poor would cost? How else can we develop sensible attitudes to the transplant game?

The development of morality also entails the acceptance of guilt: one may very well see that motives for taking action in a particular case may outweigh the continuing possibility that the act may not be the right one. It is better to recognize the fact, than to pass the buck to an unassailable body which accepts only symbolic responsibility. It might surprise my opponent in tomorrow's debate to learn that I desire free abortion clinics, abolition of censorship, spontaneous sexual relations, in the interests of morality.

Contraception – 1972

Sunday Times, 12 March 1972

One of the vulgar errors that most frequently appears as an objection to abortion law reform is the notion that perfectly reliable methods of contraception exist and should be used, rather than wantonly allowing a foetus to come into being only to destroy it. 'You girls have got tubal ligation, pills, IUDs, diaphragms, foams – and you're supposed to be reasonably intelligent. Why can't you manage the relatively simple matter of contraception?' The question is rarely put by anyone who is actually using the Pill or the diaphragm, who is usually dismally aware that most methods of contraception are no more reliable than their users, and the lovemaking situation is not the most clear-headed.

Tubal ligation obviously works, and nowadays it can be performed very easily with the aid of the laporoscope. It is offered gladly to women of the Third World, poor women with too many children, and even forced on women in some countries, who are told to undergo the operation or be denied welfare. The woman who personally and deliberately decides that she does not want any, or any more children, will have a good deal of trouble in finding a doctor who is willing to perform the operation. If she is unmarried she can forget it. The doctor will argue that she might meet the man of her dreams and change her mind or have it changed for her. She might then be moved to sue her doctor for mutilation or for taking advantage of her state of mind. Like vasectomy, tubal ligation has the disadvantage of being irreversible. Even a married woman who has not had children, or not had very many children (I knew a woman who was denied sterilization after her eighth) or is not yet within sight of the menopause, is quite likely to be denied tubal ligation.

The Pill is supposed, by those who have nothing to do with it, to be the perfect contraceptive, regardless of side effects, short-term and long-term. Somewhere there is a pill for every woman, specially adapted to her particular hormone balance, a pill which does not nauseate, bloat or depress her, does not cause breakthrough bleeding, will not activate any disposition to thrombosis. The trouble is that the woman herself has got to find it. She may go on for years experimenting, waiting three months for side effects to settle down and finding that they don't, while her doctor finds, in the suggestion that she change her pill, a panacea for all her ills. No method of scanning an individual woman's hormone balance in order to prescribe the right pill has yet been devised. In order that one process be inhibited, a multitude of other interrelating processes are disturbed. Some upsetting effects of this disturbance are regarded as too trivial to be mentioned in discussions of the way the Pill works, but women are distressed by the efflorescence of brown discolorations around their mouth, forehead and eyes, and the upsetting of the hormone balance in the vagina which affects lubrication and sensitivity, and the inhibition of sexual desire itself. The Pill is a crude medication and prospects for its eventual refinement are poor.

The woman who comes to terms with her pill does not automatically emerge into the paradise of efficient contraception. Exhausted, hysterical, drunk, drugged or miserable, she still has to remember to take it. She is told to establish a routine, but routine is what enslaves us and takes all the savour out of living. Routine actions are performed without thinking, and can easily be forgotten. Moreover the Pill is destructible; it can be dropped down the plughole, eaten by the children or the dog, or lost when the airline loses your luggage, and you cannot get any replacements until you have seen a doctor, got a new prescription and gone to the chemist, and started all over again with a new cycle. Perhaps the manufacturers should append a few supernumerary ones like spare buttons for a cardigan. Perhaps the doctors should be freer with prescriptions so that you have one for emergencies, but it would never be in the right place at the right time. The Pill can become tyrannical all right.

The Intrauterine Contraceptive Devices are said to provide perfect contraception for three in four women. The incidence of failure is too high to guarantee much peace of mind even for the woman who is using one and getting away with it. Horror stories of infants born with the coil embedded in the fontanelle, of complete prolapses necessitating hysterectomy, of massive abdominal infection, may not reflect the likely destiny of the one-in-four who find that they cannot tolerate the device, but tranquillity and security are important motivations for adopting any method of contraception and the IUD seems deficient in reassurance. For one thing, doctors are not sure how it works. Opponents of abortion might do well to reflect upon the possibility that loops and coils are abortifacient, in that they cause the shedding of the fertilized ovum by provoking constant irritation of the uterine wall.

Even if foams and creams and diaphragms worked better than they do, their effect on love's careless rapture would be a sufficient deterrent from using them. The volume of spermicide and its texture severely affects local sensitivity and it tastes terrible. Of course it is not intended for internal consumption, a situation that speaks for itself. The circumstances of application can be embarrassing beyond recovery. The course of D. H. Lawrence's novel would have gone awry if Lady Chat. had to rush off to fetch her diaphragm. It might have flown out of her hurrying fingers and landed in a cowpat or an anthill. One can grow to love one's diaphragm, but it is hardly worth the effort.

There is a newish alternative. In New Zealand many women are having three-monthly intramuscular injections of Depo Provera 150, the trade name of medroxyprogesterone acetate, which inhibits ovulation and menstruation, and so controls fertility. There are side effects in eighty per cent of patients in the first month, but these taper off with continued use of the drug, which is not recommended for short-term contraception, because its effects last longer than the three-month period which is accepted as the safe margin for continued protection.

The women who are using this method are jubilant, and once more I hoped that Depo Provera would be the answer to a non-maiden's prayer, but it is, after all, no more than a delayed-action dose of synthetic progesterone. It relieves women of the day-to-day fuss of contraception, and of menstruation, but it interferes with other processes connected with physical comfort (for continued spotting is a nuisance) and sexual pleasure (it has a marked anti-oestrogenic effect on the vaginal epithelium).

The possibilities of effecting birth control by manipulation of the female reproductive system seem, after all, to be limited. The brightest hope for the future may well be chemical abortifacients, to be used as vaginal pessaries as soon as the menstrual period is thought to be delayed. This method represents the least possible interference in the general health of the woman, but those people who believe that any removal of the fertilized ovum from the womb is murder will probably use all their considerable influence to ensure that such a comfortable situation never eventuates, although it may well be that it is the only way in which women may maintain their own hormonal rhythm and endocrine balance, and the spontaneity of their sexual behaviour.

Raped women in refugee camps

Sunday Times, 9 April 1972

The heroes of the Hindu epic, *Mahabharata*, sprang from the loins of Queen Draupadi, a woman so extraordinary that five brothers decided to marry her, in order that their line be sure to incorporate hers. The fortunes of war so chanced that the five of them lost her in a gambling match with an invading king. When she was presented to him as war booty, Draupadi denied her husbands' right to dispose of her, claiming that she was a person in her own right and could only lose herself. The stranger king mocked her claims, pulled her on to his knee and snatched at her sari, so that she might be seen naked by the soldiers and humiliated. Draupadi prayed to Lord Krishna to protect her and as the infidel tore at her sari it unwound and unwound eternally. Upon it were woven miraculously the stories of the *Mahabharata*: Queen Draupadi and her issue were not dishonoured.

Genocide has two manifestations, as the story from the *Mahabharata* might be taken to illustrate. As well as the massacre of the menfolk, babies in arms and especially those who might prove leaders, the women must be impregnated with the spawn of the conqueror. From all accounts the West Pakistani troops in East Bengal obeyed both parts of the order to the letter. Among the evidence in the forthcoming war-crimes trials are said to be written memoranda from commanding officers recommending that the Punjabis redeem the inferior Bengali race with a plentiful injection of their nobler blood.

Mrs Budrunnesa Ahmad, one of the seven women elected to the National Assembly of Pakistan, claimed, even before the liberation of Bangladesh, that women were the worst sufferers during the massacre by the Pakistani Army. The organizers of the refugee programme in West Bengal were well aware of the problem of raped women, but even in the relatively controlled camp situation they found that there was little that they could do to alleviate the sufferings of women whose lives had been destroyed with the destruction of their personal honour and self-esteem, their *izzat*. The lot of the women who made it across the frontier, some of them hideously wounded with sharpened bamboo stakes and bayonets, was, on the whole, better than that of the women kept to serve the Pakistani army as cooks, body servants and whores. Even so, the Bengali women who were sent into the camps to seek out the women who needed surgical intervention or psychiatric care found that the raped women would not talk. As long as they could do so furtively, they came for abortions, but any attempt at a public campaign proved futile. In the special camps where unaccompanied girls from Bangladesh were taught skills, the ones whose pregnancy began to show were quietly removed.

When Mother Teresa went to Dacca two days after its liberation, she found the embarrassed Indian Army trying to care for three thousand women who had been found naked in the bunkers abandoned by the Paks. Their nakedness was not solely the result of Pak eroticism; their saris had been taken away so that the women could not run away, or hang themselves in them. Many of them were no sooner given saris than they did hang themselves. Many of them, after months of indiscriminate sexual usage, were heavily pregnant. Mother Teresa found the problem so urgent that she devoted her efforts in Bangladesh to it. An international inquiry committee was called for at a public meeting presided over by the poet, Begum Sufia Kamal. The Planned Parenthood Federation set up abortion clinics in Bangladesh. Mother Teresa found houses where the women could await the offspring of hate, and adoptive parents for them in Germany and Switzerland.

The exact extent of the problem is not known. Peasants in a border district near Tripura tell of Pak soldiers bringing naked women roped together down to the river to be washed. A youth, saved from machine-gun massacre by the bodies of the other men in the huge group with whom he was travelling to the border, told Colonel Luthra, Secretary for Refugee Rehabilitation, that when he crept out from under the corpses, only the old people and the children in the huge group remained. All attempts to trace the women with whom they had travelled have been in vain. The World Council of Churches estimated the number of abducted women at two hundred thousand; another official estimate at three hundred thousand. Some Indian officials quote the figure of half a million, which, when one considers the possibilities of nine months of rapine by ninety-three thousand men, may not be as unrealistic as it seems at first. The only people who know, the women themselves, are not talking.

Some of the insolubility of the problem is the result of the fact that, unjustly, rape is the one crime of violence which throws more shame on the victim than on the perpetrator. Sheikh Mujib tried to address himself to this aspect, when he besought the young men of Bangladesh to honour the tortured women as war heroines and to marry them. The Bangladesh Women's Rehabilitation Programme announced proudly that hundreds of young men, many of them graduates, had come forward in response to the call. Nevertheless, the sheikh's attempt to equate sexual bondage with heroic resistance is unconvincing and marriage for pity's sake is hardly a good augury for lifelong cohabitation. Bengali women were so oppressed by brutalizing toil and repeated childbirth, that it is too much to expect that some of them did not capitulate to their captors, or did not feel ambivalently towards this new form of servitude. In any case, the suspicion will abide, because they did not take the option of death. If they had been educated in resistance, they might have murdered their oppressors in their weaker moments and died for it. As it is, they are now taking the tragic option of suicide.

Bangladesh is paying, as other nations have paid before, the price of having reared its women in a tradition of powerlessness and servility. Sheikh Mujib has announced that women will be brought to fully equal status in Bangladesh and that religion will no longer condemn them to ignorance and a housebound existence, but for too many women that promise is an impossibility and a cruel mockery.

In the chaos that is Bangladesh, new guilts compound the old. Even the women who chanced upon Mother Teresa's loving care are running away to the hospitals where European doctors are perfecting techniques of late-term abortion by Caesarean section. Destitute women in isolated areas are walking away from new-born Punjabis or smothering them.

Many women will love and care for children whose tell-tale features will condemn them to a lifetime of proscription. Still more are desperately lying, trying to blot out the memory of the nightmare of 1971, which the war-crimes trials will regurgitate for years to come.

If ever you doubted that women must be capable of self-defence and fighting alongside their men for a measure of liberty and self-determination (and I must confess that I doubted it myself), then the time gives it proof. It behoves the students of sexual politics not only to examine the psychology and the politics of rape, but also to commit themselves to a policy which would make rape impossible. We cannot now, and we could not ever, trust to Queen Draupadi's endless sari or the intervention of mystical religion. Psychopathic bullies must not inherit the earth.

Abortion i

Sunday Times, 7 May 1972

It was predictable that the Catholics and proto-Catholics would mount an anti-abortion campaign, and little short of inevitable that their first public demonstration should take place in Liverpool, where abortions are almost impossible to get. However dubious one may feel about the Catholic bishops' belated discovery that the foetus is not the only one with problems and mother could do with a hand, at least the Thomist position has the relative merit of rigour and consistency, neither of which characterizes the utterances of the newly formed 'Liberals Against Abortion' group.

Doubtless the sentiments behind the Catholic initiative to talk mothers-to-be-or-not-to-be into having their children is saintly and disinterested, but if even Mother Teresa cannot resist the temptation to religious imperialism, and places the Pak-Bengali children born in her homes only in Catholic families (thus totting up one more something beautiful for God) it is unlikely that the Bishop of Leeds will do otherwise.

In most cases of sudden and unwelcome pregnancy, the intrusion of some celibate or senile, reformed reprobate persuading you to have the baby is the last thing you desire. The friends of the foetus are not the ones who are going to go through the changes in mind and body which accompany pregnancy or the trauma of birth or the sudden bereavement of adoption or the day-to-day struggle of bringing up the fruit of their persuasions.

The pressure which these interfering Christians bring to bear upon the pregnant woman is not different in kind or less excusable than the charade daily mounted by those doctors and psychiatrists who decree therapeutic abortions. The woman who persuades herself that her abortion is justified because a gaggle of professional men have said so is in just as serious trouble with herself as the woman who knows that she does not want her baby but has been overawed by the Bishop of Leeds and his apostles.

The question, as in all matters of sin and innocence, is one of will. None of us is morally adult until we can take responsibility for our own actions; the abortion law, in its present ambiguous state, pre-empts the woman's right to decide and vests it in a (most often male) group who have no opportunity and less desire to investigate and take responsibility for the results of their *ex-cathedra* decisions. By the time a woman comes to ask for an abortion she has made her personal decision and even if the doctors and psychiatrists to whom she talks should set it aside, she is still stuck with the guilt of her own attitude. Her decision is most often a completely rational one, but in order to have it ratified by the medical Sanhedrin, she must behave as if she is incapable of a rational decision, pretending that her sanity is threatened by the birth of a child. If she is highly skilled in the manifestations of hysteria, she might even manage an abortion on the National Health.

That is what 'therapeutic' abortion most often amounts to.

The compromise notion of 'therapeutic' abortion is a feeble-minded evasion of the fact that a woman who does not want her child will try her hardest to destroy it, and if she fails she will none the less be as thoroughly inculpated as if she succeeds. The woman who does not manifest by outward gesture her resentment of the child which has invaded her body, is more, not less, likely to be beset by guilt and malice in her relationship to it. Day by day the petty crimes of inarticulate misery mount up. The unwitting child becomes an occasion of sin. If Malcolm Muggeridge and Leo Abse and James Dunn and the Most Reverend George Beck are so anxious to salve their own consciences, what do they propose for the mother who is condemned by them to sin diurnally? If Malcolm Muggeridge can make the audacious connection between abortion and euthanasia, how can he not see the much more likely one between unwantedness and the fact that most baby-battering mothers are pregnant at the time of the offence and battered children are most often illegitimate or born within nine months of marriage?

The rigorous Catholic position is that there is no real difference between battering a conscious, sentient child piecemeal to death and sucking a lump of jelly with remarkable potential out of the uterus. Both are murder most foul. Casuistically we may allow sickly creatures to die but we cannot interfere in the course of nature to kill them, even *in utero*. Nature is thereby equated with the will of God, although it is also nature's way to shed as many as one in three fertilized ova because they are genetically or otherwise defective.

The Catholic argument seems untenable, but not entirely contemptible. 'Liberals Against Abortion', on the other hand, wallow in myopia and confusion. To be sure, the present abortion law is calamitous, but not for the reasons that Kevan Logan and his muddle-headed (male) friends suppose. At the moment it is possible to get an abortion, but if abortion is right in principle then possible is not good enough, it must also be cheap, quick, safe and easy. Those who object to that idea, need not undergo the procedure; it is hardly coincidental that few of them could reasonably expect to.

The notion that Logan, Mumford, Walsh and Wilson have somehow got, that the present situation amounts to abortion on demand, is absurd. Abortion on the National Health is virtually impossible to get, for reasons as irrelevant to medical considerations as may be. The hospitals are overcrowded with willing mothers; abortion patients must find themselves on a waiting list, if they are lucky enough to persuade the doctors that an abortion in their case is justified, which is much harder than it is in the case of private practitioners, most of whom are not simply greedy, but incidentally in favour of abortion in principle as well. Then demand is translated into exorbitant payment. The National Health patient does not have to pay money, but she does have to pay in humiliation, delay and uncertainty. Most girls do not even bother to try to manipulate such an unpromising situation.

Belated abortions, and hospitalization and antiquated methods in National Health abortions are a gross waste of public money. Properly performed abortions do not necessitate hospitalization or even use of general anaesthetic. The fact that high prices are being paid to doctors who are becoming full-time millionaire abortionists is a natural consequence of leaving the decision in the hands of medical cartels. Closing of private clinics will simply mean that we revert to the situation as it was before the law was changed; abortions might even cost less because the practitioners don't have to pay taxes or do so much paper work.

The truth is, despite the fantasies of the Liberals Against Abortion, that abortions are more expensive and more laborious to get than they were five years ago. What we need is a mass of people for abortion.

Abortion ii

Sunday Times, 21 May 1972

The friends of the foetus are a contentious lot. No sooner had they twigged that my last column was written in favour of abortion than they sprang to their escritoires and dashed off screeds full of quaint formulae which a less charitable soul than I am would simply dub misspellings. Many of them seemed to have an idea that the Bishop of Leeds was running a day-nursery. One woman announced that 'a woman's power lies not in her readiness to jump into bed with every Tom, Dick and Harry to prove how emancipated they are, but in their ability to stay out of bed at all costs,' a notion which seems at least to suffer from a paucity of alternatives, not to mention a certain grammatical blight.

It is easy for the pro-abortion lobby to sneer at the polemical flailings of the anti-abortionists, but their cause will suffer for their complacency, as it already has in New York, where the amended abortion laws were recently repealed. Well-known humanitarian Richard Nixon, at the same time as he was authorizing bombing of non-military targets in North Vietnam without consent of Congress, announced his support for the Catholic position on abortion.

Intellectual incapacity is not a disqualification from power. Truth will not out unless everyone struggles to discern his own truth and fight the armies of sophistry and vulgar error. And so I do repeat myself, for I about must and about must go to climb the crag of truth, even though those readers who have kept the knickers column I did a year ago fast in their wallets, have the impression that my mind never rises above my belt. (I do occasionally stand on my head.)

If anyone else sends me a picture of a sixteen-week foetus, with the disingenuous question whether or not it looks like a lump of jelly, I may run amok. It is so much easier to grieve over the 'innocent' homunculus, than to consider the sinful, sexual creature who carried it in her womb for sixteen weeks. She may have lost a wanted child, a sad business and infinitely muckier and more destructive than a medically induced abortion (yes, yes, both have happened to me), in which case the object of pity is not the undeveloped humanoid thing which she has shed, but herself, as every hospital knows. Or she may have had an abortion, for which she has waited three months, poor soul.

The guilt of destroying sixteen-week foetuses is not that of the women who would terminate their pregnancies, but of the cumbersome system which forces them to wait so unnecessarily and to submit themselves futilely to the gamut of changes that lead to parturition. The essence of moral abortion practice is speediness. Delay is danger, guilt, misery and waste.

I am romantic enough to believe that bearing a child is a marvellous, as well as a taxing experience; rather like climbing Mount Everest or learning the Bible off by heart, it is only rewarding if it is spontaneously undertaken. A man forced up Mount Everest at gunpoint or because he could not earn a living any other way, or the miserable child conning his Bible text for fear of the rod, has no knowledge of the pleasure in achievement which could attend the operation.

It is not as if our society greets the newborn with joy and makes of the mother a heroine, as it once did. Girls who become midwives because of their delight in bringing infants into the world are often baffled by the apathy which greets the new arrivals. Once born, the child's chief function is to inhabit the children's ghetto, to be not even seen by adults, let alone heard. An Indian wandering through the streets of London on almost any day, might be pardoned for imagining that the British had abolished childhood. Women's liberation means, among other things, the liberation of mothers and children to full participation in society. Imagine, women bringing their children to work, like the road-building women of India do.

It is not women who have downgraded motherhood, but Western society itself. Those people who in their raging letters to me most extol the joys of motherhood, are the same who glare at the woman on the tube because she cannot keep her child quiet and still. A society which pretends to honour motherhood while it forces lactating women to hunt for hiding places where they may give their infants the breast is utterly hypocritical.

Compulsory motherhood is not ennobling, although the friends of the foetus are at pains to point out that most women denied abortions end up loving their issue just the same. Whether they love them *just the same* as they would have if they had wanted them is of course unverifiable; most women are not so perverse and unjust as to punish their children for the crimes of society (their fathers), but the oppression of their circumstances is real notwithstanding. For the oppressors themselves to take credit for the women's magnanimity is sickeningly smug. The compelled mother loves her child as the caged bird sings. The song does not justify the cage nor the love the enforcement.

One of my correspondents was more rigorous than usual: 'With her progressive ideas,' she wrote, 'I wonder why she doesn't encourage her followers to buy themselves a Karman cannula to enable them to abort themselves ... it would save our overworked doctors (and nurses) from being pressurized ... into breaking the enlightened Hypocratic (sic) oath and turning themselves into butchers.'

The assumption that I have followers is unjustified, and so is the idea that I do not support self-help in abortion. Women's liberationists would limit their use of the Karman cannula to themselves. Women are already training as paramedical workers who will use the cannula and teach its use to other women. They are prepared to go to gaol for using it, if the formulation of the abortion laws includes the techniques of menstrual extraction among criminal practices.

I am prepared to help finance such a programme, to work in it and to go to gaol for it, if necessary.

Abortion iii:
Killing no murder

Spare Rib, July 1972

This essay ought to have been the third in my abortion trilogy in the Sunday
Times, *appearing on 4 June. When it was dropped without explanation, I offered
it to* Spare Rib, *who commented:*

> *Germaine Greer has had a regular column in the* Sunday Times *for a year. In recent weeks she
> has been discussing abortion and her proposal for a women's health centre. Why did the* Sunday
> Times *suddenly refuse to print the following column on June 4th?*

'She,' wrote one of my harassed editor's correspondents last week, 'is
capable of killing and many of us are not.' Yes, indeed, I am capable of
killing but so, I would have thought, is the writer of the letter, and so are
you, dear reader.

I grew up in an atmosphere of carnage. Because flies clustering around
the eyes give children trachoma, and crawling on food give them gastroen-
teritis, we were brought up not to 'chase that fly!' but to bash, mash and
poison them whenever possible. The unauthorized entry of a blowfly into
the house had us vowing bloody murder, holding our breaths until that
mother-to-be was gasping her last, while her young streamed across the
windowpane from her ruptured womb.

With blithe disregard of the food chain we bombarded mosquitoes with
DDT, because little kids scratch the bites until their legs are pitted with
purple craters.

But the commandment makes no exceptions. 'Thou shalt not kill,' is
what it says.

One of the more memorable massacres of my early youth concerned a
colony of red-backed spiders living in a rockery which my mother, in the
spirit of a sergeant major at Puckapunyal, told me to shift. My small sister
was fooling around me as I toiled back and forth with the rocks, while the
spiders streamed out of the clefts which I unearthed. The bite of that
spider will kill a small child, and perhaps a big one, so I chased every one
before Jane could pick it up and thumped it with a piece of Lilydale rock,
until the underside of my weapon was thickly larded with mashed corpses
and waving disembodied legs. Their entrails were a warm caramel colour.
My sister has grown up to be the mother of two beautiful sons, one of
whom is called after Archbishop Mannix.

The next hardening of my spirit occurred when I went to stay with a family who earned a good living on Lord Howe Island, by farming and butchery and fishing. I was sent off to plunder the rock pools of a double-header cod, because one of our customers particularly required that form of protein. To my despair, I learnt that the only bait the cod would take was a live crab. For the first twenty minutes I presented the crab to the hook, hoping that they would join without any direct violence on my part, but at length I stabbed the barb into the underside of the crab's belly, and then damn me if the creature didn't wave its eyes about in distress and clasp the line with its pincers.

And I caught my double-header; the next day I landed a twenty-five-pound kingfish on a twelve-pound line, bloody to the elbows and cut to the bone by the handline. The fish would pant and suffer in the sack because we had to keep them alive and so fresh. On such hecatombs is human superiority nourished. To the primitive abattoir I dared not go, but I ate the cows I had milked, with relish.

Kill then, I can, but only just. If I had been a Roman slave commanded to hold my master's sword while he fell upon it, I should surely have bungled it. The noble suicide would find the weapon in his eye or his knee. That's the horrifying part, the pusillanimous failure of nerve.

Dozens of sick cats have found their way to the mercy-killing vet in my hands, except for one which chose to be injured on Good Friday when not a vet in Sydney was answering his phone. I should have split its skull with a hammer, but I couldn't so I threw it off a very high bridge. It swam for two or three seconds.

Once in Calabria I spent a whole night trying to kill an inoffensive gecko, because the peasants had assured me that it was a salamander, whose bite would make me swell up all over and die. Holding my oil-lamp above my head I beat away at it with the broom, sobbing to it to die, but it struggled on until I crawled off to bed and dreamed of bloating to an awful death. Morning found it horribly swollen and still not dead. The small child who polished it off with his toy spade told me offhand, '*Bisogna chaivarlo ben in testa*' (an untranslatable joke for you Italian speakers), so no wonder I couldn't do it. The gecko is, of course, harmless, and, as the friends of the foetus say, innocent; I could have been subject to what the editor's correspondent calls 'murky feelings of guilt and self-dislike' if I had been sufficiently irrational and masochistic.

Irrational and masochistic to a point I certainly am. The only time I was ever assaulted, I urged myself to counterattack quite uselessly. 'The carotid artery . . .' I thought desperately, as my head rang from the blows, 'the testicles . . . pressure points . . .' but I also thought 'but you might kill him'. I should have been thinking, 'He might kill me . . .' But there you are.

If some friend of mine asked me in his agony to help him to end his life, my only reason for refusing would be, not fear of imprisonment or imagined fealty to a commandment I have broken, wittingly or unwittingly all my life, but because I'd be afraid of such a failure of nerve, afraid to botch it. For even if we interpret the commandment as meaning 'Thou shalt not kill (human beings)' it is hugely disregarded, and by living in the civilizations in which we do, we condone this disregard. The baffled soldier, following orders originating *in coram populo*, accepts breaking the commandment as an occupational risk, regardless of his own guilt and horror. In fact the commandment does not even say 'Thou shalt not kill (anybody else)'. The nuns taught me that it also means 'Thou shalt take proper care of thy own health and life'. People sin against that part of the commandment every time they light a cigarette or eat saturated fats or drink too much or hit their favourite drug, be it caffeine or cocaine, or overwork themselves, either for mere money or for Oxfam. The woman who submits her body to the powerful and mysterious chemistry of the contraceptive pill commits a sin against the commandment every time. Childbirth, inasmuch as it is much more dangerous than abortion, especially if we consider what proportion of the abortion risk is due to anaesthetic procedures, is a greater sin against that part of the commandment.

Abortion is killing right enough, but killing what? Is it more like killing a fly or killing a Vietnamese peasant? Or is it like torturing the fish for nourishment? How much regret is appropriate? Such difficulties have been called inconsistencies, but really they are paradoxes. Those of us who hope to be moral beings cannot shirk the discomfort of the paradoxes and skulk in the security of a rule, especially not if we intend the rule to apply mostly to other people's behaviour. It does seem that the killing of a foetus involves more the later it happens; it might have something to do with the development of the brain synapses in the organism, as well as its developing potential for separate life. The distinction is something like the one we make between the death of a fly and the death of a cat and the death of a child. I would flatly disallow the killing of born human beings against their will on any pretext, judicial or military or hygienic. One of the paradoxes is that most pro-abortionists are anti-war and most anti-abortionists are not anti-war. Fellow killer, how does it seem to you?

Hippies in Asia

Sunday Times, 27 August 1972

The reign of the flower children was inevitably short. Within a year or two rock groups were producing sentimental intermezzi called 'Summer '67' and using the term 'hippie' pejoratively. Nowadays the Underground prefers names which are boring for a different reason, like 'the alternative society' or 'youth culture'.

However jejune, not to say weak-minded, the hippie alternative may appear from this end of the telescope, it had its unforgettable moments, like Woburn Abbey in '67 and the 'Legalize Marijuana' rallies. The time of our time then coalesces into a long afternoon suffused with golden light, when Eric Clapton would have been God if it had not been for Jimi Hendrix, and women wore their hair floating, after a generation of bouffants and beehives and urchin cuts, and people passed the joint from hand to hand and row to row, even in the Paramount Cinema.

Brief though the reign may have been, its marks are upon our society still, and many of them are good ones. Marijuana is basically a good habit, or at least a better habit than the blues and black bombers that preceded it among the kids, or the alcohol that their parents absorbed. You would have thought that because marijuana is most often an aphrodisiac and sedative in its effect, the authorities would have set up cannabis farms, but all they did was to forfeit the respect of the young by talking palpable nonsense about something they too clearly knew nothing about, so undermining the sway of law and order in the unformed mind. And even when the lotus-eaters perceived that whatever is, is not necessarily right, those of a less somnolent disposition decided that whatever is, is wrong. The conservative character of youth was radically altered and that impetus continues. It makes no odds that the radical young are a minority, although any teacher knows too well that they are; for most political purposes a minority will suffice.

Phenomena which are in themselves superficial may have profound effects. When young men grew their hair, a great many pin-headed or coarse-featured people became suddenly finely proportioned. Being unexpectedly beautiful they found themselves able to behave unexpectedly well. Long hair and the mystique of gentleness brought the sexes together quite unconsciously and so other developments became possible. People made better love, and more of it, than before, for which relief much thanks.

The uniformity of long hair has receded to a less slavish adaption of hair lengths to the individual's own notion of his best looks, which must be a good thing in that it reduces the amount of ugliness in the world. The way was beset with pitfalls, like the megalomaniacal Pancho Villa moustaches which the less secure struggled to put forth, but they too will wither away except where their becomingness overrides the tyranny of fashion. It is something to be grateful for, that men are so much better-looking than they were.

Clothing is no longer a single cult which all must practise in the same way, only well or badly. One may now dress quixotically or sentimentally or satirically or gorgeously, at will. It is no longer necessary to wait for a costume party to get out the thirties dressing-gown embroidered with hollyhocks or that ragged Tunisian wedding dress. Everyone wears motley.

So much for the superficial observation of the way in which the pluralism of society absorbed the mandates of hippiedom. Ecology was a hippie issue, and its taking up will leave very little that is fundamental unchanged. Diet became a narcissistic fetish of the hippies, but the effects of new consciousness about ruinous Western eating habits will proliferate. The hippie balance-sheet has much solid value in the credit column, but there is, after so much, something else to be said.

The hippie is the scion of surplus value. The dropout can only claim sanctity in a society which offers something to be dropped out of – career, ambition, conspicuous consumption. The effects of hippie sanctimony can only be felt in the context of others who plunder his lifestyle for what they find good or profitable, a process known as rip-off by the hippie, who will not see how savagely he has pillaged intricate and demanding civilizations for his own parodic lifestyle. Those who fled and still flee their homelands to wander in India or Nepal or Mexico or Bali are grotesque parasites upon peoples who cannot afford them and have nothing to learn from them. The hollow-eyed youth begging in Connaught Place in a travesty of a dhoti will take money from the poorest people in the world, although when they are forced to go to war as an indirect result of the policies of his homeland, he can and does cable home for more money than they can ever hope to see in a lifetime, by way of an air-ticket the hell out of there.

The smugness of hippie communities disporting themselves wherever the weather is good enough, regardless of the political climate, is repulsive and unpardonable. Their disregard of the customs and the decorum of the civilizations which they invade is no better than contempt. For all their reverence for the ecology, they cannot see themselves as pollution. Hippie assumptions of saintly poverty are compromised by their forms of commerce, buying up local drugs and artefacts at the cheapest price, to flog them at inflation rates in another country. The function of the tourist, however lamentably, is to provide foreign exchange; the hippie cannot claim even this service for the cultures he invades. Only the hippie has the arrogance to suppose that he is part of the solution rather than the problem.

No cruel ignorance is greater than that of the Western maharajah posing as a beggar, who says with utter complacency, 'Oh man, I don't have any news media in my house. I've got to hang loose', as if life were a mere matter of scoring and staying high. Marie Antoinette went to the guillotine for less.

The Other Woman

Sunday Times, 10 September 1972

I have it on the authority of one of the senior ladies of Fleet Street that 'If wives don't make the big effort to keep their men at home, there is absolutely no shortage of other women only too willing to make a takeover bid.' It really is time that somebody spoke up on behalf of the Other Woman; these wifely journalists have had things their own way for far too long. It is understandable that loving wives should imagine that their meal ticket is absolutely desirable, and I dare say it shows a touching loyalty, but it is not at all short of raving paranoia to suppose that the world throngs with rapacious women ready to swoop at the first sign of conjugal boredom and carry the guileless males off to their lairs.

Let it be first of all established that more sagging husbands fancy unattached women than are fancied by them. Other Women have to listen to more maudlin and dishonest tales from husbands about their wives' shortcomings than they ever willingly elicit, and few gambits are more repulsive. More passes are made at unattached women by attached men than vice versa, but you will never convince the sob-sisters of that simple fact.

I may perhaps be permitted to cite an example from real life, of how wifely paranoia distorts reality. Because the bus service in the Midlands town where I live is notoriously inadequate, I usually hitchhike to the university. Anyone who is going my way and feels like offering me car room is my prey and my object is no more than that – a lift. At a university social one of my colleagues from another department reminded me that we had already met, when he had given me a lift. His wife sailed into me at once; she seemed to be convinced that my motive for hitchhiking was to waylay her husband, to oust her and to steal her children's father away. Perhaps I ought to have been flattered, she was so sure that I oozed fatal charm, but instead I was uncharitably mystified that she should have thought her cringing husband such a catch.

To be sure, now and then your Other Woman does fancy somebody's husband, but she usually cares only to borrow him for a night or two, perhaps a month or so. If she is an Other Woman by choice (strange as it may seem to a devoted housewife, she is not the universally envied creature she imagines herself – there are indeed women who have other ambitions) she does not leap into bed with a husband view matrimony, but simply view bed. That simple specificity constitutes the Other Woman's most attractive characteristic for most husbands, even those who are not at all bored with their marriage situation. When sex is degraded by being used as a lure or reward for the breadwinner, great strength is added to the Other Woman's hand, because she likes sex for itself, but Mrs Journalist-and-Mother can only counsel more of the same.

Apparently, the way to pacify a restless husband is to treat him like one of the mackintosh brigade. 'When he comes home from work, be wearing only one of his shirts, black tights and high-heeled shoes.' So there you are, looking like a reincarnation of Zizi Jeanmaire 1958; it is not at all clear whether foot fetishism or nostalgia is being invoked here, and even less clear whether the Grand Lady of hack journalism has tested the method for herself. Later on she advises cooking the dinner with nothing on but an apron, a risky procedure if you're frying anything or fetching things out of the oven, let alone if you usually wear spectacles, like she does. 'Shop around for a suspender belt and black stockings. Scatter a few girlie magazines round the house.' What do you do if he is insulted by such a coarse view of what turns him on? What do you do if he is only turned on by multiple amputees?

A marriage to be saved must be turned into a coarse burlesque show, according to this champion of the threatened wife. Of course, she is not alone in her belief that male sexuality is as commercialized and predictable as what is offered the deprived strip-show audiences at inflated prices. She might have directed her avid readers to an unforgettable book by Libby Jones, called *How to Undress in Front of Your Husband*. The only things missing in this account are the old man's comments as Jones's pupil goes through her tedious paces, say, turns her back and, bending slightly at the knees and swaying the hips, works down one side of the panties at a time to the top of her cleavage. Then she is to grab the sides of the panties firmly in both hands and work them below her buttocks in a series of short wiggles. 'Stop! Give him one of those "Are you still with me" looks (he will be)' and so on until the panties are off and being scrunched 'modestly' over the mons. The account of pantie removing ends 'You're on your own from here' – you couldn't blame the old man for slipping off to the pub.

If coming on like an unimaginative professional tease doesn't inflame a husband's desires, and buying boots and wigs and rubber undies and knouts and scourges and nuns' habits proves useless, then apparently you've to make the poor fool jealous, short of actually getting into any but the connubial bed of course. There follows a series of transparent stratagems for setting the hapless husband at it, sending yourself flowers and chocolates and billets-doux, praising his family, his driving, his football team, making love in unusual places, such as the bath and the floor (which, it is assumed, you have never tried before). The children must be banished during these manoeuvres, for they are assumed to be deadly anaphrodisiac.

As an Other Woman of long standing I ought to congratulate myself that marriage should be so threadbare and tawdry, if I were able to act in character, that is. Most often, would you believe, the Other Woman finds her strange libidinousness rejected eventually for the comforts of home and the sweetness of children. Most husbands, however their wives agonize over their extracurricular activities, cannot handle a mistress, in or out of the house. Most husbands who are not making love to their wives are not making love to anybody, black stockings and suspender belts regardless. And despite all the Grand Lady's care for the morals of the monogamous housewife, a great many Other Women have husbands of their own.

The Big Tease

Harper's Monthly Magazine, October 1972

The weather in Miami reminded me of Vietnam, the same rank heaviness in the air whacking sullenly against the rotor blades of the military heli-copters and the same filthy skirts that the airliners trailed across the livid sky. The fumes that clouded the freeway came from the exhausts of vast carapaces of metal shielding their soft-bodied drivers, instead of the million Hondas that infest South Vietnam, but the root cause of the ecological disaster is the same. The soldiers billeted in Miami Beach High School had the faces of American soldiers anywhere, and the non-delegates lived like refugees in their pup tents in Flamingo Park. The whores threading through the gloaming of the plush bars used the same lines and chewed the same gum.

Saturation bombing and defoliation and cloud-seeding are not the only disasters that the USA has inflicted upon Vietnam; they may not even be the worst. American money is the central reality in the war-made metro-polis of Saigon; it reaches into every area of life, civil and military, so that it has almost destroyed the last vestiges of an individual civilization. The withdrawal of every last American soldier will not eradicate the traces of big business and gangsterism, even though the money will depart when the soldiers can no longer protect its interests and consume its heroin, and when the military supplies no longer stock the black market and there are no more lucrative currency deals to be made. America will leave behind a nation of whores, pushers, beggars, spies, petty spivs, racketeers, cripples, and disaffected mercenaries who have learned how to use their guns for robbery and looting.

It is not only American policy that has laid waste Vietnam, but the nature of the American economy and the cast of its civilization. Buy or die is the message. Those who buy the free enterprise system escape massacre and economic ostracism, but their culture grows leprous with the absorption of cannibal values. Imperialism is not a vice practised by certain depraved characters, but the mode of operation that characterizes economies that must keep expanding in order to survive. To blame Richard Nixon is weak-minded; to hope that a nice man from South Dakota will reverse the process is plumb crazy – but that is what I and thousands of other radic-libs did.

Who knows? Economic analyses of American hegemony might be false, might be emotional reactions caused by an overaesthetic response to Holiday Inns and Thick Shakes. Perhaps distrust of international corporate capitalism is but a feeling after all, seeing how few radicals really understand it, business know-how on that level being a prerogative of the practitioners.

It has become for many of us essential to believe that there is a way out. Humanists are not anxious to accept the idea that man is now ruled by the machine. Democrats believe that the people can take power again in the name of the Constitution, notwithstanding Nixon's accomplishments without a Republican majority in either house. If the President's personal power makes him virtually uncontrollable, the solution is not to abolish the office, it seems, but to choose a good man for President (as if Nixon were not himself, by his own lights, an extremely virtuous person, appalled by dirty words, if not by dirty money). The most cynical of us needs to sing 'We Shall Overcome' occasionally. After years of guilt about our standard of living and education, the colour of our skins, and our unconscious assumption of ethnic superiority, the middle-class radic-libs desperately need a chance to feel *good* again.

I struggled to retain a modicum of Marxian good sense, but the drag of desire pulled me away so many times that despite myself I began to hope madly that McGovern was a superman, that the convention was open, that the people were really the people, autonomous and honest, and not mere pawns for the men who were marketing McGovern. From the first time I had ever heard the man's name, he had been praised by people I loved and respected, Americans Abroad for McGovern. At best, so it was said, he was incapable of lying, at worst he was our Only Hope.

If I were going to hold hard to my economic analysis of American politics, then I could most easily be seduced into support for McGovern by a better economist. When Kenneth Galbraith beamed on me with all the tender optimism he had been amassing during the campaign, irrational hope gained another toehold. When Arthur Miller explained fervently how important it was that McGovern get a chance to realize the issues for which American liberals had been fighting against tremendous odds all their lives, I felt like a destructive child wrecking my own source of happiness. Amerika cannot be willed out of existence, so it must be changed. Violent revolution is more likely from the military-industrial complex than from the faction-torn, informer-ridden, rhetoric-stoned Left, whose futile gestures towards it simply provide the sanction for more grinding forms of repression. Non-violent revolution would require more time than anybody thinks we have. McGovern offered a chance, albeit slender, of a change for the slightly better: more Nixon threatened a change for the much worse. Arthur Miller announced the familiar warning: 'If this man wins another term, the Supreme Court will be castrated, and the *New York Times* will be a single mimeographed page.' Upon reflection, neither eventuality seemed as unlikely as it should have.

For many, McGovern appeared like a new prophet, a healer of society who could not function without faith. 'You gotta *believe,*' they would say. Flo Kennedy, the black attorney from New York who had arranged the Feminist party activities at the convention, explained it in her own vivid way. 'Honey, this man McGovern is like a paper cup. You turn him up empty and put a chair leg on him and he'll collapse. You fill him up with sand and put a lid on him and turn him up, and he'll hold the chair and anyone who sits on him. The people are the sand; they've gotta make him what they want him to be.' Lack of faith in McGovern was lack of faith in oneself, or loserism, as Flo calls it. 'There's a whole lotta people out there who are afraid to win because they don't think of themselves as running the show. They've been niggerized, the only way they know is suckin'. They'll bitch their own people and chop down their own supports. It's all part of horizontal hostility, see.' Maybe part of my dubiousness about McGovern stemmed from that sort of feeling. Kurt Vonnegut said once that there was no worse experience than seeing the guys who were in high school with you in charge of the world. As a small-time academic, McGovern came from a class I was contemptuously familiar with; I did not want to think I mistrusted him on that ground.

The myths of the Republican regime are repulsive. Nixon has survived on the notions that the poor remain poor through their own fault; that America lacks the resources to assure every American the fundamental necessities of life; that national health services are too expensive to maintain; that unemployment is essential to the American economy – and that all these notions shelter beneath the banner of the New Prosperity.

The New Mythology of the Democratic Party is more attractive, although softer-headed, than the nastiness of the GOP. 'Power to the People' is a slogan that will warm the heart, especially when set to music by John Lennon and bawled in the streets by the young, the gifted, and the black. We would all so very much like to agree, to feel our energies flow for altruism, and to believe that the issues are not so complicated as to evade our grasp. 'Intellectual pseudosnobs' are ill-equipped by their cultural traditions to accept dialectical materialism that denies the individual will, is anti-Protestant, substitutes determinism for heroism. Such a philosophy is dehumanizing, degrades the individual, phallus and all, to mere reagency. The middle-class radical can easily be persuaded to forgo it in his fantasy, and the best educated are the most vulnerable in this respect. The cultural revolution that Marxism entails is an unbearable impoverishment, a forfeiting of the intellectual's most cherished heritage; Yevtushenko and Solzhenitsyn remind him horribly of the price that the proletarian dictators must exact, in return for the least amelioration in the condition of the masses.

The softening up that the Democrats had plannned was bound to draw us in: no bourgeois Marxist really sees himself as an anomaly or expects to be massacred by the proletariat; he has not the sense of grievance necessary to believe that he could cut the throats of the White House incumbents, although they could turn the M16 rifles of the National Guard upon him without turning a hair. His intellectual passion for truth and justice and equality and tolerance cannot join in battle with the irrational hostility of a race brutalized for generations by anality, competition, and sexual repression. The idealist Democrat cannot kill for his ideals. We all needed so intensely to believe that our case was not hopeless and that we were not totally hypocritical in our well-fed radicalism, we were so ready to love the man who would agree to represent us (yes, me too) that within hours of arriving in Miami Beach we were all maudlin and ripe for being screwed in every orifice of the mind and heart.

At a meeting of the National Women's Political Caucus on the morning after I arrived, I caught sight of my fellow Yippie, Abbie Hoffman, covering the meeting for the book he is doing with Jerry Rubin and Ed Sanders. Abbie looked odd with the unsolicited nose job he had as a result of a police beating in Washington last May, but odder still was the something soft and questing, even mawkish in his expression. 'Ah, come on, Geegee,' he pleaded with me. 'Don't be so down on everything! We gotta chance this time, Geegee!' 'But Abbie,' I replied faintly, 'it can't work this way. What kind of bargaining power have these people got? Remember your Marx, man, and the nature of capitalism.' 'Aw Gee, I never read Marx, but Lenin woulda liked it.' I realized with a guilty creak of the heart that Abbie was sick of trashing and being trashed, tired of the feds infesting the staircase of his apartment, tired of informers and spying, too intelligent not to see that most of his activities had had the net result of intensifying oppression while revolution remained as far off as ever. Besides, he loved America.

'It's terrific, Gee. We're inside the hall this time. All these women and blacks and young kids, it's terrific! Ya been down to the Park? Ya gotta come down, and there's a poetry reading – ya wanna read a poem?'

I had been to the Park – the night before, with a young reporter who had lurched at me with his lips puckered when we were on our way in the cab. I ducked; he asked me why. I thought the overriding question was why he had lurched in the first place, having received no encouragement. What I did not realize is that a political convention is still a convention, that all the males-away-from-home expect to let their hair down, make love to strange women, dance all night and all that.

I have seen a good many People's Corrals in my time, and Flamingo Park must rate as one of the nicest. It was warm; there were lavatories and even a swimming pool, and the retaining wire was hidden by blossomy hedges, and Green Power was handing out nourishing food. Best of all, there was hardly anybody there. A drug entirely appropriate to the strategies of containment had appeared, a muscle relaxant called Quaalude. The non-delegates sprawled about, enervated and content. The Democrats could expect little needle from that quarter.

By way of relating to the disenfranchised poor of South Beach, the slogan of the non-delegates might have been 'Think Jewish', not the Jewish of Meyer Lansky or Moshe Dayan or even Trotsky, but the Jewish of chicken soup. Allen Ginsberg was into wearing a yarmulke and intoning Yiddish mantras. Abbie Hoffman produced a poem abusing Nixon in Yiddish. The Zippies were fed up with the schmaltzy complacency of the Yippies, and a few abortive trashings ensued, but the truth about Flamingo Park was that nothing was happening there. As Jerry Rubin said when I met him on the convention floor, 'The action is here, man. The Park is a drag,' and he went off to secure himself a nomination for the Vice-Presidency from the New York delegation. It felt like the end of an era.

The non-delegates' finest hours were spent in the Doral Hotel lobby demanding an explanation from nominee McGovern of his words to the POW and MIA families: 'While I am fully confident that there would be no such need, I would also retain the military capability in the region – in Thailand and on the seas – to signal and fulfil our firm determination on this issue [the release of all prisoners and a full accounting of all missing in action].'

The irritating thing about that statement was the impression it gave that McGovern had only recently grasped the practical difficulty of withdrawing from Vietnam, and that only in the vaguest way. He was saying what the families of POWs and MIAs wanted to hear, just as he constantly produced the stirring promises that the anti-war lobby wanted to hear, regardless of US commitments in south-east Asia and the size and scope of the American operation there. Five hundred people marched on the Doral to hear his explanation. They arrived at noon; McGovern could not be coaxed from the seclusion of his suite until nearly seven o'clock. A little straight talking could have had them on their way in minutes, and yet the Democrats were amazed and impressed that McGovern agreed to talk to them at all, and overcome with admiration of his cunning in getting it together for prime-time viewing. LIVE!! I stood and waited with them for a couple of hours off and on. Arthur Miller was standing near me, appalled by the self-consciousness of what he saw. A demagogue from the Park came up to me and asked for $60 to buy the people food. I dug my last $37 out of my pocket. 'That's no good, man,' he wailed. 'I need sixty.' 'You're damn lucky to get more than half of it at your first touch. You get and raise the rest, you asshole,' I snapped. 'They're publicity hounds, provocateurs,' Arthur was saying miserably.

The most vociferous of the invaders of the Doral were probably no more than self-seekers and stoned demagogues, but there were more perilous infiltrations into the ranks of the non-delegates. The Yippies smelled a grand jury and more conspiracy trials in the offing and clammed up, but the vets, the most persuasive antiwar group in the country, were not so fly. As a result of the infiltration of their open south-east regional planning meeting held in Florida a month before, more than twenty vets were served with subpoenas to appear before a federal grand jury in Tallahassee on Monday morning, the first day of the Democratic Convention. The scale of the operation was unprecedented, the number of men expected to testify on one day apparently preposterous.

The Democrats' wholehearted support of the vets was a mark in their favour, even if one considered that it was more closely connected with anti-Nixon feeling than a genuine understanding of the issue. Anti-Nixonism is probably the main reason the convention was so ready to accept the contention of the People's Coalition for Peace and Justice that US Air Force jets have been repeatedly and deliberately bombing the dikes in North Vietnam, despite official disclaimers from the White House and the Pentagon. By the last night of the convention, the dikes had become an instant *cause célèbre*; the vets marched silently through the streets carrying torches and bags of sand to patch a symbolic dike. A huge banner appeared in the convention hall: STOP BOMBING THE DIKES. A journalist standing near me asked, 'Is that a Gay Liberation sign?'

The Democratic Convention also represented the first emergence of women as a significant group in electoral politics. The National Women's Political Caucus was only a year old, and its first big opportunity had arrived. There was almost no hope that it could have developed voting strength and practical strategies in such a short time, but in the unkind way of history it was about to be tested and a precedent set. The intensity of my irrational hope that the course of American politics could be changed with respect to its foreign policies was compounded by the fervidity of my desire to see the women distinguish themselves and win some representation in the party platform and some power to implement their own will. After several days of following their activities I found myself in a morass of passionate wishing and utter disappointment.

When I got to the National Women's Political Caucus meeting in the Napoleon Room at the Deauville Hotel on Sunday morning, Gloria Steinem was speaking, and the controlled jubilation of her tone pushed my tormenting hopes up to fever pitch. She spoke of councilmen being ousted by housewives, of women forming forty-six per cent of the attendance at precinct meetings in one state. 'The political process has been changed,' she sang, 'and it will never be the same again.' Women had challenged their way to being forty per cent of the delegates, with thirty-eight per cent of the vote; they had made the McGovern-Fraser guidelines work for them. Of course, some delegations had simply stacked themselves with token females, wives and daughters and whomever, in order to escape a challenge, and for them at least new activism among women had nothing to do with it, but the atmosphere was so electric, the women's enthusiasm so contagious, that I for one could not keep my heart from beating faster.

Bella Abzug took over, vowing staunchly that Yvonne Brathwaite Burke was not going to be Lawrence O'Brien's right-hand man, that women would not be McGovern's sacrificial lamb, coming down heavy on every last syllable as if to nail her meaning to the Democratic masthead.

A bevy of women paused in the doorway, their heads moving with odd self-consciousness, and minced extravagantly to a row of empty seats. One of them, a delegate from New Mexico, festooned with Zuñi jewellery, her hair elaborately teased into a modified braid, was smoking a small blue enamelled pipe. Her eyes slid round the room, under their carefully slanted false eyelashes, Fifth Avenue Indian style. The blonde next to her suddenly said, in a skittish, unnecessarily piercing voice, 'Ah think we'd do a lot better down in our room' – at which signal they rose, clattering and clinking and excuse-meing at the tops of their voices. Even Bella paused in her oration to demand the cause of the disturbance, but the ladies, swinging their rumps like ponies, were gone.

Bella brought up the question of the minority report on control of one's reproductive destiny. To bring abortion into the Democratic Party platform might seem unwise, she argued, but the issue concerned a fundamental human right that could not be denied by those who chose to live by a different code. There was a brief debate on the subject: some delegates argued that it was a state matter, and inappropriate therefore in the party platform. Another woman said she was against abortion and she was sure that more than half the women there were on her side. A show of hands was called for; five went up. A tension had crept into the high-spirited meeting. Bella's attitude had been doggedly apologetic, and she did not expound any strategy for the defence of the abortion report. Her windup left us in even more doubt about how the women were to proceed: it was our overriding priority to dump Nixon, she said, even if we had to waive the immediacy of certain demands. 'Womanpower is a growing thing that must live.'

Betty Friedan, introduced as 'the mother of us all', took the floor and reminded us that in 1968 there was not one word about women in the Democratic Party platform. Women had figured as miniskirted greeters or invisible wives who had lunches with each other. This year, she announced proudly, 'women are gonna make policy, not coffee.' The women's duty at the convention was to make 'what may not be realistic today, realistic tomorrow.' Her words suggested another possible strategy for the women, to make sure that abortion entered the Democratic party platform, because the Democratic candidate was unlikely to win in '72: by '76 they would have had to develop a way of handling it. I wondered if abortion would have a chance if Kennedy ran in '76. By this time it was obvious no clear guidelines for feminist action at the convention could be expected from the NWPC. Most of their talk was self-congratulation for what had already been achieved, but it was early days yet and the meeting was very small.

In the days that followed I went to many women's meetings. Women for McGovern debated the credentials' challenges, which I had great difficulty in following and for which, in any event, the strategies would be directed by telephone from the McGovern campaign trailer. The caucus met again on Sunday afternoon to discuss strategy, but while I was there I heard only Bella's oratorical chariot riding over the voices of dissent. Gloria and her cohorts withdrew to the Betsy Ross Hotel to prepare for the meeting with the caucus of women delegates and to throw a fund-raising party, while I went down to the Shore Club Motel for a sing-in with the Feminist party, whose various educational activities, such as public burning of anti-feminist religious quotations, went largely unnoticed. (Apparently the fires in the Playboy Bunny wardrobe were caused by electrical faults: such a symbolic conflagration could have been claimed by a women's guerrilla organization notwithstanding, but it wasn't.)

The Feminist party had arrived at the Shore Club only to find that the motel had netted some bigger spenders than the poor women who had come by bus and train to sleep two or three in a room and eat fried chicken out of cardboard boxes; their block booking had been summarily shifted to another hotel. They had printed all their literature with the HQ address of the Shore Club, so Flo Kennedy announced her intention of squatting bag and bagging in the foyer until the Shore Club honoured its obligation. The bastions fell at one blast of her trump, and the women moved in.

Jammed together in a steaming cardroom, the Feminists relieved their hearts by roaring, 'I'm tired of bastards fuckin' over me,' and 'Move on over or we'll move on over you.' We allowed ourselves the luxury of believing that sisterhood is strong, although the events of the day had left me feeling that the mere fact of femaleness does not constitute sisterhood, and sisterhood itself does not automatically confer power.

The next morning I dashed down to the Carillon for the big womanpower meeting of the caucus of women delegates. This was going to be it: here I would see forty per cent of the delegates emerging as a powerful voting bloc, disciplined and agreed on all essential points. When I arrived, Gloria Steinem was calling the roll. The delegates sat at tables set in semicircular tiers and sprang to their feet cheering themselves whenever the name of their delegation was called. Their jollity was infectious, but I was feeling slightly appalled that the business of the day seemed to be self-congratulation and laurel-counting rather than hard plotting for the long nights ahead. There were even a few indications that some wheeling and dealing was being attempted offstage, contrary to the stated spirit of the proceedings. Even Gloria's relentless prominence in all affairs began to disturb me and most of all her occasional wistful mention of the 'smoke-filled rooms where the decisions are made.' Either this convention was going to drag the naked screaming decisions out of the smoke-filled rooms, or it was going to be defeated in its essential purpose. It was hard to be pessimistic with the women howling with glee as their states were named, leaping in the air and beaming all round, but I persisted in wondering how many floor leaders were absent because they were at McGovern briefings on the night's strategies.

The miserable fact was that the women's caucus was not a caucus in any meaningful sense; the McGovern machine had already pulled the rug out from under them. Even if they had had microphones on the floor at their meetings and had thrashed out the issues, polled the women present, and based a feminist strategy on the results of the poll, they would not have had much more bargaining power than they had had before they ever attended a precinct meeting. They were in Miami as cards in McGovern's hand, to be led or discarded as he wished, not as players at the table. He could rely on the intensity factor to work them hard and stack the hall with his supporters and he was not obliged to offer them a bent nickel in recompense: they would vote him to the nomination because they had no alternative. The right wing could threaten him with secession, but not his captive women, blacks, Latins, and kids. They were just not cynical enough to grasp that fact, or else they would have considered an alternative play, a vote for Humphrey or even for Nixon. As Flo said bitterly, 'Honey, if you'll fuck for a dime, you can't complain because somebody else is getting a fur coat.' Womanlike, they did not want to get tough with their man, and so, womanlike, they got screwed.

I began to fear that I could no longer maintain my journalistic pose of calm impartiality, and so I bolted from the room to the Latin caucus next door. It was every bit as muddled and bombastic as the women's. Later glimpses of the black caucus and the youth caucus indicated what I had feared all along. None of the caucuses really existed as policy-making bodies or influential entities on the convention floor. A spurious leaderism ripped them all off and masqueraded as the collective voice, without one firm position sanctioned by the collectivity out of which a hard deal could be made. Spokesman after spokesman claimed to have secured this or that, on a collateral of hot air, and the women's caucus was no exception.

When I got back to the Carillon, newspeople were scurrying everywhere, like bedbugs when you turn the light on. A clot of men in suits was moving like the Blob From the Swamp towards the room where the women's caucus was. I squirmed through the cameramen up behind the Blob. In its heart was McGovern: it was the first time I had seen him since I arrived, except for a glimpse of him, as coquettish as any sultana riding in her palanquin, as he was borne out of the Fontainebleau after a press conference. I had seen a smallish man, with an engagingly shy list to his head, his teeth as well capped and his jowls as well shaven and powdered and his shoes as shiny as you would expect of one who is desirous of being a Presidential candidate.

McGovern was eventually decanted from his escort's collective embrace and faced the women's caucus. They threw themselves at his head, cheering, climbing on chairs for a better look at him, yelling endearments. If ever he doubted that he had them in the palm of his hand, he could no longer doubt it. He might be an expert in the techniques of coquetry, but his women were a pushover. I raged inside, to think what such spontaneity and generosity could cost them. Liz Carpenter introduced him with a gesture so fulsome that it almost overbalanced itself. A woman beside me muttered, 'What a hypocrite. Everyone knows she was for Humphrey.'

Liz said, 'We are all here because of him.' Cheers and tears. McGovern took the floor, and uttered the boo-boo that revealed that he had utterly no understanding of the temper of feminism. To have passed off responsibility for the women's presence from himself to Eve would have been bad enough, with all its pious reference to the anti-feminine Judeo-Christian tradition, but to put it down to Adam! He must have been reassured, for the women forgave him at once. There were a few cries of 'Shame!' and 'Pig!' but you would have thought they were more endearments. He swung into an explanation of the California delegate dispute and on into his stock speech on Vietnam. Suddenly there was an interruption. Jacqui Ceballos, deadly pale, was on her feet just below the stage.

'What about the right to control our own bodies?' she cried. 'We'll never be free until we have that!'

I could hear her from where I was standing, halfway down the hall, but Bella and Gloria stared glassily out into the room, as if they were deaf or entranced. Without a microphone, Jacqui could not hope to compete with McGovern's hugely amplified voice. He faltered, and in the brief silence Jacqui's voice wailed, 'We must control our bodies, otherwise we'll never be free.' McGovern resumed, sailing crescendo into the familiar finale: 'I want us to resolve that once that tragedy is put behind us, never again will we send the precious young blood of this country to die trying to bail out a corrupt dictatorship.'

I would have been happier if he had also said that America would never again send her precious intelligence to set up corrupt dictatorships, but everybody else was deliriously happy with McGovern's oratory. He and his acolytes proceeded past me, women reaching out to touch him and take his hand. Shirley MacLaine trod softly behind him, her eyes awash with tears. The women's last chance to negotiate had been washed out in a tide of soupy emotion.

Why had Bella and Gloria not helped Jacqui to nail him on abortion?

What reticence, what loserism had afflicted them then? I wondered if they had already made some sort of a deal. They may have thought they had: perhaps they had agreed not to embarrass him with the minority report on reproduction, but what on earth would they get in exchange? South Carolina? What could be worth it?

What happened on the first night of the convention is now a matter of record. McGovern's nomination was safe before the official proceedings had even started, when he and Abraham Ribicoff had persuaded Lawrence O'Brien to rule that the credentials issues should be settled by a majority of those delegates eligible to vote. South Carolina, *pace* the women, was thrown out to avoid a ticklish dispute over the definition of a majority before the California vote was settled. It was, after all, a numbers game. The delegates did as they were told; onlookers who marvelled at their biddability ought to have spared a thought for their lack of any organization except McGovern's. I hardly understood what was happening, my eardrums perforated by Sammy Spear's hypodermic sound, penned in a dark gallery on the wrong side of a TV cat-walk where you couldn't see the convention floor or the large TV screens. I had read that George Wallace's campaigns were a new kind of carnival, which mixed revivalism, jingoism, and populism in a new and heady brew, and it seemed to my unseasoned eye that the Democratic National Convention had modelled itself on his scenario. An overamplified choir had screamed rousing songs in bursts for an hour or so; flags had paraded around the hall to shrieking brass, a cleric had prayed for the proceedings. God, whom I had thought of as a Nixon intimate, was continually invoked.

The presentation of the New Mythology was as remorseless and simplistic as any advertising campaign. I had become familiar with the principal gimmicks by watching the telethon the night before, and in Lawrence O'Brien's opening address we got most of it over again. Like all marketing techniques it worked by manipulating emotions, at the most accessible level, and even as you recognized the facileness of the technique, it got to you. God, Conscience, Sincerity, the dead Kennedys, the suffering Vietnamese, and, above all, the People were all on the side of the Democrats. Gloria Steinem said that the McGovern-Fraser guidelines had had the effect of making the convention floor 'look like the country': the Democrats cited this single factor tirelessly in their own praise, but actually the change stopped right there. The convention floor only *looked like* the country. The presence of women, blacks, and youth was visible; what had changed was the party's *image*, so crucial in the age of media politics. The attributes one could not see, like class, income, and education, are more fundamental to politics in many ways than the obvious sexual and ethnic differentiations, and when it came to representing these less obvious categories the Democratic National Convention was markedly inadequate. More than two-thirds of the delegates came from the over $15,000-a-year bracket, which accounts for only twenty-three per cent of the American population; thirty-nine per cent of the delegates had done postgraduate work, when only four per cent of the population has enjoyed that privilege. The insolvency of the Democratic Party had affected its ability to bring the lower-paid workers to Miami Beach, just as the lower-paid workers have not the expensive leisure to undertake political campaigning. One delegate told me that the first question the party had put to her, when she announced her desire to become a delegate, was her name; the second was, 'Can you pay your own way to Miami Beach in July?' Some of the delegations had been subsidized not, it seems, by the party but by the McGovern machine.

The Democrats knew that the faces of the delegates were their most valuable stock-in-trade (closely followed by the pious memories of the Kennedys and the quotability of JFK). They used them over and over again, in their official publication, 'Democrats in Convention', in the telethon, then in Lawrence O'Brien's opening address. The precedent was well established for depiction of the vital, glowing eager faces in all the news media. The long nights that followed were bearable only because the eye could be guided from the dreariness of the rostrum to the ferment beneath. Film of prettily lit, prettily shot faces of every racial cast, but all of them agreeable, fleshed out the platitudes of O'Brien's opening speech. The dialectic was that of sentient flesh and soul against the giant machine; the language was the same that Goldwater had used, of moral revival, righteous disquiet, and the groundswell of public feeling. The Democratic Party was the party-of-the-smaller-man-than-ever-before.

In depicting the people, the image-makers for the Democratic Party allowed no dissident voices, no one who said, 'If we don't fight them in Vietnam, we'll be fighting them in our own backyards,' as the people can be heard to do, not a queer-basher or a law-and-order addict among them. The people on the convention floor were only too happy to applaud this charming image of themselves as simple folks; direct, honest, and profound in their candid appraisal of the political malaise of America, tolerant of all human failings, but hell on institutions. A great foam of enthusiasm rolled off them, and O'Brien's speechwriter worked them further, using that special variety of meaningless language that can elicit a consensus response. 'It comes from the people up,' he intoned with a throb in his voice, 'these simple direct words sum up what many people have been saying ... In good men – good women – good ideas – and good works, the Party of the People is unmatched.' What was the use of drawing a polyglot convention from the intellectual élite, when you had to talk to them as if they were sentimental, tasteless, pious idiots?

Suddenly I realized that the most significant aspect of the convention was being lost on me, precisely because I was present. O'Brien was not speaking primarily to the delegates; he was speaking to the nation-at-large on prime-time TV. The delegates were no more than the studio audience, kicking the show along by cheering and laughing whenever the signal was given; O'Brien was not after all wearing pancake make-up for our benefit. In the fact that almost no significant contender for office appeared in public without cosmetics I found an interesting insight into the methods of political parley. Just as the man's face, authentic and expressive as it was, could not be allowed to make its own appeal to the public and stand or fall by the response, so also a politician's arguments could not be allowed to be clearly and faithfully expressed, but must cloak themselves in jargon and the fake resonance of the pulpit. To get people to believe the truth, the admen believe, it is necessary to lie. Before the convention had ever nominated him, McGovern's personality and beliefs were being falsified by those who sought to make the people buy him. His meaning had to be puffed into vagueness, because consensus politics means that you cannot afford to give the many-headed beast, the public, anything to vote *against*, for voting against is what gargantuan pseudodemocracy has to come down to.

The delegates were not wearing stage make-up though, and they were not talking to each other in the fervent hope of saying as little as possible. They were extraordinary, so proud and alive and earnest and so damnably naïve that it swelled your heart and broke it to watch them, puzzling over the issues, doubting what was best to do, seeking guidance and being raked by the big guns of baloney-power. If only they had had the confidence of their own imagination and judgement instead of meekly allowing themselves to fall in line at the merest touch of a McGovern whip, he might have had to be their servant instead of their master. That is what was so maddening; there was a chance of something really new, but it was stifled at its birth.

For me, the clearest case of funk was the railroading of the abortion issue. The minority report on a 'person's right to control his reproductive destiny' was, of course, treated as an abortion plank, although it applies equally to a man's right to have a vasectomy and a woman's right to refuse compulsory sterilization. The delegates who were for McGovern first and the interests of the group they represented second argued that abortion was a state matter and had no place on a federal platform, which was irrelevant. What was in question was a *right*, to be established constitutionally and upheld by the Supreme Court. If state laws were in violation of the right of privacy, they must be declared unconstitutional; for the women who have already spent millions of dollars and years of their lives battling the state legislatures on the issue, federal intervention has become an urgent necessity. If the 'abortion' plank had been adopted as part of the party platform, thousands of people with energy and experience would have campaigned for McGovern in a positive and intense way, just as they had done in the primaries; they might lose, but they would lose honourably.

By foul means I acquired a delegate's pass to get on to the floor for the debate. Betty Friedan had told me that the Idaho delegates had had the bright idea of asking the male delegates who were not interested in the issue to give up their seats to the women delegates who felt more directly concerned. As I asked around the floor it was clear to me that many delegations were ready to do this, but many of the willing men were for the adoption of the plank in any case. Too many of the women said that they were for the plank, but that they had agreed to vote against it for McGovern's sake. At least two women defied their entire delegations, which polled their single votes *for*, with a bad grace; most gave in.

When Eugene Walsh came out with the arguments of the Right-to-Lifers, not a single opinion in the convention hall was changed. If anything, his contorted face repelled, but Gloria was furious that he had been allowed to speak at all. 'You promised us you would not take the low road,' she said to Gary Hart. I was at a loss to explain her distress; the friends of the foetus do not have so much right on their side that their arguments must be stifled. Even more, I was outraged to think that nonsensical promises had been made in secret sessions, when the business of strengthening the women's caucus had been neglected. Shirley MacLaine's speech to the issue made one single point, which if it had been taken to heart would have lumbered McGovern with the 'sensitive' issue he was now so anxious to avoid. Instead of speaking directly against abortion, which she could not in conscience do, despite the slot she chose to speak in, she begged the delegates to vote according to their consciences – but even as she spoke, the McGovern whips were instructing his delegates to avoid the necessity of a roll-call by shouting the minority report down. Why Bella Abzug should have been so angry with her, on the ground that a 'sister never goes against a sister', when sisterhood had not been adequate to bring Jacqui Ceballos' question to McGovern's notice, I could not understand either.

As I travelled home in the bus that night something happened that brought home to me in the most vivid way the fact that McGovern had not managed to please the sexual bigots by betraying the sexual liberals. A man sitting across the aisle from me suddenly burst out:

'What am I doing, sitting here all night letting them debate abortion? Suppose some broad does get herself knocked up, I don't give a shit!'

His wife's hands were loosely clasped on the skirt of her little-girl gingham dress. She was not listening.

A man on the other side said, 'The country's not ready for that. It's a matter of education.'

He went on for a bit in a calming way, and then suddenly overbalanced and began to say in a voice that rose higher and higher, 'That sexual orientation stuff, that's what I don't like. I don't care what they do in private,' (his voice said that he cared passionately) 'but I don't want one teaching my kid! I just don't. I mean, how would you like it if some homo is getting at your kid . . .' By now he was screaming with disgust.

The other man joined in, 'Yeah. You know, most of the elected officials in my state are *queer*! Every damn one of them.'

They yelled insanely at one another until the first man capped it all by roaring, 'You ever see McGovern walk? He's one of them, I tell you! He's one of them.'

I looked around the bus looking for signs of ridicule or dismay. A boy with a Wallace button on his hat gazed at me as unwinkingly as a lizard. The two men had fallen to commiserating on their long years of service for the Democrats, and how they would have to abandon politics. It did not matter to them one bit that the distasteful reports had been voted down; McGovern's image was tainted with them anyway. Instead of carrying his stinking dead dog proudly through politics, he had hidden it under his coat.

The official sexuality of the Democratic Party has not, of course, changed. The politicians' concubines sat in their seraglio at the side of the rostrum each night, until the debates got too tedious and they began to lose their beauty sleep, when they melted away. They were all coiffed and plentiful of eyelash and fixedly smiling. If you asked for information about any of them from their aides, the answer came, 'She is lovely, truly lovely,' or words to that effect. On all symbolic occasions the wives appeared, standing beside, behind, below, and smiling. The heterosexuality of the politicians was in plentiful evidence, but their virility was almost as important. Ladies of the Wallace persuasion, worried perhaps that the Gov'nah might not appear to be holding his own, volunteered the information to me on three separate occasions that 'he has all of his sexual faculties *unimpaired*.'

According to Rocky Pomerance, Miami chief of police, the Democratic Convention had not attracted the usual number of whores; a mere 18,000 had bothered to make the trip, and, said Pomerance, 'That'll be 18,000 votes for Nixon.' The ladies implied that they had been undercut by amateur competition from the large number of women delegates, but the fact of the matter is that few delegates or press men had the time or the energy for whoring. I hung out with the ladies who work the Fontainebleau one night, trying to get their angle, but there were so many newsmen trying to engineer newsworthy confrontations between us that I had to give it up. The newsmen wrote their stories just the same: the *Miami News* said that I told one girl 'she was a disgrace to our sex', when really I don't think she is any more disgraceful than any politician's wife. *The Village Voice* imagined that a whore had upbraided me for prostituting myself to *Harper's* (as if they ever use the *word*, let alone figuratively). The only person who did that, in fact, was Norman Mailer.

*

The image-makers went to some pains to present Eleanor McGovern as a new sort of candidate's wife, careless of how history suffered in the process. Her least pronouncement was greeted with wonder and acclaim, as if it were remarkable that she could speak at all. One afternoon in the Doral, a woman for McGovern grabbed my arm: 'Quick, Mrs McGovern is going to speak, down there,' and she spun me off down the lobby. 'No, no,' I heard them say crossly when I arrived in the room. 'Mrs McGovern is not going to speak,' and they shrugged as if the whole notion were preposterous. I had got pretty used to Mrs McGovern as the traditional smiling mute and was preparing to leave when my arm was grabbed again. 'Come and meet Mrs McGovern.' I was dragged into the scrum that hid her tiny form from view. The press of advisers and trainbearers parted and catapulted her into my midriff. I took her hand, as cool and dry and still as a dead bird. 'It must be so nice to be covering the convention,' she said faintly. I choked on the desire to say that it was unmitigated mental torture and bleated something about how I'd rather have been involved. 'Oh no,' she said, 'much less exhausting. So much tension.' Bending over at the waist to bring her voice within earshot, I felt like an intolerable, sneaking bully. 'The Senator says Eleanor has an energy problem,' someone said. A gigantic bouncer appeared from nowhere, clearing the room for the next non-event. Incredibly he was wearing a clergyman's dog collar.

Of all the extracurricular events Mrs McGovern might have attended, the one she chose was a fashion show put on by Governor Askew's wife. I had come across it by accident, after seeing the tiny demonstration that trudged round and round in the Americana Hotel forecourt shouting, 'The poor need food, the poor need clothes. What do we get? Fashion shows!'

I ran the gamut of the security men and was gingerly welcomed by the hostesses. Until I saw the complimentary orange drink among the samples of suntan lotion and scent on the tables, I could not fathom why the hostesses were balancing giant orange paper roses on their heads, or why in that heat they were draped in orange capes with bobble trim. Even Mrs Askew was starring in an imaginary commercial for Florida in her orange, green, and white dress, oversewn with orange blossom. She mounted the podium to present the distinguished guests: 'I want you to meet the women behind the men behind the wheels of the Florida government,' she said.

Then she introduced us to all of her female relatives, in blood and in law: 'It is a very special pleasure that we have our mothers with us at this convention.' Mrs Wilbur Mills and Mrs Terry Sanford and a bevy of assorted wives were present, but the star had still to come. Eleanor McGovern's arrival was signalled by a panic of photographers. Under cover of the confusion, a few poor women laid down their $3 and moved quietly into the ballroom.

A small voice arose in the din: 'This is what the poor woman is wearing this year, cut-down dungarees and Levi jacket –' The genuine poor is more likely to be found in a wash-cotton dress and trodden-down slippers, but the women had a point and they were making it with a little wit. Crash! The security men moved in, lifting the girls bodily off the floor. One of the women had a very small baby. The police in their space-age helmets came running down, batons akimbo, to help. 'You rich women—' one of the girls began to scream, but her voice was choked off in the rush that carried her clean out of the room. Mrs McGovern curled a small white-shod foot around the leg of her chair. The Florida matrons clicked their tongues. 'Publicity-seekers', they opined sagely. The models came out and gangled down the catwalk in ready-made stocklines from Saks Fifth Avenue. The poor had been phoney poor, and the rich were not rich. Nothing in Miami was what it seemed.

As if I had not fallen foul of enough bamboozlement and forlorn hope in Miami Beach, I also had the misfortune to entangle with the Star. I was introduced to him in an elevator, so there was nowhere I could take cover when he bent his full charm on me. That charm is a work of kinetic art, and I am not one to sneer at artistic achievement. The raw material is not contemptible either; there are few flaws in the marble out of which the Star has hewn himself. We achieved the fifteenth floor and I prepared to make a dash for reality, but the Star caught my arm. 'Can I have a meeting with you?' he asked as he drew me aside into a chair. 'Do up that button,' I said crossly. 'You don't have to come on with your tits hanging out.' Bless my soul if he didn't put his perfect fingers to the second button on his shirt. 'I wasn't serious,' I amended feebly. The Star leaned close. 'Do you know I have been trying to find you? I even called the Chelsea.' My palms began to sweat.

I don't remember too much of what ensued. The Star was upbraiding me for voicing my misgivings about the American political system on the Cavett show. He was leaning so close to me that I began to worry about my toothpaste, mainly because it was still in London, and I hadn't cleaned my teeth in days. I snatched at a toothpick and stuck it in my mouth. The Star leaned further forward, nipped the end of my toothpick in his perfect teeth and bit it off. I was so rattled I forgot the cash value of a toothpick curtailed by the Star and promptly broke it into tiny pieces and left it in the ashtray. The Star took my gnarled paw into his smooth hand.

'Why do you want to go to that meeting?' he asked. (Shirley MacLaine's voice was echoing from the meeting I had been on my way to attend.)

'Because I'm on an assignment and I like to be serious about serious things.' I wasn't really too sure that the Democratic Convention was serious, but I was still giving it a chance.

I bolted from the chair. The Star ran after me. 'Call me,' he said. 'Any time.' He gave me his room number, which I instantly forgot. I could just see myself trucking round Miami, sniffing at the Star's warm trail like a bloodhound. I knew I was being challenged, but I squirmed away. 'Look, I'm pretty busy. Can't we play the game according to the old rules? You call me.' I cut and ran.

When I tottered home to my air-conditioned nightmare that night, two messages were waiting. One said simply, 'Please pursue.' The more I thought about it, the more I thought that the whole encounter was phoney. I was being vamped for McGovern, or maybe just so that the Star could test his artistic creation and find it still good. The next morning I sent him a dozen red roses and a note, 'Sorry I was out when you called.' The Star was not to be so easily snubbed. At length he left a note, 'Can we go on like this?' Heartsick and teased beyond endurance by what the convention had become, I still managed to resist the promise of an intimacy that still struck me as illusory as everything else at the Democratic National Convention. I could see it as part of the whole process, the wooing and winning of vulnerable and hopeful people, for somebody's good, but not their own. I withheld belief, but I could not avoid him for ever. We met again. He pleaded with me not to play into Nixon's hands by helping to destroy McGovern's credibility with the people who were the hard core of his support. I wanted so much to believe, found my scepticism so desolating, that I almost threw myself sobbing into his arms and signed on for the Presidential campaign trail, but the Star tired of his conquest before it had quite taken place. I was right after all, although he laughed uproariously when I accused him of vamping for McGovern; I was right, but I wished with all my heart I hadn't been.

The last night of the convention seemed to me the culmination of outrage. All week the McGovern machine had been soliciting for prospective candidates for vice-president with connections among the labour unions and the Catholic Church. At the eleventh hour, Tom Who? came across with so much alacrity that suspicions must have been aroused. There was no time by then to check these out because the delegates had to be organized out of saddling McGovern with some woman or black or pot smoker. McGovern was running out of arm's reach of his core supporters to angle after the centre and the centres of organized tyranny, but the exhausted delegates, after a week without sleep and a diet that should have given them kwashiorkor, were still supporting him as trustingly as ever. When the charade of voting was over and Teddy Kennedy had summarized the glorious traditions of the Democratic Party, I walked among the delegates while they greeted their hero, issuing forth after three days in the tabernacle. I remembered how Valerie Kushmer had seconded his nomination, putting her suffering as a POW's wife at his disposal in simple words, her nakedness almost obscene among the blarney that surged about our ears for so many days. It had seemed to me then a blasphemy to make such wanton use of sincerity and fervour in a vulgur tourney for power. Coming after her awesome act of faith in McGovern, Walter Fauntroy's speech sounded as false and mannered as any fraudulent preacher's pitch. The Philistinism of the famous litany shocked me almost to tears. Even the hard-bitten newshounds around me had looked sick. Respect for the language, for communication, is essential if ideas are to be respected: truth could never prevail in the guise of hucksterism. People around me laughed at my expression of consternation. 'You're just not used to American politics. You have to learn to accept the ballyhoo.'

'I won't and I don't,' I said unsteadily, 'especially when your precious party makes such a big song and dance about its new candour.'

McGovern came among his people, painted the colour of pigskin and gleaming with sweat. High on the podium, facing the raunchy disorder of the convention hall, he looked like a disposable paper man compared to the people who sent up such a blast of enthusiasm to him. Walking among them as they drank in his words was like moving about during the National Anthem. Perhaps tiredness had a good deal to do with it, but many eyes brimmed with tears of joy and thankfulness. I wanted to warn them that they were being teased and played upon, to beg them to keep some reserve, but I was too close to hysterical tears to speak at all. McGovern's words, the regulation mix of jingoism, pietism, and populism, were aimed at their heartstrings, working them over and over so that emotion roared about the hall in waves.

> Come home, to the affirmation that we have a dream.
> Come home to the conviction that we can move our country forward,
> Come home to the belief that we can seek a newer world.

I should not have been surprised that Fauntroy's bombast had supplied the McGovern movement with a slogan, vapid as it was, or that McGovern was reduced to quoting jingoistic songs or that America was still committed to warlike policies everywhere else but Asia, as far as he was concerned. I passed a young black delegate, his hands clasped to his breast, his eyes shining adoration at the man who would bring him home. My resentment at the whole horrible travesty became unbearable. As I turned to get out of there before the kissing could begin, I heard McGovern intoning:

> May God grant us the wisdom to cherish this good land and to meet the great challenge that beckons us home.

When the shouting was all over, I realized that despite the secret dealings, the hypocrisy, the tantalization and the bamboozlement, the coarsening and cheapening of every issue, the abandonment of imagination and commitment for the grey areas of consensus, there was no alternative for American liberals but to let McGovern tease them a little while longer. In their alienation, their impotence and their guilt they have no other alternative. Through the disappointment and the dismay that clouded my mind, another flicker of hope began to burn, against all reason and probability. I wish and painfully hope that the women, the kids, the blacks, the Latins, and the 'intellectual pseudosnobs' bring off the impossible for him in November, in spite of himself, his baloney machine, and his Machiavellis, even though they will take the credit for it. The Big Tease has just begun.

Not a time to die

Sunday Times, 3 December 1972

This is a terrible time to die. Death has never been so mysterious, so obscene or shameful an occupation as it is in our time. The dying are at a loss how to behave themselves, and their families are even more confused about the meaning of what is happening and the proper decorum for the proceeding. There are few ceremonial expressions of bereavement and mourning is considered absurd. I know a man who wept publicly for a young suicide who was very dear to him, and his university tutors suggested that he ought to go into a psychiatric hospital where they would try to cure his grief, as if it were a disease.

Death has not always been obscene. Dying used to be a public activity, and the features of the grim reaper were familiar. Most families had assisted in the course of one lifetime at a score of deathbeds. Landlords visited their dying tenants; ladies of gentle breeding helped the poor out of the world, and making a good end was a conscious and orderly activity.

Perhaps such a committed attitude to leaving the world was morbid. Brooches and rings of the hair of the dead may seem a barbaric ornament to us, but our incomprehension and fastidiousness about the end of life is hardly less unreasonable. When I was a convent schoolgirl, my forehead was anointed once a year with ash, and the priest murmured to me: 'Dust thou art and unto dust thou shalt return'. When a nun died, she lay in state in the chapel and we were all told to file past and take a good look, but I had a note of protest from my mother. I stayed in the classroom and speculated wildly until the others came back and said disrespectful things about how the cadaver smelt and what expression was on her face. Then we would all sing her requiem and the more polished hypocrites among us would squeeze out a tear.

So, here I am, well on my way to the grave and I have never seen a human corpse. If my progress out of the world should suddenly turn out to be faster than I anticipate, I have no idea how I should behave. If any member of my household announced that the end was in sight I should be cast into utter confusion. I have known people who died, but because death is so thoroughly offstage, they did not tell me much about it. Indeed, the correct decorum seemed to be grisly cheerfulness and a mad pretence that the obvious was not happening.

When I was in hospital once, I used to hear an old lady crying out in

146

terror all day and all night long that the end would come and she would be on her own. She spilt her orange juice in the bed and threw her things on the floor and tore off her dressings, all in a desperate attempt to lure the nurses into her room, so she wouldn't be alone. I asked if I might sit with her and the nurses were disgusted.

Making a good end is harder now than it has ever been, because the manner of dying is usually not in the sufferer's power to choose. An old Italian lady, whom I had to tell that she had terminal cancer when I was a hospital interpreter, broke out in joyful prayers because her suffering was nearly over. Within seconds a nurse had sedated her so thoroughly that she could not speak at all. She was, after all, in a public ward.

Hospitals generally prefer people not to die in them. It disturbs the other patients and depresses the nurses. Some hospitals used to be so intolerant of death's ministrations that the dying no sooner ceased to breathe than they were flung on the floor and their hearts violently massaged so that their agony might last a little longer. Other hospitals send the dying home to families who are helpless and baffled about the nature of the process, unable to cope with incontinence or pain or terror. Our censorship of death has resulted in phobias and ignorance which our vestigial religion will not suffice to counteract.

The problem has assumed national proportions. This week a one-day national symposium on the care of the dying was held at the Royal College of Physicians. Learned and compassionate men met to discuss ways of guaranteeing the dying 'freedom from suffering, the preservation of personal dignity, compassion and peace'. Would that it were within the power of the National Health Service to supply them.

The problem of the dying, especially of those who are a long time dying, is simply an extension of the problem of the aged. Our tiny, short-lived families are less and less able to deal with the older generations. The houses and flats they live in are quite unsuitable to the constant vigilance and the back-breaking labour of caring for the enfeebled. It was not easy for George Eliot to sit up at night easing her father's pain with hot stones and changing his soiled linen and waiting for lucid intervals when he needed to talk to someone, but for most women nowadays it is utterly impossible. The community services which might ease the problems of hygiene and routine medical attention simply do not exist. Most people die in improvised circumstances of harassment and confusion, whether in hospital or out of it.

The national symposium on the care of the dying recognized that the trend is towards dying in hospital rather than at home, although the consensus is that death is a family event and ought to occur at home. The fact that most families are not united, and that most homes cannot bear such a burden was not confronted, even though the circumstances of old-age pensioners in this country are well known. The smallness of old-age pensions would not be such an outrage, perhaps, if old people were still living in the bosom of a family, if lonely old women did not make up the majority of geriatric patients, and if so many geriatric patients were not confined in psychiatric hospitals for want of a better solution.

It is as difficult to persuade medical workers that helping the dying is a worthwhile activity as it is to persuade a government that citizens who do not work are entitled to a dignified lifestyle. Philosophic acceptance of death is as rare among the medical profession as it is among the general populace.

The need seems to be for special hospitals in which care of the dying could be properly exercised, but as long as we regard death as an alien function, even to the extent of taking upon ourselves the responsibility of concealing from the dying their condition, people will be prevented from availing themselves of their help. Dying is, after all, a service to the community and ought to be honoured as such.

A seasonal wish

Sunday Times, 17 December 1972

My Christmas wish is that every child might find, when he is most needed, a Mr Hare. To qualify as a Mr Hare one needs to be rather old, a little lonely, to have something to give and something to get through the friendship of a child. The results of such a friendship can alter the course of a child's life and sweeten an old age.

I was lucky enough to find my Mr Hare when I was thirteen. I was quite properly taught to be afraid of strangers, especially old men, so although Mr Hare lived only two doors away, I was almost unaware of his existence.

He was a piano tuner by trade and his house was full of pianos: uprights, a Bechstein and a little white grand piano, all perfectly in tune. And each piano stool bulged with music sheets. He was not a performer; he had never succeeded in playing the piano or any other instrument well, but he loved music and was happy to serve it in his own way.

In my parents' house there was no piano. Not even a record player. The only music-making instrument we had was a small mouth organ I acquired somewhere, but its inaccurate tuning exasperated me so much that I was forever throwing it away until the desire for some instrument would become unbearable and I would fish the harmonica out of the shrubbery and try again. I scrounged my musical experience from the wireless, belabouring the ears of the family with Bartók and Wagner, until their patience ran out and the set was resolutely switched to cricket or tennis or just plain off.

Failing any instrument, I used to sing. The first hum of the vacuum cleaner or whirring of the electric mixer and I burst into the oddest renditions of every madrigal, aria or motet I had ever heard. I imagined that the noise of the appliances drowned my piping, but someone always appeared from somewhere and insisted that I shut up forthwith. I beseeched and badgered my parents for music lessons, but they stoutly maintained that I would not practise, that the money would be wasted, and so forth and so on. Eventually I gave up and contented myself with reading about opera and opera singers, and musicians and composers, until my dreams were thronged with unsavoury nonsense.

My uncontrollable shrilling was eventually completely proscribed. I was allowed to sing only if I buried myself in the depths of the vegetable garden, when the rampant pumpkin and marrow leaves could deaden the impact of my piercing sounds. I used to perch on a sawn-off tree-trunk where we chopped wood, and sing every air I could remember for hours at a stretch, striving vainly to keep it soft in case the neighbours should complain, but always forgetting or yielding to the music and roaring away like one demented. As I did not know the words, I sang a nonsense tongue, with no proper consonants and vaguely Italo-Germanic sounds.

All the time I yearned for music, for resonance and harmony. At school we sang wonderful music, but since I could not read music and could never learn any special part, I simply sang away with the body of the choir and kept my renditions of the obbligati and solo parts for the vegetable garden.

Then came the day when Mr Hare could stand it no longer.

He came to the door of our very discreet, not very approachable house, and knocked. My mother opened it and looked at him enquiringly. He found it very hard to explain, but eventually my mother understood he had heard the child singing and would like to teach her music, for nothing, understood? Mother asked me if I might like to go just once and see whether I liked it. Ten minutes later I was standing nervously in the porch of his tiny house, waiting for him to open the door.

The house was dark and smelt of age and loneliness. The pianos loomed in the dark shiny parlour; to me they were like so many science-fiction machines. Mr Hare had already bought my piano primer, a red book called *Teaching Little Fingers to Play*. My fingers were nearly as big as they are now, but Mr Hare brushed aside my embarrassment. Within minutes the treble clef was no more a mystery and I was sitting at the baby grand, picking out tunes and singing the airs faster than my hands could play them.

The greatest moments came when Mr Hare would produce the music of something special that he believed I should and could sing, and he would beam at me from the end of the keyboard as I filled my lungs and sang as loudly as ever I had wanted to. Nearly every evening I would sing the Countess's aria from *The Marriage of Figaro* for him, doubtless very badly, but for me it was a new horizon and he was proud to have shown it to me.

Because of Mr Hare's patience and his enjoyment of my efforts, I came to know one of the purest pleasures of humankind: the pleasure of singing in concert, tuning the voice in harmony with other voices, experiencing the happiest co-operation, in making music. I became a member of my school consort, singing Beethoven and Pachelbel and Palestrina, and of various consorts and choirs in universities and cathedrals. I moved away from my parents' house and never saw Mr Hare again.

I dare say I thanked Mr Hare prettily every evening after I had finished plunking away on his pianos, but I never managed to thank him for the greater debt. He never knew the full extent of the change he made in my life.

We no longer think of old people as wise, but there are many older people who have much to impart to the very young and no young around them to impart it to. Mr Hare might as well have taught me fishing or drawing or carving or how to make an omelette. Families do not always supply everything that children need and they often reject their old people completely. There is a great well of tenderness and concern in older people which children might tap, if only families were not so suspicious of outsiders, and there is a great power in children to give ample reward.

So I wish all children a Mr Hare this Christmas.

Seduction is a four-letter word

Playboy, January 1973

Once in a hot courtroom in New Zealand, I had occasion to ask a lady who was giving evidence against me for saying 'fuck' in a public meeting, whether she was as disgusted and offended by hearing the word 'rape' used in a similar context. She wasn't. I asked her why. She thought for a moment and said happily, 'Because for rape the woman doesn't give her consent'.

My little linguistic enquiry opened a sudden peephole on the labyrinth of crazy sexual attitudes which we have inherited from our polyglot traditions (although it did not prevent my being sentenced to three weeks' gaol). The craziness extends into our (mis)understanding of the nature of sexual communication and thereby finds its way back to behaviour. Our muddled responses to the word 'rape' have their source in the sexual psychosis that afflicts us all, especially the policemen and judges who are most vindictive in their attitudes towards those few sexual criminals who have sufficient bad luck or bad management to fall foul of the law.

Otherwise quite humane people entertain the notion that women sub-consciously or even consciously desire to be raped, that rape liberates their basic animality, that like she-cats they want to be bloodily subdued and savagely fucked, regardless of their desperate struggles and cries. Women are thought to provoke the sexual rage of men who in turn may need to add bloodlust to their sexual desire in order to achieve full potency. Darwin is sometimes quoted as the ideological ally of the rapist and forcible impreg-nator – how else but by his marauding activities could the survival of the fittest be assured?

Yet many women are terrified of rape as of nothing else. Women who have been raped may be too terrified to leave their house by day or night, as a consequence, or so distressed by male nearness that they cannot take a job or get into a crowded train. There may be some truth in the notion that the lonely spinster who is terrified of intruders is actually longing to be violated, but her subconscious wish is of the same order as the wish of a mother to destroy her children which is chiefly expressed in her fantasies that they have come to violent harm. The fury that a father feels against the man who rapes his daughter might as profitably be construed as jealousy. For all practical purposes what the spinster experiences is a fascinating terror which may become an obsession. The man who actualizes her fantasy is in no way gratifying her or benefiting her, except in his own overweening estimation. The extent to which all men participate in this fantasy of violent largesse can be dimly detected in their willingness to laugh at Lenny Bruce's description of his aunt going into Central Park each day for her appointment with the flashers, or the sneering assumption that older women and unattractive women are disappointed if intruders or invading soldiers don't rape them.

Many (men) believe that rape is impossible. The more simple-minded imagine that the vagina cannot be penetrated unless the woman consciously or subconsciously accepts the penetration, and so the necessary condition of rape cannot be fulfilled. Doubtless such a view reflects upon the potency of those who hold it; there are cases of vaginal spasm in which the vaginal sphincter closes tight around the penis which cannot therefore detumesce and so cannot withdraw, but this is a rare occurrence and most often occurs during coition, not before. The difficulty of getting a fully erect penis into the vagina is in direct proportion to the difficulty of overcoming the woman, either by physical force or by threat (holding a gun to her head for example) or by drugging her or taking her by surprise.

The idea that rape is impossible may be an invalid extension of the view that all women subconsciously desire or provoke rape. It is certainly true that women do not defend themselves against rapists with any great efficiency. Even though they know that a sharp blow to the groin will incapacitate a man, or that a high heel smashed into the temple will have a certain effect, they seldom take advantage of what forms of self-defence may be accessible to them. The fault lies not in their suppressed lechery or promiscuity but in the induced passivity which is characteristic of women as we have conditioned them. Feminist encounter groups have developed routines in which a woman is encouraged to fight off a would-be rapist. Even strong heavy women had a struggle to overcome the passivity which impeded the release of energy in self-defence; passionate urging from the other members of the group was needed to take advantage of their own strength and determination.

Without special help, most women have no idea how to defend themselves and no concept of themselves as people with a right to resist physical misuse with violence. They are like children being beaten by their parents and their teachers, or slaves being brutalized on the plantation. Their physical strength remains unexploited because of the pathology of oppression. Women are poorly motivated to be as aggressive with their assailants as their assailants are with them and so rape is easier than it should be, but this cannot be held to justify the contemptuous attitude of the rapist. Women's helplessness is itself part of the psychosis which makes rape a national pastime. Encounter groups have not yet developed the kind of psychic energy which can defeat a gun or a knife or the frenzy of drugs.

The fear of sexual assault is a special fear: its intensity in women can best be likened to the male fear of castration. As a tiny child I was utterly unafraid of the derelict old men who drooped their pallid tools at my mother and me when we sunbathed in the beach park, but I remember an occasion when much less sinister behaviour provoked wild terror. A young man simply came up to me and offered me a sweet; his kind smile was the most hideous thing I had ever seen. Usually I invoked my parents' rage because I consorted so readily with strangers, but this time I recoiled from the bribe, speechless with fright. Then I was running and running until my lungs were screaming, and I fell down and cowered in the grass, desperate not to look up for fear I would see that indescribable smile. Whenever I saw that man hanging out in the lane below our apartment, looking up my six-inch skirts as I went up or down the stairs, I was terrified. When I tried to explain to the grown-ups why I loathed that man I had no words for it, but I know it was the greatest fear of all, worse than spiders or octopuses or falling off the roof of the flats. Devoted sadists might argue that my terror was terror of my own innate femaleness, but it would be bad Freud, because I was presumably in my phallic phase and unaware of my vagina, and if such a view is not to be justified by the great apologist of female masochism it is not to be justified at all. What I was afraid of was rape as Cleaver described it, 'bloody, hateful, bitter and malignant', even though I had no clear idea of what it entailed.

Sexual intercourse between grown men and little girls is automatically termed rape under most codes of law. It does not matter whether the child invites it or even whether she seduces the adult; he and he only is guilty of a serious felony. From the child's point of view and from the common sense point of view, there is an enormous difference between intercourse with a willing little girl and the forcible penetration of the small vagina of a terrified child. One woman I know enjoyed sex with an uncle all through her childhood and never realized that anything unusual was toward until she went away to school. What disturbed her then was not what her uncle had done, but the attitude of her teachers and the school psychiatrist. They assumed that she must have been traumatized and disgusted and therefore in need of very special help. In order to capitulate to their expectations she began to fake symptoms that she did not feel, until at length she began to feel really guilty about not having been guilty. She ended up judging herself very harshly for her innate lechery.

The crucial element in establishing whether vaginal penetration is rape or not is whether or not the penetration was consented to. Consent is itself an intangible mental act; the law cannot be blamed because it must insist that evidence of absence of consent be virtually conclusive, so that a woman who has not been savagely beaten or terrified by threat of immediate harm and was not unconscious has little chance of proving to the satisfaction of the law that she has been raped. Consent is not a simple procedure; it may be heavily conditional or thoroughly muddled, and the law cannot allow itself to be drawn into ethical conundrums. Most of us do not live according to the bare letter of the law of the land, but according to moral criteria of much greater complexity. Morally, those of us who have a high opinion of sex cannot accept the idea of passive consent sanctioning all kinds of carnal communication; rather than rely on the negative criterion that absence of resistance justifies sexual congress, we must insist that evidence of positive desire alone dignifies sexual intercourse and makes it joyful. From a proud and passionate woman's point of view, anything less is rape.

The law of rape was not made with a woman's pride or passion in mind. The woman is no more and probably even less the focus of the law of rape than the victim is the *raison d'être* of the law of homicide. The crime of rape is rather considered as an offence not against the woman herself but the men who made the law: fathers, husbands and kin. It is a crime against legitimacy of issue and the correct transmission of patrimony. The illegitimate sexual intercourse constitutes the offence; what the woman who complains must do is primarily to dissociate herself from any suspicion of complicity in the outrage against her menfolk. This she must do by making a complaint immediately. She is regarded as the prosecutrix of the rapist and he has all the recourse against her accusation that any defendant has against the State Prosecutor, and then some. Only a girl child escapes the ordeal, because she is automatically deemed incapable of consent. An adult woman is actually called upon to prove her own innocence in the course of a rape prosecution, as well as managing to establish that the circumstances of the man's behaviour are as she alleges.

A man has to be very unlucky to be convicted of the crime of rape. He has to be stupid enough, or drugged or drunk enough, to leave a mile-wide trail of blood, bruises, threats, semen, screaming and what-have-you, and he has to have chosen the kind of woman about whom the neighbours have nothing but good to say, who nevertheless has enough chutzpah to get down to the precinct at once and file her complaint, and if it results in a trial, to face down public humiliation, for hearsay evidence about her morals and demeanour is admissible. The most the court will do for her is to rule that evidence emanating from a district other than the one she actually lives in is inadmissible. Then the jury must feel confident that no element of consent entered into the woman's behaviour.

Nevertheless, men do go to gaol for rape, mostly black men, nearly all of them poor, and neither the judges nor the prosecuting attorneys are hampered in their dealings by the awareness that they are rapists too, only they have more sophisticated methods of compulsion. A deprived man forces his way into a woman's body by pressing the point of a knife against her throat; a man who owns an automobile may stop on a lonely road and tell his passenger to come across or get out and walk. The hostility of the rapist and humiliation of the victim are not necessarily different despite the difference in the circumstances; indeed they could both be worse in the latter case, and that sort of thing happens every day. Probably the commonest form of non-criminal rape is rape by fraud – by phoney tenderness or false promises of an enduring relationship, for example.

The woman who is assaulted and raped by a total stranger may suffer less than the woman who endures constant humiliations at the hand of people she is trying to know and love. The inadequates and psychotics who are arrested for rape have been known to select their victims and lie in wait for them, and other criminal rapes may involve women who are known to or even related to their assailants, but for the most part the selection of the victim is as fortuitous as it might be in an automobile accident. That element of haphazardness can help the woman to avoid permanent psychic damage, because she is not compelled to internalize the experience and so to feel guilty and soiled as a consequence of it.

One of the great injustices which the victims of criminal rape must suffer is the necessity of reliving the experience in minute detail over and over again, from the first complaint to the police to the last phase of the trial. By attempting to prosecute the man who has raped her, a woman dissociates herself from the crime and endeavours to reconstitute her self-esteem, but it is a rare woman who is so independent of the evaluation of others that she can survive the contemptuous publicity that her attempts will draw upon her. If she fails to make her accusation stick, so that people assume that she is malicious or hysterical or that she enticed her rapist, she is in more serious psychic trouble than before. The odds against her succeeding in her prosecution, even after the police have reluctantly agreed to charge her assailant, are rather worse than four to one. If a woman's only concern is for herself and her eventual recovery from her experience, then she is much better advised not to prosecute. Rape is a habitual crime, however, and any woman who decides not to prosecute ought to spare a little thought for the women who will be raped as a consequence of her decision.

It is true that women have attempted to frame men for rapes that were never committed. Some have done so out of fear of punishment for an illicitly sexual relationship which has been discovered. Others have done so because they needed abortions, for revenge and other ulterior motives, for politics or policy. Some studies of rape quote a percentage of phoney rape charges as high as twenty per cent, but it is important to remember that the essence of the frame is that it is public and that a good deal is left to the discretion of law enforcers in deciding whether a woman has been truly offended or not. There are not too many pro-feminists in police stations.

Criminologists believe that less than one in five rapes are reported, making rape the least reported crime on the books. Those figures are, I believe, conservative, even within the terms of their narrow legalistic definition, which refers to the second gravest crime in the statutes – what we might call Grand Rape. The punishments for Grand Rape are very savage but it was not women who decided long ago that rapists should be blinded and castrated, or hanged with benefit of clergy (as they once were) or sentenced to jail for life (as they still are). Nevertheless, even from a woman's point of view there are instances in which rape is an injury just as serious and perhaps more so than homicide. A black friend of mine spent years of passionate effort to see that the seven white youths who raped her when she was sixteen years old and a virgin spent the maximum time in gaol, for they ruined her life by cursing her with a child whom she could never leave and never love. (The wonder of it is, of course, that a white jockocratic court convicted on the evidence of a black girl.)

It is in the interests of everyone involved that the connection of rape with pregnancy be resolutely severed. This means that all women claiming rape must be entitled to abortion, long before the offence could be proved. To wait for any legal process is to increase the degree of physical and mental trauma involved. Nowadays a raped woman has a pretty good chance of getting an abortion, especially if she can supply reasonable circumstantial evidence of the offence. However, the women who are most traumatized by rape are religious and sheltered women, who are not likely to be much helped to recover from their experience by the necessity of committing what they devoutly believe to be a mortal sin as a result of an act committed upon their person against their will. In cases of scrupulous religious conscience, religion can be the woman's only consolation, but most cases of normally muddled morality would be best aided by the adoption of a protocol by medical officials confronted with rape cases. One practical solution would be to offer the removal of the contents of the womb by aspiration as part of the diagnostic procedure. This would diminish the element of psychic intrusion and relieve the woman of the necessity of making a difficult moral choice arising out of circumstances beyond her control. The procedure, which is the same as biopsy aspiration, is commonly practised and need occasion very little discomfort.

The woman who is not impregnated or significantly physically injured as a result of rape, may nevertheless suffer acutely. The idea, so commonly entertained, that women somehow enjoy rape is absolutely unfounded, and a further indication of the contempt that men feel for women and their sexual functions. One might as well argue that because most men have repressed homosexual or feminine elements in their personalities, they enjoy buggery and humiliation. Women are, as a result of their enculturation, masochistic, but this does not mean that they enjoy being treated sadistically, although it may mean that they unconsciously invite it. Because of this masochism, women frequently take the whole burden of horror upon themselves. I know personally of a case in which a woman has been repeatedly raped by her mentally retarded brother for thirty years and has never sought any protection from him because of the distress that the knowledge would cause her parents. Her struggle to cope with the situation alone has had a marked effect on her psychic balance and yet it is not beyond a law-enforcement officer to argue that she is guilty of collusion, that she is an accomplice in effect.

Bored policemen, amusing themselves with girls who come to them to complain of rape, often kick off the proceedings by asking if they have enjoyed it. Rapists often claim in their defence that the prosecutrix enjoyed herself, that she showed evidence of physical pleasure or even had an orgasm. Most of them are lying. Some are sincere, but men are notoriously incapable of judging whether a woman is feeling pleasure or not, and women are not so unlike men that terror cannot cause something like the symptoms of erotic excitation in the genitals. Even if a woman were to have an orgasm in the course of rape, it need not necessarily lessen the severity of the trauma that she suffers. This, it would seem, is quite understandable in the case of rape suffered by a man at the hands of women, which although not an entity in law is still a possibility. Malinowski describes with thrills of disgusted horror the rape of a Melanesian male; if the clear evidence of the victim's sexual excitation makes any difference to his sense of outrage, it is to intensify it:

> The man is the fair game of women, for all that sexual violence, obscene cruelty, filthy pollution and rough handling can do to him. Thus, first they pull off and tear up his pubic leaf, the protection of his modesty, and, to a native, the symbol of his manly dignity. Then, by masturbatory practices and exhibitionism they try to produce an erection in their victim and, when their manoeuvres have brought about the desired result, one of them squats over him and inserts his penis into her vagina. After the first ejaculation he may be treated in the same manner by another woman. Worse things are to follow. Some of the women may defecate and micturate all over his body, paying special attention to his face which they pollute as thoroughly as they can. 'A man will vomit and vomit and vomit,' said a sympathetic informant. Sometimes these furies rub their genitals against his nose and mouth and use his fingers and toes, in fact, any projecting part of his body for lascivious purposes.

For Malinowski the trauma is directly connected with loss of dignity and obliteration of the individual's will, at which his body actually connives. Women too, have been known to vomit and vomit, to wash themselves compulsively, to burn their clothes, even to attempt suicide, after a rape. Nightmares, depression, pathological shyness, inability to leave the house, terror of darkness, all have been known to develop in otherwise healthy women who have been raped.

Malinowski was writing from the point of view of the rapee. The injury, for him, lay not in an outrage to his tutors and guardians, or in injury to his body, or in an unwanted pregnancy, but somewhere even more fundamental, in his will, and thence in his ego, his dignity. In this perspective the legalistic category of Grand Rape fades into unimportance. Sexual rip-offs are part of every woman's daily experience; they do not have the gratifying strangeness of disaster, with the special reconstructive energies that disasters call forth. They simply wear down the contours of emotional contacts and gradually brutalize all those who are party to them. Petty rape corrodes a woman's self-esteem so that she grows by degrees not to care too much what happens or how. In her low moments she calls all men bastards; she enters on new relationships with suspicion and a forlorn hope that maybe this time she will get a fair deal. The situation is self-perpetuating. The treatment she most fears she most elicits. The results of this hardening of the heart are eventually much worse than the consequences of fortuitous sexual assault by a stranger, the more so because they are internalized, insidious and imperceptible.

The idea that a woman has merely to consent or give in to sexual contact provides the basic motivation for petty rape. Silence or failure to resist is further misconstrued as consent. Then, by a further ramification of blunder, passive silence is thought to indicate pleasure. The breakdown in sexual communications occasioned by acceptance of these related vulgar errors can be illustrated by an example.

A young Cambridge undergraduate at a party in London missed his last train back to Cambridge and so asked around the other guests at the party for a bed for the night. A female guest, who lived near the party and near the railway station, said he might use her spare room, not making any odds of the fact that her husband was away, for the young man and all his family were well known to them. She duly drove him to her apartment where clean towels and pyjamas were laid out for him and he was wished a good night's rest in the spare room. She had had rather a lot to drink at the party and was feeling giddy and rather ill, so she was grateful to slide between the sheets and pass quietly out before she began to feel any worse.

It was beneath young Lochinvar's dignity to stay in his room though, and she was just slipping through rather swirling veils of sleep when he climbed into the bed beside her. She resisted, but there was little point in making much to-do; having the police called to the apartment would have made a scandal, upset everybody and left her in a ridiculous situation. The law would take only one view of an unaccompanied married woman's invitation to a young man to stay the night, regardless of the fact that Victorian sexual paranoia is gradually ebbing from other spheres of activity. She scolded and pleaded, exaggerated the degree of her drunkenness and even resorted to being sick, but the young man's ego would give no quarter. Like a Fascist guard in Mussolini's Italy, he woke her every time her eyelids began to close. Then he made his little show of force. She offered only passive resistance and so got fucked.

It was, of course, a terrible fuck. She was exhausted, distressed and mutinous; he was deeply inconsiderate and cruel, although he fancied himself as a nipple twiddler and general sexual operator and believes to this day that he gave her the fucking of her life. He has boasted of his conquest just often enough so that the fact of his talking about it has come to her ears and reduced her to acute fear and misery. She has never told her husband of what happened because of the sheer unlikeliness of his being able to exonerate her from any taint of desire for the little shit, however nobly he decided to behave. Worst of all, she must see her enemy frequently at dinners and parties in friends' houses and endure his triumph over her time and time again. She has not allowed the circumstances to corrode her self-esteem to any serious extent, but her enemy cannot lay the fact to his credit.

What has happened is just one kind of the zillions of forms of petty rape. There is no punishment and no treatment for offender or victim in a case like this. It just has to be crossed off as another minor humiliation, another devaluation of the currency of human response. The woman in this instance revenged herself by striking the man out of her list of friends, but he hardly noticed. His account of the affair, needless to say, is very different.

The attitude of the rapist in such an example is not hard to interpret in terms of the prevailing sexual ideology. A man is, after all, supposed to seduce, cajole, persuade, pressurize and eventually overcome. A reasonable man will avoid threats, partly because he has a shrewd idea that they will not produce the desired result. A psychotic rapist is quite likely to desire fright and even panic-stricken resistance and struggle as a prerequisite of his sexual arousal or satisfaction, but not your everyday pusillanimous rapist. He simply takes advantage of any circumstances that are in his favour, to override the woman's independence. The man who has it in his power to hire and fire women from an interesting or lucrative position may profit by that factor to extort sexual favours which would not spontaneously be offered him. A man who is famous or charismatic might exploit those advantages to humiliate women in ways which they would otherwise angrily resist. In cases like these, mutual contempt is the eventual outcome, but what the men do not realize is that they are exploiting the oppressed and servile status of women. The women's capitulation might be ignoble, but it is morally more excusable than the cynical manipulation of their susceptibility.

One of the elements which is often abused in the petty rape situation is the woman's affection for the rapist. This might not even be a completely non-sexual affection: there is a case on record in Denver in which a woman who was brutally raped explained to the judge that she would have been quite happy to ball with her assailant if he had asked her nicely, but as soon as they got into her apartment he beat her up and raped her. The parallel in petty rape is the exploitation of a woman's tenderness, which would involve eventual sexual compliance for a loveless momentary conquest. Because a woman likes a man and would like to develop some sort of a relationship with him, she is loath to behave in a trouble-making manner when he begins to prosecute his intentions in a way which alienates her. Her enemy takes cold-blooded advantage of that fact. For lots of girls who slide into promiscuity, this is the conflict in which they are defeated time and time again.

In all but the most sophisticated communities, a young woman who wishes to participate in the social life of her generation must do so as a man's guest. Dating is a social and economic imperative for her. This situation is the direct result of her oppressed condition and however venal her motives may seem to be she is not totally responsible for them. For her, the pressure is disguised as pressure to fall in love and go steady; he may see it as a kind of being on the make, corresponding to his own fairly impersonal desire for sexual gratification. If she gets raped as a result of her dependence upon a man as an escort, neither party thinks that she has anything grave to complain of, and yet a great wrong has been done.

For most young women who set out on the dating road to marriage, petty rape is a constant hazard. The fact that a man pays for the night's entertainment, that he owns and drives the car, that he has initiated all that has happened, means by extension that he is also entitled to initiate and to set the pace of the physical intimacies that will occur. She would probably be disappointed if he manifested no desire for her, but she also has the problem of not seeming easy while keeping him interested. His self-esteem prompts him to achieve as much intimacy as he can, before she 'draws the line'. The element of petty rape appears when he threatens to throw her over if she doesn't come across or whenever he decides that he does not like her well enough to move gradually through the stages of intimacy as she desires them, but will force the pace to get as much as possible out of an otherwise unsatisfactory encounter. His use of the vocabulary of tenderness becomes fraudulent. He may even fake an excess of sexual desire.

A group of law students at my first university had a competition to see who could fuck the most women in one semester; one ploy that they all had in common was a trick of heavy breathing and groaning, as if they were writhing in torments of desire. As they were after quantity and not quality, this was not often the case. It worked very well in the main, but partly because they were exercising the class prerogative of the rich bourgeois and wantonly disrupting the lives and expectations of women situated in less fortunate circumstances, like the hero of *My Secret Life*, but more callously.

The man who won that competition was an expert in exploiting women's fantasy and vanity, and their tendency to delude themselves that the contact they were experiencing was a genuine personal encounter and not a crass sexual rip-off. He and his friends were proud of their mastery of the gestures of tenderness, but their use of them was utterly self-centred. They were simply exercising a skill like angling, drawing silly women to their own humiliation. The only way to earn their respect and friendship was to resist them, and so they wantonly encouraged toughness and suspicion in this cold world. The girls they had never realized they'd been victims of petty rape until they grasped the fact that the first time was also the last.

For such rich and handsome young men, petty rape was a sport which, by virtue of their privileges, they played with great success. There were occasional uglinesses which marred the light-heartedness of their proceedings. One of them was threatened with a paternity suit, but all his friends turned up in court and testified that they had had carnal knowledge of the plaintiff and so he got off. They committed perjury in fact, but it did not disturb their sleep.

The group-bonding skills of males will always defeat the interests of isolated women. Men will conspire to see that acts of petty rape are successful. Many women would be appalled to learn just how their most intimate behaviour and physical peculiarities are discussed by men, and this supplies a further dimension of petty rape by blackmail. There is no point in resisting a man's advances if he is going to talk about how he had you in any case, especially when your word is generally less respected than his. I was once pestered for three or four days by a detestable male chauvinist who explained my consequent dislike of him as pique because he refused to fuck me. When sex is an ego contest, women get fucked over all the time.

Petty rape is sometimes called seduction, which is not regarded as a contemptible or particularly damaging activity. A woman who capitulates to a seducer is considered to do so because she really wanted to or because she is too silly or too loose to know how to resist. It might even be thought to be in her interest to overcome her prudishness or priggishness about sex. The man who excuses his unloving manipulation of women's susceptibilities in ways like these cannot honestly claim to have the women's interests at heart. His assumption that he knows what is good for them is overweening even if it is sincere, which it usually is not.

Some men decide that it is their prerogative to punish a woman in a sexual encounter, either for her looseness or for teasing or for lying and evading the issue. The distortion of an erotic response into a chastisement is pathological, but not uncommon. An economics student, son of a high-ranking public official, boasted to me once that he had punished a girl who had lied to him that she was menstruating, by raping her, buggering her and throwing her out of his rooms in Cambridge in the small hours of the morning, knowing that she would find no kind of transport to take her back to her home in the country. He had absolutely no understanding of her motives for lying to him; she had done it because he would take no stalling while she needed time to get to desire the intimacy that he was forcing on her. She could have walked out earlier, or screamed and brought the housekeeper to her rescue, but that would have meant rustication for him and a summary end to any developing relationship. Either course would have required positive hostility, which she simply did not feel. She had very little understanding, for her own part, of the sexual hostility that he did feel, which underlay a good deal of his sexual response, especially in casual affairs.

The men who do cruel things to women are not a class apart; they are not totally incapable of relating to women. In nearly every case I have described, the details were told to me by the men, who explained their comparatively humane attitudes towards me as a result of my own respect for myself and my own straightforwardness in sexual matters, both results of my unusually privileged status as a woman; I was also older than most of them. But I have not entirely now emancipated myself from the female legacy of low self-image, self-hatred and identification with the oppressors, which are part of the pathology of oppression. The girls who have been mistreated in the ways that I have described, take the fault upon themselves. They think that they must have made a mistake somewhere, that their bodies have provoked disgust, that they were too greasy in their conversation. The internalization of the injury is what makes petty rape such an insidiously harmful offence against women. What the men have done is to exploit and so intensify the pathology of oppression.

Many petty rapists do not wittingly dislike women or hate them; they do not revenge themselves upon their mothers through other women's bodies in any conscious way. Group therapy sessions at treatment centres for sex offenders are producing results which seem to indicate that repressed hostility towards the mother is one of the most common unconscious motivations for violent rape, but these conclusions ought not to be regarded as particularly enlightening; if an analyst is seeking evidence of an infantile trauma involving women, it is almost inevitably going to involve a mother or a mother surrogate. It is small wonder that our civilization manifests a psychotic attitude to women, when children are thrown upon the mercy of one woman almost exclusively during the formative years between one and five. Women's hostility to each other may be explained by the same phenomenon, at least partially. Teachers at any time, women in authority over men in any capacity, attract a good deal of antagonism, some of which masquerades as affection.

There are other discernible motives for active sexual hostility in the male. Religions which rely upon guilt mechanisms for their hold upon the faithful, build up an image of the female as an occasion of sin. The nuns at my Catholic primary school prepared the children for raping and being raped by treating even the littlest girls' bodies as dire inducements to lasciviousness, even to the point of forbidding us to bare our upper arms or our collarbones, and begging us all not to look at our 'private parts' even when we were washing them as perfunctorily as possible in the bath. This wanton stimulation of sexual tension still goes on in religious schools. If scientology and other forms of psychic manipulation for eventual control can be declared illegal, then some attention should be paid to this process, enacted without fear of reprisal upon the very young.

Undue aestheticism in representing sexual behaviour can also have harmful effects. The inauthenticity of sexual fantasy as it is stimulated by commercial representations of the woman as sex object leaves many immature men unable to cope with the eventual discovery that women do not feel smooth and velvety all over, that their pubic hair exists and is not swans'-down or vine tendrils, that a woman in heat does not smell like a bed of roses. Most convicted rapists who have been subjected to any degree of analysis have shown an exaggerated dislike of menstruation. For most men, sexual experience begins and persists throughout the years of most intense libidinous activity – the teens – as fantasy and masturbation, rather than actual physical confrontation with the object of their desire. It is not surprising, then, that the imagery of their puerile fantasies continues to interpose itself between the ego and the reality long after their active sexual life has begun in earnest. What the permissive society has achieved, in fact, is merely the proliferation of inauthentic sexual fantasy, with virtually no degree of emancipation of the sexes into genuine communication and mutual understanding.

Women are not yet consumers of commercial soft-core pornography; they do not have the same fetishistic attitude towards men's bodies that men have towards women's. Instead, they are further alienated from the area of male sexual orientation by their own culture of romantic fantasy. Attempts to duplicate the marketing of images of women's bodies to men, have been made with men's bodies, without much success, and similar inauthenticities were represented. When my husband posed for the gatefold in *Cosmopolitan* (UK), it was found necessary not only to cover him with body make-up and hide his penis behind his upraised thigh, but also to airbrush his navel and the wrinkles on his belly clean out of the picture. Men trying to understand feminists' reactions to the commercialized stereotype of women ought to study their own reactions to the degradations and desexualization of Paul du Feu.

Those who hate women most are often the most successful womanizers. The connection used to be recognized in common parlance by the expressions 'lady-killer' and 'wolf'. Sylvia Plath describes a crucial encounter with one such in *The Bell Jar*, leaving it to the reader to estimate the role that this humiliation plays in Esther Greenwood's eventual collapse.

> Marco's small, flickering smile reminded me of a snake I'd teased once in the Bronx Zoo. When I tapped my finger on the stout cage glass the snake had opened its clockwork jaws and seemed to smile. Then it struck and struck against the invisible pane until I moved off.
>
> I had never met a woman-hater before. I could tell Marco was a woman-hater because, in spite of all the models and TV starlets in the room that night, he paid attention to nobody but me. Not out of kindness or even curiosity, but

because I'd happened to be dealt to him, like a playing card in a pack of identical cards.

Young Esther has no hope of beating Marco at the game he has been perfecting most of his adult life. He sweeps aside her tremulous attempts to remain independent. On the dance floor he forces her to give up all idea of independent locomotion:

'What did I tell you?' Marco's breath scorched my ear. 'You're a perfectly respectable dancer.'
I began to see why woman-haters could make such fools of women. Woman-haters were like gods: invulnerable and chock-full of power. They descended and they disappeared. You could never catch one.

Marco's excuse for treating all women like sluts is an impossible love for his first cousin (probably a narcissistic fantasy) who is to become a nun. After he has assaulted Esther, and she has partly beaten him off and he has partly given up, saying 'Sluts, all sluts . . . yes or no, it's all the same', Esther goes back to her sex-segregated hotel, climbs on to the parapet of the roof and feeds her wardrobe to the night wind. Marco has brought her to the beginning of the end.

In all cases of petty rape, the victim does not figure as a personality, as someone vulnerable and valuable, whose responses must not be cynically tampered with. So great is women's need to believe that men really like them that they are often slow to detect perfunctoriness in proffered caresses or the subtle change in attitude when the Rubicon has been crossed and the softening up of the victim can give way to unilateral gratification. Not all woman-haters can belie their feelings of hatred and contempt successfully throughout the duration of a sexual encounter. When their situation is secure, say, when they have the victim safe behind the hotel door and know that she is not about to run screaming through the lobby in a torn dress, they may abandon all pretence of tenderness and get down to the business of hate-fucking, and yet still the wretched woman attempts to roll with the punches. Her enemy may use physical and verbal abuse, even a degree of force to make her comply with forms of sexual intercourse which she does not desire. Mostly he retreats into an impersonal, masturbatory frame of mind. After the loveless connection is over, he cannot wait to get rid of her, either by giving her her cab fare or shutting her out of his mind by going to sleep, or pretending to.
Guilt and disgust may follow. The man may be sorry that he went with such an abject creature, but he will not blame himself for the poor quality of the sex he has had, any more than when he finds the woman unresponsive because her sexual submission has been extorted from her. If he is distressed by the crassness and perfunctoriness of the love he has made, or embarrassed by the willingness and generosity of the love he has been given, he will abuse the woman in his mind. She is a dog, a pig, goes with

anyone, so dumb she wouldn't know you were up her till you coughed. Like the Grand Rapist, he excuses his conduct on the grounds that she asked for it, by her lewdness, her willingness to discuss sex, her appetite at dinner, the money she made him spend, the dress she had on, the size of her breasts. If she has enjoyed and responded to caresses up to a point when they became brutal and struggled to escape, then she is a tease who leads men on and then wants to chicken out when he gets to the nitty-gritty. No punishment is too severe for a tease.

Some men who are very well aware of their own preference for force-fucking and their hostility to women, may doubt that women's sensibilities are elevated enough to perceive their own humiliation. Feminists are at last beginning to spell it out for them, but too many men do not realize that the slogan 'An end to rape' does not so much refer to Grand Rapes committed on the crime-ridden streets of the cities, but to the daily brutalization of contact between brother and sister, father and daughter, teacher and pupil, doctor and patient, employer and employee, dater and datee, fiancé and fiancée, husband and wife, adulterer and adulteress, the billions of petty liberties exacted from passive and wondering women. The solution is not to be found in the castration or killing of the rare rapists who offend so crazily that they can be caught and punished, but in the correction of our distorted notions of the nature of sexual intercourse, which are also the rationale of the law of rape as a felony.

Women are now struggling to discover and develop their own sexuality, to know their own minds and bodies, and to improve the bases upon which they can attempt communication with men. The men who continue to assume that women must be treated as creatures who do not know what is good for them, to be cajoled or coerced or punished at the will of a stiff-standing cock, seek to imprison women in the pathology of their oppressed condition. Some women are coquettish, although far fewer than the mythology of rape supposes; the only way to put an end to such fatuous guile is to cease to play the game, simply by taking women at their word. The woman who says no when she means yes and so loses a man she wants will find a way to see him again to tell him that she meant yes all the time – if she really did mean yes, that is. If she didn't really mean yes, then she is better left alone.

Any man who realizes that he likes screwing mutinous women, that he is bored at the prospect of only balling women who want him, had better be aware that he finds resistance and tension essential to his satisfaction: he is a petty rapist and should look to it.

The abandonment of the stereotype of seduction, conquest, the chase and all, increases the number of erotic possibilities rather than diminishing it. Once the rigid course of sexual manipulation is disrupted, the unexpected may occur, some genuine erotic development can take place. Even the rapist author of *My Secret Life*, whose sexual activity was entirely dependent upon the possibilities of exploiting lower-class women, was aware that coercion and insistence were not in his best sexual interests, even when he had paid for the use of a woman's body and was in some sense entitled to it:

> A custom of mine then, and always followed since, is putting down my fee, – it prevents mistakes, and quarrels. When paid, if a woman will not let me have her, be it so, – she has some reason, – perhaps a good one for me.

Nothing that I have said should be interpreted to mean that no man should try to make love to a woman unless he is prepared to marry her or to undertake a long and serious affair with her. A one-night stand can be the most perfect and satisfying sexual encounter of all, as long as there is no element of fraud or trickery or rip-off in the way in which it develops. If women are to free themselves from the necessity of deploying their sexuality as a commodity, then men will have to level in their dealings with them, and that is all we ask. There is still room for excitement, uncertainty, even antagonism in the development of sexual friendship, but *if you do not like us, cannot listen to our part of the conversation, if we are only meat to you, then leave us alone.*

As women develop more confidence and more self-esteem, and become as supportive towards each other as they have been to men, they also lose their reluctance to denounce men for petty rape. Where before they respected men's privacy a good deal more than men respected theirs (despite phoney claims of chivalry) they are now beginning to tell it how it is. A theatrical impresario, well-known for his randiness, recently invited a leading women's liberationist to his hotel for a business meeting. To her amazement, for she had thought such gambits long out of style, he leapt on her as soon as he had her fairly inside the room. She held him off until suddenly he ejaculated all over the front of her dress. Gone are the days when she would have slunk out behind a newspaper. Her dress is a museum piece of the women's movement in her country and the joke will be around for years.

Rape-crisis centres are being set up by groups of women more interested in self-help than vindictiveness. Here a woman who has been traumatized by a sexual experience can come for counsel, for medical and psychiatric help. She is not regarded as a culprit, or challenged about the length of her skirts or the thickness of her eye make-up; her word is believed, as the first step to reconstituting an ego damaged by sexual misuse. The victim is encouraged to externalize the experience rather than to entertain feelings of guilt and shame, and she is also taught how to defend herself against future assault and brutalization, even from her husband, who by law has the right of rape over her. Menstrual aspiration will also be practised as the technique becomes better known and the instruments more widely available. Force-fucking is being phased out.

The new feeling of solidarity among women will render petty rape quite futile. Women who used to rejoice to think that their men treated other women badly cannot accept it once their consciousness is raised. A musician returning to his feminist old lady after a protracted tour abroad boasted that he managed to be faithful to her (something she had never demanded) by making the adoring groupies give him blow jobs and then get out. He was proud that he had never even kissed one of them, let alone balled her. To his amazement, his old lady walked out on him.

Women are finding, in the stirring words of women's advocate Florynce Kennedy, that 'kickin' ass and takin' names, talkin' loud and drawin' a crowd is better than suckin' '. Our weapons may be little more than ridicule and boycott, but we will use them. Women are sick to their souls of being fucked over. Now that sex has become political the petty rapist had better watch his ass; he won't be getting away with it too much longer. How would you feel if a videotape of your last fuck was playing at the feminist guerilla theatre? We didn't start this war, but we intend to bring it to an honourable settlement, which means we have to make a show of strength some time. People who are fighting for their lives fight with any weapons that come to hand, so it is foolish to expect a fair fight. Sex behaviour is becoming as public as any other expression of political belief: next time I write an article like this I'll tell you all the names. So don't say you weren't warned.

Women tied down

Sunday Times, 13 February 1973

Perhaps women should be glad that Mr William Hamilton's Private Member's Bill to render illegal discrimination by employers on grounds of sex was talked out in the Commons on the twenty-eighth of January. For one thing, the manner in which a division of the House was rendered impossible by Mr Ronald Bell made it perfectly clear that the men who rule us are no longer concerned with the appearance of democracy in their everyday dealings. One man's manoeuvre was able to secure the defeat of the bill against the wishes of the majority present at the debate. The four o'clock Friday deadline proved more intransigent than any other factor. All the combatants trooped off to tea. Mr Hamilton's bill has been killed partly because he does not have a favourable position in the Private Members' Ballot – in other words, the cumbersome machine that governs us in our day-to-day dealings is run on principles of compounded serendipity. It must be better to know this than to live blindly on in the hope that there is a divinity that shapes our ends, governments being *vox populi, vox dei*.

It is also as well to see clearly the intolerance and contempt which exists in our society towards women. If Mr Hamilton's bill had been passed, a great many people might have been led to suppose that England displayed an exemplary attitude towards women, having freed them from all significant forms of discrimination. In fact, no significant amelioration in the condition of women need have followed. Since equal pay became law in most European countries, the difference in male and female earnings has grown, not diminished. The female-dominated industries are still backward, their workers the most exploited in industry. When a woman cannot attract employment by virtue of the fact that she is cheaper than a man, she is as likely as not to find that she cannot find a job. In the industries dominated by women, pay is low, conditions are poor, so men do not bother to compete, except at the highest level. Polarization in employment increases. The women who drive the sewing machines enrich the designers who are men, and so on.

All that Mr Hamilton's bill could have accomplished would have been to make expression of the prejudice which exists against female employees an offence. It simply imposed a form of censorship which would have clouded the contours of the situation from the view of the egregious women in search of a decent job. Where the employer was not allowed to specify sex in his advertising for a job, he was not obliged, unless the bill was more cunningly formulated than I can well believe, to employ any of the women who applied to him. His reasons for rejecting female applicants could always be expressed in terms which had no direct connection with sexual discrimination. Moreover, his criteria of suitability for the job need not be altogether spurious: the progressive disqualification of women for exciting and responsible positions in industry or the professions begins as soon as they are born. By the time they come to apply for gainful employment the process is completed. Mr Employer may claim, say, that Ms Applicant is tentative and unsure of herself when dealing with strangers, and he may well be right. He will not be expected to employ her to the disadvantage of his business, pending her development of the qualities that he wishes to exploit. If Mr Hamilton's bill had demanded that all employers show an equal distribution of men and women in all parts of their enterprises, it might have forcibly wrenched asunder the vicious circle of women's position in the workforce, but it would also have wrecked what remains of the British economy. None of the liberal MPs who were so hot for Mr Hamilton's token legislation would have voted for it.

There is another way of dealing with the problem. In America a woman who feels that she has been rejected from a job for which she feels she was qualified, in favour of a male candidate, may bring her case to the attention of the Department of Health, Education and Welfare, who in turn will approach the employer and ask him to justify his hiring policies. As a result of these inquiries, Harvard and Columbia universities have had to offer to reform in this regard, to bring the proportion of women they hire into line with the proportion of women who are qualified to take up teaching posts. Columbia is now under sentence of closure, having failed to alter their policy significantly in two years. This solution has the advantage of taking the burden of action off the shoulders of the individual woman, but it can hardly be as effective outside academic and research establishments, where job qualifications exist clearly on paper, and in some other cases where potential, ability and experience can be more or less accurately assessed.

We are still faced with the problem that women's conditioning disqualifies most of them from competing in the job market. Not only are they often not motivated to seek independence and self-respect as a permanent part of the workforce, but even when they are eager to make themselves a different kind of life from *Kinder, Küche, Kirche*, the stress of continually opposing conventional pressures often results in disturbance and impairment of efficiency. No form of words tabled before Mr Selwyn Lloyd can offer serious resistance to the million threads which tie women down. In all too many cases the legalistic approach to women's demands for a freer life will founder on the discovery that oppression cannot be legislated out of existence.

That Mr Hamilton's Private Member's Bill was dealt with so shabbily is a shame and a disgrace to the Conservative government. Not the least saddening aspect of it was that out of twenty-six women of all parties in Parliament only fourteen actually attended the debate. Mr Sharples's arguments and the sneers of Bell of Bucks were as grotesque as could be hoped, but even the speech of the bill's mover left much to be desired as a testament of seriousness and commitment to the women's cause. Mr Hamilton begged us to let him say this about women's liberation: 'I do not believe in the throwing away of women's apparel either above the belt or below the belt. I do not think it makes any contribution one way or the other, but having met some of them in the past week or two, I have been impressed by their intelligence, courage, determination and courtesy.' What Mr Hamilton's 'them' can refer to is anybody's guess; one supposes he means members of the Women's Liberation Movement. Why he had not met any long before when he was drafting his bill is also anybody's guess. Why he should refer to throwing away apparel below the belt may possibly be because he read a frivolous column in this paper many months ago and mistook it for a Women's Liberation Manifesto. The combination of ignorance, presumption and inarticulacy in this utterance makes one tremble for the bill. Nevertheless, the treatment of this bill in debate should provide reason to tremble for the Tories, for pseudo-democracy and the so-called rule of law.

King Cophetua and the beggarmaid

Unpublished

Throughout the latter part of 1972, relations with the Sunday Times *were becoming more and more strained. My column had been run alternately with a column by Jilly Cooper and the feeling seemed to be that mine should be as frothy as hers; I tried mixing serious columns with flummery but the editor of the 'Look!' pages dropped everything but the flummery.*

'Please – if you have any ideas help me – I'm going round the bend.' Her problem was not as unusual as she thought, for she is one of many wives who scrimp and plot to run a household on next to nothing while her husband plays the big executive on five and a half thousand pounds a year. He wears custom-made suits and keeps his hair well-cut and his shoes gleaming, gliding around to executive lunches in an impressive car, for the good of the firm's image, while she prowls the supermarkets in search of bargains, and has too little left after buying the children's shoes to buy herself a new summer dress. He lives, with the help of the expense account, at one level and she at another, a much lower one.

A husband may have a moral duty to 'maintain his wife according to his condition or estate in life or according to his means', but he has absolutely no obligation to do so. His wife has no legal claim on any of his earnings; to continue in the jargon of the law books, 'Those chattels, personal in possession, and specific chattels in the hands of third parties, which before the marriage belonged to the husband, continue to belong to him exclusively after the marriage, the *communio bonorum* being unknown to the marriage law of England.' 'The mere fact of marriage gave the wife no claim to participate in her husband's personal estate during coverture, nor any indefeasible right to share in it, after his death.' What is true of his property at the time of marriage, is also true of his earnings during the time of his marriage. He cannot be forced to settle any proportion of his income upon his wife for maintenance of the household, unless, of course, his wife sues for divorce, when he may eventually go to gaol for failing to pay her more than he had ever let her have during the period of their cohabitation.

Of course, women do share joint bank accounts with their husbands, and are given half shares in the conjugal dwelling, but not of right. It is simply a personal arrangement and as such a matter of luck.

There was a time when even the property which a woman owned in her own right had to be held in trust for her by a man: her father, her guardian or her husband. The Married Woman's Property Act of 1882 changed that, and for the propertied classes it proved to be a change for the better. Moreover, a wife whose husband gave her a separate allowance for her own use, pin-money, was entitled to save it if she chose and to dispose of it as she wished. If she received nothing but a housekeeping allowance, she was not entitled to claim a penny of anything she managed to save. The Married Woman's Property Act of 1964 decreed that, 'If any question arises as to the right of a husband or wife to money derived from any allowance made by the husband for the expenses of the matrimonial home or for similar purposes, or to any property acquired out of such money, the money or property shall, in the absence of any agreement between them to the contrary, be treated as belonging to the husband and the wife in equal shares.' So out of every penny she managed to retain by dint of clever and assiduous economies, a wife may claim a half-penny, as of right. This too might have been welcomed as a significant reform by those housewives whose husbands gave them ample housekeeping money, but even then it affected only those who did not automatically spend the lot on the house and the children, because that was how they saw *their* duty.

No reform has ever given a wife the right to know what her husband earns, or what he claims on his tax return, or to insist upon a certain amount as due to her. One of the inconveniences of the confused notion of marriage as a true love match, which we have inherited, is that few brides would insist upon assurances about the level of their maintenance before they said the clinching words. Everybody hopes that justice will be done, but no attempt is made to ensure it.

Where earnings are low, the proportion made over to the wife is much greater than it is among the middle classes and white-collar workers. It is the kind of tradition often honoured in the breach among the working classes, that dad makes his weekly pay-packet over to mum, who then lets him have an often ill-spared allowance for booze and cigarettes. Because low earnings need careful husbanding, the wife is decently consulted in the manner of it, but not always. Many working wives in England are actually supporting the family on their earnings alone. If they don't like it, they can lump it.

It is not easy to see how legal reform could supply an answer. From the juristic point of view, such a reform would have to cut across the whole common law tradition of the role of feme covert, because England is almost unique in Europe in having no tradition of common property between spouses. The repercussions throughout the law of property could be enormous.

Practically, few women would be emotionally prepared for the embarrassment of litigation against their husbands. The effects upon the domestic atmosphere would be disastrous.

Meanwhile, in the actual world, the phenomenon of the split-class family grows commoner. The rising executives who accustom themselves to *haute cuisine* at the firm's expense have wives at home feasting uncomplainingly on baked beans on toast. The occasional climax of injustice comes when the firm's white-haired boy admits that he has no further use for a wife who serves the boss with shoulder of lamb and frozen peas, instead of Chateaubriand and *pommes dauphinoises*.

Nowadays, most women who marry do not own property in their own right, and do not have any independent income. Their financial independence can only come from the work of their own hands, which two thirds of them give up, more often sooner than later. They give up their earnings (which they are easily persuaded to invest in the family anyway) because they are doing other work, for which they are not entitled to earn a specific reward. That they must also perform this work within the terms of a budget which their husband has sole right to determine seems verily outrageous, but the regular method of determining just practice in the particular case is readily conceivable.

One small guerilla tactic suggests itself. As a further aspect of a wife's status of virtual wardship, a husband cannot repudiate her debts. Perhaps some of those desperate women who have written to me might consider the naughty expedient of not struggling any more to pay those household debts, and try running up a few more, like Blondie used to with her hats. It is not a dignified alternative, but it might bring about a change in the law of housewives' financial serfdom more quickly than any other expedient.

But my correspondent's question remains unanswered: 'How can I establish my rights without breaking the family up?'

'Unhelpful to the workers' cause'

Unpublished

After months when half the columns I sent in failed to appear, I decided to go for broke with this column. It was rejected on the bizarre grounds that it did not advance the wage claims of nurses or teachers. It was perfectly obvious to me that a paper edited by Harold Evans was most unlikely to publish a strike call, especially when those being urged to withdraw their labour are those we have left in charge of our children and our aged and sick. Neither nurses nor teachers have ever taken really militant action and the pay, conditions and prestige of both professions have continued to deteriorate.

Some people are canny enough, when they are very young, to ride the rapids of our education techniques with their faculties intact so that they do still have the option of doing some genuine work for the community. They ignore the massive bribes that are offered for instant relinquishment of the right to develop, they decide not to be unskilled or semi-skilled labour, selling nothing but their powers of endurance, but to do some challenging work. Too many of them do not realize that they have no right to make the biggest contribution of which they are capable; that the opportunity is a privilege for which they will have to pay dear.

Doctors, lawyers and even accountants have always understood that they would have to stand firm, functioning as a solid group protecting its own expertise and hence its earning capacity, from the tendency of all merchants to buy cheap and sell dear. They made of their special knowledge a rare and valuable commodity, insisted on a mystique and protected each other by an immovable professional code. They were cynical enough to know that if they were once cast in the role of public martyrs, working harder and more generously than most other groups of workers, they would be left with nothing but masochism, exhaustion and despair to show for their labours. Like successful trade unions, who have always worked on the principle that the job is worth whatever you can force the employer to pay for it and not a penny more or less, they understood that nobody was going to pay them their fees out of gratitude, that if they left it to the man whose life they had saved to pay them what he thought fit, they would wind up with half an old penny.

Which is about what the nurses and the teachers have wound up with. It is universally acknowledged that they do a marvellous job, that without them society would crumble, and for that very fact of indispensability they are required to *pay*. The spiritual satisfactions of doing such noble work are thought to be so significant that they replace the need for a house to live in, a car to travel in, clothes for the children, an annual holiday or meat on the table.

The teachers were long ago swindled in a now-historic attempt to curb inflation. They accepted a principle of parity, as the jargon of the day had it, and had to spend the whole financial year watching every other union defying the policy and holding the employers and the government to ransom for wages much higher than what most teachers would have been earning, even with the increment they had agreed to forgo. They were supposed to feed on their own selflessness, on the sheer prestige that their 'professions' commanded in society, and for too long they fell for the gambit.

The harsh fact is that in a materialistic society the poor command no respect, even if they do a noble and self-sacrificing job for the community. The teachers have become the Harijans of England. The Untouchables were essential too, they carried off disease-bearing excrement, swept streets and kept the rich from infection, and for it they were despised. The school-children are quick to see that the nice man with the haggard face and the darns in the elbows of his Marks & Spencer's jersey is a loser: the rivalry between school and home is sharpened by the contrast between the wages of drudgery and the wages of work. A schoolboy whose pocket money provides him with luxuries beyond his harassed teacher's reach does not scruple to abuse him, or even to attack him. The teacher is nothing but a sucker and his inability to take care of himself is clear from his manifest inability to protect his standard of living. Schoolroom violence is not the result of some mysterious debauchery of the underground press or of the availability of porn of all sorts; it is a direct result of the degradation of the teaching profession into genteel and impotent poverty. The powerless get beaten up. The teacher now plays the role of the puny kid with specs. Not only is he prevented from defending himself against classroom violence, he is also subjected to violence of a more sophisticated kind from his superiors, who may humiliate him and chastise him by reprimand or staffroom discrimination, even dictate his dress and appearance, without any fear of retaliation.

The National Union of Teachers has two-thirds female membership. Everything I've said about *him* could have been said about *her* and then some.

It has even been argued that it is because of the masochistic passivity of the women who have come to dominate the teaching profession that the prestige of the profession has declined so much. It might as profitably be put down to the liberal optimism of the average bourgeois teacher or to fatuous idealism or to the effects of teacher training in brainwashing docile employees. Few training schemes would be allowed the ideological content of the disciplines of teacher training.

Other people's callousness and greed are already driving the best teachers out of the profession. Gradually, the competence and spontaneous devotion of teachers will decline as they become more and more overworked as a result of understaffing. Soon, only those people who had no other option will be making a drudgery of teaching. It will no longer be dignified work, but a shallow, time-wasting, humiliating procedure, a sort of witless game. Perhaps that time has already come.

There can be no doubt about the cynicism of a society which dares the indispensable servants of the community to withdraw their labour, knowing that they will eventually capitulate to the reiterated reproaches of the press and the public. Even the pinkest newspapers have strike editorials which point out that the irresponsible workers are causing suffering to the poor, while the withers of the rich are unwrung; that nurses and ancillary workers can only strike at the direct expense of the sick; and teachers' half-hearted attempts to protect their standard of living only penalize the children. The government is not required to have a heart: it actually hopes that there will be deaths which will instantly be blamed upon the strikers, although the government must bear an equal part of the blame, so that the strikers will be shamed and blackmailed back to work.

Blackmail has been so successful with nurses and teachers that it has been used in situations where the connections are more tenuous. The power workers were constantly confronted with the spectre of old people freezing to death. Old people freeze to death every year for want of the wherewithal to pay for adequate heating – now these casualties were to be considered as murdered by the power workers. The newspapers have been hunting for a *corpus delicti* in their case against the gasworkers. One woman, panicked by the dire warnings of unsafe levels of pressure, bought a camp stove and blew herself up with it. The screamers came out within minutes of her demise: 'Gas strike claims first victim.' They might as profitably have read 'Newspapers cause woman's death' or 'Government intransigence causes tragedy'.

The dire prognostications have lost their force. The threatened deaths have not ensued. If they don't happen soon they will have to be invented. Meanwhile, the ancillary workers, disabused of the liberal delusions of the nurses, struggle to prove that the fact that his services are essential is not a reason why the labourer should forgo his hire. If virtue is to be its own reward, virtue will be starved out.

What turns women on

Esquire, July 1973

Heterosex will probably survive the eventual liberation of women. Some idealists even believe that the liberation of women is the only hope for the future of heterosex. Permissiveness and the Pill have worn away the glamour of sin, secrecy and risk that for aeons made second-rate sex worth the trouble: now most free sexual encounters seem even more pallid and predictable than the inventive maliciousness of monogamy. Only some radical new stimulus, even a hostile one, can possibly put the adventure back into sexual intercourse. Some cynics in the ranks of lechery hope that women, by way of taking the initiative, will become even more punctilious geishas, even less demanding sluts. Others dream of the liberated woman standing over them in jodhpurs and jackboots, whipping them for their unregenerate chauvinism.

Helen Gurley Brown is doubtless an idealist. It would be mean-minded to argue that her motives for running the first male nude pin-up in the gatefold of *Cosmopolitan* magazine were purely commercial. No doubt she wished to demonstrate a point of ethics: the 'liberated' or careerist woman is entitled not only to her own key to the executive washroom, but also to treat the younger, prettier male bodies as sex objects. All cheaper imitations of the *Cosmo* optative format saw the rationale and adopted the same course. Male pin-ups flooded the news-stands; *Ladies' Home Companion* went eleven better in producing a calendar of twelve naked beefcakes. One Australian magazine ran a gatefold of a blond hairy actor, posed exactly like a Titian nude, covering his genitals coyly with one hand.

The convention of the playmate dominates the presentation of the female pin-up in the glossies. The heightened colour, the roseate light, the suntan marks, the backgrounds opulent but hip have become basic requirements of the genre. The debut of the male pin-up saw the same elements transposed, the same atmosphere of health and wealth, the same all-over skin colour of coralline beige which signifies soundness in men and in pork chops, except where the swimming costume had screened out the healthful rays and left suggestive bars of paleness. The backgrounds featured wood panelling, books, furs, potted plants and other paraphernalia of conspicuous consumption or the expensive freshness of the great out-doors. Variety being the spice of life and the staple of pornography, *Ladies' Home Companion* obligingly alternated hairy men and smooth men, black, brown, yellow and blond men, outdoor summer men and indoor winter men, but all the surface variations served only to emphasize their basic similarity. All were passive, all pleasant, all bland and wholesome as cottage cheese. Moreover, they all looked silly, especially the rather plump gentleman wading into the shallows and peering through a jauntily cocked telescope. The calendar did not turn me on and although I have not heard how many *Ladies' Home Companion* managed to unload, I am prepared to bet that other women were not turned on either. Even if the calendar did sell millions, which I am prepared to bet that it did not, it would not have been because it turned women on.

If what was sauce for the gander had turned out to be sauce for the goose as well, vast fortunes would have been made overnight and vaster ones would be sweeping to maturity. Women outnumber men absolutely; they also outnumber men rather more as magazine readers. The publisher who finds the formula for the pin-up that turns women on would quite soon be able to make Hugh Hefner look cheaper than a postcard peddler in Port Said. And yet, despite a smattering of glory for Burt Reynolds, nothing of the sort can be said to have transpired.

Apparently, men are easy to satisfy. All they demand is, in Lenny Bruce's phrase, tits'n'ass, ass'n'tits, tits'n'ass. After generations of saturation bombardment with tits'n'ass, all they seem to want is more tits'n'ass. (As for beaver they can take it or leave it.) Nothing is more inevitable than that the male photographer of naked men for the female view should imagine that women would turn on to male pectorals and gluteals with the same fervour. But men have been posing for pin-up shots for about as long as women; the images that result are calculated to gratify the voyeuristic requirements of other males. The average woman, confronted by a pouting boy, clad in nothing but black leather gloves and motorcycle boots, toying with a riding crop, is not likely to swoon or salivate. She might burst out laughing. The male sex object as marketed to the male consumer is utterly coy and passive: women have been conditioned for centuries to turn on to the opposite. Even if they succeed in throwing off the shackles which have bound the free expression of their own spontaneous sexual desire, it is doubtful whether they would ever respond to the servility and insipidity of these images. It will take a good deal of masculinization (which is not the same thing as liberation) to turn women on to the charms of plump boys gazing soulfully through chicken wire, or lying naked in the straw doing a pout directly copied from Jane Russell's in *The Outlaw*. Gay pin-ups are on display on all the stands and the chaps, limp or semi-tumescent, are on full-frontal display inside them, but women do not buy. Perhaps they dare not loiter long enough on Forty-second Street to take them in, perhaps their wages are too scanty to afford the blackmailing prices, perhaps they feel ashamed and embarrassed. Perhaps – but nearly all of these considerations apply equally to those men who do buy *Gym* and *Boy*. We must conclude that women are tuned into a different sexual wavelength.

Mass-circulation magazines do not enjoy the same freedom as over-priced, sparsely distributed hard-core pornography. They cannot extort astronomical prices from the members of vulnerable minorities and they must use the postal services. The glossies have had to reproduce the already passive gay formula without showing penises, and so are even more emasculated rather than less. The gay formula had no pretensions to wholesomeness or beauty; the heterosexual version fell foul of both.

Paul du Feu claims that when he posed for the gatefold of *Cosmopolitan* (UK), he demanded rather more money than he eventually got and he stipulated that the picture he was to pose for would not be in good taste. He is a very sexy man, in a battered and nuggety sort of way, and subsequently the underground press did manage to run very louche and tasteless pictures of him, but for *Cosmo* he was as thoroughly camouflaged as any playmate. He was spray-painted buff all over, and the scars on his cheek-bones and all else that gave character to his face were obliterated with make-up. His hair was streaked and shaped and lacquered. They laid him on the highly polished floor of a swank apartment, lifting up the thigh nearest the camera to hide his penis and propping him on his elbow. The result was still too raunchy, so they brushed out the wrinkles on his belly, the same wrinkles that were considered an indispensable attribute of the beautiful *kouroi* of ancient Greece. In the frenzy of cosmetic airbrushing, nobody noticed until after the magazine had appeared on the stands that they had inadvertently removed his navel. When the banners came out screaming that inside *Cosmo* Germaine Greer's husband revealed all, I seriously considered bringing an action against the editors and publishers under the Trades Descriptions Act.

Neither Mr Reynolds nor Mr du Feu was a pioneer in the field of male pin-ups for female viewers. Singers and film stars have long adorned the insides of schoolgirls' desks and working girls' lockers and bedroom walls, but they are not the meaty males that sophisticated publishers might expect. They are David Cassidy, Donny Osmond, Engelbert Humperdinck and Tom Jones, and they have their clothes on. They were Frank Sinatra, first heart-throb of the bobby-soxers and Paul McCartney, the baby face among the otherwise rather saturnine Beatles. Tom Jones used to be a rugged construction worker; when he became a pin-up he had his nose (absurdly) bobbed. The key to their success would appear to be glamour and a strong appeal to sentiment, laced with a dash of strictly potential sex. The sex ingredient may be reinforced; many singers favour a twist of hemp in the trousers or even a rubber tube.

P. J. Proby used regularly to split his trousers on stage, until he was forced to abandon the act. Jim Morrison used to perform with a genuine erection if he could manage it, until the dire day when he actually flashed it. Rock-and-roll audiences are composed of all sexes and the big pin-ups, like Mick Jagger, Robert Plant, Roger Daltrey and Marc Bolan, are pin-ups for everyone. Their imagery reflects the eroticization of the male form which is one of the most gratifying effects of pseudo-permissiveness.

Men's hair may not be sacred, but it is sensuous and enticing especially when worn in riotous curls, shining and perfumed. Partial nakedness, sheer, shiny and furry fabrics, slight piquancies of sadism and polymorphous perversity, and suggestive movement are all utilized by the dynamic sex objects of rock and roll, whose greatest resource is the music itself. White rock-and-roll stars learned these forms of blandishment from the blacks. James Brown is still the undisputed master of the arts of male enticement: he showed the kids the human equivalent of the mating dances of the bowerbird and the peacock, and he still does it better than anyone else. All Mick Jagger's outrageousness is a less vigorous version of James Brown's.

These sexual displays are not related in any way to beefcake. Instead of exposing passive flesh, they celebrate phallic energy, the male in his pride. The way the singer moves, the pulse and boom of the music, the guitarist's affair with his instrument, the exhibitionism of the drummer, all demonstrate the power of the libido. The display is not limited to men, although comparatively few women have been motivated to get into it. Tina Turner has been called the sexiest woman in the world, although any picture of her tits'n'ass would be as anticlimactic as a picture of Jimi Hendrix in a bubble bath. The pin-up picture of any rock-and-roll star since Elvis is no more than an *aide-mémoire*; it works by virtue of a remembered response to a past stimulus suggested by the picture. Nonentities don't make it. No class of males remarkable for nothing except the pleasing pattern of curves and shadows that their bodies might provide in photographs has yet come into existence. So far, women persist in loving people and not shapes.

Nevertheless, the body is an object. Whatever else it may be, it is a material thing which can be perceived; it has tastes and smells and textures. It can be an object of desire and a source of pleasure. It would greatly enhance our lives if everyone who lived inside a body was careful to keep it as pretty and sweet-smelling and attractive as possible, and this means men as well as women. Such a duty is considered, in our time, to be servile and effeminate, and so men have largely laid it aside, while women have found that not only is it their duty to attract, it is their primary and even their only duty . Moreover, strict rules and conventions governing the kind of beauty they must exhibit have been laid down, even though they are not suited to the mass of women. The pleasing procedures of self-expression through adornment have become a relentless discipline of dieting, dying, depilating, injecting, tanning, cleansing, painting and so forth. The functional man and the artificial woman are both unsuccessful sex objects. The man does not know the pleasures of narcissism, while for the woman they have become an addiction.

The revolt of women against the exclusiveness of their role as sex objects is perfectly understandable; any man who tried to speak sensibly to a woman who stared at his crotch or simply watched his lips moving would soon become exasperated. Men resent being whistled at or groped in the street much more than women do, because their own sexual anxieties and repressions have caused them to treat sex objects with disdain. Most such men, hard-working, decent members of the community, would find it quite impossible to plan ways of making themselves sexually attractive.

The utter identification of women with sex objects coincides with the historical phenomenon of the polarization of the sexes. Men are seldom, if ever, considered as sex objects at all. Except among groups of comparatively recent formation, men have for the last hundred and fifty years gradually been required to suppress all the erotic aspects of their appearance. Beards and whiskers disappeared, hair was cut back to the skull and limbs were hidden in drab clothes which were neither loose and flowing enough to enhance nor tight enough to reveal the wearer's shape.

The fear of being treated as a sex object derives not so much from masculinity itself as from sexual insecurity. Sexual insecurity is the result, at least partially, of a highly competitive performance ethic. The man who sets out to attract might find himself seduced into a degrading role because without his masculine armour he cannot carry through the bluff of omnipotence. Demands might be made which he could not gratify. In so far as display leads to comparison, men are afraid of it. Women have suffered for a long time because of the invidious comparisons they were forced to make between themselves and the pneumatic young bodies that were offered as examples of what was really desirable. Men will not allow the same disparity to become apparent. The comparison could only be made more invidious by the effects of photographic distortion.

Not all male groups are so timorous. It is often pointed out that the most virile groups in the community are those least afraid of physical display. Manual workers often bare their bodies, without supposing that the fact of their near-nakedness gives passers-by the right to take liberties. The cowboy, in his tight trousers, high-heeled boots, low-slung belt emphasizing the crotch, and further embellishments of scarves and silver studs and buckles, has always been allowed a measure of sexual display which the young executive would not risk. My mates and I picked out Charles Bronson years ago as the type of the male sex object, because he moves with the most desirable grace, precision and power, he looks both savage and susceptible and he is as inarticulate as could be wished. Bullfighters, pugilists and pimps are allowed as much flamboyance as they desire and women capitulate. D. H. Lawrence's gamekeeper assured

Lady Chatterley that the cause of sex would be well served if men would revert to the exhibitionism of the male creature in nature, because then women could be rescued from their own profound and desolating narcissism.

'An' I'd get my men to wear different clothes; 'appen close red trousers, bright red, an' little short white jackets. Why, if men had red, fine legs, that alone would change them in a month. They'd begin to be men again, to be men! An' the women could dress as they liked. Because if men once walked with legs close bright scarlet and buttocks showing scarlet under a little white jacket: then the women 'ud begin to be women.'

Not everyone would agree with Lawrence's overbearing notion of a uniform which would excite women's sight and so stimulate their capacity for pleasure. It is hardly necessary to apparel men like waiters to effect the stimulus that Mellors describes, but there is some point in demanding visual titillation for women, in exchange for that which social mandate forces them to supply for men. Women would respond to it, although not as uniformly and predictably as men, who have been programmed by the print media into a series of very limited aesthetic expectations. In so far as psychological testing can be trusted to reveal sexual differentials at all, it seems to have shown, so far, that women are more responsive to colour and other visual stimuli than men.

The Wife of Bath married her fifth husband for his lovely legs; he cannot have been wearing anything so defensive as a three-piece suit.

'As help me God! whan that I saugh him go
After the beere, me thoughte he hadde a paire
Of legges and of feete so clene and faire
That al myn herte I yaf into his hoold.'

Most likely he wore a doublet

'not long enough when he stands upright to cover his privities and buttocks'

like the ones condemned in the Chronicle of Saint Denis. On the pretext of covering the revealing gusset in the front of his hose, he may have sported a braguette, tied with decorative bows and points, or even a codpiece or one of the large leather pouches that the gondoliers flaunt in the paintings of Carpaccio. He may have exaggerated the curves of those lovely legs as they did, by stripes and contrasting colours and decorative gaiters, slashings and rosettes. He might have bleached his hair into a great golden cloud and stuck a cap jauntily over one eye. He might have extended his shoulders or his sleeves or his feet, exaggerating and embellishing his whole body in a fashion as impractical as the spread of the peacock's tail, for excess and extravagance and frivolousness are essential to the amorous message he conveyed. His like stares impudently out of many a fresco, shamelessly soliciting the viewer's appraisal, even while his companions are nailing Christ to the cross.

Later ages took to padding out the chest and shoulders with bombast, carving through layers of encrusted velours to reveal the great insolence of a decorated codpiece. Hips and waists came and went, bosoms were even plumped out with small pillows, the high stock forced the chin up to an impossibly arrogant angle and tumbled curls of real hair replaced the formality of wigs. Perfect cut and better fit replaced lace and satin, embroidery and jewels. It was all most exciting, until the cut-away coat dropped into the frock coat and the Inexpressibles were gone for ever. The super-narcissist Corinthians were the last of the male sex objects, until the present generation.

The current fashion for jeans and bum-freezer jackets is a return to long-vanished kinds of display. Flared trousers were worn by the Incroyables of the Empire, and the purpose is now, as it was then, to make the thighs seem more lissom and the buttocks perter. Tight, high-waisted trousers are almost as revealing as the delicately coloured Inexpressibles which were hauled taut over the genitals by the first suspenders. Hipster pants with heavy belts and important buckles perform the same function as the low-slung belts and rapier cases of the seventeenth century. In England, men have begun to wear immensely high-heeled boots with huge platforms; walking in them causes a rollicking roll of the hips that would have made Marilyn Monroe blush.

One of the mistaken assumptions behind the failure of the playmales was the belief that nakedness is of itself erotic. Men dress and undress in a way which is not meant to provoke sexual desire. The underwear is simple and functional; indeed, no more repellent garments than boxer shorts have ever been devised. There is nothing rare and strange about male exposure, unless it be exposure of the penis, but the pin-ups have not even been able to supply that. It is doubtful whether a flaccid full frontal is any more exciting than a hand over the crotch though, because a limp penis is not just not positive evidence of sexual readiness, it is specific evidence of unreadiness. Nothing very erotic about that. Besides:

> 'When you have all done, *veniunt a veste sagittae*, the greatest provocations of lust are from our apparel . . . *Primum luxuriae aucupium*, one calls it, the first snare of lust . . .'

Burton was convinced that outward ornament was of more force in inciting to lust than natural beauty. For one thing, the use of 'counterfeit colours, headgears, curled hairs' and suchlike reveals the desire to please, indicates that someone is trying. Women in our time have a virtual duty of daily face-painting, something never before demanded of them, but men, short of making themselves clean, refuse any measure of self-beautification. Egyptian men kept their faces meticulously hairless, painted their eyes with kohl, malachite, crushed lapis and antimony. The warrior princes of

Assyria, the Ashurnasirpals and Ashurbanipals, dressed their beards and thick black tresses in rows of perfumed, stiffened curls and hung huge stiff ornaments of gold in their ears. The symbols of their virility and authority were also their chief blandishments to love. The heroes of Greece were bathed and rubbed down with fragrant oils, their hair and beards cut and curled, and they donned fresh silken tunics before presenting themselves in banqueting hall or bedroom. Rinaldo, the conquering paladin, languished in Armida's bower in 'garments light and wanton soft attire', 'of Civet, Balm and perfumes redolent', his sword bewrapt in flowers.

The greatest paean ever written to male sexual attraction is probably to be found in the 'Song of Solomon', and it may have been written by a woman. The lover sings:

'My beloved is white and ruddy, the chiefest among ten thousand.
His head is as the most fine gold, his locks are bushy and black as a raven.
His eyes are as the eyes of doves by the river of waters, washed with milk and fitly set.'

Clothing and cosmetics are erotically pleasing; artifice is enticing. Because men have refused or been prevented from using these forms of blandishment, a number of anomalous conditions have arisen. One is that women, who know that they are turned on by their own and other women's sensuous appearance and delicate garments and perfumes, find that their sexual fantasies centre on these same things and hence upon their own sex. Nell Dunn confessed to Edna O'Brien that she found other women's petticoats erotic and Edna wondered, 'Isn't it strange that, on the whole, women are more touched by the external things of women, like petticoats or dance shoes or something, than by the external things of men . . . Does that make us a little lesbian?' Eroticism is connected with pleasure, with intricate, impractical, fragile and vivid things, with preciousness and rarity and hiddenness. Women dress to attract, men do not. Anyone desirous of being attracted will think of the attractive, even as a narcissistic prelude to a completely heterosexual experience. The rigid allocation of all sensuous appeal to the person and accoutrements of women does not solely affect women. Some men resent being deprived of the pleasures of self-adornment: they treat themselves to frilly satin undies beneath their grey flannel suits or dress up secretly in their wives' clothes, suffering torments of guilt and confusion the while. The high-stepping black dudes who cruise Forty-second Street in part-coloured jersey cat suits and huge woolly hats and high boots are making a mockery of both kinds of anxiety.

Marc Bolan, who is the idol of British teenyboppers, wears iridescent eyelids, lamé trousers, feather boas and spangles on his cheeks, but he always reminds the mouse-coloured reporters who interview him that he is a very tough cookie and very well-endowed. His exhibitionism is both erotic and male; it is only just becoming possible after a hundred and fifty years of repression. The way the little girls scream out for him might remind us of the jubilant bacchantes of antiquity who sang out of their divine lover:

'Flames float out from his trailing wand
As he runs, as he dances,
Kindling the stragglers,
Spurring with cries,
and his long curls stream to the wind!'

Young Dionysos, his cheeks flushed with wine and the spells of Aphrodite in his eyes, is coming on earth again.

Very few women have ever felt secure enough in the ranks of artists, predominantly male, to write in any way frankly about their direct apprehension of male physical beauty, but when they do so they very often select the same characteristics to praise in their male subjects as their male counterparts do in women. Aphra Behn, credited as the first Englishwoman to earn a living by her pen, celebrated the men in her circle as young and lovely and gracious as any woman could ever be.

Then there was lucky Mr N. R. V. whose beauty was praised this way:

'If anything can add a Grace
To such a Shape and such a Face . . .
His shoulders covered with hair,
The Sunbeams are not half so fair . . .
On's Cheeks the blushing Roses grow:
The rest like whitest Daisies grow:
His Lips, no Berrie of the Field,
Nor Cherries such a Red do yield . . .'

Very few of the depictions of the nude, male or female, in European art have been erotic in intention. In classical Greece the secondary sexual characteristics were virtually suppressed in depictions of the human body, because they were considered disproportionate and unpleasing. Nevertheless, the dedicated man fancier can find some fuel for fantasy. Before the dictates of classic art made them as fat and epicene as bullocks, the Greek *kouroi*, sculpted figures of youths, were juicy and male and beautiful. Stiff bodies, with high buttocks and long legs, tight bands around their waists and their hair curled into formal shapes, they gazed boldly ahead, with the trace of a languorous smile curling their lips. In the rhythm of the sculptures the penis assumed its just importance, slung in a girdle running from the sacroiliac crest, full and tense under its crown of stylized hair. The alternation of smooth and rough, hard and soft, creates a fine tension, like pleasure: the sexual attractiveness as sculptures and as emblems of human dignity. Gradually, the subject matter of these sculptures became identified with Apollo, 'like to a man, lusty and powerful, in his first bloom, his hair spread over his broad shoulders'. Other figures of virile and beautiful

Greek youth appear on Greek pots and vases. A kylix in the Fitzwilliam Museum in Cambridge shows a young athlete stooping in his bath. The rapturous motto round the dish says, 'The boy, yes, the boy is beautiful'.

At the hands of the Romans the ambiguity of the Greek tradition became outright perversity. Apollo the sex object became Apollo the freak, or the hermaphrodite. His hips spread and he swooned over his lyre like Liberace, wearing his rare *pietra dura* like a gold lamé dinner jacket. The fine amorous energy of archaic Greece had become vulgar passivity and coyness.

When the Catholic Church dominated the visual imagination of Europe, painters had to express their interest in the erotic appeal of the male body under various guises. The favourite was Saint Sebastian; young, naked, his eyes misting in the languors of death, he was the least ambiguous emblem of amorous desire. Even the arrows that pierced his idealized form might have been shot from Cupid's bow. The curves in his body, and indeed the tree to which he was tied for the penetration ceremony, were directly copied from classic depictions of the boy god, Bacchus, or, as we have already had occasion to refer to him, Dionysos. His dying body described all the undulations that we would ascribe to orgasm, and bewitched painters recreated him thousands and thousands of times, until Carpaccio finally ran amok and painted endless variations of the theme in the Diecimila Crocifissi del Monte Ararat. It is worth a trip to the Accademia in Venice just to see the myriads of young male bodies gasping and coiling in every extremity, draped over rocks, trees and the harsh earth, their lips gently parted by the expiring breath.

Renaissance humanism rescued the painters from the necessity of disguising their ideal young men as martyrs. Apollo and Bacchus came once again into their own; their traditional postures became those of Michelangelo's slaves sinking back into the stone. Antiquarianism provided the excuse for uncompromising eroticism. It became possible even to depict the male *in ore*. Andrea del Briosco decorated the side of an inkwell with a relief of a male bacchant, his throat arched in ecstasy, his lips curving in that old lecherous grin and his penis pointing proudly to the sky.

My favourite Renaissance sex object is fully, even heavily dressed. He is not visible at all below the waist, so that the state of his sexual readiness is a mystery to the beholder. He wears a voluminous jacket with lappets of some luxurious fur, like lynx. On his left hand he wears a soft grey leather glove, with a slit at the back above the button, through which his skin glows like a pearl, and with that hand he draws through the lips of his coat the bulbous pommel of a rapier. The expression on his face is noncommittal, but his lips seem to quiver with the beginnings of something more significant than a smile. Perhaps he means to disarm and let his heavy coat slip to the floor; perhaps he does not. He is a Man in a Red Cap painted by Titian, and he hangs all day and every day in the Frick Museum in New York.

It is possible, then, to create images of the young, handsome, vigorous male body which women would find attractive, but that is not to say that a female market for formula images of the male nude will emerge. Women are not yet so alienated from tenderness and respect that they can appreciate the male body separated from its soul, or even that they could take any simple voyeurist attitude which might lead them to seek pleasure from contemplating an arbitrary disposition of curves and contrasts. If liberation means that women will make the same arbitrary demands of men that men have for generations made of women, it will be a sorry outcome for the human race, which is not universally young, vigorous and beautiful. If women are to be as contemptuous of the unbeautiful and unyoung among men as men are of women who are past their first youth and cannot boast the vital statistics of the current stereotype of beauty, then sexual hostility and resentment will increase.

It may be that men will have to be treated cold-bloodedly as sex objects before they will realize how desolating such behaviour is. The Dolly Minas of Holland who whistle at men in the street are probably carrying out a valuable activity as sexual guerrillas but there is the ever-present danger that what begins as an emergency tactic becomes an immovable element of ideology. It would be truly terrible if, instead of liberating the women who are forced to regard themselves as sexy zombies, we simply created a group of men who had equally to consider themselves dishy and mindless, and to allow their prettiness to be exploited by the female rivals of Hugh Hefner.

In fact, erotic appeal is not strictly genital and is not strictly controlled by considerations of gender. It is part of the aesthetics of everyday life. We have a duty, men and women, to delight each other's eyes and increase the pleasure quotient in our common lives, in a spontaneous and co-operative way, and not so that a tiny group of entrepreneurs can make empires out of it. Men and women, old and young, fat and thin, energetic and languorous, all ought to be able to find a style which expresses their own particular beauty. The day that the male pin-up becomes a commercial commodity will be the day that such a possibility for the human race is utterly extinguished. We need, not coy males clutching their genitalia in glossy gatefolds, but a whole new erotic art.

Review of *Conundrum* by Jan Morris

Evening Standard, 25 April 1974

You cannot help liking Jan Morris and she poses her *Conundrum* in great style, a bit purplish and hazy perhaps, but she does so love having such an excuse to go on about herself that one is, willy-nilly, caught up. Puzzles are enjoyable ways of consuming the time, even if one does find oneself objecting at the end that, for this poser, there is not and never will there be, any solution. Others, of a more rigorous turn of mind, will object that Jan Morris's conundrum will not work out because the problem has been wrongly formulated.

Jan Morris is a man who has eaten a great many pills, artificial hormones and the crystallized essence of the urine of pregnant mares, a man who has had his penis cut off, but a man nevertheless. It is only courteous to call him *she* because she wishes to be called so, and to be treated as a woman. In so far as femininity – if not femaleness – is a product of conditioning, Jan Morris is well on the way to being a woman. Her description of the changes in her own personality which have come about because of other people's changed attitude to her is very convincing.

In calling Jan Morris *she* I am only extending the courtesy that is given by all Italians to each other in polite discourse, where the *she* stands for the unspoken *your Excellency*. Jan Morris's *she* stands for the abstract concept of the feminine, the anima of Jungian psychology, the maternal, nurturing, delicate, passive aspect, which is only a part of the female personality.

For Jan Morris femininity means being on the side of the angels. The girlishness of angels in most representations is really meant to express the theological fact that they have no bodies. James Morris seems to have thought, like a typical male, that his body was his penis, and that in getting rid of it he was changing over. However, such a view, expressed in his description of himself taking a last look at his male self (already altered strikingly by the hormone treatments) is phallocentric and not very comprehensible to a woman.

James Morris revolted against the pressure upon him to concentrate all his capacities for pleasure in his genitals. He seems to have enjoyed all his life the diffuse carnal responsiveness which is typical of the infant and the feminine female. He was as interested by 'buildings, landscapes, pictures, wines and certain kinds of confectionery' as by amorous intercourse, a preference not so much angelic as infantile. He did not want to concentrate all this voluptuous susceptibility in one tag of flesh so peripherally attached to his person. Once that had gone, he was clean, integrated, whole, pure: he was Ariel. He became she.

Jan Morris believes that the soul, having been created in eternity, comes to inhabit a body for a time, cribbed in the finite world while yearning for 'God who is our home'. Morris carries this belief of fundamental separateness of soul and body to fairly grotesque lengths. She says of the death of her child Virginia:

> I felt she would surely come back to us, if not in one guise, then in another – and she very soon did, leaving us sadly as Virginia, returning as Susan, merry as a dancing star.

James Morris believed that he had been fitted with the wrong body. If his Christianity had been more than merely sentimental and spasmodic, he might have arrived at a sort of sublimation of his very real suffering, but he preferred the course adopted by the Skoptsi, castration.

Women have long been considered saints. Quite reasonable men are more disgusted by drunkenness and foul-mouthedness in women because they think of them as above the ordinary coarseness of mankind. The puzzle was not that Morris adored sainthood in women, but that he had to be it in himself. There is in *Conundrum* no adequate discussion of the origin of James Morris's obsession with femininity. While anyone can understand that Morris rejected the barbarity of aversion therapy and electric shocks, and was fastidious about unliberated homosex, it is not easy to understand her total ignorance of the nature and purpose of psychoanalysis. Some guided and rigorous self-examination might have filled in the voids in her story which are only webbed over by self-indulgent, impressionistic prose. Part of the answer may be found in the way the story begins with Morris's mother playing Sibelius, and ends with the observation that the Blüthner now stands in Morris's own house, where neither she nor any of her acquaintance has the skill to play Sibelius upon it.

Another teasing aspect of the book is Morris's failure to be at all frank about what her 'new' body looks like and how it works. It is all too clear that she considers all such perfectly normal curiosity prurient and vulgar, even while she recognizes that she must make some attempt to explain why such a reorganization of her plumbing was necessary to her. Apart from a passing reference to the lady wrestlers who frisk women in Indian airports, it remains a mystery. Poorer boys make do with a cross between a dance belt and a jock strap which would fool even the Indian security officers, but Jan Morris had to have it off.

The failure to describe what is so central to her obsession is part of Morris's enduring contempt for genitality in men or women. She calls some woman who tried to seduce her (when James, I mean) a nympho, a jibe every bit as coarse minded and ungenerous as the ones she is seeking to forestall by writing this book.

Even more disturbing is Morris's sketchy account of how she came to be recognized officially as a woman. The legal precedent of Corbett *v.* Corbett, when the judge humiliated April Ashley by declaring her a man and therefore a transvestite catamite instead of a married woman, seems to mean that Jan Morris is, for all judicial purposes, including his own divorce, a male. If policies have changed, and genetically normal men who eat pills and have themselves castrated are to be admitted to the female sex (needless to say by *men* who have not consulted the actual members of the sex so honoured) then the situation had better be made public. Let the privilege be extended to all the prostitutes and bar-girls who are boys at the police station, and not just to a well-connected journalist with the gift of the gab.

Dimly, through the silken trammels of Jan Morris's verbiage, moves the figure of Elizabeth, James Morris's wife, now Jan Morris's sister-in-law, unsatisfied as a lover, and deeply versed in the anguish and ambiguities of real womankind. So often when husbands are trumpeting, one wonders what the silent wife is really thinking. In the same way, as Jan Morris plucks at your sleeve for a girlish heart to heart, you wonder about Elizabeth. Her unbroken silence is the truest measure of Jan Morris's enduring masculinity.

On population and women's right to choose

Spare Rib, March 1975

This statement came out of my experience at the World Population Year conference in Bucharest in 1974, when I observed first hand the nature and motivation of the pressure on Third World women to limit the number of their children. Some of that pressure was being exerted by people who called themselves feminist. Spare Rib, who were given this copy, were loth to publish it, attempted to edit it and eventually ran it as submitted, to outcry and general incomprehension from British feminists.

Only a few years have passed since women first took to the streets to assert their right to control their own fertility. To some, that battle may seem to have been almost won. Free family-planning advice is widely available. Abortions are gradually becoming easier to get, even if they are still unnecessarily traumatic, still cost far too much and are subject to too much interference and bureaucratic control. This very circumstance should waken our suspicions.

We have used no force or coercion to bring about acceptance of our demand for the means to control our own fertility. Our oppressors have not put such means within our grasp because we wished to have them, but because they, our oppressors, wished us to have them. Our rulers simply decided that what we were shouting for on the streets was in their own interests. Permitted contraception and abortion simply indicate that our rulers find population control a congenial idea. The day that they change their minds, contraception and abortion will be as inaccessible as they ever were, in fact more so, for we will have forgotten all the self-help know-how of former generations of women.

The crucial issue, that of the individual woman's right to choose her own reproductive destiny, has been recognized by no enactment, by no precedent in law or in practice. We are still manipulated according to the plans that others have made for us, as any childless woman who desires a sterilization is only too aware.

Now that the rulers of the world have taken up the notion of global population limitation, the battle for the right to control our own bodies may now have to take on a different form. Where once our banners read 'Free Abortion on Demand' in large letters, and 'No Forced Sterilization' in much smaller ones, we may find that we have to reverse the emphasis. We may have to struggle for the right to be pregnant, and pregnant as often as we want to be – especially if we are unemployed, unmarried or have no A-levels. The ways in which the right to be pregnant can be eroded are many; they range from the 'advice' of a doctor, to his taking matters entirely into his own hands, as in the cases where doctors performing abortions on girls whom they considered 'mentally retarded' seized the opportunity to sterilize them. Social and bureaucratic pressures can vary from counselling (which will eventually include genetic counselling) to the kind of coercion suggested by various law projects in America, in which it is suggested that welfare payments be denied to any poor mother of four children if she will not accept sterilization (which is already the practice in Singapore).

Many women are convinced that there are too many people in the world. Nevertheless, no feminist can allow forcible abortion or compulsory sterilization of women who are not convinced that it is their moral duty to deny themselves wanted children. The principle at stake, that of control over one's own body, is an integral and essential part of feminism. No act of faith in the oracles of demography can overrule it.

Women who reject the fashionable convictions about 'overpopulation' are not irrational or immoral; the case has not been proved and even if it had been it would not justify wholesale interference in the reproductive behaviour of the individual.

There is a world food shortage, to be sure, but when one quarter of the world's population wolfs eighty-five per cent of the world's resources, the food shortage can at once be seen to be owing primarily to an appallingly unjust economic (and hence political) system. This system is actually reducing the productivity of the world by raising the costs of modern agriculture. Megadeaths from hunger will affect all the demographers' projects for the year 2000, meanwhile people suffer from oppression, not from their own reproductive irresponsibility. The ones most sinned against are the ones who will oblige us by dying, leaving our ghastly, gargantuan lifestyle to flourish unchecked, except by its own poisonous wastes.

Western complacency wishes to be spared the spectacle of the deaths of thousands of women and children; besides, famines lead to unrest and the overthrow of established authority. People with nothing to lose are terribly dangerous, so it is perfectly understandable that the imperialist countries would prefer that the poor would cease to be born.

In countries where the infant mortality rate has fallen because of imperialist medicine and therefore may as quickly rise again; where death in early childhood from starvation is an ever-more-probable possibility, and where there is no provision for old age except a surviving son or two (for females have no financial independence), it is crass to assume that large families are not desirable. The failure of 'voluntary' birth-control policies in these countries was utterly predictable. Yet that failure, directly caused by the ignorance and insensitivity of the planners of other people's families, could be avenged by *compulsory* birth-control programmes.

All fascism assumes a state of fictitious emergency, a threat of invasion, of civil war, of the black and yellow hordes taking over. The new fascism relies upon a phantasmagoric view of the future as universal Calcutta.

Many of the nations who paid lip service to the idea of a rational population policy at last year's UN conference in Bucharest, actually promote birth in their own countries by denying women access to family-planning amenities (as, for example, the host country itself, Rumania). Between the extremes of national chauvinism and international hypocrisy stands the individual woman whose womb has become a vehicle of government policy. The name of feminism itself has been co-opted in the service of her manipulation and persecution. Issac Asimov declared that, in view of the seriousness of the population situation, 'women's lib' would no longer be the priority of a 'splinter group of activists', but 'the settled and serious policy of society as a whole'. 'Liberation' would be forced on women whether they wanted it or not. International Women's Year was, the pundits opined, the logical outcome of World Population Year.

Feminists cannot accept crude numerological analyses of the behaviour of women who have never spoken in the first person in their lives. They cannot permit the dissemination of a crude and misleading view of feminism as an ideology opposed to childbearing and the family. Within our own countries we are the unexplored, undeveloped, speechless population, systematically undeveloped by our conquistadorial society. We are the 'Third World' at home; we must represent the alien population beyond the factitious boundaries of states; bamboozled, manipulated and exploited by the same forces that have held us face downwards over the lavatory bowl and the sink. That any superpower should give the name women's liberation to the boot that he is preparing to place upon the necks of Third World women, ought to call forth the most appalling exhibition of women's rage that the world has yet seen.

International Women's Day, International Women's Year (1975)

New York Times, 8 March 1975

Despite the fact that all the nations represented at the United Nations oppress women in all degrees and in all manners, many to the point of slavery and mutilation, and are truculently uninterested in forfeiting the privilege, some good guys at the Secretariat decided that 1975 should be International Women's Year. It is typical of the special brand of UN Pollyannaism that they did so regardless of the fact that hiring policies at the Secretariat are grossly discriminatory. So pervasive is woolly-headed hypocrisy in the corridors of the UN that it is doubtful whether anyone felt egg upon his face, when the women of the Secretariat presented their petition on the day of the first international event of IWY.

The decision to have a women's year was simply a belated recognition of the fashionableness of feminism in the West. Western lifestyles dominate the UN self-image, despite their manifest irrelevance to most of the people at present living upon the planet. Thus, women from countries where the majority of the female population is pregnant and performing unpaid hard labour in the fields, are quite happy to discuss 'marriage or a career' in terminology culled from *McCall's*. IWY is a simple extension of Madison Avenue feminism: the agricultural labourers of Asia and Africa might as well lay down their hoes and light up a Virginia Slim.

1975, like 1974, will be a year when tens of thousands of girl babies will die because of discriminatory feeding practices, when thousands of women will have their external genitalia mutilated and hundreds of thousands will be manipulated and medicated and castrated in the service of population control. Wars will take their customary toll of women by slaughter, rapine and prostitution. In 1975, the US of A will manage not to pass the Equal Rights Amendment. Women's chances of controlling their own fertility will retreat instead of advancing. Unperturbed, the UN will arrange hours of chatter about 'Women: Equality, Development, Peace'.

This year of disgrace began willy-nilly; half the member nations of the UN had failed to give IWY even the lip-service of ratification. Only twelve of the 138 member governments had promised cash to the voluntary fund set up for IWY and only half of them had actually parted with the money, in derisory sums: $50,000 from the United States, only five times as much as Finland. The promised total is less than $1,000,000. Next year's Human Settlement Conference in Vancouver already has millions in hand; the mini-budget of the IWY is expected to fund six regional conferences and the two-week international conference in Mexico (19 June–2 July). Information about the conference is available from the Women's Year Information Centre at the UN, or rather was, for in March its funding ran out. The failure of the voluntary fund would have been less of a disaster, if the UN had not 'forgotten' IWY in drawing up its own budget. $250,000 was scraped up out of petty cash.

Women control neither the UN, nor its member governments, nor the multinational corporations, nor the purse-strings of nations, nevertheless the débâcle of the IWY will be blamed upon them. The foolery and botching of the UN Secretariat will be taken as evidence that there is no public concern for the plight of women.

The UN has no power to force governments to cease oppressing the helpless and no amount of shop-window funding will disguise that fact. The UN is too fearful of the power of its various blocs to risk offending individual governments by so much as motions of censure. Representatives of nations which forbid women passports, shackle their legs and veil their faces, where husbands have the right to kill their wives, are not so much as requested to explain these practices, especially if they produce (as they always can) tame women delegates skilled in the showy pro-feminist verbiage of UN debate. The Consultative Committee which draws up the Population Plan of Action was headed by the twin sister of the Shahanshah of Iran, Princess Ashraf, whom no one would have dared to offend by asking for news of Mehry Manoutcherian, Iran's first woman lawyer, who resigned her post as a senator because Iran's new passport law requires a husband's express permission before his wife may leave the country.

Maddeningly, women have not even the option of ignoring the UN muddle because there is a real possibility that given feminist formulations will creep into the UN declarations of pious intent and there ossify into immovable definitions. The callousness of last year's Population Plan of Action alerted many women to the ignorance and frivolity of the UN's attitude to half the population of the world, and their last-ditch struggle to humanize the linguistic slop-bucket which is the diplomatic doublethink of the UN, was fruitless. The resolution on 'Women and Food' sponsored by Bangladesh, Egypt, the UK and the USA at the Food Conference in Rome last year was principally concerned with women as feeders of children, especially by 'maximum lactation', as if the nourishment of children was women's *raison d'être*. In a world beset by problems of food supply and birth rate, the conviction that women who are not feeding children might as well starve, was only lightly veiled. Women all over the world are conditioned to eat less than men, after men have had their fill, but no UN utterance betrays the least concern about differential nutrition. At what Helvi Sipila calls the 'macro level' women do not exist as ends in themselves, but simply as means to it. Four of the regional conferences are on 'Women and

Population'. Women, dammit, *are* the population, but IWY will not recognize the fact. It simply carried on where Population Year left off. As Elizabeth Reid said in the 7 March seminar, sedulously ignored by all the media except the UN back-slapping brigade, IWY looks like being 'one long Mother's Day'.

If the IWY had been properly planned, adequately funded, the research materials prepared in good time, women might have had cause to bless the day that Helvi Sipila became Assistant Secretary General for Social Development and Humanitarian Affairs. We might then have had accurate and comprehensive information about the half of the world's population that is speechless, about its health, its morale, its workload, its contribution to national economies, its work evaluation, the effects of social and economic change upon its lifestyle and social status – all the prerequisites for realistic discussion which we do not have. Follow-through studies of women in population planning programmes, of women as war casualties, of women as pressure groups, might have been undertaken in time to give those conferring in the various parts of the world some inkling of what the women of the world need. Perhaps some of the 500,000,000 illiterate women in the world could have been given a voice. Some of the hundreds of millions of unpaid family workers might have readjusted our naïve materialistic views about the importance of being integrated in the processes of production.

Notwithstanding that none of the necessary conditions for a successful IWY exist, women are struggling to prevent the worst consequences of unlimited discussion of women's lives by the predominantly anti-feminist United Nations. The question is not now 'What do you women expect IWY to do for you?', but 'What do you fear that IWY will do against you?' Our only way of controlling the situation is, in the way of UN egregiousness itself, to work for it, and to swallow our gall in appearing to support it.

World Conference, United Nations' International Women's Year, Mexico City, June 1975

Chatelaine, September 1975

There were three parts to the World Conference of the United Nations' International Women's Year and never the three did meet, which was only disconcerting to the participants in the least regarded part, the Tribune. The Tribune is where NGOs or Non-Governmental Organizations, which is UN jargon for people without power, might meet to discuss such subjects as 'Processes of Formation of Attitudes and Socialization', 'Law and the Status of Women', 'Agriculture and Rural Development'. Anybody who could think of any organization to which he or she might belong, be it a sewing circle or a trade union, could gain admittance, unless the anyone in question was Mexican, when she had to apply to a special registration centre that was closed before the conference began. No organization representing Mexican working-class women had been able to get in.

When Betty Friedan addressed a gratifyingly full lecture hall at the Tribune on the second day, she dismissed the activities of the government delegates at the main conference and its committees as 'rhetoric'. The significant activity, she opined, was taking place right there – women were talking together in the first person. Hence she proceeded to execute a brilliant rhetorical display of her own. The Tribune had been stacked with mildly interested housewives from the fashionable suburb of Coyoacan, who were fascinated by the details of the life that Betty so contemptuously took for granted. The *amas de casa* murmured among themselves when Friedan spoke of putting powder in the dishwasher and heating TV dinners. Hounding the fifty per cent of the Mexican female workforce that is in domestic service is doubtless more taxing than dealing with machines, which are not likely to go to sleep standing up in the pantry out of sheer exhaustion, or to steal leftovers because their wages are so low.

By the fourth day, the middle-class housewives had given up their half-hearted attempt to attend the Tribune sessions. The speakers (some of whom were well worth hearing) struggled to talk sense to a two-thirds empty room. The free discussion time at the end of the short lectures had degenerated to a sloganizing free-for-all. A discussion on 'Health and Nutrition', was followed by a rousing speech on the fate of women in prison in Bolivia ('kicked and beaten, raped, made pregnant, kicked and beaten till they miscarry, raped again . . .') which was followed by a request for the condemnation of slimming pills.

Periodically the Tribune was convulsed by the enraged demand why there were no means by which Tribune decisions (of which there had been none) should be heeded, recorded and even ratified by the main conference. None of the people there would have presumed that they should have a voice in the political assemblies their compatriots had elected, nevertheless it seemed logical to some of them that they should have had a voice in an international assembly of government delegations. At length it was proposed that the NGOs should march upon the main conference.

This situation would seem to have been foreseen, for the Tribune, which was grudgingly mentioned as 'a parallel but independent activity to be held upon the occasion of the conference' on the last page of the government delegates' information booklets, was so far from the main conference that it did not even figure on the delegates' map of Mexico City.

The geography of Mexico gives itself to containment and the painless dispersal of energy, for the city is one of the worst cases of urban sprawl in the world. Paseo de la Reforma, the main street, is thirty-six miles long and every malodorous yard of it is traffic chaos. The delegates spent one third of their waking hours imprisoned in their official cars, glumly wondering if their mental stupor was another effect of the altitude or how long they could hold out in the endless traffic jams before setting off on foot in search of a toilet. The virulent Mexican version of tourist tummy laid low some of every delegation all of the time. The fourteen hotels which housed the delegates roared like Niagaras as they strained the plumbing to the utmost.

The sheer physical difficulty of moving about the city was not the worst of the delegates' problems. The timing of the conference would have been problematic even if the delegates had been able to find food at the conference site, and were not invariably late to the afternoon sessions. It began on a Thursday and had not begun before it was disrupted by a two-day halt (for no meetings were scheduled on Saturday), and had hardly gathered momentum again before it stopped again for two more days. All speeches in committee were limited to absurdly short times but even so, precious time was lost in pointless enumerations of irrelevancies.

The opening of the conference was a spectacular affair, mainly because the women from the dozens of African delegations had indulged in an orgy of nationalist flamboyancy. Many had had their draperies printed with the stylized dove which is the emblem of the year. Others had had their hair woven into fantastic shapes. As the conference dragged on, we were to realize that many of them were late to afternoon sessions because they had been devising a complete costume change. Some of the delegates seemed very young and decorative: one does not wish to be ageist, but nevertheless it is hard to see how the experiences of a seventeen-year-old would equip her to deal with the bureaucratic tedium and manipulativeness of a UN conference, especially if, as in one case I observed, she spoke only her own brand of Arabic and enough English to say 'Bring me orange' to a waiter.

As we arrived at Gimnasio Juan De La Berrera, where the opening ceremony of the conference was held, we were welcomed by a small group of Mexican women under a banner proclaming them as 'Mexican Women's Liberation'. We were also given key rings as mementoes of the IWY lottery in Mexico.

The entrances were policed by a troupe of Mexican police girls, all exactly the same height and weight, with identical make-up and coiffure, and, wonder of wonders, pale blue-grey uniforms with miniskirts. During Kurt Waldheim's speech, he was obliged petulantly to call for order as the press stampeded from the galleries to catch the memorable sight of the miniskirted police people resisting the onslaught of the working-class Mexican women who, having been given an inch, thought they may as well take a mile and come all the way in.

Host-President Luis Echeverria's address at the opening meeting spelt out the dilemma facing the conference and indicated the way in which the second and third would approach. He agreed that women were everywhere oppressed: 'Discrimination against women exists among all social classes, from the privileged classes in the rich countries to the oppressed classes in the poor countries. In the former case they are the dependent subjects of a way of life in the development of which they have had no active part, and in the latter they are the proletarians of the proletariat.'

The adroit way in which he ranged the nations of the world into haves and have-nots, while blurring the face of class struggle in all nations, is typical of the agility of Echeverria's mind. He was bidding for the leadership of the UN majority, and the whole sorry affair at Mexico was staged for that and that alone. He spoke brilliantly of stereotypes, of personalities assessed by what they do not do, rather than what they could do, but then he abandoned this skirmishing and turned to his own political baby, the New International Economic Order. The women who are most oppressed, he maintained, are those 'who lack medical care for their children, hygienic housing in which to shelter them and adequate training to prepare them for life'.

So much for women. The focus had suddenly blurred and women were being defined, as usual, in terms of their children. God knows, in most countries of the world the sterile woman is the most savagely discriminated against, but Echeverria, for the same reasons that other men oppress the sterile woman, ignored her.

His argument made perfect sense – it is idiotic to speak of women demanding equal education opportunities in countries where there is no education, and so forth, but the corollary of his argument was that discussion of the specific phenomenon of sexism would have to wait on economic redistribution.

Nobody yet knows what the New International Economic Order is, or how it might come into being. Basically, the haves will have to share with the have-nots, but as the have-nots have not the power to force the haves to share, they will have to rely upon guile or good will. Simply raising the prices of raw materials will not help, because the developed countries are still the greatest producers of them as well as everything else. However, the mere mention of the New Economic Order seemed to provoke gales of enthusiasm from Third World delegates, especially those who hailed from countries where a hundred families control all the economic activity. They were only too pleased to abandon the unpleasant task of confessing the sexism of their own societies and indulge themselves in their favourite pastime of ganging up upon the 'West'.

The next day began reasonably well, with an enormously long speech by Sirimavo Bandaranaike in which we were induced to believe that women in Sri Lanka had nothing further to ask for (except perhaps a living wage for picking tea, some form of industrial organization to represent them, and literacy and a decent diet, but on the statute books they were doing fine). Well, Mrs Bandaranaike is a head of state so there was a reason for her being the first to address the third plenary session. The second speaker was Her Imperial Highness Princess Ashraf Pahlavi of Iran, twin sister of the man who repudiated a wife because she did not bear him a son. That was a little harder to understand, but Princess Ashraf had headed the consultative committee which had worked on the Draft World Plan of Action of IWY. Besides, she paid a million dollars for the privilege. Imelda Marcos, wife of the President of the Philippines, preferred to spend her money on presents for all the delegations. The head of each delegation found upon his desk a prettily tied bundle of books, including an expensively produced picture book on her carefully coiffed and painted self and another quaintly entitled *The Compassionate Society*, which, one hopes, did not purport to be a depiction of the gangsterland of the Philippines.

Mrs Marcos's entry was spectacular. Becomingly late, she drifted in in the palest blue silk with butterfly sleeves, flanked by two oddly conspicuous men who may have been bodyguards. One was entrusted with a minute powder-blue satin purse, too weighty, one supposed, for the tiny hands which warded off an assassin's bullets just before the last election. When her moment came she ascended the podium like a film star and told us all that men were strong and women were beautiful, at least in Asia, however deviant the horrid West might be. The effect was rather spoiled because she had to speak American English, after a rather unpromising start in Spanish. As women grow most of the food in Asia, carry all the burdens, build the buildings and the roads, Mrs Marcos's pussy-power routine was slightly miscalculated, but the average lady delegate, sweating in her wig or batting her eyelids at the camera, was very impressed.

The other star of the morning was Jehan El-Sadat, who made a half-hearted attempt to convince us that Islam was good for women (nobody laughed) and then, beating the air with her false eyelashes, embarked upon a bombastic attack upon Israel. Mrs Rabin, neither so young nor so beautiful, drew nervously upon her cigarette. She had to wait four days for the privilege of being walked out upon. Instead of a conference about women, we had all been duped into attending a débâcle, where women who had come to prominence through their relationships with men were employed by those men to further their policies at the expense of the women of the world. It was disgusting. One wondered helplessly who had allowed it to happen.

The best speech of the day was given by Elizabeth Reid, head of the Australian delegation. It was interpreted as an attack upon the Mexican President's speech, because she argued poignantly that there was a phenomenon of human behaviour called sexism, and there were certain abuses and tortures to which women *qua* women were subjected, which were in direct contravention of the doctrine of human rights as propounded by the United Nations, and could not wait for the fiction of the New Economic Order to become fact. It was stirring stuff and well argued, but the delegates were restless, partly because Mrs Sadat was having a pamphlet about herself, complete with pin-up cover picture, circulated through the meeting, and partly because it was well and truly lunchtime.

The UN *modus operandi* for these functions is that the full session of the main conference listens to speeches from all the delegations (all of whom have instructions from their governments to say that everything in their garden is lovely, even though women may be mutilated, forbidden to travel without their husbands' or fathers' permission, or beaten, ostracized and killed with impunity), while committees deliberate the business of the conference, which is principally the acceptance of a World Plan of Action. The plan satisfied no one (except the Secretariat, which had produced it after two false starts) and the tabled amendments numbered more than 900. The emphasis was upon women as agricultural producers and the rearers of children; no mention was made of the sufferings of women subjected to the grosser forms of torture, either as hapless victims of mass family-planning campaigns, or as the urban poor, or as the scapegoats of sexist religion and customs.

Yet we learned, as the rainy days slid past, that there would be no time to discuss the amendments, mainly because the working party formed to discuss the amendments was a committee of the whole of the plenary session, so it was too unwieldy to function in the time allotted, let alone the time that the delegates actually spent at their posts.

The third part of the IWY Conference had been the seminars organized by the American Association for the Advancement of Science, which were over before the conference began. In that forum, conscientious women had told the truth that was hidden behind the policy speeches of the official delegations. Moroccan psychoanalysts asked how they were meant to function as analysts in a country where most of their patients needed cosmetic surgery to repair broken hymens more urgently than they needed to understand their own problems. Indian doctors asked how they would reconcile the pressures of population with the physical and mental sufferings of women in whom the Lippes Loop had been inserted. The AAAS meetings were not open to the public.

The women of the world have been mocked by the jamboree in Mexico City. The UN declaration of human rights derides them by its witless confidence that no one shall live in slavery or servitude or be subjected to cruel and inhuman treatment. Even less was accomplished in Mexico than might have been if the conference had been held five years from now, if the UN had been less hypocritical in its own employment policies and more rigorous in the drawing up of its own verbal forms, if Luis Echeverria had been less interested in being the next secretary-general and the moral leader of the Third World, if nations had been given precedence because of their proven concern for women instead of their riches or their power, or the fact that some of their delegates shared a bed with the head of state, if . . .

We have another chance. This fall, an international tribunal to hear the cases of crimes against women is being set up in New York and Berlin. Perhaps one of the accusations ought to be that the UN Secretariat, in mismanaging IWY, has brought half of the world's population, of whom perhaps one per cent actually know that it is women's year, into undeserved disrepute. Nevertheless, the UN is not itself to blame, perhaps, for insuccess in arriving at any useful statement, when such a statement must be based upon a consensus and no consensus exists. Moreover, feminism is a revolutionary movement and cannot reasonably expect to find its interests served by governments which have come to power in the traditional masculine ways.

Women's year has been a non-event so far, on the international front, but many feminists who were in Mexico have gone home early to roll up their sleeves, more than ever convinced and determined, and clearer than ever about their priorities.

A modest proposal

Spectator, 14 January 1978

The recent uproar about the activities of Dr Sopher, who artificially inseminated twelve women designated 'lesbian', highlights the disgracefully irresponsible use we make of that priceless natural resource, the nation's sperm. When Dr Rhodes Boyson points out that the State must take action to control the use made of it, in the case of lesbians, he is only gesturing towards the greater problem of haphazard waste. Most sperm is decanted far from a fertile ovum, but even if the concept of a world laved in oceans of dying sperm – for there are said to be four hundred million potential human beings in each ejaculation of a healthy male, whether 'normal' or not – were not itself horrifying, the problem of those spermatozoa which find themselves in the vicinity of an ovum must preoccupy every thinking person.

As long as men may go about dispensing this potent liquid as they list, we can have no safeguard against the proliferation of undesirable human beings, or conversely, against the condemnation of millions of innocent children to be brought up by sadists, mutilators, Moonies, murderers, spelling reformers, subversives, proof readers, immigrants, the unemployed, pederasts and pairs of women.

The legislation proposed by Dr Rhodes Boyson in the case of frozen sperm should also apply more broadly. Control of all varieties, frozen or fresh, would solve the problems of absentee parenthood, broken marriage, child poverty and multifarious abortion. If Dr Rhodes Boyson intends to hasten slowly in the matter of husbanding this national resource, I do *not*, for the matter is a pressing one, and the solution is within our grasp. It must be nationalized.

What we need to do, quite simply, is to take a number of samples from all males in, say, their seventeenth year and commit them to the safekeeping of a National Sperm Bank, after which the males must undergo vasectomy. At such time as any male wishes to father a child, he must find a willing female, then both apply for access to his sperm, which may be withheld upon any grounds deemed expedient at the time. Thus, at a blow, all the problems of uncontrolled parenthood are eliminated. Males wishing to become fathers will have to sign contracts binding them to fulfil the duties of parenthood either as defined by the State or as agreed between the contracting parties – the only way left to us now to shore up the ruins of the marriage ethic. Reproductive rights could be forfeit as an automatic consequence of criminal convictions or any other proof of chronic unreliability, such as unpaid parking fines or three endorsements on a driving licence.

By this means only, can fatherlessness, justly described by Dr Rhodes Boyson as a 'great evil', be eliminated, provided of course that the other departments of State could be deterred from the antisocial practices of sending fathers to war and to prison, allowing them to die and so forth. No itinerant workers, such as air stewards, diplomatic couriers and the like, ought to be allowed to become fathers. One has only to reflect upon the careers of the many British statesmen whose upbringing was left to groups of women, widows, military wives, grandmothers, aunts and nannies and matrons, to understand at once what an appalling evil fatherlessness is.

Men ought to welcome this solution because it represents the only way that a man can be guaranteed paternity, in that the insemination is controlled and no alien sperm can find its way to the ovum first, provided of course that the civil servants entrusted with this charge fulfil it faithfully. Moreover, men will not be menaced by the development of Celebrity Sperm Banks, which are already being set up by private enterprise, which will supply the sperm of matinée idols and pop singers to their female fans at enormous expense, thus severely reducing reproductive opportunities for poorer and less famous men.

Women will welcome the scheme because all men except the very young (with whom intercourse will be illegal) will be sterile and they will be freed from the necessity of upsetting their metabolism by powerful, continuous medication, or harbouring curiously designed pieces of metal and plastic in their uteri. Freed from anxiety, pill-induced depression and so on, they might take more confident steps towards asserting themselves.

More important in the long run is the fact that this method of State regulation of sperm distribution can eliminate at source all those genetically determined disabilities which place such strain upon the health services; not only serious congenital disorders, but commoner and hardly less costly ones, like myopia, prognathousness and flat feet.

Doctors ought to welcome the measure. As the churches lose their power to trammel the anarchic sexual energies of the human race in guilt, the duties of regulation of reproductive behaviour have gradually been hived off on that least qualified of groups for such business, the medical practitioners. Already struggling in the toils of the hypertrophied National Health Service, and further oppressed by the volume of technical information which they are expected to learn and unlearn week by week, the unfortunate doctors are now being asked to decide who shall be allowed to reproduce and who shall not. They are expected to decide for fatherless children in some instances by denying access to abortion, and in others they are required to refuse access to the source of procreation because the result will be fatherlessness.

The exigencies of National Health practice mean that few doctors have time to check whether their patients are *physically* able to undergo pregnancy: that they should be expected in the short time at their disposal to come to some conclusion about the social suitability of patients for parenthood is clearly absurd. It is no small commendation of the National Sperm Bank scheme, that it would relieve the long-suffering practitioners of some of their more god-like functions and therefore of some of the causes of their own ill-health.

The principal beneficiaries of the scheme would, of course, be the children. No one would be born who was not guaranteed a stable nuclear family and continuing support. Perhaps no one would be born.

Eternal war: Strindberg's view of sex

Spectator, 3 June 1978

There has come into existence, chiefly in America, a breed of men who claim to be feminists. They imagine that they have understood 'what women want' and that they are capable of giving it to them. They help with the dishes at home and make their own coffee in the office, basking the while in the refulgent consciousness of virtue. Not only do they call women Ms and let them open car doors for themselves and pay for their own food in restaurants, they write books called *The Liberated Man* and *Male Chauvinism: How it Works*. A few of the more intrepid travel about preaching the new religion of sexual equality to any who will pay to hear.

Such men are apt to think of the true male feminists as utterly chauvinistic. Having successfully trivialized the problem of male-female hostility in their own cases, they are quick to denounce the more perspicacious men who have glimpsed the archetypal conflict in all its terrible grandeur. One such is Buñuel, whose film *Cet obscur objet de désir*, shows in the simplest and most astonishing way the utter inability of either sex to comprehend the other. By contrast with the implacable, eternal war of the sexes, which cannot find truce until our civilization is completely changed or completely destroyed, the petty outrage perpetrated by male on male for ephemeral political motives is banal. Buñuel is a feminist because he finds the sexual conflict to be radical, tragic and overwhelming – not simply a peripheral question.

Strindberg, an episode from whose anguished life is the subject of Per Olov Enquist's *The Tribades*, was another who understood that the expression of the radical enmity between men and women in social or political action would have appalling consequences. Like Buñuel, he embodied his vision of internecine sexual war in archetypes so simple that they could appear preposterous or simply perverse. It is useless, faced with a situation like that of *Dance of Death* (which will open at the Aldwych on 13 June), to demand explanations of why Edgar's and Alice's marriage does not work, for Strindberg is at pains to show that such an arrangement can never work. Above all, the men in Strindberg's writing cannot be found to blame for their own and their wives' sufferings. Strindberg understood, although his public hardly ever understands, that the most unpardonable privilege that men enjoy is their magnanimity

As a character in *The Tribades*, Strindberg shows outrage because his wife and her friend, the tribadists of the title, forced him to play whist every evening without ever bothering to learn the rules. This is the kind of libel which most riles the pseudo-feminist of the twenties who believes that women would become gentlemen like himself if only they knew how, ignoring the sad fact that those who play the game are greatly outnumbered by those who keep the green and pour tea in the pavilion.

While Enquist is commendably careful to avoid the crasser kinds of explanation of the anguish that Strindberg and his wife caused each other, he cannot avoid some of the more voguish reductions of the essential enmity of men and women. Where Strindberg is mocked and maddened by the very inscrutability of the female body compared to the pathetic exposure of male libido, an essential and instransigent difference between the sexes, Enquist renders his anxiety as an unusual degree of concern about his own genital endowments. Such a method is closer to Ibsen's method than to Strindberg's for it implies journalistic explanations which adduce accidental causes, when Strindberg's agony stems from essential things. It is probably true that Siri Strindberg and Marie Caroline David were or became lovers, and that Strindberg underwent a self-imposed virility test, but such matters do not help us to understand Strindberg's vision of the whole conflict and may positively hinder us from grasping the nature of our own dilemmas. In so far as Enquist's play might lead us to interpret *Dance of Death* as the crooked fantasy of a severely disturbed man, one might wish it had never been written.

Susan Hampshire is warmly to be commended for undertaking the role of Siri von Essen, although her sweet voice and far-fetched profile make the character seem even more long-suffering than Enquist meant her to be. Georgina Hale, a curious choice for Marie David, was more hampered by Enquist's slightly obtuse sympathy. Crushed by the weight of Enquist's view of his sexual and emotional inadequacy, Enquist sees Strindberg as a casualty of the nineteenth-century stereotype of conquistadorial male and a cliché of neo-feminism. Strindberg's own vision goes further out, and deeper in.

If one expects no more of Enquist's play than one might from any dramatized biography, *The Tribades* is exceptionally good. If Enquist's intention is to be more than journalistic, some references to the 'Hansen affair' and to 'what happened in Grez three years ago' could have been entirely submerged, for the audience was simply teased and baffled by them. The photomontage which began the play, otherwise almost entirely naturalistic, more so in this production than Enquist might have intended, placed it in the context of current feminist debate, to which it makes a far less significant contribution than did that tormented theoretical misogynist ninety years ago.

1980 – 1985

Chemistry and fertility:
review of Carl Djerassi

Spectator, 7 June 1980

Carl Djerassi is Professor of Chemistry at Stanford University, author of 650 scientific publications and the man who synthesized oestrone and oestradiol from diosgenin, which is to say, he is the man who found out how to regulate female fertility by an oral route. He is not the sole begetter of the Pill, for Russell Marker's work with yams, and Rosencrantz's work with Marker's work, preceded Djerassi's work with Rosencrantz's work, but he has the largest share of the responsibility and he is not at all shy of taking it, especially as Searle pinched his idea, modified it slightly and beat him to the line.

What a man who had so much to do with the birth of the contraceptive era thinks of the phenomenon twenty years later must be important if only for the inadequacies and blind spots in his vision. *The Politics of Contraception* is an essential document, even though it deals with only a fraction of its subject, namely the vicissitudes of the manufacture and dissemination of oral contraception. Professor Djerassi is very much aware that there are other, non-oral forms of contraception, and he lists them punctiliously before mounting his own hobby-horse, but it is clear that he feels that they will not do, but why he should feel so is nowhere examined. Coitus interruptus, he agrees, is not contraceptive hardware; indeed, as he says, 'that is its greatest virtue', and he is too scrupulous an empiricist to repeat the assertion that it is not effective, but he greatly obfuscates the issue by including Francis Place's erroneous description of the method, after simply stating that 'it clearly detracts from sexually satisfying intercourse'. Notions of sexually satisfying intercourse are remarkably protean, as the extraordinary spectrum of human paraphilias demonstrates, but Djerassi cannot see that his nominal subject includes the reasons why he, and men like him, consider that intravaginal ejaculation is the only satisfactory kind. His assertion that the success of coitus interruptus 'depends heavily upon practice and sexual discipline' does not distinguish it from all sexual intercourse. If it were to be suspected that female sterility, temporary or permanent, is a permit for perfunctory, drunken, selfish, nasty, brutish and short intercourse, it is itself a contributing factor in the death of passion.

The rhythm method is likewise dismissed because people are not 'motivated enough to try it'. One reason why people are not 'motivated enough', and it is a reason which Djerassi ought to have considered, is that they have been sold on a pharmaceutical method of control. Besides, saying that people are not 'motivated enough' is simply jargon for saying that they are unwilling; in this case, unwilling to forgo intromission for a limited period as a way of avoiding an unwanted pregnancy. Within that scope there are a number of motivations or lacks thereof, and it would be part of Djerassi's topic to consider just what kinds of conflict result in the phenomenon of taking chances.

Djerassi is too honest a scientist not to admit that prolonged lactation together with demand feeding are more effective in keeping human numbers down than anything Western technology has been able to devise, but he muddles this issue too, by not including the common concomitant practice of sexual abstinence by lactating women and their spouses. He would find the fact that millions of people abstain from intercourse during pregnancy similarly difficult to deal with, for the unexamined premisses which underlie his life's work are that everybody ought to be free to have intercourse whenever he feels like it (and he ought to feel like it often) while the possibility of pregnancy, rather than enhancing intercourse, spoils it.

Nearly all the people who will read Djerassi's book will share these assumptions based upon their own experience, but any serious discussion of the politics (or the ethics) of contraception must account for the fact that birth rates in the developed world fell, in some cases, below replacement level, long before Djerassi felt the need to devote himself to the pursuit of an oral contraceptive. Djerassi's own success was the immediate result of the popular enthusiasm which hailed the Pill as the perfect birth-control technique. We will not understand the situation into which this blind faith has catapulted us until we examine the social and cultural factors which led to Pillolatry, nor will we have anything but the haziest notion of the impact of our proselytizing fervour in countries where this demand has to be artificially stimulated.

Notwithstanding his own parental interest in the ideology of the Pill, Djerassi advocates positive promotion of the condom as a glamorous and groovy (literally) contraceptive, but he does not confess the role of his invention in the current worldwide epidemic of sterilizing disease in juveniles, or refer to the fact that the only people to have any success in controlling the incidence of venereal disease were the Swedes, who mounted an effective condom programme.

Battered by current anti-Pill propaganda, he forces himself to say, with conscious nobility, 'I do wish to emphasize that on safety grounds, the diaphragm is clearly the best female contraceptive.' Be that as it may, women abandoned the dreadful thing without a pang. Professor Djerassi could, if anyone could, develop new sperm incapacitators which did not rule out all oro-genital contact, and were not bulky, clammy and cold, but he is not really interested. He is not concerned either to tell the puzzling story of how the diaphragm beat the superior cervical cap out of the market, or why – both questions of the politics of contraception if ever there were any.

Under his general heading of contraception, Djerassi discusses the IUD, but does not reveal the historical facts behind the collapse of international IUD programmes or the impressive array of legal suits against the manufacturers of the devices. Abortion functions as contraception in Djerassi's overview, as does sterilization, but Djerassi does not spare a thought for the precipitous rise in the number of routine sterilizations being performed in the United States, where sterilization has been responsible for the definitive limitation of more families than any other method. The signs are that we are already nearing the end of the contraceptive era, for new developments are more likely to be abortifacient than contraceptive. (Djerassi's own projection of a luteolytic 'contraceptive' is close to probability but he does not care to explain the difference between disrupting pregnancy and preventing conception.) Meanwhile, the number of sterilizations continues to increase rapidly.

The most interesting part of the book's nominal subject matter lies buried, undeveloped, in Chapter 2. Thereafter, Djerassi is concerned solely with his baby, the contraceptive steroid Pill and the obstacles which prevent its improvement and even wider acceptance, principally impossibly protracted and expensive testing, which postpone the marketing of a new Pill until the patent has run out.

The Politics of Contraception is an outpouring of Djerassi's frustration and, as such, perfectly understandable, if rather tiresome. Many of the anxieties which lie behind virulent (his word) criticism of the Pill are the result of our frightening ignorance of exactly what such a potent drug is up to besides suppressing ovulation. This statement of the situation comes from no disgruntled Pill user but from a fellow scientist:

> Steroidal contraceptives have now been administered for more than twenty years and world usage was recently estimated at over eighty million women . . . one would expect our understanding of the clinical pharmacology of contraceptive steroids to be comprehensive and sound. Yet, rather the opposite appears to be true . . . At present, relatively little is known about the exact influence of a multitude of factors governing the bio-availability and metabolic fate of synthetic steroids, e.g. drug formulation, route of adminstration, absorption processes, enterohepatic recycling, binding plasma proteins, catabolic events, modes of excretion, etc. Even less data are available on the relationship between steroidal pharmakinetics and such variables as ethnic background, nutrition, climate, disease states, simultaneous administration of non-contraceptive drugs, etc. (H. Hammerstein *et al.*, 'The Clinical Pharmacology of Contraceptive Steroids', *Contraception* Vol. 20. No. 3, September 1979, p.193)

For all Djerassi's ingenuity in finding an oral contraceptive, it now seems obvious that much smaller doses of steroids are more effective if administered in other ways, while the ingested Pill is largely wasted, or worse, quite harmful. Djerassi may gnash his teeth over apparently silly bits of information, such as that oral contraceptives reduce the secretion of ear wax, but they are indications of a systemic effect and biological pathways which are unknown.

The great red herring in all discussions of contraceptive steroids is cancer. Djerassi repeats all the old arguments, that popping your Pill is safer than smoking, much safer than being pregnant and a thousand times safer than sitting in a moving automobile. Women, like other people, will run risks if they consider that the result of their risk-taking is an enhancement of life. Women are giving up the Pill in favour of electrocautery of their entrails not because of the chronic trivial side effects, which are, after all, not so trivial – changes in mood control, the struggle to keep weight down, the disruption of the vaginal environment and the resultant recurrent infections, chronic bacteriuria and recurrent cystitis, fluid retention, headaches, facial mottling and so forth.

Djerassi knows that the generalized systemic effects are real. His frustration is, in the last analysis, a professional one; he wishes that the oral contraceptive steroid had been a better idea. So does the present generation of women. Their children may have even greater cause for wishing so.

The Dalton Syndrome

Unpublished

In 1981, it was demonstrated in two criminal trials (R v. Craddock and R v. English) that the defendants were suffering from PMS, premenstrual syndrome. Craddock had been placed on probation for the stabbing of a barmaid in May 1979, and stabilized by the administration of 100mg of progesterone daily. She appeared in court in 1981 when she broke the conditions of her probation as a consequence of not being given the steroid. English killed her lover by driving her car at him and crushing him against a lamp-post. PMS was part of her defence. Dr Katharina Dalton gave evidence that PMS was a disease of the mind as defined by Section 2 of the 1957 Homicide Act.

The recent emergence of premenstrual tension as a *cause célèbre* has left feminists uncertain whether to laugh or to cry. On the one hand, some good has been done: two women have been kept out of gaol, which is a good thing, gaols being both very costly forms of accommodation and utterly unlikely to lead to anything but a gradual deterioration in the character and conduct of their occupants. Better still, both women have evidently been rehabilitated by the medical treatment they are receiving at the hands of the expert witness whose testimony kept them out of gaol. Even while feminists and their fellow travellers known as 'humanists' are rejoicing at this gratifying turn of events, they are also horrified at the inference drawn by the popular press that the menstrual cycle turns docile women into werewolves or something worse. The outlook for women desirous of piloting Concorde has never looked bleaker.

What Dr Katharina Dalton sought to show in her testimony was that the two women were not responsible for the quite terrible things they had done because they were suffering from an acute form of what doctors have been taught to call Premenstrual Syndrome, which the press took up by a commoner name which actually refers to a milder phenomenon, premenstrual tension. Dr Dalton herself includes symptoms arising at times other than the premenstrual period in her definition of PMS, so even that name turns out to be a misnomer. It would be less confusing if we decided to follow the procedure usually adopted in such cases, and named the syndrome after the woman who has devoted the last thirty years of her life to tracking it down and treating it, simply, the Dalton Syndrome.

In order to suffer from the syndrome, which Dr Dalton describes in one of the latest of her dozens of publications on the subject as 'the world's commonest, and probably the oldest, disease', it is not sufficient, nor is it necessary, to menstruate. What the patient profile must show is a pattern of recurrence, corresponding to the menstrual cycle, of one or a number of symptoms, which may be of almost any kind, grave enough to cause disruption to professional or social or family life, interspaced with symptom-free intervals. No matter what kind of symptoms appear, 'bloatedness, weight gain, oedema, backache, sinusitis, glaucoma, tension, depression, irritability, lethargy, headaches, epilepsy, fainting, panics, nausea, exhaustion, aggression, asthma, rhinitis, urticaria, upper respiratory infections, tonsillitis, acne, styes, conjunctivitis, boils or herpes', if they are caused by the Dalton Syndrome, they will respond to administration of progesterone. (Perhaps the most unique aspect of the Dalton Syndrome is that it was identified from the therapy backwards.) Whether the symptoms occur in pre-pubertal, post-menopausal or hysterectomized women, they will respond to progesterone. They are also quite likely to respond to adminstration of a placebo, of pyridoxine or of *Vitex agnus castus*, but although the placebo effect is always significant in the treatment of PMS, progesterone does have a clear edge.

Rather more of the nasty things that women do, or that befall them, do occur in the paramenstruum than would if all factors were equal. Most women know that when they are under stress, the added stress of the lead-up to menstruation will produce whatever symptom their particular psyche has inflicted upon the soma, be it a pimple or a blister or vomiting and blind rages. Most women would readily agree with Dr Dalton that the paramenstruum is a time of vulnerability, but that is not at all the same thing as giving up any attempt to control it. Even given the period of vulnerability, women get up to very little mayhem compared to men, who have no cycle at all. Perhaps the predilection of men for rapine and slaughter should be interpreted as meaning that men are premenstrual at all times.

When it comes to allaying human suffering, Dr Dalton's record is impressive. Recent publicity means that new patients will wait eight months to see her privately, or two years on the National Health. She has very generously published full descriptions of her therapy which is well within the competence of the average GP to perform. However, there is deep resistance to Dr Dalton's methods, and there are good grounds for it.

There is clear evidence of the physical changes taking place in the body during the menstrual cycle, but what is far from clear is by what mechanism those changes are experienced by some women as unbearable and lead to the formation of severe symptoms. The high placebo response indicates that the problem is in part psychogenic. Moreover, we know that stress produces a rise of prolactin in the blood and that prolactin has a direct effect upon secretory activity which leads to lower circulating levels of various hormones, including progesterone. All our endocrinological functions are synergistic: disrupt one and all have been disrupted. Attempts to deal with the prolactin excess in PMS sufferers by administering bromocriptine were less successful than treatment with progesterone, and the reason seems to be that rather than attempting to attack a link in a chain which is only half understood, progesterone suppresses the whole process by inhibiting ovulation itself. Although Dr Dalton states quite categorically that there are no counter-indications for the administration of progesterone, the simple fact is that we do not know the long-term effects of regular large doses of this powerful steroid.

Although it is clear that Dr Dalton is very aware of the psychogenic factor in PMS, in her published writing she has concentrated upon the syndrome as an 'endocrinopathy'. Unfortunately, the raising of public awareness by the recent sensational events is likely to lead to an increased sensitivity to the inconveniences of the paramenstruum, and an increase in the number of women seeking tender loving care plentifully laced with progesterone. Dr Dalton is too good a doctor to dose women with the steroid because they present her with a herpes four or five times a year, but if they report *misery* accompanying the sores, which are certainly painful and disfiguring, they are likely to qualify for injections or implants. The potentiality for distortion in the situation is massive: when we read in Dr Dalton's book *The Premenstrual Syndrome and Progesterone Therapy* (Heinemann Medical Books, 1977) that children born to mothers who were given supplementary progesterone during pregnancy, appeared 'to possess enhanced intelligence and educational attainment' we must begin to suspect an acute case of radical experimental bias.

However, all the bids are not yet in. There is one school of thought among endocrinologists which has begun to consider the possibility that the abnormality in the PMS picture is the constant recurrence of frustrated ovulation. If women are genetically programmed to undergo numerous pregnancies and the high levels of progesterone which accompany them, the regular administration of progesterone may be a good way of restoring the balance. Nevertheless it must always be borne in mind that dosage with synthetic forms of naturally occurring hormones is usually disproportionate because the mode of administration is inefficient, and the biological pathways taken by the drug poorly understood.

The most depressing aspect for a feminist of the current twitter about 'PMT' is that it continues the tradition of extremely negative response to the phenomenon of the female cycle. There is no space on the questionnaires, which researchers send out to carefully chosen female populations on their tolerance of menstruation, for a positive reaction. We do not celebrate the menarche; we do not recognize the fact that segregation of menstruating women in traditional societies gives them cherished days off from labouring in the fields and preparing food. Our blindness to the positive aspects of the cycle is the concomitant of our rejection of the female in our culture. What the 'PMT' scandals showed us was that our misogynistic disgust was very close to the surface and went down very deep.

The Pulitzer divorce

Forum, June 1983

In October 1982, multi-millionaire Herbert Pulitzer brought divorce proceedings against his wife, Roxanne. On 29 December, a punitive judgement was brought in, giving the father custody of the two sons of the marriage and awarding Roxanne Pulitzer less than $50,000 in alimony.

For the general public who read the highlights in the gutter press, the Pulitzer divorce case may well have seemed entertaining; for those who were obliged to listen to the sordid tale for eighteen days the glamour must have worn off completely. Judge Carl H. Harper's is a hell of a way to make a living. His verdict reflects partly the anomaly of Florida State Statutes 61.08 (1), which specifically allows for the bringing of evidence of adultery and other skulduggery by both parties regardless of the state's no-fault divorce law, and partly his own sympathy for a part-time playboy whose arteries have turned on him at the same time as his wife. It is idle to speculate whether justice was done. When two mad dogs are at each other's throats, there is no point in deciding which dog caught rabies first.

Judge Harper presents less of a problem to me, for he fairly predictably found for his own kind, than do those judges who bring in bizarre verdicts which appear to sanction the parasitic role of women and indeed to suggest that a year catering to a millionaire's sexual and other whims is worth half his forty years' accumulated capital. To this observer at least, American case law is a jungle, where unworkable precedents are too often set and stand for years because the parties to the the litigation have been so expertly pillaged by their lawyers that they cannot afford a shoeshine, let alone another court case.

What lies behind Judge Harper's decision is not only irritation that such cases can still be brought, complicated by down-home sexism, but the moral corruption of the legal profession, whose most successful pleaders demand and get grossly disproportionate remuneration for their labours. Pulitzer was not only under attack by Roxanne, he was also being blitzed by the legal profession. While the mad dogs rip at each other's throats, the vultures sit by, ready to feast royally off both corpses. Harper was concerned to see that in his courtroom, they went away empty. I sympathize, but I do not necessarily approve. The only reason that top lawyers work for penniless women in divorce cases, is that there is a good chance of a punitive settlement. Other women may have to pay for the humiliation of Roxanne Pulitzer.

Judge Harper, in his summing up, chose to dwell on certain aspects of the Pulitzers' relationship, which he interpreted as the exploitation by a dizzy twenty-five-year-old of a hard-working – and evidently naïve – forty-seven-year-old millionaire businessman. According to him, Roxanne Pulitzer is the errant spouse who destroyed a marriage and wishes to be treated as if she had been a faithful wife. The world where jaded middle-aged businessmen seek sexual excitement and rejuvenation in second marriage seems to lie beyond Harper's ken. It seems to me that Pulitzer married Roxanne because he wanted cunningly varied fun and games, and that he must have taken an active part in the process of her corruption. The possibilities are two, either she was a hot number, used cocaine and elaborate sexual ritual when she met him, in which case that must have turned him on, or she developed these tastes under his tutelage.

No housewife with no income of her own can buy very much cocaine without a certain bulge appearing in the household accounts. The businessman Pulitzer can hardly have failed to notice what was going on, and he must have countenanced it, if he did not actually initiate it. I should have liked to hear evidence from the Pulitzers' dealer myself. Even in Harper's formulation it seems clear that Roxanne Pulitzer's first duty was to keep her husband entertained. The alcohol, the cocaine and the nannies were all part of the deal. The trouble is that ageing millionaires who marry twenty-five-year-old part-owners of mobile homes in search of rejuvenation don't get rejuvenated. They get worn out.

Pulitzer didn't marry Roxanne because he wanted someone to meet him on the doorstep in her apron and drive him into ecstasies with her meatloaf, but he simply could not keep up with the pace that she actually developed. She began to leave him out of the high-jinks department. When he tried to retreat into a more manageable middle-aged life, Mrs Pulitzer hung on to the high life to which she had become addicted. It is possible that the drugs produced a character change in her, but frankly I doubt it. Pulitzer once liked her brassy hardness and world-wise swagger: he was the one who changed.

The evidence against Roxanne was intended to disqualify her as a fit mother for their two sons, although most of it was irrelevant to the job of parenting. Children can handle parents' adultery and flightiness and drug-use very much better than they can handle quarrelling. Moreover, if Pulitzer is the early-to-bed early-to-rise workaholic and man's man that Harper thinks he is, the boys will be deprived of both parents when they are deprived of Roxanne.

Harper's verdict dramatizes the fact that in our world men control women, especially women like Roxanne Pulitzer. What she learnt in the courtroom was what some of us already know, that women are not equal with men before the law, and that the poor are less powerful than the rich even when they marry them. She thought she had a right to plunder Pulitzer but in reality she only had a sporting chance. She wagered heavily on that chance and lost. It would be interesting to know just how many of the jet-set studs are still around now that the cocaine bill is likely to remain unpaid. Among the unavoidable conclusions we must come to is that Roxanne Pulitzer is rather stupid. Millionaires and jet-set studs will only tolerate stupidity in very young women. Roxanne is young no more. In the circles in which she moves, losers have no friends. Judge Harper's confidence that she can earn any kind of a living seems to be misplaced.

So, while I welcome the fact that Judge Harper's verdict is true to the reality that women are still chattels even in the United States of America, conservative feminist rhetoric notwithstanding, I do not for a moment think that justice has been done. Roxanne Pulitzer is a victim, a fairly repulsive victim, but a victim nevertheless.

One man's mutilation is another man's beautification

Unpublished

In 1983, the Australian theatre designer and my dear friend, Barry Kay, showea me a book of extraordinary photographs of body art and asked me to write an introduction for it. The book was never published. In 1984, Barry's health began to fail and in spring 1985 he died.

Humans are the only animals which can consciously and deliberately change their appearance according to their own whims. Most animals groom themselves, but humans are tempted to manipulate their appearance in ways much more radical than those open to other animals, not simply because they are able to use tools upon themselves, but also because of some peculiarities in the way in which humans are made. The human body is a curiously ambiguous structure, partaking of almost contradictory attributes. For example, humans are neither furry nor hairless, but variously naked, slightly hairy and very hirsute. All these variations may be found on the body of a single individual at the same time. Humans are then confronted with a series of managerial problems: among the ways in which they express their cultural identities are the contrasting ways in which they handle these problems.

The Australian Aborigines used to conserve hair; not only did they not eliminate whatever hair was growing on their bodies, they collected extra human hair to work into a thick girdle for men to wear about their hips. We would look askance at anyone who could not bear to discard fallen hair, now that hair shirts are out of fashion, but sophisticated Western people often wear the hair of others as a postiche or toupee. Where the scalp-hunter once sought to augment his physical or psychic power by acquiring the hair of others, the literate people of the twentieth century feel that they will acquire youth and beauty through bought hair. They will even pay to have hair stitched into their scalps in a very costly and laborious development of the ancient practice of needleworking living flesh.

Some people identify themselves partly by their refusal to cut hair, as do the Sikhs, who twist the long silky hair of their beards together with what grows on their heads, tie the whole lot up in a chignon and cover it with a turban. Others insist on the removal of any hair, wherever it is, and they too may choose a turban, this time to hide a bald head. Western conventions of hair management often appeal to younger or recalcitrant members of societies with strict rules for hair management because they find them more convenient; in fact, they are very subtle and difficult, requiring minute calculations of the degree of shagginess which is appropriate to age, and economic and social status. The rejection of traditional modes of hair management has less to do with convenience and common sense than with the desire to break out of the confinement of the group. A shaven Sikh might object that he is as much Sikh as ever; he may claim that his elimination of his identifying marks was simply to pour out the bath water while retaining the baby, but in fact he has summarily loosened his ties with his religious group in order to be accepted into another group. If he keeps his steel bracelet, which will be recognized by other Sikhs, it is because he does not wish to lose all the advantages connected with belonging to that group. When a Sikh takes his employer to court for refusing to allow him to wear his turban at work, it is not a mere formality. He is making a serious bid to limit his employer's power over his life.

The impact of technological culture can be measured by the degree of acceptance of Western conventions of body management throughout the world. Fashion, because it is beyond logic, is deeply revealing. Women all over the world have adopted, often in addition to their traditional accoutrements, four Western conventions: high-heeled shoes, lipstick, nail varnish and the brassière. The success of all of these fashions, which are not even remotely connected with comfort or common sense, is an indication of the worldwide acceptance of the Western notion that the principal duties of women are sexual attraction and vicarious leisure. The women who have accepted these fashions will justify their decision by saying that all four are more attractive than the alternatives. All that they are really saying is that they themselves were more attracted to alien styles than they were to the styles adopted by their mothers and grandmothers. To give the full answer would be to expose the tensions which are destroying traditional lifestyles all over the world. There is a slight traffic in the opposite direction. Distinguished lady professors of economics may reject high heels, lipstick, nail varnish and brassière, and adopt the dress of a Punjabi peasant labourer; Iranian girls may resume the chador. In each case the motive for the change is clearly political; what is not so often realized is that it is equally political when it happens the other way around.

Because what we do with our bodies is so revealing we try to insist that it has no meaning at all. A man whose hair is cut regularly and at great expense, who shaves his face in a careful pattern, will say that he is not concerned with his appearance, while a man with a beard will maintain that he simply cannot be bothered shaving, but the truth is that both have selected an image which they feel best expresses their characters and chosen social roles. The man with a beard probably shaves some part of his face and neck quite regularly, and definitely trims the beard itself. He may frequently be seen grooming it with his hands, patting and stroking it into his preferred shape. Between the shaggy bearded man and the smooth clean-shaven man there lies a vast range of tonsorial modes, all of which have meanings relative to each other. The man who grows his sideburns long is expressing something about his class and his age group. The man who lets his cheek whiskers grow in tufts or shaves his sideburns off is also projecting some part of a chosen self-image. All kinds of curious facial topiary are accepted provided that they have some pedigree within our cultural tradition. The associations of such variations as curled and waxed moustaches, Mexican revolutionary moustaches, pencil moustaches and toothbrush moustaches are endlessly subtle and constantly being remade.

In the recent past we came to accept long flowing hair as a possible masculine alternative; with the passing of time our initial reactions of outrage have softened into acceptance. Men's long curls are now a sign of nostalgia for the sixties, the last quiver of hippie energy, which was never anything to be feared. By contrast, the man who completely shaves his head still shocks us. It is as if he is flaunting a violence that he has done to himself. Other men, hairless through no choice of their own, may have wigs on the National Health to hide their embarrassing nakedness. Western youths whose heads are shaven in accordance with the practice of oriental monastics will wear wigs when they go to badger people in airports because shaven heads are so alienating to our sensibilities. The man who shaves his head and does not cover it is indulging in a form of indecent exposure, the purpose of which, as usual, is intimidation.

The shaving of women's heads is considered so disfiguring that it seemed adequate punishment for women who collaborated with the Nazis in the Second World War, and yet there are many cultures whose women shave all or part of their heads and would feel dirty or unkempt if they did not. Girls who shave off all the hair except what grows on the crown of their heads are doing no more than the Turkana women of Kenya have always done, but by doing it in a society where such styles have never been seen, they defy the accepted norms and court rejection. The coxcomb and its variants, sometimes called the Mohawk or Mohican hairstyle, imitate the intimidating shapes of the advanced crests of fighting birds. A less daring version, for it can be tamed into smoothness when the wearer is in the haunts of the smooth, is the teased mop. The ferocity mimicked by the hairstyle is further expressed in the studded belts and armlets and earrings in the shape of a skull, but it is clearly a mere affectation. The camp aggressiveness of the display stands in inverse ratio to the social power wielded by the group. Their cultural uniformity is actually competitiveness and does not lead to solidarity.

In most societies which modify the body, the visible changes are outward signs of the fulfilment of the rites of passage. The acceptance of the new-born into the community at a naming ceremony or its equivalent may be marked by a ritual haircut, the shape of which may indicate his or her clan or totem. The approach of puberty may be signalled by circumcision or scarification or the adoption of a new hairstyle. The prelude to marriage may require further scarification or tattooing or fattening or a period of special body painting, while marriage itself may be signified by drastic changes in appearance, especially for women. The birth of children, achievement of elder status or the death of a spouse bring the last changes. In classless societies where property is either held in common or kept to a minimum, all changes in status must involve changes in physical appearance. Where no one carries an identity card which will, say, permit him to drink in the company of adults, everyone who may must be distinguished by a sign. The achievement of these signs is one of the most important satisfactions of such societies. Before imperialists brought mirrors, such people could not confer the signs upon themselves: the recognition of a transition was given dramatic form by the ceremony of the conferring of signs in which the interested parties all acted as a group.

In Western society the outward signs of social status have withered into mere vestiges. Pubescent boys may live through intense dramas of hair cultivation, struggling for a moustache or bushy sideburns or simply longing to shave every day. Little girls may covet high heels and brassières and long for the day that they can wear make-up, but the menarche will not be marked in any way: marriageability will be signified only by the absence of an inconspicuous ring on the fourth finger of the left hand. In Jewish society, circumcision is still a rite of passage, but once the barmitzvah is over, the initiate cannot be recognized by any other outward sign. Married women used to be expected to dress differently from girls: a pale echo of the sixteenth-century custom which required married women to wear closed bodices and hide their hair under a cap. This persisted into the twentieth century when married women were expected to wear hats on social occasions, but has now died out.

The disappearance of distinguishing marks of social status in industrial societies is not meaningless, nor can it be construed to mean that human beings have outgrown such childish things. It is an accurate reflection of the fact that social relationships, particularly kinship relations, have been and are under intense pressure from economic relationships. The one insignia that is worn, in the United States more than in Europe but the strengthening of the trend is apparent, is the insignia of the employer. The family is no longer the dominant group and human beings are no longer differentiated on the grounds of their status within it. Instead they are differentiated by their consumer behaviour, employment status, income and possessions: the contrasts are so striking that it is considered indiscreet and tasteless to flaunt them by display of wealth. Instead the degrees of difference are signalled, more or less subtly, by grooming and by some carefully chosen attributes; hints to those who know how to take them are conveyed by the watch, the pen, the attaché case, the note case, the cuff links. Along with the indications of success are clues to other allegiances, the college ring, the lodge pin, the old school tie. Democracy and uniformity in outward appearance are necessitated by the extreme differentiation in economic circumstances, which might otherwise become a source of tension.

In tribal societies, where economic activity is static, limited as it is to the repetitive daily functions of survival, there is time to elaborate the paraphernalia of status considered in all but economic terms and immense satisfaction connected with doing so. The individual who proceeds through the stages all duly solemnized has conferred an elegance and order upon the struggle, and within that wider function there is scope for individual expression and aesthetic concerns.

The motives for Western beautification are very different. Most of the figures in this book are people who are excluded from economic activity, but they cannot compensate by celebrating other forms of status for these have been eliminated. Unhappily, as the social roles which evolve out of family relationships ceased to command respect, the number of older people condemned to live for many years outside the sphere of economic activity in conditions of mere survival increased and will go on increasing. Among the displacement activities which this group must now concentrate on in order to beguile the time between retirement and the grave, there are a number connected with futile imitation of the group from which they have been excluded. As there is no prestige or power connected with being old, it is important to deny the ageing process itself. Where once humans celebrated the achievement of seniority and longevity, they now invest as much energy or more in trying to resist the inevitable. Where hair colouring used to be done for fun, it is now done for camouflage.

A full head of strawberry blonde curls is only acquired by a sixty-year-old after regular orgies of dying, setting and backcombing, all of which actually speed the degeneration of the scalp and the hair shaft. There is a good deal of pain involved as the dyes bite into sensitive old skin and the hot dryers tighten the hair, driving the pins still further into the old scalp. The ordeal is worth it if the sufferer sees herself rejuvenated by it; the suffering is an essential part of the prophylaxis, but it must be accompanied by words of tenderness and filial care from the torturers. We are not surprised to see the hairdresser as a shaman, hung about with amulets, his face suffused with long-suffering compassion. The payment of money for his services guarantees that the job has been well done; an old lady with a fifty-dollar hairstyle is still a person to be reckoned with.

The photographs in this book may be divided into two kinds, those which depict the struggle for acceptance and those which show the revolt against the cultural norm. The most disturbing pictures are those which show the violation of bodies which are not sick in order to bring them into line with a stereotype of youth, beauty and health. We are frightened, not by the truculent attitudes of those who want to shock or impress us, but by the desecration of the bodies of those who want to be admired. We are in the midst of a cultural upheaval in which the body, which for aeons was a holy thing, its excretions and its orifices feared and revered, is becoming reified. It is becoming a toy, an asset, a commodity, an instrumentality for human will, and the pace of the change is much too fast. The intolerability of pictures of stainless steel meticulously carving out faces and breasts, isolating the unwanted and throwing it in the trash, tells us that we are still superstitious. We still suspect that the fantasy which is being imposed upon the body is less potent and less various than the body itself. Yet we cannot ease our anxiety by sneering, for we know the callousness which characterizes our treatment of the old and obese. We can understand why people who have the money will endure pain and risk death rather than go on living inside the bodies which bear the marks of their own history. Cosmetic surgery is the secular version of confession and absolution. It has taken the place of all our lost ceremonies of death and rebirth. It is reincarnation.

Most societies reject the grossly deformed. All societies have notions of beauty and fitness to which they aspire: relatively non-neurotic societies tend to admire characteristics which are well-distributed among their people, because distance from the culturally recognized norm causes suffering. We are affected by our bodies just as our behaviour marks them. Peculiar looking people tend to behave peculiarly. Criminologists have known for many years that cosmetic surgery may do more for a social delinquent than years of custody and psychiatric care, when it comes to rehabilitation.

Once we begin to sculpt the body to our own aesthetic requirements we enter a realm of shifting values to which there is no guide. In essence, beautification and mutilation are the same activity. The African women who practise genital mutilation do so primarily because they think the result is more attractive; the unreconstructed genitalia are disgusting to them. Very few Westerners really find the female genitalia beautiful, but most of them would be horrified, even nauseated, by the sight of an infibulated vagina. None of them, by contrast, would cry out in disgust at the sight of a mutilated penis, stripped of its foreskin; all of them would be unpleasantly affected by the sight of a sub-incised penis.

Some mutilations have an ulterior purpose; the biting off of little finger joints of the newborn by Aboriginal mothers may be a way of deflecting the attention of evil spirits who would covet a perfect child. The custom of branding sickly infants in India may incidentally eliminate the feebler ones before too much energy has been invested in their care, and even, perhaps, activate sluggish resistance to the pathogens in the environment. In any event, the brands are carefully placed. The endurance of pain, especially in poor communities where pain and discomfort are daily realities, is another important aspect of beautification/mutilation. Scarification is valued not only because it is symmetrically placed about the body and not only because it implies the achievement of new status, but because it hurts. Where survival is only achieved by constant effort, stoicism and willpower are immensely important. The young woman who lies unflinching while the circumciser grinds her clitoris off between two stones is proving that she will make a good wife, equal to all the anguish of child-bearing and daily toil, not only to the witnesses of her bravery, more importantly, to herself.

Industrialized society is the first in which endurance of physical pain is not a condition of survival. We have identified pain as our enemy and have done our best to eradicate even its most manageable manifestations. Scars have no value for us and their aesthetic appeal has perished alongside their moral value. A few women might confess that they feel strangely drawn to men with scarred faces (or eye-patches or limps) but it is generally considered to be an aberrant taste. Yet, augmentation mammoplasty is no more after all than a raised scar. The great difference between ancient and modern beautification/mutilation procedures is that nowadays we must conceal the fact of the procedure itself. The association of sculpted breasts with pain is anaphrodisiac, so much so, that a man who guesses that what he is admiring was produced by a knife, may lose all interest. Some women may boast of their cosmetic operations, but this is a safety valve against the possibility that they will be found out.

Most mutilations which have been accepted as beautiful are so by consensus; historically the most astonishing distortions have been admired, necks so elongated that they could not hold up the head unless supported by brass rings, teeth filed and knocked out, lips stretched to accommodate large discs, ear-lobes stretched until they hung down in large loops. However *outré* the punks may appear they are the merest beginners in the arts of mutilation. The admiration of certain disfigurements is an important part of the process of self-definition: contempt for the same practices is one of the ways in which other groups insist upon their separateness. We are not surprised to find the greatest contrasts in groups living side by side. When genetic equipment and economic status are both very similar, contrasting cultural practices become immensely important; they become the expression of the group's introverted altruism. In most tribal societies the attitude is more or less pluralistic; a group of labret wearers, for example, will simply define themselves as labret wearers, without making any attempt to impose labrets on others or to deride them for being without them. Western industrial society, deluded perhaps by its own vastness and uniformity, is not pluralistic, but utterly convinced that its own practices are the product of enlightenment and ought to be followed by all progressive peoples. Thus Western women, fully accoutred with nail polish (which is incompatible with manual work), high-heeled shoes (disastrous for the posture and hence the back, and quite unsuitable for walking long distances over bad roads) and brassières (which imitate the shape of a pubescent non-lactating breast rather than the useful organs to be found in most of the world) denounce female circumcision, without the shadow of a suspicion that their behaviour is absurd.

Yet within this bland but crushing orthodoxy there are spores of something different. Our unemployed young have reverted to tribal practices. They indulge in flamboyant mutilation/beautification which is not understood, let alone appreciated in our common judgement. Teenage daughters come to their parents' dinner parties covered with blue spots, with blue hair standing on end. Deviant groups cemented by shared ritual intoxication or guilt or ordeal or all of these are budding in our rotting inner cities, terrorizing us with raucous music and insulting doggerel. If they had the power to grow like a malignant organism and invade the whole of the body politic we might have reason to be afraid. Like millions of generations of body decorators before them, they have no economic activity beyond survival; they could be toughened by the necessity of existing on the little that society will mete out to them so that they accumulate the collective power to strike at its unprotected underbelly. Or they could fritter away their spare energy in intercommunal war, as gangs have always done. The body art of the urban deviant is unlike any which has appeared on earth before in that it has no socially constructive significance. There is in this book no image of mutual decoration; no young warriors apply magical designs to each other's backs. No priests and witches or mothers and aunts confer new powers upon an initiate. The only human interactions we see are commercial. The manicurists, the cosmetologists, the surgeons, the hairdressers, the tattooists are all professionals. Between the dancer and the dance has been interposed the mirror; the clients have come to the professionals after long and lonely contemplation of the self which dissatisfies them. Individuals do not modify their bodies to please others or to clarify their relationship to others. Rather they inflict changes upon themselves in order to approximate to narcissistic needs which may have been projected on to putative others.

Inside the bodies they have reconstructed, the body builders live incommunicado. The illustrated men disappear behind designs imported from a highly structured alien culture into which they themselves could never be accepted. The body building, the tattooing, the cultivation of cockscombs, the driving of rings, bolts, barbs and studs through labia, lobes, cartilage, nipples, foreskin are all displacement activities. A caged bird suffering from loneliness and sensory deprivation will turn upon itself and pluck out all its feathers or peck off its own leg. Middle-aged women rejected by their children will turn to surgery, restlessly beautifying/mutilating to no purpose, and a good deal of their activity will be directed against their sexuality. The body builders will proceed until they have become epicene monsters, all body hair shaved off so that the light can catch the slick greased muscles. The illustrated men make toys of their genitalia in a strange parody of continual castration. Many societies have given great attention to the penis, have infibulated the foreskin and tied it to a cord around the waist, have hidden the shaft of the penis in all kinds of structures from the discreet to the preposterous, but the kind of derision and punishment that we see in these photographs is new. One of the most potent symbols among all natural symbols is the breast, not only the female breast but by the extension the male simulacrum. Only groups doomed to extinction have ever attacked the nipples; cutting, piercing and distorting them, as may be seen in this book, is something hideously strange, as if the Skoptsi had come on earth again, with their special brand of suicidal body-loathing. Attacks upon the genitalia and the secondary sexual characteristics are attacks upon the continuity of the species; they are only conceivable in lives which are confined to their own duration, on bodies which must be their own gratification, among human contacts which are fleeting and self-centred.

It might be said that the isolation and inarticulacy have been imposed upon the subjects of this book by the photographer himself, by his choice of pose and frame and the coldness of the medium. To be sure, it is Mr Kay's own policy which has deprived them of names and associations and Mr Kay's is a camera which seeks out the bizarreness of the visual image with relentless precision, but as such it is merely an extension of the mirror by which most of his subjects live. The sympathy of his eye is stirred by gifts most like his own, sophistication, skill and control. One young woman has transcended the limitation of the situation and turned the techniques of self-adornment into something more. Working within her own subculture, but very much aware of the subtleties of the long tradition of human self-decoration, she has turned her own head into a work of art. While she is evidently free from the desire to conform to the externally imposed aesthetic norm, she is not distracted by any desire to shock. The object of her exercise is a completely successful design, balanced, expressive, perfectly adapted to the shape of her skull, and delicately executed. Next to her quiet contemplation of her cranium as an aesthetic challenge, the crude daubing of the other subjects is as violent a contrast as the Hallowe'en mask of the model makes with the face of the Nuba warrior in the same shot.

Her seriousness leads the thought away from the depressing impasse of the closed life and into a strange future. The right to economic activity is no longer a right which our society can guarantee to everyone. We are on the brink of an era in which most people will be condemned to a life of enforced leisure and mere subsistence. It may very well be that these displacement activities will have to evolve into legitimate art forms involving a strong and healthy body decorated with skill, sophistication and meaning. Perhaps human worker bees will some day be delighted by the displays of squads of human butterflies bred and trained to dance the drab streets as living works of art. It would be a great pity if the dazzling tradition of human body art were to perish in a waste of dreary conformity on the one hand and neurotic self-distortion on the other. It is to be hoped that this book is not its epitaph.

The São Francisco

From *River Journeys* (BBC Publications, 1984)

Twelve hours before I left England for Brazil, on the other side of the world, my father died. He had wanted no fuss, and there was none, but the reality of the Brazilian Nordeste scraped on a sensibility more than usually raw. It was not the poverty that caused the flinching, but the dignity, simplicity and courage of people quietly coping with inhuman adversity, and equally quietly failing to cope. In the last few months of his life I had come to recognize a certain expression that often appeared on my father's face, an almost indescribable look which contained elements of trust and puzzlement, of scepticism and innocence. It was as if all the veils of social attitudinizing and defensiveness had been stripped away and for an awful moment I could see into my father's soul. Too often that look gave way to a terrible grimace of distress as out of the gathering darkness in his brain, his old anxiety neurosis rose up and laid hold of him.

It might be said that what I saw in my father's face was pure humanity, stripped of personality as his brain dissolved, so that his eyes became like the eyes of a child or an idiot. All I can say is that the look is not at all contemptible or vacant or uncommunicative. I was to see it many times in the valley of the river São Francisco, and each time it seemed to speak of the inexpressible sadness of the human condition and the irrelevance of all our cherished notions of progress. Perhaps the quality of this look will be better guessed at, if I provide some examples.

In the market at Juazeiro, an old man is selling wild honey that he has collected in the *caatinga*, the dry scrubland that takes over beyond the narrow alluvial strip along the river. The volatile oils from the tough little shrubs that grow there make the air of the *caatinga* as heady as wine, if any wine could be so hot and so thin. The flowers of the *caatinga* are either short-lived or tiny and sparse, and the bees are an extremely select society. The old man has collected the honey in litre bottles which he has stopped with whittled wooden corks, round which the honey oozes in the heat, full of charred particles left from the murder of the bee community. Stupidly I ask if he can sell me just half a litre. The old man, who has tramped in from the back blocks lugging his six litre bottles, which must have grown heavier each step as the sun rose scorching from the first instant that it showed above the horizon, has stood all day hoping to find someone rich enough to buy his precious elixir. He looks wordlessly up at me and over his seamed face steals the look.

Newcomer that I was, I did not yet grasp how poor the poor of the Nordeste are. The old man had no way of finding two half-litre bottles. He made no attempt to explain the situation, but simply shook his head and looked into the distance. I laid down my 5,000 cruzeiros and touched his sleeve. He did not smile as he folded up the bills and put them in the inside pocket of his tattered jacket. I carried that sticky bottle for thousands of miles before I finally gave it away.

A little boy with parotitis is listening to his mother tell the missionary doctor how his father was sent home from the hospital to die of a cancer his family has known nothing about. The mother is giving her grief and shock their proper, dramatic expression, but the little boy's face is completely distorted because his cheek protrudes like the nose cone of a rocket. Only his eyes tell the story. The look intensifies as the unqualified doctor prods his hard cheek and confidently declares the necessity of taking a tooth out. The child cannot know that he is wrong, but the eyes tell me that he has no expectation of his being right. The look intensifies as the doctor indulges in a sermon on the importance of not living in the past. (The child's father has been dead three days and there is no money for a decent burial.)

The neighbours told me that the little boy supported his family by fishing all day in the river with a hand-line. A good throwing net would have done more for the parotitis – and the look – than an unnecessary tooth extraction, but the wearers of the look, both old and young, know that official aid does not recognize their reality. Instead of giving him a throwing net, official aid would insist that the child go to school.

The people of the Nordeste of Brazil are descended from exterminated Indians, escaped slaves and European adventurers, in varying proportions. The result is a fantastic array of human types with extraordinary and exotic combinations of colouring and feature, living side by side even in the extremity of poverty. Smooth-faced girls with perfect Ethiopian features may have golden eyes and hair like curled golden wire. Others with night-black skin may have straight hair and grey eyes. A very few have the beautiful ruddy skin and tiny hands and feet of the vanished Indian tribes. Under the *vaqueiro*'s greasy leather hat, you may find a face as Irish as Magillicuddy's Reeks, encrusted with skin cancers. This bewildering variety is orchestrated by the Nordestino smile, wide, spontaneous, uncalculating, shy and friendly at the same time. Other people are not yet an instrument for one's own ends in the Nordeste. Each meeting is a recognition of another person as unique and interesting as oneself, and the Nordestino smile expresses a mixture of surprise and delight not often met with at cocktail parties.

That smile is often to be seen in conjunction with the look. A beautiful man with skin as black and smooth as jet is smiling as he tells another doctor in another clinic how he fell while working on a water tower for the town council. He has crawled and hopped into the room, clinging to any handhold he could find. In his face there is no mark to show that he is forty years old, father of nine children, with nothing to expect from life but pain and destitution. Occasionally he coughs a short, dry cough. His smile does not waver as the doctor tells him to drag himself somehow to the TB clinic miles away down river. The smile is dazzling but the eyes are appalling.

Other people did not seem to see the look. I may have imagined it after all. Perhaps my own guilt about my neglect of my father's obsequies caused me to see the ghost of his look in so many places. It is embarrassing to admit that I think I saw it in the eyes of a funny-looking wading bird with a ragged topknot, and in the eyes of the small boy who had hoped so hard to sell it to the hotel menagerie in Pirapora. (When he discovered that some foreign ladies are so dotty that they will pay twice the asking price to have the creature returned to the backwater it came from, the little boy's look changed to one of gratified cunning.)

Perhaps I was simply haunted and that might be why the Valle do Rio São Francisco seems to me to be the worst example of fake development and the modernization of poverty that I have ever encountered. I was not so upset by Calcutta; even in the refugee camp at Salt Lake in 1972, pity and despair were effectively held at bay. In the slums of Bombay or Bangkok or Port Sudan it seemed to me that the people had a future. Certain values adhered, certain structures cohered. The people, however scrambling and desperate, seemed to have a chance of surviving as themselves. The worst of Penedo, Juazeiro, Bom Jesus da Lapa and Pirapora is paradise compared with these vast, pestiferous warrens, and yet I found it deeply depressing. It seems only proper to explain that I am not a camera and may have seen everything asquint.

The São Francisco river rises in the well-watered state of Minas Gerais and flows northward. By the time it crosses into Bahia, springs and tributary streams have all but disappeared and for most of its 2,660 kilometre length the river flows through the 'drought polygon' where the annual rainfall amounts to only 400 mm and the inhabitants may rely on 2,800 hours of sunlight a year and an average temperature of twenty-five degrees centigrade. In these latitudes the sun passes close to the zenith and the thin, dry air can do little to blunt the burning edge of its steep rays. Sun-bathing along the São Francisco is a dangerous pastime, nevertheless you may see provincial ladies of leisure, well basted with smelly oils, grilling themselves by hotel swimming pools in the burning middle of the day when everyone else has taken shelter. It is only a matter of time before someone decides to build a tourist complex on Sobradinho dam, but it will need its own burns unit.

The minute rainfall arrives in summer; in the winter the sparse forage for the scrawny cattle, which are the chief industry of the *sertão*, must be supplemented by cutting cactus which is actually cultivated, planted out in neat rows inside thickset hedges of thorn or *avellós*. The sandy, stony soil of the *sertão*, which contains no humus, cannot produce enough vegetation to support the cattle population at the density which five hundred years of lordly ranching have imposed unless the *vaqueiro* serves the animals hand and foot. The meat yield is comparatively poor and there is no export market. The *vaqueiro* sees himself as a member of an élite, but he lives in a windowless mud house without sewerage or clean water and he eats manioc and goat's meat and he cannot read or write. His house and his land usually belong to his master, the *fazendeiro*. If an animal in his care breaks a leg he will be turned out. The *vaqueiro* is very much aware that the culture of the *sertão* is his culture, as he quaffs his *cachaça* and sings his improvised songs of flattery to his oppressors or tightens the bearing rein and pulls his little horse's mouth to pieces in order to clatter past a group of onlookers with all his fringes flying. He is proud, charming, powerless and pathetic.

We happened upon the Bacia do Rio São Francisco at a fortunate time, for the rains, such as they are, had just fallen. The desert was blooming in clumps of vivid flowers which had popped out of the stony earth like feathers out of the barrel of a toy gun. Within a week most of them had completed their life span; their stems had crumbled into dust and their seed capsules had burst, leaving their cargo to lie dormant for another year, or more, if the rains should fail, as they often do. The air was so thin and clear that ridges sixty miles away stood out as if cut from the blanched sky. We travelled, as do all those rich enough to travel at all in the Nordeste, in a small aircraft, skimming along the crystal air, hiccupping occasionally on the thermals. As Juazeiro came in sight the air was thickening slightly with the approach of evening. The oblique light struck off the surface of the river in a thick, white band. Fifty kilometres upstream the band became a blaze which filled the whole horizon, Sobradinho, the largest man-made lake in the world.

Next to me on the plane sat an Italian wine-grower from Rio Grande do Sul, going to Santa Maria da Boa Vista to check on the progress of his new table-grape plantation. He was full of optimism, for none of the diseases that plague wine-growers in the South can flourish in the dry air of the *sertão*. By regulating the availability of water to the different sections of the plantation, it should be possible to ripen grapes in every week of the year. The valley of the São Francisco river could be a new California, a new Israel. If I had known more I would have asked him why the government of the state of Pernambuco had approached an entrepeneur from the South in order to develop grape growing, and how the deal had been set up and how many local people were employed on the project. A neighbouring project, Bebedouro, developed by CODEVASF, the São Francisco Development

Company, employs a small number of *families*, who are allowed to settle in the project area only after they have satisfied 'carefully established criteria: the admission requirements thus include a study of their past life, scholarship (primary school at least) and, finally, a trial period, during which production capacity, ability to learn agricultural techniques and behaviour in community will determine whether or not they are qualified for the project'. In return for displaying conspicuous fitness, the families are allowed to work long hours on intensive agriculture for the profit of others. They are tied to the land, living 'in comfort in small villages especially built for this purpose'. On the island of Cabrobó I saw such a small village, mud huts roofed with thatch, with no cleaner water and no better plumbing than anywhere else. Where the independent farmers could spend a good deal of time sitting dreaming before their house door when the short growing season was over, the irrigation workers had to shoulder their mattocks every day, though the heat blistered. By the time I saw the captive 'Indians' of Cabrobó, for the people of Cabrobó are corralled even more securely in what passes for a reservation, I knew how to interpret the fact that almost all the irrigated crops I saw were salt-tolerant luxury items (as are table grapes) destined for the tables of Rio and São Paolo at competitive prices. By the time I left Brazil, I had come to loathe watermelon as a symbol of useless frittering away of human resources, but on that first afternoon on the plane slithering into the airport at Petrolina, I caught my companion's enthusiasm. The blinding glare of the huge dam on the southern horizon was the emblem of that new future.

As we drove in from the airport we passed houses made of the Nordestino version of wattle and daub, sundried red mud forced between closely planted wooden stakes. Come rain or high water it would simply wash out again. The houses, roofed in carnaiuba palm, were half-hidden behind walls of the same closely planted wooden stakes that held up the mud walls, these exposed and bleached silver by the sun. Within the compound the red earth was swept clean of every turd, weed or stone, so that it could function as an extension to the tiny house. At the back you might see the cooking place, which was no more than three stones set in a triangle. The pot sat above and the firewood was fed in from the sides, burning frugally at the tips and carefully extinguished when the cooking was done. Already it was obvious that wood was both an essential commodity and in short supply. Before the house door stood a shade tree, the only stout and permanent feature of the whole arrangement, and under it sat the inhabitants, peeling manioc or pounding grain or playing with their babies. In line with the open front door of the house, stood a back door, likewise open, creating a draught which dried the sweat and cooled the skin of those sitting under the tree. The principle was simple and, I was to discover, very effective. Women moved through the courtyards with the studied languor of those for whom energy conservation is a prime consideration. The gathered skirts of their washed-out print dresses often hung high in the front, pushed out by a pregnant belly. Around the houses stood fields of manioc and sugar cane and a forage called *capin*.

Abruptly the fields ended, cut off by a chain-link fence stretching further than the eye could see. Inside this vast enclosure, cheek by jowl, marching in formation up and down the low hills, was row upon row of identical semi-detached houses, each pair so minute that the façades had room only for the two doors and the two windows. Here was no shade tree, no yard space, but simply a hermetic box for living in, with no gap between wall and roof for cooler air to circulate. Electricity would provide climate control, even if cooking (with electricity) were to be done inside the house. Here were sewerage and clean water, but here was neither privacy nor individuality nor character. The rows of houselets were more like a military camp than a suburb, or some cheaper version of the slave housing built on plantations in South Carolina and Louisiana two hundred years ago. Moreover, they appeared to be deserted.

I was to see these *casas popolares* in urban centres large and small all along the Rio São Francisco. In every case the construction was mean, the design stupidly regular and symmetrical, the allocation of space meagre. The idea of providing cheap permanent housing with power, sewerage and treated water and establishing a Banco da Habitação which would finance mortgages and rental purchases was a good one, but it was not working, not because the people rejected the official notion of what would be good for them, but because, while the monthly payments rose in step with an inflation rate of the order of 120 per cent a year, employers evaded the government regulation which stipulated that wages be automatically adjusted by firing and rehiring their staff at lower rates. Besides, qualifying for a *casa popolare* was rather like getting a job in a government irrigation scheme, only suitable types would be accepted. The housing projects were terrible emblems of new forms and new norms of social control. In a society riddled with patronage and its inevitable concomitant, corruption, a provident man could do better informally than by becoming a pawn in a government scheme; the improvident man, whether sick, disabled or landless, was not eligible for inclusion in the scheme in the first place. The only person I met who lived in a government housing project held down three jobs and earned his monthly rental-purchase payment in a day. Money has been made out of the schemes by those who sold land, awarded contracts, supplied materials, subcontracted labour and distributed the units, but the pattern is the familiar one: a few made fortunes to add to the fortunes they already had while the many lost. To the houseless hordes of Petrolina-Juazeiro the myriad pitched rooflets which pinked the skyline might as well have belonged to houses on the moon.

Before breakfast next morning I took a car and went off into the pink heat shimmer to see where the people really did live. The nucleus of

Juazeiro is a grid of tight, painted façades behind which chains of narrow rooms open one out of the other in a vista of glimmering tiled floors and a welter of gimcrack furniture bedizened with crocheted mats, doilies, antimacassars, coasters, runners, plastic flowers and gaudy images of popular cult figures, Padre Velho, Padre Damiano (who foretold the bursting of the Sobradinho dam which is now rather overdue) and the Queen of the Sea (who looks a lot like Hedy Lamarr). Nothing could have been squeakier clean than these long wedges of house, crammed not only with pot plants and birdcages but with people of all sizes, mostly small. The noise level was unearthly, for not just every house, but every occupant of every room in every house, had a different idea of the exact kind of popular music that would make the day go with a swing. In order to be heard everybody screamed like a macaw. In case any chink of silence should remain to disfigure the perfect din, most houses kept a pair of green parrots with clipped wings that peeped out from their homes under refrigerators and gas cookers and shrieked until the sky rang.

There were no print dresses or bare feet to be seen here. The ampler middle-class matrons of downtown Juazeiro preferred to squeeze themselves into shiny lycra leotards as tight as sausage skins. The nether quarters were carefully hidden in stiff new jeans, but the upper areas were in full view. Brown bosoms oozed round the strapless, one-strapped, frilled, shirred and altogether most inventively tarted-up and mostly fairly transparent leotards, so that the entire female population seemed to be on its way to an audition for *Fame*. The ensemble was completed by an elaborate, hieratic head-dress of coloured plastic curlers, over which the hair was pulled so tight that the skin at the temples was pleated. These fashions were to be observed all up and down the river, but it was some time before I managed to ask a young woman who had worn her curlers day in, day out for a week why she never removed them. When she did, the result was a rather ragged little ponytail, which, as long as there was no kink in the tightly drawn-back hair, she found perfectly satisfactory. By evening the curlers had reappeared. Conventional wisdom had it that the women were trying to look European, but I persisted in thinking that the real aim was to look as Indian as possible. Certainly the few women whose hair did hang like blue-black silk were inordinately proud of it.

The car crashed from pot-hole to pot-hole, as the old, cobbled roads gave way to sluices of sand in which it yawed and slewed and slid, the motor coughing as the carburettor breathed in more sand to add to what already swirled up and down the fuel line. The lycra glamour and commercial cacophony of the centre were soon left behind. The ruins of grandiose town-planning schemes lay all about. Grids of paved street stood up above the seas of sand, while the traffic wove itself through the breaks in the tumble-down ramparts. Broad carriageways led their rows of empty lamp standards slap into blank walls. Scrawny cattle of mixed race, mostly zebu, picked their way daintily through the mess on their way to graze on the river flats. A huge bus station with quays and platforms and shelters and even a *Lanchonete* stood cut off from the roadway by a ten-foot drop. Up by the tarmac sat a small crowd of hopeful passengers under an improvised tarpaulin. Although their bundles of bedding and smoky cooking fires betokened a long stay they all gazed fixedly up the road as if a bus was due in five minutes.

Makeshift shelters began to proliferate. The driver was puzzled by my insistence that he plough further and further from the paved road, where there was no sign of regular streets and he had to navigate by following vague tyre tracks in the sand. The people crammed into the tiny shanties stared out at us. Pigs rooted in the human excrement in the road. We passed files of women with kerosene tins of water on their heads. We saw other women too, sitting open-legged by the roadside, gazing expectantly as we dragged our dust trail towards them. Even at a quarter to seven in the morning their demeanour was unmistakable. The Bishop of Juazeiro was to tell me three times in a single conversation (and I myself had not brought up the subject) that there were two thousand prostitutes in Juazeiro. If by prostitute he meant any woman struggling to live any way she can, including by offering sexual services for money, the estimate was a conservative one. If he meant women actually making a living by prostitution, the estimate was fantastic. Juazeiro was a town of would-be prostitutes without clients. The manners of the younger leotard wearers in town were as free as those of their role models from the Avenida Paulista in São Paolo, which they studied continually on television and in the glossy gossip magazines. The men they rubbed up against under the trees along the river quays were the ones who might have brought a few cruzeiros to the desperate women in the mud huts out on the vast fringes of the city. Wherever the men in the film crew went, girls called out to them, ogled them, accosted them, hid amorous notes in their baggage. The men preened, correctly interpreting the lovesick chorus as a tribute to their conspicuous success in being rich, employed, healthy and white, preened and did nothing beyond a little mild showing off. For all the atmosphere of extravagant willingness, sex is still a serious matter in the Nordeste, if only because contraception in any form is practically unknown. First births occur early and most unions are informal, in the pattern familiar to us from other post-slavery societies. Some of the priests struggling against this sexual chaos refuse to baptize children unless their parents agree to marry at the same time. The threat is toothless because Nordestino religion is only partly based in Catholicism. Given the real magnitude of the problem, the humanitarian enterprise of the Diocese of Juazeiro, which undertakes to teach 'prostitutes' needlework as a better way of making a living, is simply ludicrous.

We began our river journey in the middle of the river rather than at the source or the mouth because we had to rendezvous with our paddle steamer for the journey upstream to Pirapora. The boat, the *São Francisco*, was the star of our show and the film crew, understandably, were very keen to get to know her. From my hotel balcony I could see her yellow-painted funnel and her upper storey as she rode, or rather sat, at anchor beside the basalt-paved slipway, part of the elegant system of quays built in an earlier era, when the river carried goods and passengers and some of the wealth generated by sugar and leather percolated to the river towns. There was little or no activity on the river now. It flowed full, fast and turbid towards the rapids below Santa Maria da Boa Vista. I was not to learn for some time that this high level was artificially maintained, or that the exigencies of feeding the six hydroelectric stations 350 kilometres downstream at Paolo Afonso had caused devastating floods in Juazeiro for three years in succession. The São Francisco had never been a sleepy, silty river, but a swift and sandy one. In the days when the *remeiros* poled their long boats down it, the voyage back upstream was a terrible ordeal, for the *remeiros* had to force the boats against the strong current by jamming the punt pole hard against their breast-bones until their chests were laid open. These fearful wounds were cauterized with boiling tallow in an agonizing ritual.

The *São Francisco* had begun life on the Missouri River in 1913; to ply the São Francisco she needed a special piece of equipment, a large anchor hanging from the prow. When her flat bottom ground to a halt on the shifting sandbars of the 'Velho Chico', as the river was affectionately called, a sailor would wade out with the anchor, to which a winch-cable was attached, until he found deeper water. He would drop the anchor and the steamer would pull herself across the bar by winching in the cable. Apart from our boat, and another hulk rotting beside her, the only paddle steamer doing business in Juazeiro was working high and dry in one of the town squares as a restaurant. We had been told that there was a monthly boat carrying general passengers upstream and crossing another on the journey down, but, although the people who told us this appeared to believe it, and many citizens repeated the information, no such boats existed. When our paddle steamer, or *gaiola*, came in sight of the river towns, she was the first they had seen in three years. What we eventually came to realize as she panted and waddled ever more slowly, making a bare five or six knots and burning whole forests to make even that, was that she was also the last they would ever see. She had been refurbished for us, which is to say that the rust had been given a few coats of silver stove paint and the woodwork brightened up and the BBC had subsidized the cost of passage so that real people could travel with us. She seemed to me as trumpery as any stage set. I was afraid that once we were borne away from the confusion and the squalor on the broad, cool river, sipping *caipirinhas* (wonderful drinks made with *cachaça*, whole limes and sugar) on her shaded upper deck, the reality of the Nordeste would slip beyond my grasp. Once the *São Francisco* arrived in Pirapora she would make short day trips for the tourists staying at the hotel there, if indeed she would do so much. Despite frantic attempts to maximize the tourism potential of the valley of the São Francisco, and the determined exploitation of anything even faintly picturesque, the tourist industry has failed to take off.

Instead of visiting our star steamer, I prowled about Juazeiro, trying to estimate how important the river was to the people. It was important to the cows daintily refraining from eating the fat curare plants on the river flats. It was important to the women bashing clothes at the water's edge, and it was important to the children who splashed in the shallows beside them. The Diocese, mind you, seemed to think the women would be better off washing the clothes in a shed on the other side of town, where tubs and water (but not washing machines, despite the cheap hydroelectricity for which their town had been three times flooded) had been provided. Never have I encountered a population which did more washing than the Nordestinos, washing of heads and bodies, washing of plates, washing of clothes, washing of goats' entrails, washing of cars, washing of floors, even washing of walls. Some of the finest houses in Juazeiro were covered all over with bathroom tiles, so that the outside could be as efficiently scoured and polished as the inside. The people without piped water to their houses washed in any water they could find, including the river. A man with nothing to his name but a pair of shorts, would wash his shorts and wait in the water until the scorching sun had dried them. The importance of washing is not to be confused with an understanding of hygiene, for the Nordestinos would fish, wash and pee in the same river, as well as throwing rubbish into it and drinking from it. Decaying fragments of animal carcasses and human excrement fouled the alleyways where children played, and maggots teemed in the open drains.

Rather, washing seemed to have ritual importance. The Nordestino religion, called among other things *macumba* or *candomblé*, is a patchwork of voodoo, spiritism, animism and debased Catholicism, but the central ritual is cleansing. On the strange market stalls hung with leopards' paws and jacaré skins, the array of soaps, washes, lotions, fumigant powders, douches and astringents, all mendaciously labelled as being concocted from plants of the African coast, give evidence of religious observance principally composed of endless ablutions. Unofficial religion has got itself mixed up with unofficial medicine, and the same stalls sold herbal remedies based on European and Indian lore. Both the religion and the medicine existed for the same reason, because the people had no other resource. (Although the Catholic Church has claimed responsibility for the souls of these heathens for the last five hundred years, the Nordestino apostolate has been thoroughly neglected. Even now most of the priests working in the vast parishes of the interior are foreigners. Only now that the prospect of radicalization spreading out from Cuba via Central America has frightened the spiritual lords of Brazil have they begun to take their task seriously, but now they are obliged to teach the doctrine of the church with regard to social justice. It remains to be seen whether the church can make religion socialist before Marxism takes over the church.) Wherever we went along the Rio São Francisco we saw people engaged in the contemplative, time-consuming washing ritual that, for women especially, could take up as much as a third of their waking life. If every tattered cloth they owned and every battered tin dish was washed within an inch of its life, a sort of order had been imposed on chaos. Even little children stood in the river and scrubbed their legs and their flip-flop sandals. Only when I saw a group of women struggling to wash in an encrusted puddle no larger than a tea tray did I begin to understand the importance of washing to these people and then more than ever I cursed the kind of development which brings electricity and the twaddling soap operas of TV Globo to the poor and will not, cannot, lay a water pipeline to save their babies' lives.

So, while the crew investigated the boat and gauged the level of its picturesqueness, I haunted the less salubrious purlieus of the city, peeping in at doorways where dozens of sweating people sat entranced by 'Pane, Pane, Beijo, Beijo' or 'Louco Amor' in rooms not ten feet square, peering through the gate at the exclusive country club, so exclusive indeed that it appeared to be derelict, always coming back to the market, where it seemed to me I could see athwart the economic reality of life in the interior. The very first film we shot was in the market, at the worst time of day, when the mid-morning sun blazes away on the awnings. The cameraman had a terrible time trying to get the camera to see in the contrasting shade. Emboldened by my fear of becoming the prisoner of the paddle steamer, I insisted, in case the opportunity should not present itself again. There was not much buying and selling going on. The vendors waited, and crowds of small boys waited by their wheelbarrows, hoping that someone would pay them to push her purchases home. Occasionally a matron resplendent in leotard and curlers sailed by, with a barrow boy in her wake, struggling to keep his barrow with its towering load of watermelons and yams from tipping its costly cargo into the maggoty muck underfoot. The sinews on his little arms stood out like bowstrings.

We bought a jackfruit so that it could be opened for us to film. When we had done we gave it to the boys who yelled with pleasure. Somehow they fumbled in their eagerness and the great squashy thing plumped to the ground. Before anyone could rescue it another labouring lad had charged across it with his loaded wheelbarrow and it was ruined. Over their faces came that look. In so far as it was readable it said, 'Ah well, I never really expected to eat one anyway.' Silently they picked up their barrow handles and trudged off in the endless hunt for clients.

It would have been surprising if the Brazilian government and most of the functionaries we met had not assumed that we had come to Brazil to make a tourist film. It would have been even more surprising if they had imbibed the idea that the film was not only about the river, but about a particular person's experience of the river, namely mine, especially as the Brazilian liaison who had set our itinerary up had failed to grasp the idea, and rather floored me half-way through filming by asking me what kind of books I wrote. Brazilians, even the poorest and most isolated, are intensely aware of the media. We had only to let our eyes, let alone the camera's eye, rest for an instant on any individual, for him to start performing, even if all he was doing was washing his car or scratching his crotch. Everyone we met had his own idea of what we would want to see, and no scruple whatsoever in rigging it up whether we encouraged him or not, and then demanding a fee for doing it. When I began asking about infant mortality rates, or parasitic infestation, or the resurgence of malaria, or the unrestricted sale of dangerous drugs and baby foods or antibiotic abuse, everyone lost interest. As I was a woman, it was difficult for any Nordestino to imagine that what I thought about anything was of any interest to anybody. At times I despaired of ever putting together an intelligent film, and never more than in those early days in Juazeiro. The chief cause of my misery was that ghastliest of all the ghastly manifestations of fake folk art, the *carranca*.

In the days when cargo boats plied the river, some were decorated with grotesque figureheads, a circumstance which no one found particularly remarkable. When the river trade languished, the boats rotted and the figureheads rotted with them, until an enterprising collector realized that they were eminently collectable. In the time-honoured fashion of the art impresario he began a systematic study of them, pointing out correspondences (of a fairly inevitable kind) with figureheads from Phoenicia and medieval Turkey. Amidst all the brouhaha there emerges one *carranqueiro* of genius, Francisco Guarany, who began making *carrancas* in 1901 at the age of seventeen, and by 1940 had made about eighty of them. When the *carranca* cult developed he was persuaded to parody himself and make figureheads for boats which no longer existed. A tribe of *carranqueiros* who had never seen the genuine article began to produce thousands of *carrancas* which may be seen in every curio shop in Brazil, hideous perfunctory things made of unseasoned wood, crudely lacquered in red, white and black and of all sizes, some tiny enough to fit on pencils, others huge. One, outside Juazeiro, stands 3.5 metres tall. Compared to the exquisite Indian artefacts sold in the FUNAI shops, these objects are crude, soulless and utterly spurious. The common prejudice against the Nordestino people can only be reinforced by them.

The thought of being forced by circumstance to treat these objects seriously in our film produced in me a sensation not unlike panic. We were committed to struggle out into the *sertão* in the blinding heat in the 'Kombi' which boiled and threatened to leave us stranded on the blistering macadam at any moment, to play homage to a *carranqueiro* called Xuri. His *carrancas* were only half a notch better than the usual rubbish, but still I was not sorry that we were there, or that the director of the film had commissioned a huge *carranca* (although I prayed that we would not actually have to show it in the finished film). The beautiful thing about Xuri was not his spurious craft activity but his whole life. He lived in a tiny house, with two tiny rooms and one larger one with door fore and aft. The whitewashed adobe was velvety cool to the touch, and the mild draught through the tiles and the gaps between walls and roof kept the air fresh. In a miniature fenced compound before the house his wife grew a few flowers, four o'clocks and African marigolds, lovingly cosseted with used water. She was tall, upright, smooth-haired and brown-skinned, with that quality of stillness in her repose that comes with Indian blood. One daughter was away at school. Another sat in a beautifully made folding chair, made to a design which has not changed since its European original was made in the mid-sixteenth century, trailing delicate fingertips over the armrests with all the aplomb of an infanta. The littlest was feverish. Her hacking cough had been around for too many weeks.

In their vegetable garden, corn, melons, marrows and cucumbers struggled against the looming drought. Already the growing season was almost over. As the cruel sun slid down the sky, and Xuri's trees began to cast long violet shadows towards the little house, and his wife slipped out with a dish of something for the green parrots that Nordestinos love so well, it seemed a good and dignified life. The cattle and goats clanked past on their way to their stalls. An occasional *vaqueiro* tipped his fringed hat as he rode past. We were the false note, begging Xuri to play his accordion or chip away at a *carranca* for the camera. Xuri obeyed silently, but in his eyes I thought I saw the look. His lady patroness, who had led us to him, told us loudly how one *carranqueiro* whom she had rescued from destitution took his first pay cheque and spent it on drink and drugs, abandoning his hungry family. 'Amazing. These people.' Her house was full of the worst bad art it would ever be possible to see, debased embroideries, abominable carvings, gross daubs of sentimental subjects. Clearly she could see no reason why a man reduced to making a coarse fool of himself in lieu of making an honest living, should throw up everything and embrace a slow death. I thought if Xuri did not do such a thing, it was largely because of something I saw in his wife's eyes, a wise, disabused, mischievous twinkle.

As Xuri's patroness could not be prevailed upon to hold her tongue during the takes, she was sent off to take me to visit other protégées, a family of lacemakers. Once again I was reluctant, for I had seen the lace, which was a meagre remnant of European tradition, uninteresting and irrelevant to everyday life. The women, all without men for one reason or another, were supposed to live by their lacemaking, but with a metre of lace, a week's work, selling at 300 cruzeiros (about 15p) they clearly did not. Their house was rather grander than Xuri's, for it was faced with brick and had rooms opening on both sides of the main one, but the beds of the three sisters were all to be found in one room. Another served as a store for their family possessions and the other two were empty. In the fenced compound behind the house was a low, round mound about four metres across of smooth quartz pebbles, where washing would be thrown to dry and bleach in the sun, but if the gentle ladies were forced to survive by taking in washing no one mentioned it. I didn't like to ask. It was not until my second visit that I realized how close to going under the old ladies were. Chronic malnutrition is not so easy to detect among the elderly. In their calm and lovely house floored with silver sand brushed every day into a fan pattern, the nun-like sisters with their charming manners were practically starving.

Still trapped in the tourist convention, we went next day to a *vaquejada*, the Brazilian version of a rodeo. A truckload of little steers was penned at the top of a sandy run. At a signal, one of them was driven out of the corral and ridden down by two horsemen, one of whom had to grasp the fleeing creature by the tail and flip it on to its back within a zone marked out with flour. Then the fallen steer was pushed or dragged to its feet and driven into another pen, to be reloaded on to the truck and taken back to the corral at the top of the run. By the time we arrived the steers were exhausted. Often they would lie motionless where they were thrown while the riders spurred their horses to trample them into getting to their feet. It seemed impossible that tail-twisting to throw such a heavy animal could be painless. Just as I was making up my mind to stop watching a display which involved little skill and no courage, a fat, bespectacled competitor, a weekend *vaqueiro* if ever there was one, rode up to the judges holding the tip of the steer's tail in his hand. The exposed vertebra shone in the dusty sunlight like a pearl. Another man, involved in some dispute with the judges, did not notice that he had ridden his horse against a dislodged fence rail so that its legs were on both sides of it and it could not answer the spur. The horse tossed its head desperately as the spurs banged into its flanks and the fence rail gouged its belly. Nobody who relied on his horse for a livelihood could afford to be so stupid. Genuine *vaqueiros* drive their horses hard, and although they use a cruel bit, they are likely to unsaddle and wash their horses from head to foot in precious water before they see to themselves. Everywhere we looked people were showing off, spurring their horses to ride at full pelt into the crowd and pulling them up so short that they reared and almost fell, then turning on a sixpence and dashing off in some other direction, a procedure which seemed to me even more dangerous than it was pointless, especially as the performers were growing steadily drunker. When two of the drunkest began singing improvised songs of praise to the two *prefeites* of Juazeiro and Petrolina, who sat looking modest and kindly for the camera, it seemed time to go with a vengeance. I longed for the river beyond the dust.

Next morning the *São Francisco* did indeed embark on her last journey up the river she was named for, waddling and shimmying as her gaily painted paddles slapped the water. We were the only passengers, except for a man who said he was a travel agent from Belo Horizonte and two journalists. Life on the river banks was very different from life in the *sertão*. Huge mango trees made great pools of shade. Beans, manioc, bananas, papaya and corn shot up out of the ground. Some farmers had diesel pumps. More ran up and down the bank with pails of water; where the bank was steep, steps had been cut in the greyish pink earth. Small boats were moored at simple landing stages which women used to bash clothes on. As our majestic bulk hove in sight everyone downed tools and ran to look, laughing, waving, shouting. If I had seen nothing but the river bank I might have thought that the Bacia do Rio São Francisco was a sort of Stephen Foster paradise. As it was I couldn't help marvelling at the luck of the people whose ancestors had settled the narrow alluvial strip. The annual flooding of the river seemed a small price to pay for a lifestyle which consisted mostly of fishing, with enough tilling of the soil to vary the regime, and fruit trees which would provide all the vitamins not to be found in beans, manioc and fish. It was mere subsistence, to be sure, but the majority of the people I had observed so far had to struggle desperately hard for a very inferior life. The children who grew up in the riverine *roças* grew strong and tall, but there were too many who did not make it, because of enteric disease and parasitic infestation and periodic visitations of *gripe*. The official infant mortality figure is about 160 per thousand live births, but as I roamed around I became aware that lots of little bodies are interred at the corners of fields and no official the wiser. Even that high figure represents considerable under-reporting.

We reached the dam at sunset. Our frail craft was wafted up in a giant lock and we were set free upon the largest man-made lake in the world. It was not meant to be the largest man-made lake in the world, but, like Topsy, it growed. The dam should have been one of a series of five, but it was simply built a little higher and a little longer and a greater area was flooded. The foreign advisers warned against doing such a thing, but the Brazilians saw that a little daring would pay off in international reputation, so, at the risk of altering the water levels as far upstream as Bom Jesus da Lapa, they went ahead. The financiers of the project, in particular the International Research and Development Bank, insisted upon resettlement of the riverine population, a notion to which lip-service is as easy as its realization difficult. There was no similar land to the rich alluvial strip available. To transplant the river people to the *caatinga* was to condemn them to slow death. Some were moved upstream to settlements called *agrovilas*, the explanation being that south of Bom Jesus da Lapa there was an annual rainfall sufficient for an industrious farmer to survive. In fact, the *agrovilas* are strategic hamlets where people from 'foci of social tension' all over Brazil have been resettled, whether the houses have been constructed yet or not. Like the *casas popolares*, the *agrovilas* are a perverted project. If they had worked they would have proved a tremendous burden for the state of Bahia to carry. As they have not worked, the people have drifted away, to São Paolo and Salvador, to Petrolina and Juazeiro, to swell the ranks of the landless poor. Many of the marginal cultivators had no official title to their holdings and were neither resettled nor compensated. Others waited so long for their compensation that the inflation rate and their lawyers' fees absorbed it all. A more obvious solution would have been to resettle the people in irrigated land, but irrigated land has to earn its keep in intensive production of cash crops. As CHESF (the San Francisco Hydroelectric Company) points out, it is not a philanthropic organization. CODEVASF, the San Francisco Development Company, has its irrigation projects, but development means the production of vast quantities of cheap ethanol for the world market; it does not mean the creation of a pampered class of independent farmers with no spending power.

When the waters began to rise, the people who had seen the São Francisco flood many times before could not believe that they would not recede. As they rose and rose gradually the people realized that the land they called their own had disappeared for ever (or until the dam burst, an event some are still praying for). At midnight, the *São Francisco* stopped to take on more wood, so much wood that the lower deck had room for nothing else. As the last pieces were loaded at first light, we saw thousands of toads who had retreated as the waters rose, hopping about frantically as their shelter was stripped away. A man and his wife stood watching, as their brood of semi-naked children bashed at the toads with lumps of wood. A few yards up the bank stood a cluster of wretched hovels. CHESF had installed a single electric light on the outside of one of the houses, but it was not on.

For most of the next day we sailed over the dead shallows of the lake. The only events were skeletal treetops and the water tower of old Sento-Sé. Scan the shores though I might I could see no sign of life, no house, no animal, no track. Far in the baking distance rose eroded scarps where once there were mines. No roads cut through the grey-green scrub. Later I travelled on the road that CHESF made from Sento-Sé to Juazeiro, and flew over the scrub, marked only by the boundaries of the *fazendeiros*' vast holdings and the scars of cattle traffic round the few waterholes. The day after I drove past the town built by CHESF for the families of the men who worked on the dam, the people who had had nowhere to go when the work was completed, some 2,000 of the population of 20,000, sacked the general store, because they were starving. The town had cost a fortune to build; development eighties style requires its abandonment rather than an attempt to set up light industry using the cheap power the inhabitants had helped to generate. Everywhere on the Rio São

Francisco the same message could be read: people are a luxury. The propaganda put out by CODEVASF, subsidized by Mercedes-Benz do Brasil SA, presented Sobradinho as having two principal functions, flood control and irrigation. A dam that is kept full must cause flooding rather than prevent it, and so Sobradinho has done, three times. The river may be more navigable but few craft navigate it. The irrigation schemes are available to entrepreneurs who can put up capital for their development, and to them also is available a vast pool of underemployed labour from which to pick and choose the handful who will slave in the fields. For days I sought the flowering promised for the *caatinga* and found only a huge alcohol plant at Casa Nova. I was told there were more fishes in the lake and refrigeration plants to keep them in, but I never saw a fishing boat until we docked at new Sento-Sé. As we waddled into the quay we minced its nets with our paddles.

At Sento-Sé we were hostages of an extraordinary personage known simply as Father Mark, an American priest from the middle West, whose apostolate seemed to have less to do with spreading the Catholic faith than with inculcating the principles and methodology of private enterprise. He did not bother with mere details like hearing confessions before distributing communion in any of his sixty far-flung parishes but gave great attention to bringing his onion crop on at a time when the supply of onions was low and demand high. Consecrated hosts were left in the tabernacles to be handed out by village-level workers, a practice which has become routine in remote parts of Brazil, while the teaching which would help people perhaps to make sense of the chaos and misery in which they live is neglected. Father Mark had secured a prime piece of irrigable land in replacement for the diocesan lands now submerged, and he put a great deal of his own and other people's energy into making it work. His American supporters sent him fifteen or twenty thousand dollars a year, which he carefully husbanded without too punctilious a concern for the Brazilian currency regulations. His workforce was not composed of the workless adults of new Sento-Sé but of school-age boys and girls who lived in dormitories in the presbytery compound. The accommodation was spartan. Boys slept four or five to a small bare room, folding up their hammocks by day and storing their belongings in trunks or boxes. The toilet facilities were primitive and over the whole hung the nauseating smell of fermenting manioc. In the manioc factory there was no attempt at dust control and no safety guards on any of the machines. The irrigation channels on the farm were unlined: evidently Father Mark believes that God will hold salinization at bay in the interests of the private enterprise system. The cattle had been doctored with steroids and the top paddock looked suspiciously like other fields I have seen which have been cleared with 245T.

It was clear, looking at his land which was the best for miles, that the *sertão* needs more than water to make it bloom. There was no humus whatsoever in the neutral soil in which the precious water sank away at once. On the other side of the lake, people tainted with socialist beliefs (the gospel of hate according to Father Mark) seemed to be doing rather better in the development stakes, for the town of Remanso was ringed with irrigated fields. We were obliged to wait there for an electric element which could not be got in Sento-Sé, although Father Mark pointed out the immense improvement in the people's lot by explaining that before the dam was built people could buy only three or four things in the store and now the supermarket stocked more than a hundred different lines. As we sat at the end of an absurdly long causeway, itself evidence that the lake was much bigger than was originally planned, the inhabitants of Remanso came out to see us. Gangs of giggling girls in the uniform of the private schools, blue trousers and white T-shirt with a printed badge on it, clustered on the quay, switching their tails and shrieking as they caught the eyes of the film crew. Amid the teenage cacophony sat a cluster of gnarled old peasants, surrounded by their earthly goods, bulging bundles and boxes, the occasional large earthenware jar, a cluster of herbs grown in tins, a germinating coconut palm. They had waited months for indemnification for the loss of their lands and now they were joining our last voyage upstream. Five motorcyclists with brightly patterned foam mattresses rolled up and strapped to their pillions handed their bikes on to the boat with loving care. They were surveyors, working for a company subcontracted to the Banco do Brasil to measure out the properties offered as collateral for development loans. They would be gone from home for six months or more, sleeping in cheap guest houses where they supplied their own bedding and driving their trail bikes deep into the *sertão*. The boys were open-faced and optimistic about the value of their work, for which they had no professional qualification. Their leader was a tough, wary man who had nothing to say to foreigners.

By now we were becoming aware that there was nothing normal in the apparition of a *gaiola* at the ports on the Rio São Francisco. When we stopped at Xique-Xique, a town totally surrounded by an enormous wall built by CHESF, further evidence that the level of the river was permanently raised beyond the boundaries of the lake, ordinary life came to a dead halt. We walked through streets virtually deserted because most adults and all the children were standing spellbound on the wall. No sooner did the crew put down the gangplank than people swarmed on board, all screaming with delight and amazement, jamming the companionways. They continued pouring on and off until the *São Francisco* blew her steam whistle threateningly when the scream leapt the octave and they threw themselves on land, terrified that they would be borne off into the unknown. At Barra, a delightful town built by the cattle barons to a standard to which CHESF had never aspired. with piped water and paved streets and a meat market as clean as an operating theatre, and at

Ibotirama, a sprawling, filthy brothel town growing up at the point where the Salvador–Brasilia highway crosses the river, the scene was repeated, on an ever-expanding scale until our journey southwards took on the aspect of a Götterdämmerung. More pieces cracked or shattered or fell off the engine. The brightly painted funnel turned black and at one point burst into flames. Leaks opened in all systems. Hot water failed and lavatories refused to flush. Worst of all, the wood kept running out, as it took more and more to generate a head of steam. We were falling so far behind schedule there was only one thing to do. The BBC abandoned her ageing prima donna and travelled overland to Bom Jesus da Lapa, thereby running a not inconsiderable risk of not being on hand when the old girl finally sank or burned to the waterline.

Bom Jesus is a centre of religious tourism, simply because there is a series of large caverns to be found under a rock outcrop so tall that it can be seen from miles downriver. Any landmark in Brazil is instantly claimed for the church and surmounted with a statue or a cross. Bom Jesus not only crowned the heights, but created a Via Crucis up through the rock sugar loaf and filled the underground caverns with altars and shrines. The whole complex has now been taken over by a group of Polish priests whose interpretation of the economic application of God's law is markedly different from Father Mark's, for they are earnestly working for the Commissão Pastoral da Terra, which is struggling to organize and mobilize rural workers to defend their rights. A few weeks before we arrived, an independent farmer who had been resisting continual harassment for years, refusing to abandon his *roça*, had been shot by a group of gunmen, in front of witnesses. The police had been strangely unable to connect the assassins with his persecutor, the *fazendeiro*. The women who survived him had no stomach for continuing the struggle. When I saw one of the priests talking with a group of peasants after mass, I followed them to the church hall. It was the first of May, the *dia do trabalhador*, but in the hall were only old men and schoolgirls, who listened hypnotized to the earnest harangues of the young politicoes, one of whom had flown from Salvador specially for the meeting. The discourse was impassioned, the language that of infant Marxism with frequent references to *a luta da classe*, but the Polish priest who listened and carefully refrained from taking over the meeting, even when the leaders got into a tangle about minutes and motions, did not flinch. The *trabalhadores rurais* close to Bom Jesus are either *vaquerios* or dependants of the beef industry and the good graces of the *fazendeiros*, who had neither been to mass nor the meeting. Communications are so bad in the interior of Bahia that there was no way farmers in the back blocks could get to Bom Jesus. The little meeting with its fine rhetoric and its high ideals represented no threat to the status quo whatsoever. We were committed to film a festival in Bom Jesus, which we had already been asked to subsidize. We managed to talk our way out of it, almost, although the festival went ahead with dreadful inevitability, but the little meeting was in its way as unreal as the fiesta. I felt as if the Nordeste was fading away before my eyes. The only real thing was the great yellow river, writhing in its bonds.

We travelled up to Pirapora where brown boys caught the fish that flipped like coins out of the rapids, and no tourists bought *carrancas* or danced at the discotheque. I rejoined the old *gaiola* after seven hours slipping downstream in a tiny boat and slept one more night in my cabin which boomed and banged as the crew flung the last of the forests of wood she had consumed into her voracious boiler. At noon next day she nosed into the smelly mud flat by the São Francisco Navigation Company's workshops in Pirapora and the boilers were shut down. All along the bank, people had downed tools and run to follow her, effortlessly keeping up with her crippled pace. Reporters appeared from nowhere, one with a cine camera, for all the world as though she had been a real ship on a real voyage. The crew changed into dazzling whites. There was no sign in their confident greetings that from now on they were out of work. They held up their children to be kissed and admired, lavishing on them all the caresses that they did not give to their wives. Other Latins might leave everything to *mañana*; the Nordestino adores and indulges his children because he knows that the only good time of their lives is today. How can there be a future with inflation running at 120 per cent a year? Why teach children self-denial when there is no jam tomorrow? Why lower an astronomical birth rate when it will take twice as many children to keep you in your old age as it has taken your parents? Why teach the work ethic when there is no work? Better far to frolic in the river catching a hundred minnows than to learn useless skills in an expensive school or nothing at all in a free one.

Pirapora is in the state of Minas Gerais which is industrialized in the Brazilian manner, which is to say that its metal production depends upon charcoal for smelting. Hundreds and hundreds of hectares grow nothing but trash eucalypts, planted so closely that, from a distance, they look like dull green Axminster. There is no space to walk between or beneath them. For this cultivation, too, people are irrelevant. From Minas Gerais we went to the fertile coastal plain at the mouth of the river, to Penedo with its gaily painted Portuguese colonial houses and its sick children. When I asked why children died so often, the people laughed, the genuine laugh mirthless. Of the three men who crewed the *canoa* which took me upstream to Pão de Azucar, one was unmarried, one had had seven children of whom three were alive, and the other had had five, all dead. It is not an easy matter to talk to people of their lost children. Generally, the older people were convinced that matters had improved greatly. Certainly, the polio immunization campaign had been efficiently run, and malaria, even if it is resurgent, is not the scourge it once was, but the people's optimism was fragile, more like an aspect of good manners than a spontaneous feeling. Medical services existed only in theory; public free clinics were either closed or manned by incompetents, or so they thought. The people's teeth were terrible, but a filling cost fifteen or twenty thousand cruzeiros. Nobody wore glasses, including two of our drivers who could not discern turnings until they were right on top of them, but they struggled on somehow. Their mad optimism began to get to me so that I wanted to shake them and say, 'For God's sake, get angry!' but I knew that it would only make them less able to endure. Perhaps the worst moment was when a young couple came into a clinic with their two children, a newborn who was frantic with hunger but by now so weak that his cry was beginning to fail, and a little girl who could not walk for weakness and a pain in her buttock, but lay with her head on her father's shoulder, gazing sightlessly with eyes glazed with fever. The doctor (whose only qualification was in dentistry) did not notice the newborn's futile sucking movements and did not ask the mother about her milk until prompted. She laughed and said she had very little, and laughed again when she said she was giving the child cows' milk. 'Make sure you dilute it with water,' said the doctor. The village had no water treatment plant; she might as well have diluted the milk with cyanide. The doctor did not tell her to boil either the milk or the water. The little girl seemed to have polio, but the doctor did not ask if they had had her vaccinated. He treated her for worms instead. Her father kept crazily trying to cheer her up, bouncing her and joking with her, calling her '*mulher*' and flirting. The mother pounded her newborn on the back and laughed again as she told the doctor that she had already had a child die. She herself was only twenty.

I left Penedo and drove overland through the fertile coastal plain, most of it given over to sugar cultivation for ethanol production, and into the area of intensive mixed cultivation called *agreste*. Here the population was dense, and large, sprawling towns with advanced light industry appeared at every crossroad, but just as suddenly they gave way to the *sertão*, and I was back in the São Francisco heartland. Here in the state of Alagoas, cattle raising was more intensive than in Bahia. Every inch of the dry, inhospitable hills was used. Tiny houses were everywhere. I saw water trucks drawn by oxen and women washing in every mantled pool or runlet of green water. As we swooped over a rise, I saw coming out of one of the low mud houses a flock of women in clean, bright dresses, red, pink and turquoise. I turned in my seat, thinking I was seeing something like a Nordestino Tupperware party. 'A funeral,' said the driver. Then I saw among the skirts that flickered in the breeze, two little girls carrying a cardboard box with improvised handles. 'Why are they all women?' I asked, being more familiar with countries where only men attend funerals. 'The deceased was a woman,' said the driver, letting in the clutch. A woman eighteen inches long. I have seen infant death in many places, but never has it seemed more appalling than in that brisk little procession, making its way to the walled cemetery where bare mound was heaped on bare mound, with no time for grass to grow, or to make a cross or to name the mounds.

I went on to Paolo Afonso, where a series of huge hydroelectric stations harvest the power from the river yoked at Sobradinho. I was guided up and down inside its vast fabric, into its shadowless bowels where a handful of men presided over the electrification of all the cities of the Nordeste. I was shown the oasis where the élite CHESF workers are housed among fountains and exotic trees. I was shown the zoo where Brazil's original inhabitants die slowly in their own stink. It seemed a world away from that line of women making their way over the bare hill. The technical achievement of Paolo Afonso is staggering; piping water to the struggling farmers of Alagoas is a doddle by comparison. I went to Brasilia to find out what plans, if any, the central government has for this region. The senior official who spoke with me was charming. Yes, the Nordeste was discriminated against and probably on racist grounds. Yes, the Nordeste had chiefly functioned as a reservoir of cheap labour for the developed south. On the other hand, I must understand that even in the fertile plain near the river mouth the initial cost of the rice polders was $12,000 per hectare. There was no way such an investment could be put in the hands of backward farmers with no knowledge or aptitude for intensive year-round cultivation. If irrigation was developed, it would have to be done by the states in collaboration with private investors. No, such schemes would not make very much difference to the unemployment picture. As for bringing river water to the *poligono das secas*, academics had made many plans, but state and local politics are involved, and like federal politics, he smiled, these are dominated by vested interests. In Brazil, the same people own the land, the money and the power. But it was true that the river was a priceless national resource and should not be allowed to become nothing but a conduit of kinetic energy, hence the existence of PLANVASF which would co-ordinate SUDENE, CODEVASF, PORTOBRAS, CHESF, CEMIG and DNAEE and the Ministries of Agriculture and Mines and Energy . . . a new acronym to add to the storm of acronyms which designates Brazil's bureaucracy. 'The most likely result of attempting to co-ordinate all the authorities dealing with the river in any of its aspects is a number of very long and inconclusive meetings,' said I. 'Precisely,' said my friend from the Ministry of the Interior, and again he smiled. 'Perhaps you should take them all on a month-long tour of the Bacia do Rio São Francisco.' 'If they could afford to take a month off to do that, they wouldn't be important enough to make any difference to the status quo.' I supposed not. He was a very nice man, but he knew and I knew that the people of the Rio São Francisco had had it. They could continue to struggle in a declining, outmoded, second-rate beef industry or they could cling to their scraps of earth, or they could take the journey to the *favelas* of the overcrowded cities which so many of their kin had taken before them, never to return.

People crammed into urban slums lose their trustfulness and the spontaneity of their smiles, and all the other qualities that make the Nordestino people so special. I said goodbye to the river at Bom Jesus da Lapa, where the setting sun turned the water to copper. Small boys twirled their throwing nets which, as they dropped, broke up the red shimmer in flakes of verdigris. Soft brown women leaned on the parapet talking and laughing round their babies' prying fingers, squeezing their brown bottoms in their hands. The people rich enough to have proper houses with electricity were sitting spellbound by the soap operas, while their children played among the pig and dog droppings in the street. Watching the Technicolor posturing of a fictitious middle class surrounded by the impedimenta of conspicuous consumption through tumbledown doorways in a street full of scummy water and decomposing excrement, I was shocked to find myself hoping that Padre Damiano was right; perhaps the dam would burst, and the bloated river become its wild self again. The people had learned to live with the river's changes. Now that the river was controlled by man's caprice and greed, there was no coming to terms with it.

Women and power in Cuba

This essay was commissioned for Women: A World Report *published by the United Nations to mark the end of the Decade of Women 1975–1985.*

I came to Cuba with my heart in my mouth. Ever since my first contact with the 'Third World', in Jamaica in 1971, I had been aware how burningly important it is for the developing nations that Cuba not be a fraud or a failure. As the years passed and I wandered through slums in Bombay, past windowless huts in Morocco, Tunis and Yucatan, through the dust of Uttar Pradesh and the infested dirt of the Brazilian North-East and the menace of Bogota and the Guatemalan highlands, every step showed me that paternalist development aid is worse than useless. In the eighties as the external debts of the developing countries mushroom over them while their people grow steadily poorer and the number of landless multiplies daily, the need of a genuine alternative is agonizing. If Cuba had shown me nothing but the institutionalized poverty and bureaucratic rhetoric and repression that Western megamedia taught me to expect, a brain-washed militarized population living by hypocrisy and fear, the dark future would show no sign of dawn. If Cuba's was really a revolution of the people, then even if a malignant power should blast Cuba out of the Caribbean, its people will be invincible.

My arrival coincided with the fourth congress of the Federation of Cuban Women, the FMC. Billboards and posters announced it all over Havana. *Toda la fuerza de la mujer en el servicio de la revolución.* The logo was an art-nouveauish montage of Kalashnikov rifles and Mariposa lilies. I wasn't keen on the implications of either. On the Rampa, the floodlit exhibition pavilion was turned over to the exploits of women. Banked television sets showed colour videos of the history of Cuban women, and a succession of booths displayed everything from the techniques of screening for breast cancer to scent and hair curlers. Women whose bottoms threatened to burst out of their elasticized pants tottered round the exhibits on four-inch heels clutching their *compañeros* for support. Their nails and faces were garishly painted. Their hair had been dragged over rollers, bleached, dyed and coloured. Their clothes, including their brassières, were all two or three sizes too small and flesh bulged everywhere. Most people rushed past the educational exhibits to where a painted, conked, and corseted trio bumped and ground its way through an amorous rhumba. At the sight of an unattached woman, the loose men began 'Psst! Psst!' and beckoned to me, as if I had been a dog.

The next day, my minder from the Ministry of Exterior Relations (MINREX) came to take me to the Palacio de Congresos for the first session of the FMC Congress. Security was tight. I was directed to a press box in the back of the vast auditorium, with no facilities for simultaneous translation. A policeman ordered me not to put my tape recorder up on the parapet. Later I discovered that one such instrument had been accidentally knocked off and narrowly missed braining a delegate seated thirty feet below, but then and there it seemed that Cuba was determined that I would see little and understand less. The whole day was taken up with the reading of the *informe central*, the 157-page official report to the congress. The reader was Vilma Espín, president of the FMC, alternate member of the Politburo, member of the Central Committee of the Communist Party, and wife of Raul Castro, Fidel's brother. She read correctly and quietly, a calm, matronly figure hard to associate with the slender girl who had organized the medical support system during the *lucha clandestina* and joined the guerilla fighters in the Sierra Maestra. I complained that she was hardly a charismatic speaker. 'She doesn't have to impress us,' answered one of the delegates. 'We know her. She is our Vilma.'

Alongside her, in the front row of the serried ranks of office bearers on the dais, sat Fidel Castro, quietly reading through the report. I expected him to make some formal rhetorical statement and leave, as befits a totalitarian figurehead, putting in a token appearance for the Association of Townswomen's Guilds, before leaving to take care of more pressing matters of state. To my surprise, he sat there quietly the whole day long, reading, caressing his beard, thinking and listening. The next day he was there again. As one of the delegates waxed eloquent on discrimination against women in the workplace, a man's voice interjected, 'This is the heart of the problem, isn't it? Women's access to work?' I looked about wondering who owned these mild, slightly high-pitched tones. It was Castro, whom I soon learned to call what every Cuban calls him, Compañero Fidel. He was leaning forward earnestly, intent on participating in the debate, not leading but participating. If anything the discussion became less formal and more spontaneous, as delegates held up their hands for recognition and described precise problems of access to work. The women claimed that they were considered more likely to absent themselves from work, because of their family responsibilities. Fidel pointed out that men still refuse to shoulder their part of the burden of housekeeping and child-rearing as laid down by the Cuban Family Code. The women pointed out that in fact the *ausentismo* of women workers was often less than that of men, and certainly no greater. Fidel pointed out that women shoulder a double duty, which is unequal, and the women argued that they were not prepared to give it up. Sometimes, when the head of state wagged his hand for recognition, the chairperson ignored him. At other times, the delegates noisily disagreed with him, crying 'no, no!' some even booing.

I had been prepared for the chants of 'Fidel! Fidel!' but nothing had prepared me for this. I thought ruefully of Margaret Thatcher and Indira Gandhi, both incapable of listening, especially to someone who disagreed with them. And all the time Fidel made jokes, selected funny comparisons, continually pressing the delegates to give concrete, living examples. Their carefully prepared statements went all to pieces. We discovered that women did not want men to have the same leave to absent themselves from work for family reasons because they would abuse it and use the time to visit other women – or at least the delegates thought they might – and thus one of the most fascinating contradictions in Cuban sexual politics was drawn out in a public forum of 1,400 participants.

All afternoon the debate surged on, with Vilma at the helm steadily working through the order paper. And all the next day. When delegates complained that if the day-care centres closed down for any one of a hundred reasons, lack of water, pollution of the water supply, sickness of staff, deterioration of the building, communicable illness, women were called away from hospitals and factories, schools and voluntary work, to take care of their children. Because the day-care centres did not operate on the free Saturdays, which fall every two weeks, women were effectively prevented from undertaking the extra voluntary work that led to distinction and party membership. Fidel noticed that the Minister of Labour and Employment and the Minister of Education had not bothered to attend the Congress. 'They should be hearing this,' he said. 'Watch,' said one of the Cuban journalists. After lunch the chairs on the dais had all been moved up, and lo! the ministers in question had appeared to answer the women's demands. When the Minister for Education complained of lack of trained infant teachers, Fidel reminded him that he was using statistics from the Second Party Congress and updated them for him, thus destroying his excuses. Everyone but the ministers, who could fall back only on silly compliments and party slogans, enjoyed it enormously.

When the sessions rose, the women leapt to their feet, waving the coloured nylon georgette scarves and matching plastic flowers they had all brought with them, pounding maracas, bongoes, conga drums and cowbells, clapping their hands and singing fit to bust, *Para trabajar, para estudiar, para defender nuestra libertad! Firmes con Fidel! Firmes con Fidel!* Hips gyrated, scarves flashed, flowers wagged. The syncopated thunder roared round the huge building, sucking the tiredest professional congress-makers out of their offices to watch as the women put on a turn that would have shamed a Welsh football crowd into silence. They were so delighted, with the occasion, with Fidel, but above all with themselves, that I forgot how clumsy some of the women looked in their harsh-coloured and badly made synthetic suits and the crippling high heels they thought appropriate to the situation. I abandoned my posture of superiority and let myself be impressed.

Each lunchtime, 1,400 women swarmed into the commissaries of the vast building and forty minutes later they swarmed out again into group and regional meetings in preparation for the afternoon sessions. They gave hundreds of interviews for Cuban television, to be used gradually over the ensuing months, for daily papers, for women's magazines, for regional newsletters, for books. The youngest delegate was sixteen, the oldest ninety something. They were ready to work all day and all night if necessary. My questions to Vilma Espín had to wait ten days for answers, but late on a Saturday afternoon I was called to her office, to spend two hours discussing what the questions meant. The written answers and tape recording of our discussion were delivered to me the first thing on Monday morning.

The first evening the delegates were taken to a ballet. They arrived stomping and chanting, sat chatting eagerly about the day's doings, and when the dancing had started and silence was finally imposed, a good proportion of them went straight to sleep, waking up only to applaud wildly. While exhausted *delegadas* slumbered around me, I watched Dionea, a man-eating plant composed of Josefina Menendez and the *cuerpo de baile* to music by Villa-Lobos, as it ate three male dancers dressed as glittering mothy creatures, with horribly erotic gestures. This was followed by the world premiere of *Palomas*, a ballet choreographed by the Chilean exile Hilda Riveros, especially for the Fourth Congress of the FMC. The story ran straight down the party line; the dancers mimed birth, the mother mimed ecstatic admiration of her child. She was joined by her mate and mimed ecstatic admiration of him. They simulated spontaneous conjugal relations on the floor. She then went off for her militia training, and mimed something rather like kung fu in strict unison with the *cuerpo de baile*. Then she and her fellow soldiers were joined by their mates and mimed heterosexual fulfilment in unison.

The delegates snored through the whole thing but woke up with a start to watch the eighth wonder of the world, Alicia Alonso, sixty-six years old and virtually blind, dance a *pas de deux* with Jorge Esquivel to music by Chopin. Her line was exquisite, and if once or twice things went slightly wrong, such as when she slid out of a lift and down Jorge Esquivel's nose, so that his eyes streamed with tears, the audience had no intention of feeling let alone showing any dissatisfaction. Alicia Alonso came back to Cuba at a time when artists and skilled technicians were leaving in hordes. She promised her people a world-class ballet and she kept her promise. She danced in complete confidence on a stage she could no longer see, borne up less by Esquivel's strong arms than by the love and loyalty that surrounded her.

This was early days, but already I could feel something unfamiliar and very special about Cuba. The absence of theatricality that I noticed in Vilma and Fidel was part of a complex of attitudes. People did not sell themselves as they do in consumer society. Life was not soap opera, but real. There was no competition or character assassination, as people jockeyed for limelight. They spoke not to persuade or bamboozle, but to explain. They had not our prurient interest in domestic and sexual affairs. No one was quite sure how many children Fidel might have had, or, for that matter, Vilma. Public functionaries were assessed on their perform-ance of their public duty, and did not have to drag their bed partners around with them, miming domestic bliss. Life without gossip magazines and advertising seemed wonderfully uncluttered. There was no equivalent of Princess Diana's latest outfit or Elizabeth Taylor's latest wedding or the American president's haemorrhoids. Doubtless there are some Cubans who think life would be more interesting if murder and rape were reported in the newspapers and convicted criminals were paid a working man's earnings for ten years to describe their activities in lurid detail, but most of the people I met know the other culture from glimpses of Miami television and find it crazy and perverse. The slice of American culture they get from Miami includes late-night pornographic videos, which do nothing to improve the US image. Some Cubans, the ones who steal designer jeans off foreigners' clotheslines in Miramar and offer to change pesos for dollars giving five times the official exchange rate, so that they can buy ghetto blasters in the dollar shops, obviously envy the hyperstimulated lifestyle of capitalism, but all the Cubans I met and talked to were more interested in Ethiopia and Guatemala than in Michael Jackson. A Chilean exile explained to me, 'I could have stayed in West Germany. They were paying me a fortune, but what could I do with it? Invest in the latest parsley cutter? Life is exciting here, even if I have very little money. There is always something to do, and it's exciting. People are creating their own future. If I got sick in Germany I could lie and rot. Here, if I don't show up at the *tienda* for my rations people are straight round to help.' Her bath was kept permanently full of water to flush the lavatory, for Havana has a chronic and crippling water shortage, just another minor inconvenience that women have to deal with, but it made no dent in Elisabeth's fierce loyalty to Cuba. As we sat on her tiny balcony, drinking *añejo sobre las rocas*, while people flowing in and out of the tiny apartments above, beside and below us, and the old red buses, affectionately known as *guaguas*, groaned and shrieked down the hill, disgorging streams of workers, she said, 'It's a hard life, but a good life.'

The Cubans are involved after all in a much bigger adventure than sex, speed and smack could possibly supply. Their morale is towering, even if their energy should occasionally flag, as they negotiate the daily obstacle course which is life in a poor country, cursed by an irreplaceable invest-ment in a single crop, sugar, and strangled by the American blockade which has cut off the only cheap source of supply for all the goods a single-crop economy does not produce. Every Cuban will tell you that underdevelopment is a feature of minds and hearts as well as economies. As Cubans struggle to develop logistical and communicative skills, they encounter inefficiency and confusion at all levels of social organization. The response is not irritability and hostility, but tolerance and mutual assistance. Because of rationing, limited supplies of essential commodities and the unreliability of transport (given shortage of vehicles and spare parts), queueing is a way of life, but Cubans do not try to jump queues or stand guard to see that no one else does. Instead they have developed a characteristic solution to an intolerable situation. When you arrive at the *tienda*, to find fifty people already waiting for their ration of rice, beans, oil, crackers, fruit juice or whatever other commodity is on sale that day, you simply ask who is *el último*. When another person arrives, and you are asked the same thing, you are free to go about other business and return when the queue has moved up. People less pressed chat, criticize the authorities, flirt and clown around. When you come back the person who was behind you will call you to your place. This *ad hoc* system involves co-operation and a degree of awareness of other people, neither often found in rich countries. Even on my last day in Cuba, when I found a hundred people queueing at the hotel cashier's desk, I could hardly prevent myself from panicking, thinking I had no time to pack because I would be queueing for two hours or so (given the mean speed of such transactions in Cuba). However, I tried asking *el último* and went about my other chores. When I came down, the honeymooners behind me waved me to my place, by now only four from the head of the line. As I had screamed and ranted to the hotel management about their inefficiency, while they politely defended a system I condemned as hopeless, I felt truly ashamed.

It may seem that all this has little to do with women and political power in Cuba. In fact, it has everything to do with it. The people deal with constant daily frustrations with calm and co-operation because they do not feel that they are the result of corruption, caprice or incompetence on the part of a separate ruling class, but aspects of problems which afflict a twenty-five-year-old nation with a heritage of ignorance, disease and poverty.

The first priority of the Cuban revolution was to combat illiteracy, disease and malnutrition, thus bringing the Cuban population a condition where they could exercise the duties of popular government. Despite the enormous drain of human and other resources in maintaining a convincing defence posture, they have achieved those basic aims, largely by voluntary work undertaken alongside the desperate struggle to make the sugar economy profitable despite falling world prices, and to cope with the effects of the US blockade. My first duty in Cuba was to check the validity of Cuban claims about health and education, so I hired a car and slipped off into the countryside, driving through town after small town, checking the *policlinico*, the water supply, the electricity cables, the health status of the inhabitants, the intensity and productivity of the industry and agriculture. I turned up back streets, wandered into sugar mills and factory forecourts, stopped to watch militia training and the volunteer brigades grubbing up garlic and packing tomatoes in boxes. Nobody stared, nobody tried to beg, but people by the roadsides cheerfully accepted lifts. *La guagua esta mal*, was the usual explanation. Everyone I saw was healthy, busy and quietly self-confident. Occasional unpleasantnesses helped me to realize that I was not dreaming. A boarding-school cook, coming back from collecting his daughter who spent the weekend with her psychologist mother and lived with her father during the week, told me he would not let her marry a Negro. 'Oh, popi,' said the ten-year-old indulgently, shaking her head at his foolishness. Everyone was interested in the progress that was being made. They explained to me about the difficulties of industrializing sugar production, 'humanizing the work' they called it. Questions about plant genetics and animal diseases got intelligent answers, if not from parents then from the children.

In all Cuba's struggles women have been in the front line. During the *lucha clandestina* women organized medical supplies and treatment and taught school in the Sierra Maestra. Fidel has always acknowledged that without the help of women in building up the underground organization which victualled, supplied and protected the guerrillas in the fifties, they would never have been successful. Celia Sánchez, who was waiting with supplies, petrol and transport for the arrival of the yacht, *Granma*, which brought Fidel back to Cuba in 1956, became his aide in the closing years of the war, and took part in several battles. She chose to work as Secretary to the Council of State when the Revolutionary Government was set up. Every little girl in Cuba grows up with an impressive series of role models, going back more than a hundred years before the revolution: Rosa la Bayamesa, a captain in the war of independence, Paulina Pedrosa and Carolina Rodriguez, supporters of Jose Martí's revolutionary party in the 1890s, Emilia Rodriguez, leader of the Partido Popular Obrero in the 1920s and dozens more. The struggle to oust Baptista threw up more still, like Lydia Doce and Clodorinda Acosta Ferrais, who were only twenty years old when Baptista's police threw their bullet-ridden bodies into the sea. The all-woman Peloton Mariana Grajales, formed in September, 1958 and named after the mother of the maceo who led the Revolutionary War 1868–78, held one of the most exposed positions on the highway between Havana and Santiago de Cuba and was involved in some of the bitterest fighting of the war. Women fought at the Bay of Pigs; Cira Garcia Reyes, leader of the FMC in the region, lost her life there.

On 23 August 1960, the female network which had contributed so much to the rebel effort was officially instituted as the Federation of Cuban

Women, the FMC. By spreading out over the countryside, they were to consolidate the revolution by convincing the passive and fearful that they could construct a new society. Peasant women like Nadividad Betancourt Marten led groups of women who travelled from village to village in their regions, politicizing women like themselves. The FMC organized the push for literacy in Cuba, working as volunteer teachers in peasant huts up and down the island, teaching more volunteers who taught others. Women conducted the 'Battle for the Sixth Grade' and when that was won, they went on to help all kinds of people achieve the standard of ninth-grade education.

The US blockade is a disaster which popular endurance and initiative have turned into a blessing, for nothing less brutal could have protected Cuba from becoming another impoverished would-be consumer nation. The ridiculous attempt to invade, known by the Cubans as the Victoria de Giron and the Americans as the Bay of Pigs débâcle, gave all Cubans a sense of external threat and national heroism. The strangely explosive epidemic of haemorrhagic dengue fever, involving a mutant strain similar to one that is normally found in Asia, which swept through the province of Havana in 1981, producing thousands of cases within a week, was met by mobilizing all the mass organizations to isolate cases and run improvised field hospitals in all kinds of public buildings. The hypothesis of germ warfare was obvious, but the Cubans wasted no time in investigating whether it was another gift from the CIA dirty tricks department; they were more interested in their own preparedness and efficiency in overcoming it, as they did. The disease vanished from Cuba as suddenly as it came.

It would be quite wrong to imagine, however, that there was no resistance to the full incorporation of women in the development process. For many people the only notion of the good life was derived from the bourgeois example; moreover, the legacy of the past included male unemployment, especially during the seven months of the year when the cane was not being cut, while women struggled to feed their families by domestic work, by working in the tobacco industry, and by prostitution. Slave women had not been protected from brutalizing toil, therefore the right to manual labour was not one that Cuban women were on the whole particularly anxious to win. There had been opposition to the presence of women fighters in the Sierra, but for some reason, perhaps his dependence on Melba Hernández and Celia Sánchez, Fidel insisted on women's full participation in the struggle, in the victory and in the glory. In 1965 he was already defining women's liberation as 'a revolution within the revolution'. It is generally assumed that the authority for the revolutionary Cuban conception of women's role is the writing of Marx and Lenin, against 'the base, mean and infamous denial of rights to women' and inequality of sexes. To be sure, Cuba follows the Russian line on abortion, contraception, neo-Malthusianism, women in the workplace, divorce, child care, education and maternity leave. But there are aspects of sexual politics in Cuba that are distinctly Cuban, and owe nothing to the Russian paradigm.

Sexual politics in Cuba are complex. It is not enough to say that the Cuban man is macho or even extremely macho. Chances are that whatever the Cuban male is, his mother has had far more to do with the development of his personality than his father. A joke in a Cuban girls' magazine sums the conundrum up perfectly. 'Your boyfriend is terribly macho,' says one. 'Yes,' simpers the other, 'aren't I lucky!' Cuban sociology does not express itself in detailed examinations of the psychopathology of everyday life, so it was difficult for a visitor to gain any clear idea of the reality behind the body language of male-female interaction. Officially, Cuba is a totally heterosexual country. There are no homosexual unions, no people living alone, no one-parent families. There are no published figures to illuminate the reality behind this impossibility, just as there are no figures on rape and crimes against women or sex-related offences generally. Certainly, when work is over, the streets of Havana fill with couples, hand in hand, kissing, giggling, wandering through Coppelia, a complex of pavilion and garden covering a whole block and totally given over to the sale and consumption of ice-cream, or attending any of the dozens of free amusements that socialism supplies, museums, aquaria, literary *tertulias*, concerts ... The situation is complicated by a severe housing shortage, with a typically Cuban solution. People in need of privacy to make love can go to one of several *posadas*, where at very reasonable rates they can hire a room, a bed and clean sheets by the hour, and order food and beverages to the room. Nobody asks questions about the couples, who may be married to each other, married to others, unmarried, engaged or one-hour stands. The only inconvenience is that, as with everything in Cuba, there is a wait, sometimes a three- or four-hour wait. Couples sit in the waiting room, smoking, necking, chatting, until the next horizontal space becomes free. Anyone who remembers Lenin's scornful dismissal as bourgeois the demand of feminists like Inessa Armand and Alexandra Kollontai for the right of free love will see that, in this matter at least, the Cubans have gone their own way.

The Cubans have accepted that adultery is their national sport. Men boast of it. A man, otherwise intelligent, cultivated and reasonable, will tell you that when a pretty girl works for him or near him, he will do his best to get near her and 'be with her' as often as he can, but his attentions to his wife will continue at the same intensity. The implication is that he can satisfy both, and there can be no significant objection to the spreading of so much happiness by his so potent art. The men seem to be totally caught up in this fantasy, which explains why they have the temerity to call unattached women across to their sides as if they were loose puppies. A foreign woman alone in Havana might well interpret the staring and gesturing of men as signs of aggression, hostility and low esteem for women, especially if she is accustomed to the North American or North European version expressed in whistling, cat calls and sexist comments. Cuba's boast of advances in their progress towards complete equality for women seemed to me invalidated by the overt interference by Cuban men in my freedom to sit in a darkened cinema by myself or stand waiting for the lift in a hotel lobby. However, after a few days I began to realize that male aggression in Cuba was different. If I clearly expressed my displeasure or lack of interest in the proceedings, the men appeared startled and embarrassed and tended to disappear or, indeed, flee. Men told me that Cuban women quite enjoy approaches of this kind and often flirtatiously provoke them, and I did see some evidence for the truth of this claim. Women, on the other hand, told me that if I had protested, when I was harassed in the cinema for example, the people sitting around me would have taken my part. One of the men involved might have found himself the victim of a citizens' arrest and eventually subject to up to fifteen years' detention in a work centre. This is a rather different reason for not creating a scene from what prevails in England, where the people around me would most likely dismiss the uproar as evidence of my hysteria and exonerate the man for lack of evidence other than my protest. It stands to reason that male aggression towards women would be modified by the salutory reflection that any woman may be a salaried officer of the Fuerzas Armadas Revolucionarias. Most women are trained in the Militia and actively involved in the public surveillance duties of the Comites para la Defensa de la Revolución. However, male-female relationships in Cuba are different from those I grew up with principally because, like Cuba itself, they are Afro-Latin. The Africans who were shipped to Cuba left behind them intricate family structures in which the relationships of siblings and cross-cousins through the female line were at least as important as patrilineal relationships and the mother-child relationship possibly the most intense and durable of all human bonds. In the slave society, where men and women were bought and sold like cattle, women were used as brood animals, often fecundated by their owners rather than the men of their choice and prevented from setting up any viable, legitimate family structure. The legacy of this persists in all Afro-American societies where first births are often very early, where the nuptial bond is fragile and mothers and mothers' mothers supply the only stability in the child's experience. Doubtless, feminist chauvinists will sneer at an impression based on two weeks' acquaintance, nevertheless I must say that there seems to me to be less hostility in male-female relations in Cuba, than, say, in northern Europe. Cuban women would agree. They staunchly refuse to entertain a notion of sexual politics which postulates any significant degree of male-female hostility. Even when Compañero Fidel suggests that the greatest obstacle to women's complete equality is the attitude of men to the work traditionally done by women, the women prefer to stress other 'objective' factors. Cuban men, for all their flirtatiousness, seem to like and respect women. One way of interpreting the emphasis on men's strength, 'machismo' as Cubans are themselves ready to call it, is as an attempt to counterbalance the dominance of women in family and kin relations.

It is notable that one of the sources of friction in the day-to-day workings of the friendship between the Cuban cockerel and the Russian bear, is the Russians' treatment of women. Almost more important than Marx and Lenin in the genesis of the Cuban revolution is the figure of Jose Martí, the National Hero of Cuba, a man of high culture and clear and coherent political ideology who adored women. He died fighting with the Mambí Army in 1895, but his personality permeates Cuba still. When accused of being a Marxist after the attack on the Moncada Barracks in 1952, Fidel claimed that the sole designer of the attack had been Jose Martí. Martí believed that no cause that women supported could be defeated, and no side could be victorious which did not have the support of women. Martí's feminism was based in a chivalrous ideal of the pure, cultivated, disinterested woman, an ideal drawn from bourgeois notions of women as weaker, nobler and less sexual than men, but which had a special relevance in a society in which women had never been protected from degrading physical toil. His notion of male/female complementarity relied upon an extreme polarity, but he also argued that one source of the brutality of capitalist society was that it suppressed feminine feeling in women *and* in men. He found American feminism erring in its overemphasis on the same coarse self-seeking that characterized the perversion of the American dream of a free and egalitarian society. If they achieve their aims, he asked, *Donde stará l'aroma de las rosas*? Present-day Martí scholars argued with me earnestly that society needs the feminine qualities, which, when pressed, they defined as self-abnegation, sensitivity, enthusiasm, 'espirito' and tenderness. *Cual es la fuerza de la vida y su unica raiz, sino el amor de la mujer*?

To Martí's enduring influence then we may attribute the emphasis that Cuban feminists lay on femininity. Women who have been trained to kill will be wearing pearlized nail polish and lipstick when they do it. The perennial shortage of acetone in Cuba probably means that the nail polish will be chipped, unless the soldier has had time to go to the beauty parlour, for acetone is supplied to the nation's manicurists. Even the heroines of work, who cut cane, go down the mines and drive huge cranes, are depilated, deodorized and scented. One of the first problems tackled by the FMC was devising a way of supplying Cuban women with the resources for making pretty clothes out of the scanty fabric supplies. Seamstresses and tailors were trained and given the facilities for carrying on trade as licensed artisans in a state scheme. At the FMC Congress, some of the foreign journalists were intrigued that so many women were wearing suits of various styles in a particular shade of kingfisher blue Courtelle. Was it a uniform of some sort, they asked. In fact it was simply that the blue was one of the few vivid shades available, and literally hundreds of women had chosen it. For a feminist like me who considers that the combination of dazzle with drudgery is one of the most insidious ways in which women in our society are subject to stress, the multiplication of contradictory demands upon the Cuban woman is a cause for concern. Women who are expected to be prepared to kill are also expected to be flower-like; the Mariposa must accompany the Kalashnikov. The brain surgeon, the Polit-buro member and the chief of police must also be ready to sit by their children's beds in hospital, comforting and caring for them, their attention for the moment undivided. The Cuban women are proud that they can handle all this. They see theirs as the force of the flower that in growing towards the light shatters the rock. To Martí's question, *Hay hombres que se cansan, cuando las mujeres no se cansan?*, they answer *yes*.

As I travelled around the provinces of Havana, Matanzas and Pinar del Rio, alone in a hired car, I talked to dozens of women, hitchhiking without fear in their own country, to join their parents, their novios, their husbands, separated from them by the demands of the revolution. They were shy, but not frightened to talk. Pilar was typical. She is twenty-three and has nearly finished her studies in medicine at the University of Havana. Next will come work in a remote part of the island or *internacionalismo*. She had hitched a ride with me to visit her husband, studying a hundred kilometres away at the University of Matanzas. When I suggested that so much separation now and a prospect of indefinite separation to come was a bit hard on a marriage, she said, 'We can handle it. We were sweethearts for eight years, and it was always like this.' I pushed a little harder, saying how hard it was to give men the attention they demanded after a week's hard work. She grinned and I noticed how pale she was and how white her gums. 'Sometimes, I've been in the operating theatre all night and I have to grab my bag and get out here on the road. I haven't time to wait for the *guagua* and it's always so crowded, I just can't face the trip standing up.' I probably should have concentrated on the pot-holes and let her go to sleep, but instead I asked if she might not have been anaemic. She seemed slightly startled by the thought. 'Possibly. I've got an IUD.' She knitted her brows. Cuban girls can be fitted with IUDs on demand if they are sixteen or over. Pills, some made from steroids derived from locally grown henequin (sisal) are also available and there is a move to switch. IUDs in a young population are always problematic, but absolutely no publicity is given to such matters in Cuba. Juvenile pregnancy is such a pressing problem that the emphasis is all on prevention. We talked about housework. 'A man wants a wife, doesn't he? Not a maid,' she said stoutly. I got to know other women like her, hard-working party members, serious and committed in everything, including their sexual relationships. As I watched her walking towards her husband's dormitory over the burnt grass, I hoped she would find his room clean and his clothes washed when she got there. The older women told me, 'Oh no. If she wanted to be at all comfortable, she would have had to set to and clean him up.' The young women said, 'Of course,' but it sounded more like ideology than fact. As she walked away, I called out, 'Take care of yourself!' She gave me a white smile, and a slightly ironic shrug.

It would be perfectly possible to argue that Fidel Castro's revolution exploits women. Socialist revolution exploits everybody. 'From each according to his capacity, to each according to his need.' Every ounce of courage, patience, energy, determination and intelligence is needed if Cuba is to realize her own aims.

The burden ought to fall on men and women impartially. In addition to their salaried and professional work, men and women both undertake voluntary work in the service of the revolution. Men and women are involved in the constant watch kept in Cuban streets by day and night, so that the Cuban people can be mobilized from the street up, in the event of an attempted insurrection or invasion or an epidemic, and, as a by-product, crime has disappeared off their streets. Men and women volunteer to clean the streets and plant public gardens in their free time; on a Sunday morning in every town in Cuba, you may see gangs of women, gangs of men, and mixed gangs sweeping away leaves, burning waste paper, hauling trash. Such voluntary work is particularly onerous for women because in addition to their paid work, they are also working unpaid in the home. As the level of general culture and the standard of living has risen, the amount of housework to be done has increased exponentially. Cubans are fanatically clean; when it became possible to wash garments every time they were worn, because water, soap and garments were all present in sufficient supply, all Cuban garments were so washed. The traditional Cuban diet involves a good deal of preparation and long cooking, as well as the hours of waiting at the *tienda* for the monotonous supplies. The state helps by providing meals at the place of work, and in schools and day-care centres, where preschool children stay from 7 a.m. to 7 p.m. and eat two full meals and two snacks. Working women carry a card which enables them to go to the front of the food queue, not because they deserve some free time but to make it possible for them to cram all the duties expected of them into the inelastic twenty-four-hour day. There is very little time left over for even more voluntary work in the grass-roots organization of the *Poder Popular* which is the ultimate legislative power in Cuba even if we do not take into account the time and money the Cuban woman must spend on her other duty of keeping pretty and attractive. It is the more remarkable then that two million members of the FMC voted to be allowed to train with the *Milicia de las Tropas Territoriales*, the volunteer home guard, who train one Sunday a month. Women's record as *cumplideras*, with full attendance at work and invariably fulfilled production quotas, is consistently higher than men's. And yet at the first sign of *fiesta*, the Cuban woman is ready to stick a frangipane behind her ear and rhumba the night away. Even the Cuban sugar allowance, four pounds of sugar per person per month, could not generate this kind of energy in a disaffected population, although it clearly goes some way to causing a serious health problem of massive obesity, especially in women over forty.

Those people who ask, 'But in Cuba are men relinquishing political power so that women can take it up?' are projecting a curiously corrupt notion of political power on to the post-revolutionary process in Cuba. Revolutionary socialists are involved in remaking political power in such a way that it is genuinely wielded by the masses. While enemies of the revolution may persist in believing that power is still concentrated in the hands of an oligarchy, the people themselves are working hard to create the administrative structures which will promote the expression of the collective will and translate it into state policy. Outsiders may assume that Cuba is actually a dictatorship masquerading as a democratic republic and that real power is vested in the Politburo or the Central Committee of the Communist Party; such, in fact, is not the case. In 1976, Cubans voted in a referendum to accept a Socialist constitution which enunciated the principle by which the popular assemblies became the ultimate legislative power in the land. Those of us accustomed to seeing democratic processes subverted by lobbying, patronage and secret government would assume that the huge machinery of *Poder Popular*, as it is called in Cuba, could do little but rubber-stamp legislation originating in the inner recesses of the Communist Party. In fact, the grass-roots-level assemblies do originate the legislative process, follow it through and participate actively in the drafting of legislation. For such a cumbersome system to work, the enthusiastic participation of large numbers of people for frequent and long sessions is indispensable, yet the system has produced the new housing law in Cuba, which has less to do with socialist ideology than the pragmatic expression of the people's will. Rather than nationalize housing, the Cubans have chosen to own their own homes, amid a multitude of special considerations regarding leasing, letting, inheritance, all designed to protect the right to own one's home and prevent speculation or profiteering.

Democratic centralism, if earnestly undertaken, is the system which produces the least return for the most massive expenditure of human resources. Frequent long meetings, with the intervening struggle to study unfamiliar matters, such as housing law, contract, equity, conveyancing, and alternative administrative systems, as in the case of the 1985 Ley de las Viviendas, must arrive at unanimity, much as juries do, by long argument and counter-argument. The amateur legislators, for only the full-time functionaries are paid, must struggle to keep the process under control, agreeing agendas and then following them through. The process demands what Cuban women have least of, time. Yet, even so, twenty-seven per cent of delegates in *Poder Popular* are women. This is more significant than the presence of women on the Central Committee of the Communist Party; nevertheless of 119 members and 71 alternates, 27 are women, 17 of them full members. Women formed twenty-two per cent of the delegates at the Second Party Congress, which elected them, an increase of fifty per cent over the First Party Conference. The Third Party Congress this year will probably be attended by a high proportion of women and elect more female members of the Central Committee.

If we look at the profile of women's participation in leadership activities, contradictory trends emerge. From their first participation in the youth movement of the Jose Martí Young Pioneers we will see that little girls are 50 per cent of the members and 66.3 per cent of the troupe leaders. In the Federacion de los Estudiantes de las Escuelas Medias, women are 57 per cent of the membership and 61 per cent of the leadership, while at university level, they are 59 per cent of the student enrolment but only 48 per cent of the leadership. Thus as women become numerically dominant in the rank and file, they are outnumbered in the leadership. Women are only 41 per cent of the Young Communists, the highly selective organization and training ground for future members of the Communist Party of Cuba. The disparities can be understood in two ways: the increasing proportion of female leaders in the younger age groups may reflect a general tendency to increasing female participation in the future; the troupe leaders among the Young Pioneers may continue as leaders until they find themselves on the Central Committee of the CPC. (In December 1984 the FEEM elected a national committee composed of six women and three men with women for president and vice-president.) The negative interpretation of the same data leads to the conclusion that as little girls approach puberty their ascendancy over the boys, who develop social and communicative skills more slowly, disappears, to be replaced by passivity and participation only in an ancillary capacity, in proportion as they become aware of and involved in sexual activity.

The price Cuban women pay for teenage sexual activity is very high; analysis of statistics supplied in the Anuario Estadistico de Cuba (1981) shows that not only were nearly 52,000 of the nation's 187,500-odd births in 1976 to mothers aged between fifteen and nineteen, a further 10,000 of the total were unaccounted for, probably to mothers below the age of fifteen, the only category not specifically mentioned. Abortions have settled at about 100,000 per year, and about a quarter of them are carried out on women under nineteen; more than 400,000 girls of less than nineteen years old are already married, accounting for the largest proportion of divorces, currently running at about 3.2 per thousand per year, while marriages stand at about 13 per thousand. Of the nation's 3,371,000 women over fifteen, about 1,400,000 are legally married, while half as many are living in informal unions. Of Cuba's 575,000 or so girls under nineteen, 52,000 are already legally married, while 87,000 are living with a man and a further

25,000 describe themselves as divorced or separated. The data are incomplete, but they point to a situation in which young women find themselves with domestic and family responsibilities just at the time when they should be gaining professional experience and qualifications. To the problems of evolving sexuality and the contradictoriness of the female role as both active comrade and sex object, are added the divided attention of the young mother and the unavoidable drain upon her time and energy. The state gives all the help that legislation can provide with free birth control, free abortion on demand, and free day-care facilities, but it cannot alter the emotional reality of juvenile marriage, parenthood and divorce and the young women's own attitudes towards them. Babies are accepted in day care from forty-five days old, but mothers are not and should not be constrained to give them up for twelve hours a day, an impossibility in any case if they wish to breast-feed.

It must not be thought that it has taken an outsider to detect the series of interlocking factors militating against women's full incorporation in the development of the Cuban state. The FMC is a high relief organization, with vociferous representation at all levels of local and provincial, and state administration. *Las federadas* are known throughout the country, and although their demands may cause consternation, as does their present campaign to allow husbands to be granted leave from work to accompany sick children in hospital, it is understood that they will eventually have to be met. Cuba's commitment to the full social, political and economic equality of women is a fundamental aspect of Cuban socialism. In so far as the system is not one of draconian imposition but of pragmatic accommodation of the people's will and transformation of social realities at a pace with which the ordinary people who are the ultimate cause and purpose of the revolutionary process can keep up, women's full emergence into political life depends upon their own redefinition of their life aims with a consequent alteration of the psychopathology of everyday life. Put in the simplest terms, this means that women will have to demand more of men.

There are some indications that the Young Communists are leading the way in this. In sex education discussion groups involving both sexes it is generally agreed that emotional relationships should be built on a more intimate and committed basis. Cuban feminists have begun to reject the idea that men should help with women's work, and have begun to demand sharing all aspects of family building, involving men much more in the activities of parenting than has traditionally been the case. It is understood that progress towards women's equality is a struggle against entrenched attitudes and obsolete but enduring concepts of appropriate sex roles. An older Cuban man may tell you that he accepts the idea of his responsibility towards his children and their mother or mothers, and yet give curiously vague answers to direct enquiries about how often he sees his children and how much time he spends with them. He may tell you that his wife accepts his absenteeism and his sporting attitude to extramarital conquests, but it is unlikely that his wife will agree with him. The *delegadas* stoutly maintain that as women have economic independence they no longer have to tolerate humiliation and would reject any husband whose infidelity was discovered, but their anxiety about male fickleness could not be concealed. When I argued that male adultery was impossible without serious flaws in female solidarity, they refused to see the point. They would not agree either that if women were really monogamous, men would be unable to find partners for adultery or that men's promiscuity was anything but 'natural'. *El es hombre* is the sexist explanation they give for male perfidy. They could not see that women's vulnerability to men's infidelity was an aspect of sexual colonialism. The Cuban woman has all her emotional eggs in one basket; she is a psychic one-crop economy, direly threatened by male sanctions, in particular the withdrawal of affection and intimacy, but the suggestion that she protect herself by cultivating other kinds of emotional satisfaction and other sources of esteem was not taken. There was very little emphasis placed by the FMC on sisterhood. No one ever discussed the single woman, a rare creature in Cuba in any event.

There is an inherent contradiction in Cuba between the socialist ideals of the revolution and the bourgeois paradigm of the nuclear family which is what most Cubans take as the basic unit of the modern state. In the nuclear family the child is confronted by only two adults contrasted by sex. The tendency towards polarization is unavoidable. The duplication of effort in the nuclear family is directly connected to the family's role as the principal unit of consumption in consumer society. Each household is destined to acquire a complete set of all the consumer durables considered necessary for the good life and per caput consumption is therefore maintained at its highest level. In sex, as in consumption, the nuclear family emphasizes possession and exclusivity at the expense of the kinds of emotional relationships that work for co-operation and solidarity. Even the best-educated Cubans seem unaware of the arguments of Marx and Engels against monogamy. They regret the instability of marriage, and work towards enculturating young people to delay the formation of exclusive sexual partnerships until they should be mature enough to undertake long-term commitment, when perhaps they ought to be spending more time reducing the psychic damage done to young people, young women especially, by the breakdown of these early relationships, so that they are less vulnerable in future. One of the heroines of the revolution, Haydee Santamaria, killed herself after her husband began a public affair with a younger, more glamorous woman. Although she was founder of the Casa de las Americas, and widely respected throughout Latin America, she could not recover from this blow to her self-esteem; yet Cuban feminism shows no signs of any attempt to reduce women's psychic dependence upon their success in heterosexual relationships by strengthening camaraderie among women or teaching them that in order to live with men they must learn to live without them. As the standard of living rises, women's work increases and their dependence upon the sexual relationship with their husbands will increase as households diminish in size.

There are difficult days ahead for the Cuban woman, but as long as the ideology of revolution is lively and sincere, ways will be devised to deal with the new stresses. In the meantime Cuba remains the only country in the world where women may take a job they wish to do at the same rate of pay as a man, earn any qualification they are prepared to study for, carry their own weapon in the army and rise to the rank of colonel, dress as they please and accept or refuse men's attentions as they please, terminate or continue a pregnancy as they think fit, knowing that they will have help to carry out whichever course they should decide to follow. Perhaps the true extent of women's power in Cuba is best illustrated not by quoting numbers on the Central Committee, but in a homely example which shows how important women are to Cuba. Every sexually active woman in Cuba at risk of contracting cervical cancer is given her smear test at least every two years. Every year hundreds of women's lives are saved by prompt treatment, while in England, Equal Opportunities Commission or no, women are dying because they have not had their smears, because they did not have them often enough, and because they were not informed when the cells were seen to be abnormal. The British health service could not cope with the demand if all the women who should, asked for smear tests and presented for further treatment. Yet little Cuba manages it. Follow-up and recall are carried out at the street level by the FMC and the Committee for the Defence of the Revolution, while the state institutions supply the technical facilities. This may not be evidence of power as it is commonly perceived by capitalist societies, but access to the technology in order to save your own life is the kind of power women want. It is real power, unlike the authoritarian fantasies that pass for power in most of the world. And the women of Cuba struggled for it, defined it and exercise it on their own behalf. It remains to be seen now whether Cuban women will raise their own standard in the world forum and show the other emergent nations how to harness the strength and tenderness of women in the remaking of our tired and guilty world. As Cuba's leaders have always realized, survival is too desperate a matter to be left to half the world's population. We need to see federations of women of every nationality mobilizing in the streets of every city, town and village in the world, *para trabajar, para estudiar, para construir nuestra libertad!*

Resettlement, Ethiopia, 1985

Unpublished

Like an ant dragging a dead beetle up one side of a grass blade and down the other, I spent the entire month of February struggling to put together a return trip to Ethiopia, with no clearer idea than the ant has of what was driving me on. Regular telephone calls from Richard Pankhurst, Ethiopia's historiographer, and encouragement from writers like Graham Hancock and Andrew Lycett, who were as disgusted as I with the daily coverage of events in Ethiopia, were spurs that I hardly needed. Eventually I succeeded in putting together a television package, yet when it fell apart the day after my arrival in Addis, I wasn't particularly disappointed. My commission from the *Observer* was hardly less shaky, but I wilfully concealed my misgivings from myself and embarked on an in-depth study of resettlement when a moment's reflection would have warned me of the utter unlikeliness of the *Observer*'s publishing any such thing.

In December I had made the usual press trip to Ethiopia, forcing myself to watch people die, following the corpses to the washing place and the burial ground, while my photographer looked for the most stick-like limbs and the biggest eyes, in our bid to keep up the emotional pressure on a fickle public. A Danish Red Cross worker called the media binge on pictures of the dead and dying 'the pornography of famine'. The public was hooked on it; you can't sell a picture of a healthy, smiling Ethiopian for love or money, as I was to find out. Relief, recovery, rehabilitation, development – all smack of anticlimax. By the end of December, even food distribution was no longer a story. The only newsworthy events occurred when the Ethiopians screwed up in some all too predictable way, as happened, for example, at Ibnat, where overzealous officials, in a ham-fisted attempt to get the famine victims to return to their own areas in time to take advantage of the *belg* rains and remove a focus of epidemic disease in their area, burned down their straw tukuls.

Bored or exhausted after our brief orgasm of altruism, we seemed to be willing Ethiopians to fail. The spontaneous reaction of ordinary people to the spectacle of such terrible suffering borne with such dignity had become poisoned by institutional distrust and contempt. The emphasis was distorted: Ethiopia was taking flak for blunders made in the course of a genuine attempt to prevent deaths from famine, when Brazil, said to have let three million people die without making a move to help them, got off scot-free.

What was in question was the Ethiopians' commitment to seeing that such a catastrophe could never occur again. The only way to assess it was to examine, not only the highly visible feeding centres which were all most people knew of the struggle against hunger, but the whole spectrum of rehabilitation activity, and in particular the massive resettlement scheme upon which the Relief and Rehabilitation Commission embarked eight years ago, now hitting full stream.

Press visas were limited to ten days, hopelessly too short a time to get any impression of the vastness of the scheme. The Ethiopians are such novices in the art of manipulation of public opinion that they imagined that by limiting access they would decrease the scope for disinformation when in fact they increased it. More and more stories were based on the gossip to be heard any evening in the lounge bar of the Addis Ababa Hilton. I had already heard and read too much about resettlement from people who had never seen it. My first job was to secure a month's visa, the next to get permission to travel anywhere I wanted in Ethiopia. The first was relatively easy; the second was granted in principle. Making that principle work involved doggedness and ruthlessness and finally a great deal of my own money.

I left London on April Fools' Day. I was eight days into my month, about 700 kilometres south-west of Addis, before I understood anything of my own motivation. I was on my way to Asosa, the biggest resettlement project. From all I had read, except a report by Clifford May in *Newsday* which seemed too good to be true, I was half-convinced that resettlement was at best a fraud, at worst a fearful ordeal, worse even than the Falashas' desperate trek to starvation camps in the Sudanese desert. As our Landcruiser cannoned round a bend in a slew of stones and dust, three girls suddenly appeared before us, squealing and dancing up and down on their toes. I knew their blue dresses and the style of their symmetrical hair-braiding. They were from Welo, 1,200 kilometres away, where I had seen girls just like these in feeding centres. There, those straight noses were thin as knife blades, those bright eyes sunk deep into the skull, and those even white teeth too often bared in the rictus of death.

At first I had some confused idea that they had been raised from the dead. 'What are you doing here?' I asked stupidly. 'We're *safarioch*,' they said, tickled pink at my stupefaction. I kept on staring at them, practically speechless with surprise that there would be young women among the settlers and that they would have recovered teenage high spirits so quickly. In December, I watched big sisters like these lugging their little brothers and sisters for intensive feeding, helping and consoling their mothers and fathers, gravely confronting life's most intractable mystery.

Now here they were giggling at my peculiar clothes and the size of my hands and feet and ears.

'*Ama se gnalo,*' I kept saying. 'Thank you.' It was the only Amharic phrase I knew, but it was all I needed. The cold weight that had been lying on my heart since December was beginning to thaw. The spring of hope began to flow again. Then I knew why I had abandoned my work schedule and thrown deadlines to the winds. My need to find an alternative to slow death and impersonal kindness from strangers had driven me to these lengths. If I felt it so strongly, how much more strongly must they?

To get to Asosa, you climb out of the steamy cauldron through which the Dabus makes its way to join the Blue Nile, up to 1,500 feet or so, lowlands by Ethiopian computation. Silver-leafed ground cover glows blue against the blood-red earth. In the groins of the rolling tableland flow fast, full streams. The wild mango trees dotting the skyline show the water table to be high. In April the mango fruits were beginning to ripen, hanging like heavy lumps of polished soapstone at the ends of their strings, motionless while a cool breeze stirred the leaves.

The first sign of the resettlement area was a vast ploughed expanse, visible from miles away, intersected by bands of shiny elephant grass, like contour lines across the slopes, to prevent soil loss through run-off. Gangs of men hacking out the scrub with mattocks and machetes, straightened up and hooted a greeting as we swept past at the head of our column of red dust.

Among the familiar fine-featured brown faces I saw some unfamiliar blue-black ones with very pink-and-white smiles. Occasionally I glimpsed tall, almost naked women standing in compounds where everything, walls, grain bins, doors and screens, was made of plaited canes like wickerwork, expertly dovetailed and symmetrical in an architecture perfectly adapted to climatic conditions and available materials, for the long canes grow wild along the Dabus. The builders of these exquisite tukuls are the Jablawi, the indigenous inhabitants of this part of Welega province. Watching them working alongside the new arrivals, paid in food for work, I had part of the answer to one of the concerns expressed by the international community about resettlement schemes in general and the Ethiopian scheme in particular. I didn't question the Jablawi, which would have been pointless as I would have had to do it through two interpreters only too clearly associated with the authorities, but preferred to watch them as they interacted with the settlers. They seemed to be enjoying themselves and the increased social and economic activity the settlers had brought with them. Many of the settlers, who were arriving in April at the rate of about 25,000 a week, are unfit for work at first, and the Jablawi are needed more than ever. The established settlers buy calves and chickens from them, and are learning Jablawi construction techniques, while the Jablawi pop up everywhere, joining the patients waiting for the dresser or the paramedic, barracking at the football games and learning the new methods of cultivation and conservation. At the soccer game I encountered a small Tigrayan with a Jablawi throwing stick. When I asked what he was doing with it, Comrade Kumilachew, Asosa (Resettlement) Branch Secretary of the Workers' Party of Ethiopia, ex-schoolteacher, replied, 'Cultural exchange.'

Doubtless there were Jablawi who resented the arrival of thousands of ragged starvelings with their attendant diseases, but it was in the nature of the case that I didn't see them, for there are still thousands of hectares of bush for them to vanish into. The Ethiopian authorities proceed with unusual sensitivity, for the first step in opening up new areas is to provide schools where the local children may be taught in their own language. (The Ethiopian literacy campaign is conducted in fifteen languages.)

The settlement areas around Gambela in Ilubabor are protected by the indigenous Anuak, proud of their spotless militia uniforms and their cosseted old rifles. Lions can be heard at night and elephants have already trampled the settlers' huts. All the protective instincts of the Anuak are called forth by the settlers, who seem skinnier and paler than ever next to these shining blue-black, astonishingly tall and straight-backed people, who can teach them to grow stronger bones on a diet of fish which they take in traps in the many streams of the Baro system. The Anuak are astonishingly clean: an Anuak woman will go naked rather than put on a soiled dress. The settlers could profit by their example. Anuak compounds, graceful clusters of open-walled tukuls round communal threshing floors, have sprung up close to the new tube wells, for none appreciates the clean water more than the Anuak.

In some parts of Ethiopia, the indigenous peasants have run their own resettlement projects. In Horo Gudro the peasants' associations have absorbed 8,402 families, 28,890 people in all, for whom they have built tukuls and to whom they have given 800 oxen. Food is usually supplied to settlers by the Relief and Rehabilitation Commission because, obviously, the newcomers need to be fed until their own crops are adequate, although the international press corps seems to disapprove, as it continues to lament the 'massive' amounts of food 'diverted' to famine victims who have taken the settlement option. In Horo Gudro, however, the locals have taken the responsibility of feeding the new arrivals.

Such initiatives are only possible because of the development of the peasants' associations which are changing the face of Ethiopia. After the land reforms enacted by the revolutionary government, land use tended to fragment even further as each farmer was given parcels of every kind of land to be found within each association's 800 hectares. The disadvantages of such a system soon became obvious. After 'agitation' by party cadres and agricultural extension workers, new systems of co-operative farming, a notion not essentially alien to people who had always followed kin-based systems of temporary land allocation, were adopted. Now, one of the typical and astonishing sights in Ethiopia is a team of fifty or so oxen, moving in synchrony across the slopes, ploughing fields of five or six acres. The results in terms of the Ethiopian landscape are spectacular. A World Bank official told me that he expects Ethiopia to solve its food problem in ten years, and has recommended that a World Bank scheme of rolling credit for the purchase of oxen be more than doubled. The Swedish International Development Authority, after an assessment tour in April, has increased its commitment from ten to twenty-four million dollars.

Resettlement is the most condemned of all the policies of Ethiopia's embattled administration, although, or perhaps because, most of its critics know nothing whatever about it. Resettlement is generally taken to be a draconian measure to reduce population pressure in drought-affected areas, to populate border areas in the interests of national security and to undermine the power base of the rebel movements in the north. Clearly all these considerations have some weight with the PMAC, but neither in terms of historical fact, nor in the priorities of the RRC officials and party workers involved in the day-to-day administration of the schemes, do they have any relevance. Ever since the disastrous famine of 1973–4, and the localized famines that followed and continue to follow, resettlement has been carefully considered as one of the options in a strategy to abolish famine in Ethiopia. Only about a quarter of the good arable land available is actually cultivated. As the Ethiopian Mapping Institute continued its work of survey after the revolution, suitable areas for resettlement were identified and study teams sent out to assess their potential.

The first settlers arrived in the pilot project in Asosa in 1977; they were 144 'family heads', that is, unaccompanied males. We can probably safely assume that they were used as work gangs in conditions that we might consider fairly antisocial, although not more so than those commonly endured by seasonal workers such as cane cutters and shearers, or, for that matter, coffee pickers. Farmers living in areas of recurrent drought were used to walking from the northern highlands to Kefa, to make enough cash by coffee picking to return and keep their families at subsistence level until they could expect a harvest. As desertification in the north increased, the number of workers arriving in coffee-growing areas began to exceed the demand, at the same time as the coffee export price was falling. The Asosa option was by no means a soft one, but the men who arrived in 1977 probably chose it. The next year, 5,844 male family heads arrived, along with 300 women, also described as family heads. At this stage, the project directors were clearly making problems for themselves, in trying to run the project like a barracks. The Ethiopian peasant household is a unit; without the labour of women in fetching water and fuel and the lengthy preparation of food, let alone in growing vegetables and raising chickens and marketing, a peasant's life is comfortless. The early settlers were restless and their commitment to the success of the project began to flag. The women and children left at home often refused to make the journey to join them. Some of the settlers began to walk away, and, contrary to popular prejudice, there was nothing the authorities could do to stop them. Of 1,800 Tigrayans settled at Anger Guten in 1979, more than 1,300 walked back to Tigray where, seeing as they came from land considered exhausted in 1979, they have probably perished.

In 1979, the Relief and Rehabilitation Commission announced a massive scheme for the development of eighty-four resettlement units. The areas had been selected for topography and soil type as suitable for cultivation, as well as for potable water supply, disease control and access. Each unit was to consist of a cluster of villages of 500 families each, together with a farmed area of up to two hectares per household. For a country as poor as Ethiopia the scheme was staggeringly costly, but it went ahead, surveying, road-making, clearing, ploughing, until it has now cost eighty-seven million birr, a formidable investment for a poor country at war. The settlers' houses are built for them, out of materials locally available, by students, party workers and local residents, most of them working overtime without pay. The houses are what most of Ethiopia's population lives in, tukuls constructed on poles driven into the ground, with earthen floors where the cooking fire stays in day and night. The smoke cures the thatch of the roof on its way through; ventilation is drawn through the straw or bamboo or lath- and mud-plastered walls. In Asosa they had incorporated some modest improvements, hanging shelves to keep clothes and food off the floor, and a raised platform for sleeping, but otherwise the tukuls were like most of the tukuls in Ethiopia, without furniture, without means of lighting, without privacy. The most treasured of the settlers' belongings are, as in the rest of Ethiopia, yellow plastic butter-oil bottles from Holland, which, carefully threaded on sticks, are carried to the stream for water each day; the soy-bean oil tins marked 'Gift of the Citizens of the United States' that are used to hold butter oil bought in the local market; and the Canada wheat bags that hold anything but Canadian wheat. The RRC sells relief food containers on the open market: the butter-oil bottles fetch four birr each, the sacks and tins two. The sacks are split to make carrier bags or stuffed with straw for palliasses. Every single thing foreign aid brings to Ethiopia is exploited to the maximum; nothing whatever is wasted. Non-biodegradable plastics are not a curse here, but a treasure. The poverty of the RRC causes serious problems, but it also constitutes a protection, for the settlers cannot be seen to be favoured above the indigenous population, than which none in the world is poorer. As it is, settlers and locals struggle together for increased economic opportunity, and their circumstances improve mutually, if very gradually, as they sell and barter goods and services between themselves. Each tukul is set in 1,000 square millimetres of private plot, and the produce of that, whether eggs, pepper, *chat*, coffee, bananas, beans, lentils, tomatoes or potatoes, is the peasants' to do with as they please.

In the third year, nearly half the new arrivals at Asosa were wives and children. By 1980, wives and children outnumbered arriving family heads. In the last eight months, when something of the order of 200,000 settlers have arrived in Asosa, two thirds of the total are accompanying family members. In fact, most complete families have more than three members; the figure still contains a proportion of men without women and children, especially among Tigrayans. There are now seventeen settlement units in various stages of development, covering a total area of 20,000 hectares, including farmland, villages and parkland for grazing, in an area stretching from fourteen kilometres east of Asosa town to twenty-two kilometres west. Altogether, more than 62,000 households had been resettled in Welega province by mid-April, about two-thirds of them from Welo, a third from Tigray and 1,500 or so from Eritrea. In all resettlement areas in Welega, Gojjam and Ilubabor, resettlement should continue at the rate of about 100,000 people a month, a total of a million and a half by the end of the year. The sudden acceleration in the pace of the actual movement of people might give the impression that the whole scheme is a hasty improvisation, when it is actually the climax of years of planning and preparation. This is not to say that the absorption of new arrivals does not present problems. The poverty of the RRC, the social and financial burden of commandeering half the country's bus services to ferry settlers, the shortage of vehicles for the transportation of the food supplies needed by the new settlers (and in fact for almost all the settlers), the diversion of hundreds of tractor operators from state farms and other enterprises to plough the farmlands in the settlement areas and train peasants to carry on, the shortage of bulldozers and other heavy machinery, the small number of drilling rigs for tube wells, all these factors have thrown the settlers and the workers, many of whom are volunteers, back on their own devices.

The methods and aims which RRC officials and party workers involved in resettlement practise and profess have doubtless been influenced by the Bale experience. In 1980 severe social disruption was caused in the province of Bale by the flight of peasants from war and famine in the southern area along the border with Somalia. In this case, UNICEF was actively involved in the design and administration of a scheme of orderly resettlement involving 300,000 people. This massive operation has been accounted a complete success; the new settlers in the north of Bale are now considered self-sufficient, although the mechanization of their agriculture is causing problems. UNICEF still gives 'aid to settlers' although prevented from giving support to resettlement schemes as such, principally because if the settlements are to be run as state farms, they must be considered to be essentially profit-making bodies and hence ineligible for UNICEF assistance. Oxfam is also involved in special projects involving settlers. The general feeling among those few NGOs with any first-hand knowledge of Ethiopian resettlement is that the denial of development funding to the Ethiopian government, in particular the denial of support for resettlement as a bona fide attempt to restore the peasantry to dignity and self-sufficiency, is malicious and destructive. For some months, delegates of the League of Red Cross Societies have been making representations in Geneva for permission to give more active help to drought victims who have chosen the resettlement option, so far without success.

The Ethiopian authorities are to some extent responsible for the animosity aroused by the mere mention of resettlement. To begin with, they had no idea of how such a scheme should have been presented to the international community. In the struggle to maintain a degree of autonomy and to realize their own priorities, they managed to alienate the international aid organizations, just at the time when they most needed direct technical co-operation in pest and disease control. As long as the international community insisted on conditions being created for settlers which did not exist for most Ethiopians and were beyond the means of the public purse in any event, their co-operation was out of the question. Ethiopians find apologizing and explaining at least as difficult as the English do, and their unwillingness to beg for support was intensified by the antics of the international press corps in the first days of the emergency relief operation.

Nobody knows to this day where the *Sunday Times* got a story, which it did not scruple to publish, that the Ethiopian government had sold a significant proportion of the teff crop to the Soviet Union for distilling vodka. The story of the container ship full of Scotch whisky which docked at the same time as the first relief supplies, was by contrast true, but although it has run in every Western news organ and is still current, the real situation has never been explained. To the press corps in the Addis Ababa Hilton, still drinking the Scotch and paying for it exorbitantly in hard currency, the explanation must be obvious. Smuggling is a way of life in Ethiopia, where a constant revenue haemorrhage fuels Djibouti, while all government projects founder for lack of hard currency, without which essentials like petrol and spare parts cannot be got. In an attempt to milk the contraband traffic the government tried to turn bootlegger, only to be caught taking its first shipment of liquor. As it turned out, the government priced the Scotch in its duty-free shops too high, and the smugglers kept their customers, offering a service that was very much more convenient and hardly more expensive. Moreover, the government had done no market research and had acquired brands which were not popular. Instead of hard currency, the Scotch earned a year of the worst kind of publicity.

So much went into the resettlement projects that the possibility of some such serendipitous sabotage could not be countenanced. The RRC and the PMAC followed a policy of keeping the foreign press away from them altogether, thus creating an atmosphere of guilt and secrecy. Keeping the newshounds away was easier than it should have been, for the journalists were apparently content to entertain lurid hypotheses. No serious attempt was made to pressure the authorities to open up, and probably never would have been, unless of course the word got around that spectacular scenes of peasant bashing were to be witnessed. The first settlers I encountered could have been watched by any journalist who was interested, for they travelled through Addis Ababa in a conspicuous convoy of 123 buses, preceded and followed by motorcycle police on showy BMWs with blue lights flashing and sirens blaring. On almost any day in Addis, you will find special traffic police waiting to hold up cross-town traffic to let the settler convoys pass.

For the exorbitant and illegal price of two birr (a dollar by the official rate of exchange) a blue and white taxi took me to Alem Gena, where I watched for two hours as the 8,000 people on the 123 buses on their way from Kembata in Woleita to Metekel in Gojjam were given fresh bread for their lunch, and had their water supplies replenished. A doctor was on hand to give emergency aid, until they should arrive in their overnight shelter at Debre Marcos. While I was interviewing the drivers, most of whom had been driving settlers solidly for the last three months, an old cowherd came quietly up and stood sniffing the scent of the new-baked bread. He asked if he might help distribute it in return for a loaf for himself. Gravely, the drivers' assistants listened to his request; they could have worked faster without him, but they let him take the corner of a sack of loaves and run with them down the interminable line of buses. Twice he dashed up and down with them, skinny legs pumping, rags flapping. Then, with dignity, he accepted two loaves and walked back up the hill to earn his nickel a day per beast for minding other people's cows.

The convoy was one of the most stirring sights I have ever seen. When I tried to describe it to a TV journalist he interrupted, 'Did you see the Kalashnikovs?' One of the reasons I went to Alem Gena was to see if settlers were prevented from leaving the buses and if there was any attempt to terrorize or coerce them.

Watching teenage girls in Red Cross aprons trying to distribute water in half a dozen plastic beakers to 8,000 people had given me rather more to think about. The only Kalashnikov I saw was being held upside-down on its webbing strap by a policeman on the grass verge. I said so and the TV journalist shook his head, pitying my girlish naïvety. 'They use the small

Kalashnikov,' he said. He thrust a hand into the back of his designer jeans. 'They stick them down here.' The hypothesis was ridiculous. I had seen dozens of settlers desirous of relieving themselves squatting out of sight of the buses. If they chose to walk away there was little any gun could do to stop them. Crowds are not controlled by hidden guns. One shot after a fleeing settler and 123 buses would empty faster than any number of guns could cover them. The only people who could have carried Kalashnikovs, large or small, would have been the drivers' assistants, whose job is to check oil and water and air pressure, change tyres, dig buses out of rock falls, mud slides and ditches and relay settlers' requests to the drivers. I pointed out that there is little point in cluttering up the back of your underpants with a small Kalashnikov if you are wearing a boiler suit, but the point was not taken.

The question of 'voluntariness' in resettlement is complicated. Drought victims inspire a good deal of possessiveness on the part of those who care for them, who are slow to realize how irksome and even unbearable they may find such care. In one day at Asaita, the shelter authorities watched a quarter of the Afars being tended there uproot their families and make for the upland grazing, because it had rained in the hills. Many of the weakest family members must have died, but there was little the shelter administration could do to stop them, for Ethiopian famine shelters have no perimeter fences and no army of guards to stop people coming and going (unlike, say, British holding centres for Vietnamese refugees in Hong Kong). The decision to move is usually taken by the 'family head', most often a man and the strongest surviving member of the group. The decision is almost never unanimous. Throughout the journey the family mulls over the decision with tears, pleas to reconsider, dark prognostications of disaster and a general distrust of the outsiders who have come up with the suggestion of resettlement. If the travellers on the 123 buses had been euphoric, I should have suspected that resettlement had been presented to them as a cushy option, or that Eritrean claims that each family is promised an ox were true. Certainly the settlers are told that the land they are going to is fertile, but so it is. As I clambered around the buses, trying not to trample the skinny limbs of people who, having never sat on chairs in their lives, could not stay put on the slippery bus seats and gravitated naturally to the floor, I longed to reassure them and see some easing of the tension in their faces. The RRC official in charge of the stopover simply said, 'They are leaving their homeland,' and made no attempt to jolly them up or patronize them.

The Relief and Rehabilitation Commission must itself take some responsibility for the persistence of wilful disinformation about resettlement. Despite a showy three-piece, pin-stripe exterior, the RRC 'Public Relations' department is lazy, incompetent and disorganized. After a week of waiting for my itinerary and travel permits to be organized, during which I haunted the RRC PRO's office, when I finally got to Asosa, my arrival was totally unexpected. The project director was 'in the field' and his subordinates, who had never seen a journalist at Asosa before, were not at all sure that they should offer me accommodation. The project director, run ragged coping with the arrival of 25,000 settlers a week, some of them in pretty wobbly condition, would have been perfectly justified in refusing to put himself at the disposal of an unannounced visitor; my journey of 700 kilometres over unmade roads could well have been in vain. I was eventually given a bed in the RRC guesthouse where there was neither water nor light. The key to the toilet block could not be found. Even in the town, we could not find anything to eat.

At dawn next morning I was awoken by a terrific clangour which turned out to be made by a flock of red-eyed pigeons dancing on the tin roof of the guesthouse. I watched as the RRC workers emerged from the army tents they are housed in and wandered off into the elephant grass with their toilet paper. Then they washed their faces and cleaned their teeth, using a scant jam-tin of water, respectfully averting their eyes from the solitary foreign female coated with red dust, sitting on the guesthouse steps watching them. Later, someone came shyly to ask if I would like to share their breakfast of black tea and an army biscuit. By seven o'clock they had all gone off on truck beds and tractors to work. Clearly Asosa was far from being a soft option for them either, but they went to their work with a will.

Comrade Tesfaye, project director, was happy to have me see anything I cared to, but, as my presence was still unofficial, we had to consult the local branch of the Workers' Party of Ethiopia, Resettlement Section. We found it in a hut made of thatched straw. Comrade Kumilachew rose from his desk of canes laid across poles driven into the earth and put himself at my service. Then they both turned to me and asked, 'What would you like to see?' The itinerary we followed was completely spontaneous, for it consisted of me uttering whatever came into my head, and the driver turning the wheel and plunging down yet another farmtrack, past churches, mosques and clinics – all tukuls – nursery beds, vegetable gardens, model tukuls, riverside laundries, the forge, the charcoal–burning class, the pottery school, the football pitch, the tailoring school. At the horticulture project we surprised a young Tigrayan taking a bath in the little dam. As his loincloth was drying on a bush twenty yards away, he had to crouch in the knee-deep water until I had finished inspecting carrots and silver beet, onions and cabbages.

Nobody had the faintest idea that I was there to be impressed. They all assumed that I had come to help, and poured out all their grievances, which had nothing to do with their own discomforts, and all to do with the job they had come so far to do. The nurse practitioner in his tukul clinic gave me a list of the medications he was lacking. His worst problem was that acute cases had to be carried on litters to the Russian 'mobile' hospital which was firmly anchored in tents in Asosa town. The Russian hospital was the one thing I was not allowed to see, on the grounds of 'communicable disease' the Russians said. Certainly I saw far too many litters converging on Asosa town; the new arrivals had clearly brought diarrhoeal disease with them. I thought rather angrily of all the four-wheel-drive vehicles parked outside the Addis Ababa Hilton, as we passed the sweating litter-bearers trotting along the farm tracks fifteen kilometres or so from the town.

Asosa resettlement project already produces 3,000 kilos of honey a year by modern, rational methods. The hives, painted cadmium yellow, stand in gardens full of Evening Primrose and a furry variety of Catmint. The beekeepers, nearly all trained settlers, asked me for seeds of new plants to try, and took me to see their Black Medick, which was not doing so well. There was nothing for it but to discuss the possibility that they were giving it too much water and at the wrong time of day, embarrassed as I might feel at being taken for something more immediately useful than a mere journalist. On the edge of the irrigation channel I found a sinister yellow plant I know only too well. 'What is it?' they asked anxiously. 'It ruined our *noog* crop.' *Noog* (*Guizottia abyssinica* if you're interested) is one of the typical aromas in Ethiopian cooking; the failure of this crop is rather crucial for morale. The weed was Dodder (*Cuscuta europaea*). I told them the botanical name so that they could ask the international agencies for help, but I thought that any British gardener who could see how hard and how earnestly both the settlers and the RRC workers were trying, would have done whatever he could to have shortened the odds against them.

To the administrators in Addis, the notion of opening up 'virgin' land is intensely romantic; in fact virgin land produces plagues unheard of in areas of settled cultivation. I noticed that the legs of the beehives were stood in potsherds full of ash. 'Termites,' said the Forestry Officer, a waif who looked as if he could do with some supplementary feeding himself. The avenues of shade trees and clumps of windbreak he had planted were pitted by gaps, termites again. The settlers' tukuls, the storehouses, fifty per cent of the crops after harvest and even wooden bridges across streams are all being eaten by termites. In January 1984, the FAO conducted a survey and trained RRC officers to apply Aldrin in solution to the termite mounds, without endangering either the settlers or their bees or themselves. In December, Michael Miller, seconded from Oxfam to work as Special Projects Director for the RRC, wrote to Shell in Amsterdam to order $500,000 worth of Aldrin, and has never been answered. Without hard currency there is probably no deal, and the little Forestry Officer will have to look on as the settlers' houses continue to collapse within a year. He asked me if I could find seeds of more termite-resistant species besides the *Grevillea robusta* that he was planting everywhere, and I made another note. In fact the entire region selected for development from Asosa down to Jinka in Gamu Gofa is infested with termites. There are those who say with a sniff, 'Well, there you are. They shouldn't be resettling those areas then,' as if the world should be left to the thousand million ants that dwell in it, an argument unlikely to find favour with an Australian. Yet when I suggested that there was a case for direct technical co-operation with the Australian Forestry Commission, especially in the supply of termite-resistant species, an Australian official in Addis laughed at me.

In almost every aspect of the resettlement project, the problems were the same. A massive investment of work and energy from RRC workers and settlers alike was being nullified by lack of resources. Men and women were being trained in tailoring shops on machines supplied by UNICEF but the total cloth allowance for the 62,000 families resettled in Welega is less than a metre per family. The tailoring remains an academic exercise. Abesha Ferede, Women's Affairs Officer of Asosa, explained, 'Dress is not a priority.' It was the more remarkable that settlers who after months of gruelling work were still wearing the rags they had arrived in, were still optimistic and cheerful. There were babies everywhere. The women peeping from the doorways smiled when I did. Every small plot was tilled and planted. The adult education classes were full, even though the teachers were settlers themselves, unskilled in pedagogic arts, equipped with nothing but blackboard, chalk and a few tattered textbooks.

If you ask party workers and RRC officers what their primary objective is, they invariably reply, 'To save life.' Their principal responsibility is to keep the settlers fed and healthy. Food supplies are erratic, because resettlement must compete for the few vehicles that the RRC has at its own disposal. Vehicles donated by foreign aid organizations for famine relief may not be used to victual famine victims who have chosen resettlement. Nevertheless, a recent survey by the League of Red Cross Societies found that children in resettlement villages had a better weight-for-length ratio than children in control villages nearby, although the RRC has been able to distribute only wheat grain as food rations. The ration is more than a child can eat, but parents are not prevented from bartering the surplus for other necessities if and when they are available on the open market. Disease control is more of a problem, especially in Asosa, where the settlers must use surface water for drinking and cooking. The fact that all water must be fetched and carried uphill to the houses, limits the amount of washing the people are disposed to do, and flies cluster on dirty clothes and skin. The RRC does not have enough drill rigs to sink tube wells in each settlement, let alone each village. Storage tanks, such as the one being built by Oxfam at Dese transit shelter, are beyond the RRC's means. The consequences of lack of clean water supply are no worse for the settlers than they are for the majority of Ethiopians, but the settlers arrive in a particularly vulnerable condition.

The next priority in resettlement projects is the achievement of self-sufficiency, so that the impossibly expensive food lift from RRC warehouses can cease. This aim is still out of sight. Crops at Asosa must be weeded every fifteen days. To each has come its own plague: the teff, the most important cash crop, is massacred by cutworm. The sorghum is beset by rust, the wheat by mildew, and termites eat what little is harvested when it is in store. On the one hand, new varieties suitable for cultivation in relatively humid lowland, faster growing and able to defend themselves against opportunist weeds, must be developed, and on the other, the officers already trained in pest control need the equipment and the pesticide to do it. Some of the current research in biological methods of termite control could be being carried out in resettlement areas in Ethiopia.

A third priority is conservation. This year the Asosa Forestry Officer will plant more than two million seedlings. Project workers constantly stress the need for economy in the use of firewood, but when the fire is the only source of light in the tukul in the evenings, there is no realistic possibility that the people will take to the use of the closed fuel-conserving stoves they have been taught to make out of local clay. The depredations of the termites in the tree plantations are therefore doubly disastrous. Every farmer has been taught to use conservation methods, leaving uncultivated strips across the slopes to minimize run-off in the ploughed fields, ditching and draining in the pasturelands. Goats are completely banned and the ban is reinforced by the peasants' committees. Hunting is illegal for most Ethiopians; the peasants in Asosa use their guns for crop protection.

Before I left Asosa, I made a courtesy visit to take my leave of the local WPE branch. The Ideological Officer and the Women's Affairs Officer listened impassively as my minder from RRC Public Relations orated in Amharic for twenty minutes, then turned to me and asked, in perfect English, what I thought of their resettlement effort. I was about to make a formal answer, when I realized that they really cared. For some reason their earnestness threw me, and I began to stammer all the wrong kinds of words ... problems, difficulties, poverty, insurmountable odds ... It sounded as if, after all I had seen, I was going to follow the line of those who sat back in their leather armchairs at the Addis Ababa Hilton and said, 'It will never work' – those who will make the prophecy fulfil itself by starving resettlement of cheap and effective assistance. So I changed my tack and said, 'I can't believe that if people in the rich countries had seen what I've seen, they wouldn't rush to help you. You've done so much with so little. Everybody is working so hard, so far from home, in conditions of such privation and with so little hope of reward.' I thought of all the RRC officers standing about me while I quizzed them about all their failures, spelt out for anyone to see on the wall chart in the operations room, all of them struggling to converse with me in English, the language that they learned their conservation theory in, from textbooks written by Englishmen lecturing at Addis Ababa University. It seemed to me monstrous that when they maintain so high a respect for the English-speaking culture, it expresses nothing but contempt for them, giving only emergency aid when the damage is done and then pouncing on the slightest indication that any jot or tittle of it has been abused, erecting whole scenarios of perfidy on a handful of misread signs.

The Ethiopians' loyalty to 'English' values is the more striking because it has nothing to do with cupboard love, for we have denied them even the pittance of development funding which we gave in the past. In Asosa, cadres, party officials and RRC workers listened to the BBC World Service when they could, even though they often heard statements about Ethiopia which they knew to be false. They believed, as I believe, that all that was needed to repair the relationship between our two cultures was more information. Without exception, the Ethiopians involved in settlement trusted me and told me more than I could safely use without creating difficulties for them, especially where the Russians were concerned. As the Landcruiser turned to leave, the Women's Affairs Officer came shyly out to ask if I could perhaps send some English books. 'There's not much to do in the evenings,' she said, twisting her wedding ring. She didn't need to explain that her husband of a few months was working in another project in another remote part of Ethiopia. I wondered if the attitude of the British government would change if the post offices filled up with books, packets of seeds, bolts of cloth, do-it-yourself tube-well construction kits, beekeeping manuals, tins of Aldrin, cups, plates, bottles, knives – all the things the settlers need, addressed to RRC Asosa Welega Ethiopia. And I realized why I had found it so difficult to speak when they asked me. I was ashamed.

In the highlands of Welo the *belg* rains this year were abundant. When we passed through the Borkena valley, the grass was springing green through the eyeholes of the cattle skulls that lined the road. Farmers who ploughed at the first wetting had barley standing a foot tall. The dark, fine soil was split by phosphorescent green blades everywhere but on the state farm, where the heavy East German tractors had to wait until it dried out enough to take their weight. Precious top-soil, the life of the upland farmers, had been washed down into the gullies or flowed uselessly down the roadways. I saw peasants collecting it in baskets and calabashes and carrying it on their heads back up the steep paths to their fields where they were repairing bunds broken out by the rains. They were sculpting the soil with their hands, banking it against the rock walls, so the long narrow fields were dished to hold the water. Some scooped tiny trenches running along the upward side of the walls like dotted lines. Above the moulded fields stood ranks of *Eucalyptus globulus* and hedges of prickly pear or other cacti, barriers to arrest the constant tumbling of stones from the eroding hilltops. No land was ever more lovingly cultivated than this.

As the black clouds massed and burst over the people always to be found thronging the road between Kemise and Kombolcha, driving their cattle to and from the markets, walking to school and back, or standing by the hundreds of water jugs set in line to wait for the generator to power the pump, they threw up their heads and let the rain run into their mouths and eyes. The little herdsmen leapt and skipped, the split polythene bags that should have been keeping them dry, flapping around them like wings. As our Landcruiser splashed past, a young woman flung out her bare arms the better to feel the wet, and whirled like a dervish. A woman suddenly straightened up from the ditch where she was gathering water purslane for a salad and shook a handful towards us with a shining grin.

When I travelled this road in December it was crowded with skeletal figures trudging like automata, blind and deaf to everything but the death that pursued them. The weakest could no longer walk, but tried to inch forward on their fleshless buttocks. By April there were more feeding centres and dry-ration distribution centres. All along the road we passed groups of peasants heading back to the uplands with their month's provisions on the men's heads and the backs of women and donkeys. For some, the time of relief rations was nearly over, but for others it would never end as long as they stayed in Welo. Above Dese, in the *awraja* of Dese Zuriya, the population density is 181.5 per square kilometre. Year by year the exhausted earth can produce less and less to feed them. In Lasta, further north, famine has returned year after year.

For the farmers on these higher slopes the rain brought more misery. Sudden drops in temperature pick off emaciated people like sniper fire. Damp aids the flowering of myriad pathogenic organisms. In the famine shelters, health workers were fighting off disease with anything that worked, with neither time nor facilities for an exact identification. *Shigella* lurked in every ditch, attacking people in forms so virulent they caused heart distress and shock even in apparently strong people. Shigellosis can be far swifter and more lethal than cholera, unless we are speaking of *Cholera eltor*, which can lie dormant for months and then kill in hours by causing dehydration so sudden and catastrophic that no known method of rehydration can keep pace with it. As we drove up from the Borkena valley towards Dese, we passed litter-bearers trotting through the rain, carrying their sick on their shoulders. Behind them ran the relief team, ready to take over when they tired. No vehicle could stop and take their burden on board, in case they should take death aboard with it. There was no way to summon an ambulance, even supposing such things were to be found in the area. For many of those we saw, the heart-bursting run must have been in vain. Twice we passed litterbearers pulled up to wrap the body they carried tightly in a makeshift shroud.

Through the streets of Dese stumbled exhausted women carrying vast bundles of wood and thatch on their backs, all that remained of the tukuls they used to live in, pulled down to sell as firewood in Dese market. Not that they would get much for them for the market was glutted with such piles of half-rotten lumber. Thousands of families had made the hardest decision, to leave their land for ever. The town was jammed with them, sleeping in every half-way sheltered spot, unable even to live by begging, for the citizens of Dese had nothing left to give. In the road outside the branch headquarters of the Relief and Rehabilitation Commission, children and old women crouched beneath a semi-trailer, picking through the dirt for stray grains shaken from the sacks being offloaded on to smaller trucks for distribution in the highlands to the north and west. A woman sat under a tree watching them; the child lying across her lap was rigid, his head thrown back and his teeth bared in the throes of tetanus. When I lifted the bundles of filthy rags lying in the lee of urine-stained walls, I found mothers with naked newborns at the breast, too exhausted to stagger the last few hundred yards to help and shelter.

For there was help and shelter. On a tract of level ground just east of the town, they could find the Dese transit shelter, overcrowded, poorly housed in army tents, but with food, *kita* bread for adults and supplementary feeding for the children, run by Save the Children, who fed all children provided they washed before they ate. Oxfam was building a 45,000-litre storage tank for clean water, so that Dese wouldn't go the way of the more conveniently situated shelter at Kombolcha, isolated because of diarrhoea both bloody and watery. Most of the work at Dese shelter was done by volunteers working for an extra food ration of 90 kilos of grain a month which they were free to dispose of as they chose. The camp, as is usually the case in Ethiopia, had neither fence nor gates. The only guard was stationed outside the food stores. The inmates were free to come and go as they pleased, but soon they would have to move on, for new arrivals staggered into the shelter every day. The army tents were already too crowded for safety. Everyone, whether sheltered or shelterer, waited anxiously for the buses to arrive and relieve the pressure.

There were more urgent cases, however. Dese is a provincial capital; poor as it is, it has far better resources for the relief operation than smaller centres. The buses were needed more urgently at Garba, about seventy kilometres east of Dese, where the local party officials had had to find a way of accommodating thousands of famine victims who converged on their small town from the highlands to the north. They had built a couple of hundred small tukuls, with a terrific expenditure of effort, for the surrounding area is completely denuded. Even finding the bundles of straw for thatch must have involved hundreds of hours of work. Into this makeshift encampment came more than 4,000 people. The *kebele* had scraped together some food supplies, but the maintenance of any degree of hygiene in food preparation, water supply and human waste disposal was completely beyond them. The Red Cross famine relief shelter at Bati was less than an hour's walk away, but the *safarioch* waited where they were. They were free to gather firewood on the hills and to collect water from any source they could find, or to walk to the market in Bati town to barter their last hides or part of their dry ration for oil or green vegetables or cigarettes, but they returned to the transit shelter at Garba, primitive as it was. During the night of 19 April, the buses began to arrive.

When the sun came up, hundreds of people had been already marshalled by their group leaders and stood waiting quietly for the loading of their bundles of chattels to begin. The women's hair had been newly braided for Easter; some had smeared their foreheads with butter as a protection against vermin. When I tasted it to see if it was really butter, they laughed. Children clambered over the bundles to pull their mothers' breasts out of their dresses. Most people were thoughtful, but there was a vein of excitement running through their solemnity. The cadre in charge of the operation, Comrade Fitsum, a Tigrayan, came up to welcome me. 'You see, no guns,' he said. 'Their movement is spontaneous.' Then he melted into the crowd. The loading was magically smooth and quiet. The drivers' assistants and party workers climbed on to the roofs of the buses and lifted up the bundles. Once they had seen their possessions safely lashed down, the families climbed into the bus, each clasping a packet of biscuits and a calabash full of water. Some of the children seemed too weak and ill to be going anywhere, but the families tied them up tighter in their rags and bundled them on. As each bus loaded, it moved off and waited a few hundred yards down the road. More buses kept arriving until there were seventeen.

Suddenly a hitch occurred. There was a short altercation, my RRC minder appeared and told me in outraged accents that the local party secretary refused to allow me to accompany the settlers. It seemed to me obvious that if the local *kebele* had been running the operation, they ought to have been consulted about letting a foreign journalist observe it, so I allowed myself to be driven away with a good grace. In view of the fact that cynical hacks holed up in the Addis Ababa Hilton assumed that everything I saw had been staged for me, I was glad that I had been treated as a spy. Comrade Fitsum ran up to beg my pardon. 'You understand why the soldiers are here?' he asked anxiously. In fact, a truckload of soldiers had pulled up at the head of the convoy. The soldiers were sitting along the road in the shade, smoking and talking. 'Not to terrorize the settlers, obviously,' I answered and his face cleared. As the buses were to travel along one of the most congested roads in Ethiopia, jammed with flocks of sheep and cattle and strings of donkeys, it was easy to see what function the advance guard would perform. As I drove away I noticed a boy standing at the open window of the bus, playing a bamboo pipe while the soldiers smoked and listened.

My settlers from Garba moved on without me, but three days later I caught up with another group from Dese, as rainy afternoon became sodden evening, in the transit shelter at Gouder. Gouder is a paragon of temporary shelters. Its two hundred tents, made in Pakistan, gift of Saudi Arabia, are set at least a tent's breadth apart in a broad meadow below the town of Ambo. As I stood in the mud, I could hear soft chatter coming from the tents in the gloaming. When I peeped in, I saw that the tents were kept warm not only by their lining of gaily printed, mango-coloured cotton, but by clean hay spread on the earth. Comrade Kasahun, Ideological Officer, Ambo District WPE, introduced me to the volunteers from Ambo, who were preparing the evening meal for the settlers who were still to arrive. They were Amhara matrons of substance, grave and nun-like in their white shammas. 'When they saw the drought-affected people they cried,' said Comrade Kasahun, who for some reason was wearing a mad white hat with the brim turned up very high at the back and tipped over his eyes in the front. He took me to the medical tents, where a doctor, a nurse and a pharmacist were on duty round the clock.

I watched as the doctor made out a treatment card for a feverish child. 'What happens now?' 'The child stays here until treatment is completed.' I was astonished, but, as I visited the hospital tents and talked to the patients I realized that it was true.

The straggler buses were beginning to arrive. As the people stepped down from them, the party workers lined up along both sides of the roadway that led into the shelter, balancing sacks and cauldrons on low benches. As each adult came past, they tipped brimming plastic boxfuls of soused grain into his carrying cloth, one for each member of the family. Each adult was given a wedge of *kita* bread for each family member, and each child a pint of thick protein drink that steamed faintly in the cold. A man hunkered down at our feet and uncovered what he was carrying in his arms. It was an emaciated boy who, if he could have stood up, would have been as tall as the man who carried him. The boy ate his *kita* bread obediently, but clearly, chewing exhausted him. The party workers spoke quietly to the man. His voice rose in protest. 'He's been like this before. He'll be fine. Just let him eat.' The party workers did not badger him, but as, one by one, they each pointed to the medical tent, he began to waver. Anxiously the family gathered around. Watching them conferring, I began to realize something I should have understood before. All of them, including the starving boy, were desperate to move on. The party workers went on distributing food to the other settlers, and made no attempt to interfere with the family's deliberations. Perhaps what decided them was the sight of one of the volunteer ladies wobbling through the mud with the invalids' food piled up in plastic boxes in two clean pails. In each box could be seen voluptuous folds of good *injera* made with pure teff, and out of the folds bulged thick yellow *shiro*. The man turned and ran with his brother to the medical tent. Next morning, when the buses left, the boy and his mother stayed behind. I hoped they would meet up with their kinsfolk again. 'Social Committee's job,' said Comrade Kasahun. 'Actually it's not difficult. The peasants have huge networks. They can find each other quicker than we can. We'll try and keep track of them but right now our primary duty is to save life. The sorting out can come later.'

That night we all discussed what to me was the most puzzling aspect of the exercise. Neither the settlers nor their drivers yet knew where they were going. Gradually the explanation for the mystery emerged. The RRC and the WPE are responsible for the feeding of settlers until such time as they are self-sufficient. It is vital that they do not have large numbers of people arriving spontaneously in settlement areas which by their nature are difficult of access, for not only are food supplies limited, the RRC does not have enough vehicles to keep the settlement sites supplied with any amount of surplus food for such an emergency. If the Ethiopian government is to avoid the accusation that it has lured people to remote areas and let them starve, it has to keep settlement destinations completely secret for as long as possible, which, given the efficiency of the peasant telegraph, is probably not long. 'This is the reality,' said Comrade Kasahun. I asked him if he thought that the Israelis had got themselves into just the situation that the Ethiopian government is trying to avoid, and had completely miscalculated the numbers of Falashas that would respond to the rumour that the time of their Exodus was at hand. Comrade Kasahun did not know much about the bungled Falasha airlift, but he did know that peasants think nothing of walking hundreds of kilometres. A recent survey shows that the average Ethiopian peasant spends two full days a week walking to and from market; the trading networks built up in this way are one of the most important tissues connecting greater Ethiopia and stretch from one end of the country to the other.

At six next morning the peasants were up and off on the next leg of their magical mystery trip. As they filed through the feeding line they were all given a pint of milk drink. The men pulled faces and tried to hand the beakers back, but the workers gently pushed them on and doled out more. Not one person poured it on the ground, but gulped, grimaced and drank. Some of it would come back up again as the buses barrelled round the thousands of bends. (The buses were already laced and garlanded with dried vomit.)

About an hour out of Gouder we came across the convoy stopped on a muddy bend. The leading bus had swerved to avoid a broken-down vehicle and slid into the bank, hard up against a projecting boulder. An oncoming local bus had stopped and all the passengers had joined the bus drivers and their assistants in the struggle to get the big Fiat back on the road. Some of the settlers had scattered to relieve themselves. Most stood or sat snug in their blue-grey blankets watching as a hundred hands were pressed against the side of the bus. *Anda, ulet, sost!* The bus leaned a fraction and then settled back against the rock. *Anda, ulet, sost!* The motor roared, the bus leaned, and back it zoomed, clearing the rock. Then everyone ran to collect rocks, earth and thornbush to build a track up which the bus could lumber out of the ditch and on to the roadway. The settlers flew, blankets flapping, to remount the bus. Everyone waved and called greetings and we were off again.

That night the settlers were put up in a temporary shelter on the airstrip near Nekemte, a place called Gute. The rain had followed us. A dank wind blew. The only shelters were tarpaulins flung over dead trees and poles driven into the ground. Some of the settlers had lit fires and were roasting wheat grains to make *kolo*. The council water truck dispensed clean water and after the calabashes had all been filled some of the settlers took turns to wash the mud of Ambo off their legs. An old woman was suddenly at my elbow demanding '*Lips! Lips!*' 'Where are your blankets?' There followed a long and elaborate explanation of why she and the three children with her were without the blankets that had been issued to everyone. The children were all in bad shape, but the eldest seemed to me critically emaciated and only half-conscious. The party secretary took my arm and moved me away. 'She must have blankets somewhere. In any case, we have none to give her. The medical team is arriving. They will see to it.' If I had not heard shelter dwellers in other places wheeling and dealing for extra blankets I might have tried harder to follow up the case of the old woman. As I didn't, I have to share the blame for what eventually happened.

In Nekemte, provincial capital of Welega, a welcoming guard of honour had been arranged. At eight next morning the convoy began to roll through the checkpoint, to the sound of rhythmic clapping. When the buses were closer and the citizens could see the pinched and shadowed faces of the settlers, they stopped their chanting. On all sides I could hear hushed sounds of awe and compassion. As the convoy turned off the main road and pushed down the narrow road to Arjo, a more spontaneous welcome broke out. Children burst out of the schoolrooms, waving both arms and shrilling at the tops of their voices. Farmers left their ploughing and ran to the side of the road, both hands raised in the beautiful Ethiopian greeting, signifying surprise and delight. Women came to the doors of their tukuls. Some of them wore the dark blue dresses and symmetrical braids of Welo. The settlers sat still and silent, gazing at the green fields and the tall trees and the shiny brown faces of their own people, proprietors of all this beauty and plenty.

South of Arjo, the buses turned off the road again and squeezed their huge bulk along a bulldozed track and across the Didessa River, a tributary of the Blue Nile, where two hippos played, oblivious of their passing. Up the river bank and on the buses rolled. Here there was not a soul to greet them. The buses could not negotiate a deep gully with a creek at the bottom; the drivers, drivers' assistants and the stronger settlers spent a half-hour lugging rocks to make a causeway, and the buses rolled over. We were six kilometres from our destination, a place called Kone. Three kilometres further on, the buses stopped while the drivers reconnoitred a tree-trunk bridge over a small gorge. Some peasants were standing at the bridgehead. We heard a shout, saw thin legs flying, and suddenly there was hugging and kissing all round. 'Brothers,' said one of the drivers. The other settlers looked on, their faces unreadable. They may have been seeing what I saw: one of the men at the bridgehead stopped his eager questioning of the new arrivals and turned and walked blindly into the bush. The news from home had been bad.

We crossed the bridge and entered the settlement. In the bucketing buses the settlers sat frozen with tension, hardly daring to hope that they had arrived. They were almost too overwrought to notice the people who lined the road clapping and chanting the same throbbing song that we have heard when highlanders welcome the food drops, or the old man whose gnarled hands were coaxing an obbligato from his dulcimer. As the buses pulled up by the storehouses, the settlers stepped gingerly down, utterly silent. The noonday sun was merciless, but they stood still, wrapped in their blue-grey blankets as if in shock. The excitement was too much for the members of the honour guard who took off in a whirling dance, chanting and ululating and stomping their feet, hurling their dulas into the air. I pointed out one woman to Comrade Habtu, RRC officer in charge of the project. She was peering fixedly through the legs of the dancers at a group of boys on the other side, who were staring back at her. 'Come, come!' shouted Comrade Habtu, and two of the boys broke ranks and came flying across. The woman, who had risen groggily to her feet, folded them in her arms. 'Their mother,' said Comrade Habtu unnecessarily. On all sides there was clasping and kissing, and the elaborate hand kissing that is kept for more distant or senior relations, but we were all aware of the people whose gaze got wider and darker as they scanned each busload, and of others whose eager questionings were producing tears which were not tears of happiness.

Worst of all, as one bus unloaded I saw the white coats of the three paramedics flapping amongst the grey-blue blankets. Something unbearably light, bent up in premature rigor, was handed out on a stretcher. The old woman of the night before passed me, sobbing, carrying one emaciated child while another clung to her back. She must have got the girl through the night with the warmth of her own body, but the last gruelling hours on the bus had been too much. Party workers guided her through the crowd to the clinic.

Comrade Habtu led me to the official dais, a bench by the tractor shed. The people gathered quietly before us for the official speeches. I hoped desperately that no one would ask me to speak, for I could not have uttered a word, even the Amharic for 'good luck' which I had learned specially.

Looking at the 1,500 faces massed before us, some still wet with tears, all marked with weariness and privation, I felt my self-possession finally dissolve and groped for Comrade Habtu's hand beneath the bench. To my surprise he took it, gripped it and hung on. We sat like that for the duration of the speeches, which were mercifully short.

While the settlers ate their welcoming meal, Comrade Habtu took me to see the tukuls built for the new arrivals by the local people and party volunteers. I noticed that the surrounding trees had blackened trunks. Wildfire, probably set by nomads, had already destroyed eighty of the new tukuls. 'How did you manage?' I asked. 'We built them again,' said the project director, as if it was all in a day's work. In most settlement areas, the Department of Agriculture builds a model tukul, to show the settlers how to improve the basic structure so that it gives greater hygiene, privacy, ventilation and light. At Kone, a local Welega man who volunteered to join the scheme had built such a beautiful tukul, with cleverly planted fences made of cassava plants and a secluded area for his beehives, that it was used as the model instead. Another man from Welo had rebuilt his tukul on the model of his homeland, with an elegant bow-shaped roof. He showed me his seedbed crammed with tiny plantlets of red pepper, for distribution to the new arrivals to bring up in their own plots.

Besides the neat tukuls I noticed funny little square constructions in the middle of each group of four houses. 'Latrines,' said Comrade Habtu. As I had already seen him deal with a settler whose first reaction to the sight of a creek was to pee in it, I had no doubt that the latrines would be used properly. 'We have clean water too,' said Comrade Habtu, 'from two protected springs.' Then, looking across to where scores of new tukuls nestled among the native trees, he asked, 'What do you know about tsetse fly?' He might as well have asked, 'What do you know about malaria, filaria, goitre, leprosy, TB, tetanus and bilharzia?' The answer would have been the same. Without a massive increase in resources, for all their planning and dedicated toil, the RRC will make very little headway against any of them. Help for the establishing of iodizing plants will control goitre. Nurse practitioners in the settlements have more success in identifying early cases of leprosy and in seeing that sufferers take their Dapzone, than in less controlled environments. Prolonged treatment for TB is likewise feasible. UNICEF offered to provide a health screening service and a minimal survival package of vaccinations for resettlers, but on condition that the scheme was halted for three months until it could be set up. The government refused without explanation. In fact, given the pressure of popular movement and the lengths of time that settlers had already spent in inadequate holding shelters, there was not three months to waste. More-over, the health status of the local populations in the resettlement areas is so poor that any discrimination in the providing of health services would be totally unacceptable. Nothing short of a massive national campaign of vaccination against polio, measles, tetanus and TB will do. The personnel is available and in place; all that is needed is the vaccines, the training and the registration system. The thousands vaccinated in emergency relief shelters, for example, have no record of the fact, and these vaccinations will eventually have to be done again. When it comes to malaria, filaria and bilharzia, which will spread in Ethiopia if any degree of irrigation is achieved, and are already endemic in two-thirds of Ethiopia anyway, a massive, concerted and fantastically costly programme of research is needed, but as long as only poor countries suffer from these parasitic diseases, such a programme will never be undertaken.

In designing their resettlement project, the RRC has taken into account all the possible objections to the scheme, and has done its best to pre-empt them, with what is, in view of its poverty, a remarkable degree of success. What distorts the whole operation and obscures its guiding principles from the view of the international community is what I can only call the Tigray factor. Slightly more than 40,000 Tigrayans have been settled in the last six months, about half of them in Welega and half in Ilubador, where they are the majority of settlers in the Gambela area. Arguments that resettlement is simply a plot to destroy the power base of the TLF are clearly nonsensical, when only two out of every fifteen settlers are Tigrayan; nevertheless there are worrying aspects of the Tigrayan operation which are not to be found in resettlement as a whole.

International aid workers in Mekele are only too ready to describe the results of resettlement from their point of view. Virtually all of them have had to deal with cases of women whose husbands have disappeared, most of them with the ration cards which are issued for recipients of food aid in Mekele. The assumption is usually made that these men have been 'taken' for resettlement. It is at least as likely that they have preferred three meals a day and a modicum of self-esteem in the Ethiopian People's Revolutionary Forces or in the Tigrayan People's Liberation Front. A strange phenomenon involving the appearance at the Italian hospital in Mekele of numbers of young men with gunshot wounds in the hand may have something to do with the recruitment methods favoured by the TLF. It is possible too that the missing men did what they have traditionally done in times of famine in the past, simply walked away in search of work as casual labourers. There are many Tigrayans to be seen wandering in the streets of Addis Ababa: the day before I left I encountered a traffic policeman confronted with the problem of moving one of them on. Trouble was, he was dead. Despite all these possibilities, the prejudice persists among international relief workers in Mekele that missing men have been black-birded for resettlement, and so strong is this impression that they will not take the obvious step of approaching party officials and requesting information. Resettlement is mentioned in hushed tones, with knowing nods.

Chief among the reasons for the nudge-nudge, wink-wink approach is the Russian involvement. No one can get close to the Russians. They live in a closed camp at the old airport in Addis, and they are clearly under orders not to fraternize. Where the Poles are anxious that their helicopter food drops be observed by the press, the Russians prefer to shroud their operations, however philanthropic, in mystery. Their motive might be interpreted as a desire to isolate Ethiopia from her non-socialist friends by forcing her to share a secret. Or it may simply be an extension of the bloody-mindedness that causes such tension between Russia and all her allies. Ethiopian officials obliged to work with Russians find them completely undisciplined and unreliable. Some say that when the war in the North ends, the Russians will be kicked out of Ethiopia.

Meanwhile, the Ethiopians are obliged to turn to the Russians for help in moving Tigrayan settlers out of Mekele. The land route is insecure. The TLF affects to believe that resettlement is a specific attack on its power base, and has attacked settler convoys in the past. The movement of settlers has already completely disrupted routine bus services throughout Ethiopia and there is no possibility that more buses could be made available for the run from Mekele to Addis. The only solution is to airlift the settlers from Mekele to Addis, and to bus them from there. The only carriers who would agree to take the settlers were the Russians. The settlers, about 160 at a time, are herded into the cargo bay of Antonov 12s, where they sit on the floor. The cargo bay of the Antonov 12 is unpressurized. Some international aid workers say that ten to fifteen per cent of the settlers who go on board the Antonov airlift out of Mekele are taken off dead. What this would mean is that truckloads of bodies would be driven out of Bole airport each day that the Antonovs bring settlers in. Of 8,000 people shipped betweeen 9 and 13 April, more than 800 would have had to be taken from Bole for burial. As far as I could gather from quizzing the Ethiopian Red Cross, there was not a single fatality, although stress could well have accounted for one or two, given the sheer numbers flying and their poor state of health.

The obvious way to deal with such wild and destructive rumours would have been to have let me fly with the settlers out of Mekele, but although I specifically asked the RRC Public Relations Office to approach the Russians on my behalf, the request was never made. I was told that the RRC itself was worried that I might overreact to the occasional scuffle between settlers and those responsible for getting them on to the Antonovs. It is at least as likely that the RRC was intimidated by the Russians and by the possibility of ructions in the Politburo if my conclusions should be critical of the Russians, and simply took refuge in inertia. Even if I had flown with the settlers I could not positively discount apparent eyewitness accounts of men being rounded up in Mekele and beaten with sticks in order to make them get into trucks, although I do not accept that these men were necessarily being 'taken' for resettlement. Nor could I positively discount the possibility that Russians safe on the pressurized flight deck are criminally indifferent to their human cargo and fly as high as they please. For people who live at 8,000 or 9,000 feet, flying at 17,000 or so in an unpressurized aircraft is unlikely to cause problems, but in poor visibility the Antonovs may have to climb to above 22,000 feet. When I asked Colonel Ashete of the RRC Air Arm if the flight would be unpleasant for the settlers, he said, 'Decidedly.' When asked what aircraft would be better suited for the job, he said, 'The Hercules.' Although the RRC asked every air force flying Hercules in Ethiopia to help with resettlement, they all refused.

If I could not see the Tigrayans being moved from Mekele I could at least see them at their final destination. About half of them end up in the new settlement areas around Gambela in Ilubabor. In Welega they are a small minority, easily submerged among the numbers from Welo, but in Gambela there are settlements that are eighty per cent Tigrayan.

By the time I got to Gambela, after endless delays and desperate appeals to various dignitaries to help me, I was seriously worried that what I was going to see there would invalidate all the heroic effort I had witnessed in other settlement sites. I was almost certain that I would see gangs of terrorized men being forced to work by armed guards, and the whole enterprise would take a taint from the Tigray factor. RRC figures told their own story, for half the Tigrayans being resettled are family heads, a significant departure from the general pattern, which could too easily be interpreted as a deliberate attempt to remove able-bodied men, fathers and eldest sons, from a focus of social unrest. As we rolled over the tightly guarded bridge which is the only way in or out of Gambela, I was convinced that I had come to the Ethiopian version of Siberia, only as hot as Siberia was cold.

The tour that we made of the three settled sites in Gambela, Abole, Ukuna and Perbongo, was the most exhaustive of all. I had to be certain that there was no corner where the equivalent of a chain gang could have been hidden. At the end of the day I had seen all there was to see. Saddest were the displaced baboon colonies sitting perplexed on the edges of the vast fields where the Nazret tractors toiled, preparing the fat earth for sowing. I saw many tukuls where no woman tended the fire, but all their private plots were tilled. Anuak women walked along the settlement roads, carrying pots for sale to settlers, and waved to us as we passed. I noticed the settlers were growing cassava, in imitation of the Anuak, although it is not to be found in Tigray. There were guns about, to be sure, but they were carried by the Anuak and by the settlers. In view of the spoor we saw crisscrossing the roads everywhere, I would have preferred to see more of them, rather than fewer. Only a hundred yards from the settlers' nursery beds, a family of crocodiles basked on the mud flats. It was clear to me then that the Tigrayans are no different from all the other settlers I had seen, whether walking across the high pass between Debre Sina and Debre Birhan, or hitching rides on truck beds or riding the buses hired by the RRC. All they asked was a chance to build a new life and make a new home. As we passed men walking back from the fields with their hoes over their shoulders, they greeted us with raised hands, like lords of the terrain.

The British government, following the line set by the United States, has refused to grant direct development aid to the Ethiopian government. The League of Red Cross Societies, UNICEF, Save the Children, Oxfam and the FAO have all given assistance to settlers, but none will give assistance to settlements as such. It seems as if the international community hopes that the resettlement projects will fail, and the revolutionary government of Ethiopia be discredited for trying to minimize the wastage of human life that is always involved in spontaneous migration and settlement in undeveloped areas. If the carefully planned settlements in Gojjam, Welega and Ilubabor fail, our refusal of support will be one of the main causes of their failure, but we will not suffer for it. Neither will the bureaucrats in Addis Ababa. The hard-working, uncomplaining, dignified and determined people who have made the great safari will pay the price of our opinions.

In January 1986, the pace of resettlement was slowed down, for consolidation purposes according to the government. Wild rumours, originating with groups like Médecins sans Frontières, who had never been to any resettlement site, claiming 50,000 deaths among settlers, plus the disruptive activities of Oromo liberation fighters in the south-west, together with, I suspect, some greater incidence of infectious disease in resettlement areas than the paramedics could cope with, brought about what seems to be a collapse in the programme and with it the defection of the head of the Relief and Rehabilitation Commission. Ethiopia is too poor a country to be able to keep up the levels of investment in resettlement unless massive numbers of people are involved. Settlements that do not reach their optimum size are non-viable.

Ethiopia between the lines

Listener, 24 October 1985

At the end of April William Shawcross, distinguished journalist and author of *The Quality of Mercy*, a study of the Cambodian relief operation of 1979–80, made a short visit to Ethiopia. His host was his old friend, Kurt Jansson, UN Assistant Secretary General for Emergency Operations in Ethiopia, who secured for him unparalleled access. Jansson's team of nine professional monitors, all from the donor countries, keeps him constantly informed about the progress of food aid from port to final destination, but in an article published in *Rolling Stone* in July, Shawcross quoted Jansson only to dismiss him.

Jansson says of food aid in Ethiopia: 'We can account for about ninety-five to ninety-seven per cent, and that's a record. In Africa generally, because of the lack of infrastructure, because of corruption existing in many countries, one calculates that if one can keep the diversion below twenty per cent one is lucky. Here it's much less than that.'

Shawcross thinks differently: 'The government claims that over five million people have been given rations; most of the foreign relief agencies think that is nonsense.'

Shawcross's own nonsense-detector seems to have failed him in Ethiopia, for he describes the universal Ethiopian custom of partly shaving children's heads as 'a reminder to God that he has already taken several of their children and so perhaps should spare this one'. He also falls for a story of plastic bracelets worn as protection against cholera, which he describes as 'beginning to rage' in Mekele at the beginning of May, continuing in the journalistic tradition that, since last December, has regularly announced signs of the imminent outbreak of a cholera epidemic which has so far failed to materialize.

Shawcross quotes 'most of the foreign relief agencies' as the source of his conviction that aid in Ethiopia is being massively misused. There are forty-seven non-governmental organizations (NGOs) at present delivering relief in Ethiopia. None of them has access to any kind of overview. For relief purposes, Ethiopia is divided into five areas of influence: the Catholics and the International Committee of the Red Cross (ICRC) dominate in the north, Save the Children and Oxfam in Welo, the Christian Relief and Development Association (CRDA) in Northern Shoa, Care in the east and the Lutherans in the south.

One of the least edifying spectacles to be witnessed in Addis Ababa in September, was the meeting of the CRDA which purported to deal with the appearance of a new pocket of famine in Haykoch and Butajira, 180 kilometres south of Addis Ababa. Offers to run feeding programmes were invited, in a bizarre kind of Dutch auction. It should have been possible for the Relief and Rehabilitation Commission (RRC) of Ethiopia simply to transfer supplies from its nearest store, and would have been possible if the RRC had been left in charge of dry-ration distribution, but as the United States has given 400,000 tons of food to non-government organizations and only 50,000 tons to the RRC, it fell to the NGOs to try to cobble together some kind of co-operative attempt to pool resources earmarked by donors following definitions of need that were already out of date. (This situation had already caused a serious shortfall in relief supplies to Welo, for which the foreign press blamed the government; by the end of August RRC stores held a mere 16,000 tons.)

A week later, a UN Development Project officer was amazing and appalling other foreigners with a graphic tale of 300,000 starving only 180 kilometres from Addis, as if the situation was the fault of the Ethiopian government. In fact the people at risk numbered about 50,000 and 300 tons of food had arrived two weeks before, but relief workers generally have a tendency to dramatize, principally by exaggerating their own involvement and degree of responsibility. In that week I must have met half a dozen people who imagined themselves to be the sole initiators of feeding programmes in Haykoch and Butajira.

The people who have gone to help the Ethiopians in their hour of need are clearly to be admired and encouraged, but they are not always to be believed. The reality of relief work, especially for the clerical officers, is tedium endured far from home. It is usually made endurable by a battery of perks. ICRC office-workers in Addis are issued with brand-new Toyota Corollas for their own use, for example. The best houses in the provincial centres have been commandeered for relief officials; in Dese, three families were turned out of government housing, so that one foreign relief worker could be housed according to his status. Ethiopian employees of the foreign agencies do not get the expatriate allowance or the free cars and fuel allowance, but they can expect two to three times the salary that any Ethiopian institution could afford to pay them. At all levels of the relief operation there are conspicuous inequalities, between field-workers and bureaucrats, between expatriates and Ethiopians, and even among the destitute themselves, depending upon whether they are in the hands of rich or poor, large or small, efficient or inefficient agencies.

Field-workers often complain of the attitude of their own bureaucrats, especially when it comes to consultation about actual conditions in the famine areas, which office-based workers seldom visit, not because they don't want to – indeed, field trips are enviable signs of status and confer an injection of much-needed drama into the squalid tedium of life in Addis – but because travel permits can take weeks to organize and may be refused. Almost none of the expatriate relief workers speaks a word of any Ethiopian language.

There is often friction between field-workers and jejune officials. In April, a highly trained Australian nurse, with twenty years' experience of work in desert conditions, was sent back to Addis in disgrace from Mekele, because she insisted on trying to help families and to give medical treatment instead of sticking to the limited duties assigned to her as a public health nurse. A Swiss ICRC official half her age considered that she was undermining his authority. She felt that the system was inefficient and failed to meet the needs of the people. One of her crimes was, on her own initiative, to take to the Italian hospital sick people who had remained untreated, despite four months in the shelter.

The foreign relief operation has its failures too, generally less excusable than the shortfalls and cock-ups that the Ethiopians contrive for themselves, but we do not read of them in our newspapers.

Many of the agencies, in particular World Vision, are as devoutly anti-Communist as they are deeply Christian. They have come to Ethiopia, not only to perform the corporal work of mercy of saving lives, but the spiritual work of saving souls from dialectical materialism. Some of the other agencies call World Vision 'Blurred Vision' and tell bitchy stories about World Vision's notion of a 'feeding table' being surrounded by 'dinky li'l chairs'. (The best indication of the agencies' unreliability, indeed, is what they are prepared to say about one another.)

It is taken as read that World Vision is the spiritual arm of the CIA, a charge the more gung-ho workers do not even bother to rebut. Most of the journalists struggling to see anything of Ethiopia are obliged to beg rides on World Vision aircraft, a propaganda opportunity that World Vision would be foolish to waste, for its massive budget, $72 million to spend in Ethiopia in 1985 alone, must be fuelled by constant fund-raising.

Even the less evangelical agencies tend to convey the impression that their work is hampered by the Ethiopians. In a Red Cross famine shelter last December, the English doctor told me to pay no attention to the wall-charts where the Ethiopians kept track of the shelter organization. As they were responsible for the food-for-work scheme, under which volunteers were organized for grave-digging, latrine detail and the cooking and distribution of food in supplementary and intensive feeding programmes, along with every other practical detail of shelter management, it seemed to me quite likely that they did in fact know what was going on. I checked as many of the figures as I could; not only did I find that they tallied with what I could observe, the doctor was actually quoting the same figures. He saw himself as in competition with the Ethiopians for control of the camp. At one point he rushed in to tell me that the blankets that Robert Maxwell had sent him personally had been 'whipped' by the shelter administrators and locked up where he would not be able to get at them. I went to the trouble of investigating and found the bales being unloaded outside the door. 'Oh that,' he said, 'that's food.' It wasn't, but few journalists would have bothered to check.

Why would someone in this position speak so irresponsibly? Why would John Marshall, who previewed my Diverse Reports film on Ethiopia in the *Listener* last week, tell me in April when he was filing TV reports for Visnews (although on the payroll of ICRC) that ten to fifteen per cent of the peasants being flown in Russian Antonovs from Mekele to Addis Ababa, on their way to be resettled, die from hypoxia (lack of oxygen)? Mr Marshall was good enough to call me an honest and caring journalist. I particularly care when I waste three weeks of my time in Ethiopia trying to find the truth content of such loose talk. Nowadays, Mr Marshall is maintaining merely that some people die on the Antonovs: an irrefutable position. In the course of covering the resettlement programme, I saw one person die on a bus.

It is true that the cargo bay of the Antonovs is unpressurized and the journey is desperately uncomfortable, but foreigners who live at sea-level have flown with the settlers and survived with no worse than a headache. As 1,600 people are shipped each day of the airlifts, truckloads of bodies would have been seen at Bole airport, which is crowded with the air forces of the nine nations flying emergency relief supplies, most of whom are not friends of the regime. What they have seen, and all agree on this point, is the Russians hosing out the Antonovs after each day of flying settlers. Ethiopian peasants, having never travelled before except on foot or in the saddle, get frightfully travel-sick.

Marshall suffers from ICRC myopia. The ICRC can only be involved in man-made disasters, hence they work only in the war zone. Judging the rest of Ethiopia by Tigray is like judging Britain by Northern Ireland. If ICRC workers still repeating this story truly believe that ten to fifteen per cent of Tigrayan settlers die during the airlift, why have they not protested to the authorities in the time-honoured manner of the Red Cross? The present chief delegate of the League of Red Cross Societies also repeats the story and she too has done nothing about it. I have asked resettled Tigrayans about their ordeal by Antonov and they have simply not understood my concern. But then, they were under the control of the government; doubtless if I had asked Tigrayans who had fled to TPLF-controlled (Tigrayan People's Liberation Front) camps in Sudan about resettlement, they would tell me a different story

Professional journalists cannot believe anything heard in interviews that are observed and interpreted by either government or rebel cadres. They can only believe what they see. On the evidence that eighty-two refugees died in TPLF camps in Sudan, the Ethiopian Head of State, Mengistu

Haile-Mariam, is now denounced as another Pol Pot, and the resettlement scheme (in which Tigrayans form a small minority: fifteen per cent) denounced as genocide. The accusation is too painful to be ridiculous: I have met hundreds of young party cadres and RRC workers who are enduring great hardship in the struggle to make the scheme a success.

Marshall also claimed that I was 'made aware' of various accusations in April. Unfortunately, none of the accusations actually makes sense. I heard many aid workers interpreting all kinds of phenomena as having to do with resettlement, including the rounding-up of TPLF sympathizers, much as the TPLF rounds up government supporters. Marshall also attempted to make me aware that settlers were kept on the buses at gunpoint, a charge I knew to be false.

The League of Red Cross Societies is involved in monitoring resettlement; one of their monitors was logistics officer at Asaita, which, he claimed, was flooded during the rains last December, but I was there two days after the rain and it was not flooded then and had not been flooded before. Given the fact that the shelter site was not on the river bank but by an irrigation canal, and that the Awash river is controlled by dams, barrages, polder systems and the huge irrigation system sixty kilometres upstream at Tendaho, I doubt if it ever was flooded. The same man has now reported that settlers were being starved because resettlement officers were stockpiling food for the 10,500 campaigners who came to build the settlers' tukuls in August. The story doesn't make sense because the schools and universities from which the campaigners come are responsible for feeding them and have a budget for the purpose. It is very possible that he did see settlers in very poor condition in a communal hut in Perbango settlement, but the explanation is wrong. The report the monitors submitted is confidential, but the League officer told it to me in the full awareness that I was a journalist.

Nevertheless behind all this foolishness or malice, there lies a serious problem. When the RRC claims that rations have reached five million people, the corollary is, on the RRC's own figures, that they have failed to reach five million more, for the RRC estimate of the extent of famine has been consistently higher than anyone else's. With 17,000 workers in the field, the RRC is the only organization which can collect the figures.

Journalists like Shawcross on ten-day visas can see grain rotting at Assab port, although they may not register how much the handling capacity of the port has been increased in the last year. They may decide to make moving appeals on television for trucks. The problem of the uncounted dead in the remote highlands is a problem of roads. No amount of emergency relief can supply roads, especially when it is being given at the cost of robbing funds from the already laughably inadequate development aid budget. As long as Ethiopia continues to receive less development assistance aid per capita than almost any other country in the world, famine will continue there unbeaten.

It is the RRC which will count the skeletons and the graves and the abandoned villages in the remotest highlands long after the NGOs have pulled out. Because of the suspicion and mistrust so freely voiced by the intrepid protectors of our right to know, the RRC cannot hope to compete with World Vision or Save the Children at fund-raising. Money for building roads will not be forthcoming. Chief among the causes of the next catastrophe in Ethiopia will be loose talk and the kind of journalism based upon it.

Germaine Greer
Sex and Destiny: The Politics of Human Fertility £2.95

'Sex and Destiny is one of the more important books to be written this century. Let me add that it states the obvious – and that the obvious is never so until it is stated, and that is where greatness, genius, call it what you will, lies. Ms Greer's thesis is this: our Western societies are sterile and corrupt. More, we are busy infecting the underdeveloped East with our disasterous notions of what the good life is: more contraception, more abortion, more family planning, more population control, more death, in fact, less life. The power and importance of Ms Greer's book is that perhaps now, if we pay attention we will know why we want these terrible things and what is happening to us' FAY WELDON, THE TIMES

'Sex and Destiny is, in every sense of the words, a great book . . . Dr Greer has made a major contribution to our sanity'
PENELOPE MORTIMER, SUNDAY TELEGRAPH

'No reader will be left unaffected by this book. Miss Greer's passionate and intentionally provocative style either entertains or enrages. This is a feast of strongly held, strongly expressed opinions, delivered as a stern lesson from the podium'
THE NEW YORK TIMES BOOK REVIEW

'This is the work of a formidable intellectual who is not only a superb polemecist and an accomplished writer, but also one who can blend her authority with wry wit, lively personal anecdotes and a moving compassion'
THE IRISH TIMES

**The Obstacle Race
the fortunes of women painters and their work** £6.95

In her first book since the pioneering and bestselling *The Female Eunuch*, Germaine Greer considers the fascinating question of why there have been so few women painters of the first rank. Ms Greer demonstrates brilliantly that the answer is not hard to find: 'you cannot make great artists out of egos that have been damaged, with wills that are defective, with libidos that have been driven out of reach and energy diverted into certain neurotic channels'.

'Instils respect, asks bold questions, does not make wildly exaggerated claims' MARGARET DRABBLE, LISTENER

'Passionate yet lucid . . . a book that explains . . . the psychological, economic and even aesthetic reasons for the virtually unchallenged patriarchalism of all our artistic establishments' ERICA LONG